INTO THE
BUZZSAW

REVISED AND EXPANDED

INTO THE BUZZSAW

LEADING JOURNALISTS EXPOSE THE
MYTH OF A FREE PRESS

A NATIONAL PRESS CLUB AWARD WINNER

EDITED BY
KRISTINA BORJESSON

Prometheus Books

59 John Glenn Drive
Amherst, New York 14228-2197

Published 2004 by Prometheus Books

Inquiries should be addressed to
Prometheus Books
59 John Glenn Drive
Amherst, New York 14228–2197
VOICE: 716–691–0133, ext. 207
FAX: 716–564–2711
WWW.PROMETHEUSBOOKS.COM

08 07 06 05 04   5 4 3 2 1

Library of Congress Cataloging-in-Publication Data

Into the buzzsaw : leading journalists expose the myth of a free press / edited by Kristina Borjesson. — Rev. and expanded ed.
     p. cm.
Includes bibliographical references and index.
ISBN 1-59102-230-4 (pbk. : alk. paper)
     1. Freedom of the press—United States. 2. Press—United States.
I. Borjesson, Kristina.

PN4738.I58 2004
323.44'5'0973—dc22

                2004013034

Printed in the United States of America on acid-free paper

THIS BOOK IS FOR:

THE AMERICAN PEOPLE, WHO NEED TO KNOW
ASPIRING JOURNALISTS, WHO NEED TO KNOW
WORKING JOURNALISTS, WHO SHOULD KNOW

THIS BOOK IS DEDICATED TO:

THOSE WHO FIGHT AND SACRIFICE
TO KEEP AMERICA'S PRESS FREE

CONTENTS

FOREWORD

GORE VIDAL

I provided a somewhat dim preface to the first edition of Kristina Borjesson's collection of stories censored/suppressed by print editors and publishers, not to mention by those TV producers and advertisers who determine what Americans should and should not know about the products that they are expected to consume unquestioningly — from skewed States of the Union to tainted junk food. But since *Buzzsaw One* our world has changed. We have been exposed not only to a blizzard of lies from our government on matters of war and peace but to bold litigation by corporate America against whistleblowers of the sort gathered now in *Buzzsaw Two*. Borjesson is democratic in her choice of journalists: she allows such brand names as Dan Rather and Christiane Amanpour to tell us what they actually think about the awful coverage of the buildup to the Iraq War where, on the subject of those imagined weapons of mass destruction, Amanpour tells us that "the press was muzzled and I think the press self-muzzled," earning her a rebuke from the CNN Newsgroup president who plainly thinks the world of his incredible product.

Certainly CNN's idea of a lead story is a domestic murder in

Modesto, California, to be proudly peddled for months, even years, as "Breaking News," which suggests that the proper title for Borjesson's collection is "Broken News," now repaired.

The most interesting pieces are, for want of a better word, *context* pieces in which the background to a startling news item is examined. For instance, those rumors that seemed never to stop about American prisoners of war being held post-1972 by the Viet Cong were true despite the Nixon-Kissinger denials. Monica Jensen-Stevenson, who was an award-winning producer at CBS's *60 Minutes*, writes: "I first heard of Private Robert R. Garwood in 1979 when I worked for a Canadian news program." Wire reports had referred to him as a defector from the Marine Corps; worse, he was charged with being a traitor. "Because I was an American who had recently moved to Canada, it was a story that interested me intensely, particularly when a few telephone calls to Marine Corps representatives in Washington made it clear that this was a defector who had gone far beyond simply going over to the other side ideologically. The Marine Corps directed me to high-ranking officers who said that Garwood was the first Marine in history who had taken up arms against his own coun-trymen." At the end of the court-martial there seemed no question that Garwood was a "monstrous traitor." Was any of this true? Like so much else that we are assured is true by the powers that seem eter-nally to be in our media-marinated land, Garwood was no traitor. He was a scapegoat for the Nixon-Kissinger cover-up of the fact that some thirty-five hundred American POWs had been kept by the Viet-namese communists as hostages to make sure that the United States would pay the $3 billion in war reparations that Nixon had promised before his resignation. "The big question was, why had the US gov-ernment declared that all prisoners were returned in 1973, and then four years later officially determined that all but one . . . were dead?" I shall not spoil the suspense of Jensen-Stevenson's astonishing nar-rative by itemizing the cold-blooded bad faith of the US government complemented by a media all too eager to speak lies in power's name, creating a "monstrous traitor-deserter" of a Marine who had been held captive for fourteen years by the Viet Cong until he escaped, only to be seized by the American military, who forced him to undergo the longest court-martial in our history. Why was it so crucial not only to smear him as a traitor but as a deserter? He was proof, in himself (not to mention his firsthand memories), that the Nixon administration had deliberately abandoned and then erased through the media hundreds of prisoners, thus avoiding payment of the agreed-upon ransom money, and silencing those in and out of the military who had a good idea of the sinister game they played.

Borjesson has also included a valuable piece by herself on the shooting down of TWA Flight 800 en route from New York to Paris on July 17, 1996. It would appear that a missile fired from the sea off New England's coast brought the passenger plane down, killing all aboard. Eyewitnesses on the ground or at sea spoke of a fiery missile rising from the sea to collide with the plane. But that was contrary to the official story that a spark inside a fuel tank was responsible.

Where Borjesson is particularly good is in her analysis of the lies both crude and nuanced that are still being told by the military and the media. I fear that she is hard on my idol, Greta van Susteren, but let the debris fall where it must. Borjesson "deconstructs" a TV interview van Susteren conducts with a "legitimate news guest" who will follow the government's line; no guest who disagrees is to be heard on that hour. Borjesson writes: "I'll begin with the introduction Susteren reads (she may or may not have written it by herself).

"At first people thought that a bomb went off on the plane. But a painstaking search brought up most of the shattered pieces of the 747 for investigators to reconstruct. Their conclusion: an electrical spark probably ignited vapors in the jet's empty fuel tank, vapors caused by the heat of air-conditioning units located just under the tank. Just two months later, the government ordered airplanes and airplane manufacturers to change the way fuel tanks are designed, repaired, and operated." Borjesson comments: "Here's how I read the subtext to van Susteren's introduction: investigators worked their 'butts off' (that's the 'painstaking search' part) and finally concluded—although they can't prove it (that's what the word 'probably' tells you)—that an electrical spark caused the plane to explode. And they're doing something about it (albeit belatedly)." Susteren is almost ready now for her legitimate guest, but she holds a large caveat in reserve. "Is that the end of the story? And what about the conspiracy theorists who keep insisting the jet was actually shot down?" With this rhetorical question she shoots down two birds with a single phrase. Because "now she's telling you to think that anyone who doesn't buy the government's unproven theory, anyone who thinks the jet may have been shot down, is a 'conspiracy theorist.' Tacitly attached to the term conspiracy theorist are all kinds of other nouns and adjectives like goofball, nutcake, bottomfeeder. . . . Using insulting and false labels to marginalize dissenting or politically incorrect voices is a ploy that the government and corporations as well as the press use on a daily basis." Why daily? Certainly because in the real world conspiracies are the rule not the exception. Remember those tobacco companies that conspire to fool the public into thinking that cigarettes are not that harmful to health. In fact, most advertising is conspiratorial in the way it praises or denigrates a product. Finally, what on earth is a political party but a conspiracy to appropriate the powers of the state for secret ends like a preemptive war in order to annex oil fields for cronies while awarding contracts to other cronies that specialize in the demolition of cities that other companies will be paid hugely to rebuild?

Luckily, for all these conspirators (never fear to use the right word), American consumers are generally so comfortable dog-paddling in the waters of Lethe that they do not read with any care the lies much less the corrective truths that the authors of this volume have collected at some cost to themselves.

ACKNOWLEDGMENTS

As always, my deepest gratitude goes to this book's unwavering champion, Gore Vidal, and to its contributors:

Jane Akre
Ashleigh Banfield
Gerard Colby
Charlotte Dennett
David E. Hendrix
Carl Jensen
Monika Jensen-Stevenson
John Kelly
Michael Levine
Helen Malmgren
Robert McChesney
Maurice Murad
Greg Palast
J. Robert Port
Dan Rather

Charles Reina
Gary Webb
Philip Weiss

Special thanks go to James Bamford, who generously agreed to contribute his astonishing reporting to the introduction that follows.

Many thanks, too, to Steven L. Mitchell, editor in chief of Prometheus Books: Without his tireless efforts and support, this edition of *Into the Buzzsaw* would not have seen the light of day.

EDITOR'S
INTRODUCTION

Censorship, particularly self-censorship, has been a prominent feature of post-9/11 news reporting. Many journalists willingly limited their coverage of certain stories, while others chafed silently. Some, including a few major media "stars," actually spoke out about it:

> There is a corporate mentality out there, but there is also a tremendous amount of self-censorship among the press. It's like a disease. But also—they not only—they took away the edge from the press, they also muzzled the bureaucracy, they muzzled the Congress, and it's an amazing feat. We're supposed to be a democratic society, and all of those areas bowed and scraped to this group of neocons who advocated a policy. (Seymour Hersh, July 7, 2004, during keynote speech to the American Civil Liberties Union)

> It's an obscene comparison—I'm not sure I like it—but there was a time in South Africa when people would put flaming tires around people's necks if they dissented, and in some ways the fear is that you'll be necklaced here. You'll have a flaming tire of lack of patriotism put around your neck. Now it's that fear that keeps journalists from asking the toughest of the tough questions and to continue to bore in on the tough questions so often. And again, I am humbled to

say, I do not except [*sic*] myself from this criticism. (CBS Network's Dan Rather to BBC *Newsnight*'s Madeleine Holt on May 16, 2002)

Free speech is a wonderful thing, it's what we fight for, but the minute it's unpalatable, we fight against it for some reason. That just seems to be a trend of late, and I am worried that it may be a reflection of what the news [coverage of the Iraq war] was and how the coverage was coming across. (MSNBC's Ashleigh Banfield lecturing at Kansas State University on April 24, 2003)

I think the press was muzzled and I think the press self-muzzled. . . . I'm sorry to say that, but certainly television — and perhaps to a certain extent my station — was intimidated by the administration and its foot soldiers at FOX News. And it did, in fact, put a climate of fear and self-censorship in terms of the kind of broadcast work we did. . . . All of the entire body politic in my view — whether it's the administration, the intelligence, the journalists, whoever — did not ask enough questions, for instance, about weapons of mass destruction. I mean, it looks like this was disinformation at the highest levels. (CNN and CBS's Christiane Amanpour on Tina Brown's *Topic [A]* show on CNBC on September 10, 2003)

Both Banfield and Amanpour were taken to task for their comments. CNN Newsgroup president Jim Walten reportedly had a "private conversation" with Amanpour and then released this statement: "Christiane is a valued member of the team and one of the world's foremost journalists. However, her comments do not reflect the reality of our coverage and I do not agree with her about this." A FOX News spokeswoman added for good measure: "It's better to be viewed as a foot soldier for Bush than spokeswoman for al Qaeda."

NBC responded to Banfield's lecture by releasing a statement that read, in part: "Ms. Banfield does not speak for NBC News. We are deeply disappointed and troubled by her remarks and will review her comments with her."

One news executive, CNN International's executive vice president and general manager Rena Golden, did admit to institutional self-censorship. "Anyone who claims the US media didn't censor itself is kidding you. It wasn't a matter of government pressure, but a reluctance to criticize a war that was obviously supported by a vast majority of the people. And this isn't just a CNN issue — every journalist who was in any way involved in 9/11 is partly responsible."

Golden was blaming the American people for journalists failing to do their jobs. The crux of this defense is that in the midst of all the patriotic fervor, the network perceived that its audience *didn't want* critical coverage. They wanted cheerleading. So that's what they got. It would have been bad for ratings and bad for business to provide coverage for which there was little or no demand. And so in a time of extreme crisis, CNN, "The Most Trusted Name in News," wittingly sacrificed its journalistic integrity to give its audience members what they "wanted."

Others who defended their networks denied that there had been any censorship at all. Then, there was a conversation that I had with ABC *Nightline's* Ted Koppel. "I think you have to be very careful when you use the word censorship," Koppel explained to me. "Censorship has a very clear meaning to me. Censorship has the force of law. Censorship involves *the government* [my italics] saying, 'You cannot report what you want to report. You have to show us everything that you intend to put on the air and we will then decide whether you can or whether you can't. That's censorship." Koppel further explained that "the fact that the Bush administration, like the Clinton administration before it, like every administration I've known in the . . . thirty-two years that I've been working in Washington now, tries to influence what gets on the air and what doesn't get on the air — that's not censorship. That's *political influence* [italics mine]." Koppel assured me that he'd never been censored. We had our chat literally a few weeks after the Sinclair Broadcasting Company, a group of stations that reaches one-quarter of the entire TV-watching population in America, had ordered its ABC stations not to carry his program featuring the names and photographs of members of the American military who had been killed in Iraq. Koppel's disingenuous definition of censorship aside, his own experience with Sinclair illustrates why the government doesn't need laws to censor information. Ever-more-close ties between business and government have allowed a highly effective system of information suppression and manipulation to evolve organically.

While Sinclair company executives were accusing *Nightline* of exerting — guess what — political influence to "undermine the efforts of the United States in Iraq," Robert McChesney, *Buzzsaw* contributor and president of the national media group Free Press, was pointing out that Sinclair executives had donated more than $140,000 of hard and soft money to President Bush and other Republicans, and that they had a compelling business interest in not carrying any programming that reflected badly on the Bush administration.

Did this compelling business interest that McChesney was referring to keep critical journalism "product" to a minimum before the Iraq war? Judge for yourself: at the same time that President George Bush, Defense Secretary Donald Rumsfeld, and Secretary of State Colin Powell were using the WMD argument to "sell" the Iraq war to the American people; at the same time that mass media journalists should have been asking the tough questions about those WMDs, Powell's son, FCC chairman Michael Powell, was deciding whether or not he was going to roll back FCC regulations to allow broadcast media conglomerates like Sinclair Broadcasting to own an even larger (45 percent instead of the current 35 percent) percentage of properties in each broadcast market. Powell *fils* literally had the broadcast industry by the bottom line while his dad and the rest of the administration were all over the airwaves selling the war.

Award-winning broadcast journalist Jon Alpert told me this story about a colleague's experience during the first Gulf War:

> I have a friend who was working for a . . . newsweekly magazine at the time of the first war. And he refused to go into those [press] pools and was operating independently along the Saudi border. And he actually received the first surrender of any Iraqis during the war. He was wandering around in the desert when a bunch of Iraqis came over a sand dune and he was the only American around so they surrendered to him. And he brought these guys in, [and] I don't remember what his other stories were, but he was getting all these herograms from his editor, "You're just doing a great job. Keep at it. You're the best." Then all of a sudden he got a message that he should go back in his hotel room and not leave his hotel room until he joined one of the government pools. And he didn't understand this because he'd been operating outside the pools and been doing such a good job and they were telling him that. And what had happened was that the congressional liaison from the Pentagon had contacted the large conglomerate that owned his newsmagazine and said, "You know that bill, that communication bill that's going through Congress? If you would like that bill to emerge in any form that that you would find favorable, you tell your reporter to get in his hotel room and not to come out of that hotel room unless he's in a pool."

Alpert's colleague does not want to be identified because he still works in big media.

Was there an exchange of friendly coverage for a friendly FCC decision before the current war began? I can't say for certain, but the conflict of interest was real and it was huge, and coverage of the government leadership's agenda on mass media television was overwhelmingly friendly. The coverage coming out of FOX (billing itself in the summer of 2004 as "America's Newsroom: Trusted. Independent. Powerful.") amounted to cheerleading. The other networks provided wall-to-wall "official source" coverage that amounted to going along with the program. And at Clear Channel, the nation's largest radio network, a very popular show host sent this response to public relations agent Ilene Proctor after receiving Proctor's press release announcing a large peace demonstration: "I will have to pass on this one, as the station is rigidly requiring me to do only pro-war pieces."

Every corporation has a fundamental right to protect and promote its bottom line in every way it legally can. It makes perfect business sense to sacrifice critical news coverage for billions of dollars in future profits. But if a news operation that makes perfect business sense is the operating paradigm for America's mainstream media, it is absurd to expect it to consistently assume the public service role of critical watchdog and purveyor of truth to power. Why should the networks have been expected to practice great journalism and pierce the veil of government propaganda when the case for war was being made? With so much profit at stake and audiences unwilling to watch or hear criticism of the government, why should they have stuck their financial necks out or sacrificed future profits to help Americans decide whether or not it was a good idea to send their sons and husbands and wives and daughters to die in Iraq?

Michael Powell did decide in big media's favor. And just like the tougher questions that were asked *after* the war about WMDs, the hundreds of thousands of phone calls and e-mails from angry citizens protesting Powell's decision that flooded the FCC *after* he'd made it didn't matter. The Bush administration already had what it wanted: a largely compliant press when it really needed it and, ultimately, the war in Iraq.

As if reporting in the truth-starved environment created by the government/business alliance wasn't bad enough, journalists are also currently operating in a time when the suppression and withholding of information to which the public has a legal right is at an all-time high.

Tom Curley, president and CEO of the Associated Press, told me in an interview that after surveying AP bureau chiefs around the country, he determined that from the federal level on down to the local level, access to information in public offices has been drastically curtailed. Curley explained that this was the result of a memo that Attorney General John Ashcroft had written in which Ashcroft stated: "We presume all government information to be secret unless proven otherwise."

Add to government secrecy and the government/business alliance yet another virtually insurmountable hurdle for reporters: the hugely successful industry manufacturing and manipulating information, replacing relevant or suppressed information. Reporters are barraged constantly with inane, half-true public relations "product." But on matters of grave national importance, like whether or not to go to war, they are subjected to a manipulation machine that is second to none. Even worse, top reporters at powerful media outlets are part of that machine. The most prominent recent example of this is Judith Miller at the *New York Times*. Her reporting using "secret" Iraqi and high-level government sources with compelling information that turned out to be bogus resulted in headlines like "Illicit Arms Kept till Eve of War, an Iraqi Scientist Is Said to Assert," on April 21, 2003; "U.S. Says Hussein Intensifies Quest for A-Bomb Parts," on September 8, 2002; and "Iraqi Tells of Renovations at Sites for Chemical and Nuclear Arms," on December 20, 2001. In an e-mail she wrote to her colleague, the highly regarded war correspondent John Burns, Miller admitted that the now-discredited Ahmad Chalabi had "provided most of the front-page exclusives on WMD to our paper."

THE GREAT MANIPULATION AND DECEPTION MACHINE

In his must-read book, *A Pretext for War*, national security reporter and author James Bamford writes about Miller big-footing soldiers while covering the search for WMDs in Iraq: "One military officer complained that Miller sometimes 'intimidates Army soldiers by invoking Defense Secretary Donald Rumsfeld or Undersecretary Douglas Feith.'"* Indeed, Miller even managed to snag a secret clearance from

---

*All quotes in this section are taken from Bamford's book, *A Pretext for War: 9/11, Iraq, and the Abuse of America's Intelligence Agencies* (New York: Doubleday, 2004).

the Pentagon to accompany their expert teams searching for weapons of mass destruction. On one hand, it was a great coup. On the other hand, surely the Pentagon gave the clearance to Miller secure in the knowledge that she wouldn't burn them or the administration in her reports. Miller, who has a sterling résumé that includes expertise in weapons of mass destruction, seems to have made the classic journalist's pact with the devil: she got great access to high-level sources and great stories in return for shilling for those sources, which involved printing what they told her (no questions asked), and putting out — knowingly or otherwise — false information from time to time. If I were to guess why Miller's bosses are standing by her, I'd say it was because of her big, friendly contacts in the government. Anyone with lesser aces in the hole would have already been shown the door. For her superiors at the *New York Times*, the only real drawback to keeping Miller is that it might mean having to add a few more mea culpas to the two that they've already issued in the last two years.

Miller's reporting was an end product of a mind-boggling manipulation and deception machine in the Bush administration that was set up and overseen by three former advisors to the Israeli government who became senior US government officials: Richard Perle, chairman of the Defense Policy Board that advised Defense Secretary Donald Rumsfeld (Perle resigned as chairman in 2003 and from the board in 2004); Douglas Feith, undersecretary of defense for policy, the highest policy position in the administration; and David Wurmser, Vice President Richard Cheney's Middle East advisor. While advising former Israeli prime minister Benjamin Netanyahu, they came up with a plan entitled "A Clean Break: A New Strategy for Securing the Realm," which advised, according to Bamford, "launching a major unprovoked regional war in the Middle East, attacking Lebanon and Syria and ousting Iraq's Saddam Hussein. Then, to gain support of the American government and public, a phony pretext would be used as the reason for the original invasion." Furthermore, "Another way to win American support for a preemptive war against Syria, they [Perle, Wurmser, and Feith] suggested, was by drawing attention to its weapons of mass destruction program." Netanyahu didn't go for the plan, but with a little revision, the Bush administration did. "From the very first moment," writes Bamford, "the Bush foreign policy would focus on three key objectives: get rid of Saddam Hussein, end American involvement in the Israeli-Palestinian peace process, and rearrange the dominoes in the Middle East. A key to the policy shift would be the concept of 'preemption.'"

Controlling Iraq is just the beginning. There's way more to come if the Bush administration remains in charge. As David Wurmser put it, Israel and the United States "should broaden the conflict to strike fatally, not merely to disarm, the centers of radicalism in the region — the regimes of Damascus, Baghdad, Tripoli, Teheran, and Gaza. That would reestablish the recognition that fighting either with the United States or Israel is suicidal."

Right after 9/11, Wurmser was in charge of making the case to connect Hussein to the attacks. To fulfill this mandate, he set up a new arm of the White House manipulation and deception machine called the Policy Counterterrorism Evaluation Group. Bamford describes it as "little more than a pro-propaganda cell. It was designed to produce evidence to support the pretexts for attacking Iraq. This involved going through old and new intelligence collected by the various agencies and finding loose ties between Saddam Hussein and al Qaeda." According to Bamford, Wurmser's unit's "primary purpose was to come up with some basis to counter the CIA, whose analysts had consistently found no credible links between al Qaeda and Hussein." Wurmser himself "had no background at all in intelligence." This adds a striking new dimension to the intelligence failure question, doesn't it?

Meanwhile, Douglas Feith set up the Office of Strategic Influence, which, in Bamford's words, was "intended to be a massive disinformation factory." Also very busy at the same time was the Rendon Group, a public relations firm that the CIA had hired at former president George H. W. Bush's behest back in the early nineties to come up with a propaganda campaign that would vilify Saddam Hussein to the point of instigating a military coup against him. Now, having been unsuccessful at fomenting a coup more than one decade and almost two hundred million dollars later, the Rendon Group was working aggressively to promote Chalabi — one of Judith Miller's main prewar reporting sources — as Hussein's successor-in-waiting.

The Office of Strategic Influence was dismantled after a hue and cry arose about its obnoxious mission. So the mission continued elsewhere. Yet another secret office was set up in the White House in August 2002. Created by Feith, it was dubbed the Office of Special Plans (OSP). "Its purpose was to conduct advance war planning for

Iraq, and one of its most important responsibilities was 'media strategy.' [Are you beginning to see why it was almost impossible for the media to get to the bottom of anything with respect to WMDs?] Hidden away on the Pentagon's fifth floor . . . the office was Top Secret. 'We were instructed at a staff meeting that this office was not to be discussed or explained said [retired Air Force Lt. Karen] Kwiatkowski, 'and if people in the Joint Staff, among others, asked, we were to offer no comment.'" This office was so secret that even members of the *Joint Staff* [my italics] weren't allowed to know what it was doing. "Picked to head the OSP was still another longtime Perle protégé, Abram N. Shulsky," says Bamford. Meanwhile, in Israel, a mirror OSP was set up in Israeli prime minister Ariel Sharon's office. The *Guardian* (in London) reported that the Israeli OSP's mission was to give key Bush administration officials "more alarmist reports on Saddam's Iraq than Mossad was prepared to authorize." Israeli officials were discreetly coming and going from their OSP office to the Pentagon's (where their visits were intentionally not recorded) and adding their fabricated intelligence reports to those of their counterparts. One of the OSP's tasks, Bamford reported, was to target "the doubters and nonbelievers [in the government], from the CIA to the Secretary of State." "This was creatively produced propaganda spread not only through the Pentagon but across a network of policymakers," said Kwiatkowski. "OSP needed to convince the remaining holdovers, Colin Powell, for example. There was a lot of frustration with Powell, they said a lot of bad things about him at the office. . . .' She added that the OSP had a 'very close relationship' with Vice President Cheney's office." Indeed, the OSP was waging all-out war against all who wouldn't get with the program. "According to one former senior Pentagon official who worked closely with Feith's offices, their goal was not just 'how to fight Saddam Hussein, but also how to fight the NSC [National Security Council], the State Department, and the intelligence community,' which was not convinced of Hussein's involvement in terrorism." Those who wouldn't accept the OSP's fake information or go along with the agenda — like intelligence experts at the CIA and Gen. Anthony Zinni, the former commander of Middle East Forces — were attacked and put on enemies lists.

This shocking saga continues.

Meanwhile, genuine intelligence officers in Israel and the United States could find no evidence of Iraqi WMDs. Yet another secret White

House office was set up to make sure that their message was drowned out by the messages being formed and sent out by a new offshoot of the manipulation machine called the White House Iraq Group (WHIG). Chief of Staff Andrew Card was in charge of this group comprised of high-level administration officials (Karl Rove and Condoleezza Rice among them) charged with selling the war to the general public through "televised addresses and by selectively leaking the intelligence to the media," writes Bamford. Here, I must ask again, how does a reporter get past this huge and vicious information manufacturing and manipulating machine? I'd also like to point out to all taxpaying Americans that this whole operation is an example of their hard-earned money being used against them. The whole "intelligence failure" scenario is looking more and more like a post-op cover story, isn't it?

Anyway, back to the White House Iraq Group. According to Bamford, "In June 2002, a leaked computer disk containing a presentation by Bush strategist Karl Rove revealed a White House political plan to use the war as a way to 'maintain a positive issue environment.' But the real pro-war media blitz was scheduled for the fall and the start of the election season 'because from a marketing point of view, you don't introduce new products in August,' said Card. . . . In addition to ties between Hussein and 9/11, among the most important products the group was looking to sell as Labor Day 2002 approached were frightening images of mushroom clouds, mobile biological weapons lab, and A-bomb plants, all in the hands of a certified 'madman.' A key piece of evidence that Hussein was building a nuclear weapon turned out to be the discredited Italian documents purchased on a street corner from a con man."

In August the manipulation machine kicked into gear with Cheney making the rounds to sound the alarm about Saddam's WMDs: August 7, 2002, at the Fairmont Hotel, San Francisco, California, "In the case of Saddam Hussein, we have a dictator who is clearly pursuing these capabilities [nuclear and radiological weapons and biological and chemical agents] and has used them both in his war against Iran and his own people." August 26, 2002, at the VFW 103rd national convention, "There's no doubt that Saddam Hussein has weapons of mass destruction. . . . With our help, a liberated Iraq can be a great nation once again." August 29, 2002, to the Veterans of Korean War, San Antonio, Texas, "Simply stated, there is no doubt that Saddam Hussein now has weapons of mass destruction. There is no doubt that he is amassing them to use against our friends, against our allies, and against us."

At exactly the same time in Israel, writes Bamford, Ariel Sharon's office "began issuing similar dire warnings concerning Hussein and pressing the Bush administration to go to war with Iraq. Like those from Cheney, pronouncements from Sharon's top aide, Ra'anan Gissin, included frightening 'evidence' — equally phony — of nuclear, as well as biological and chemical, threats. 'As evidence of Iraq's building activities,' said an Associated Press report on the briefing, 'Israel points to an order Saddam gave to Iraq's Atomic Energy Commission last week to speed up its work, said Sharon aide Ra'anan Gissin. 'Saddam's going to be able to reach a point where these weapons will be operational,' he said. . . . Israeli intelligence officials have gathered evidence that Iraq is speeding up efforts to produce biological and chemical weapons.'" The AP's report went out to its viewing audience and readers numbering more than one billion while CBS News picked up the story and put out this headline: "Israel to U.S., Don't Delay Iraq Attack."

Little more than one week after Cheney's address to the Korean veterans, at a joint Camp David press conference, Bush stood next to Britain's prime minister, Tony Blair, as Blair dropped a big one on the press: "The point that I would emphasize to you is that the threat from Saddam Hussein and weapons of mass destruction, chemical, biological, potentially nuclear weapons capability, that threat is real. We only need to look at the report from the International Atomic [Energy] Agency this morning showing what has been going on at the former nuclear weapons sites to realize that." Then Bush chimed in: "We just heard the Prime Minister talk about the new report. I would remind you that when the inspectors first went into Iraq and were denied — finally denied access, a report came out of the Atomic — the IAEA that they were six months away from developing a weapon. I don't know what more evidence we need."

Now here was a chance for journalists to check the evidence for themselves by getting a copy of this new report and reading it. Few did. NBC's Robert Windrem was the mainstream media exception. He caught the lie and reported it on that same day. In his report entitled "White House: Bush Misstated Report on Iraq," Windrem showed that the latest IAEA report, which dated back to 1998, in fact documented just the opposite of what Bush and Blair were announcing:

"based on all credible information available to date . . . the IAEA has found no indication of Iraq having achieved its programme goal of producing nuclear weapons." But as the star *New York Times* op-ed columnist Paul Krugman pointed out later in his "Matters of Emphasis" editorial dated April 29, 2003, "for a few hours the lead story on MSNBC's Web site bore the headline 'White House: Bush Misstated the Report on Iraq.' Then the story vanished—not just from the top of the page, but from the site."

Windrem's report immediately forced the White House to admit it was wrong: "What happened was, we formed our own conclusions based on the report," a senior White House official told NBC's Norah O'Donnell. Spinning fake results out of legitimate reports and information is a classic modus operandi of the White House propaganda machine.

NBC's now-you-see-it, now-you-don't reporting didn't stick, and the White House's confession sank without a trace as Bush went ahead and repeated and expanded upon the same lie one week later on his weekly radio address: "Today Saddam Hussein has the scientists and infrastructure for a nuclear weapons program, and has illicitly sought to purchase the equipment needed to enrich uranium for a nuclear weapons program. Should his regime acquire fissile material, it would be able to build a nuclear weapon within a year."

Then came the bogus aluminum tube stories, and the whip-up-the-fear mushroom cloud myths, all sold to the big papers and TV shows by the White House's media stars—Dick Cheney, Condoleezza Rice, Colin Powell, and Donald Rumsfeld. It all went like clockwork. As I write this (late July 2004), there have been recent reports of government officials discussing the idea of postponing the upcoming presidential election in the event of a terrorist attack. On the heels of those reports, the Bush administration announced that it was exploring whether or not Iran can be connected to 9/11. After reading Bamford's breakdown of how information is parsed out by the current government's propaganda machine, I'm having a hard time suppressing this paranoid thought: Will the next terrorist attack occur around election time, "forcing" the government to postpone the election and lead us into a war against Iran after "discovering" that Iran was responsible for the attack? Past experience shows that we should be vigilant and make every effort to avoid being led by the nose into a conflict that is potentially far more deadly than anything we've experienced in Iraq.

As I end this section, I draw your attention to something you probably already noticed. The reporting in it came largely from James Bamford's book *A Pretext for War* and has been paraphrased here with the author's permission. His account of the well-planned, highly sophisticated—and sometimes brutal—operation of deception going on at the White House and Pentagon should be read by every citizen of this country. I especially hope that those who served on the 9/11 Commission, particularly those who suffer the illusion that many members of our government—particularly our leaders—lack imagination, will read Bamford's account. If you ask me, it should trigger some indictments (the names are all in chapter 12, entitled "War Room," of the book). Bamford has performed a great service in his book, and what he has done serves as a shining example of really great investigative reporting. It also explains why journalists were hopelessly behind the eight ball before the war in Iraq, particularly those with a hard-core dependence on high-level official sources.

CANARIES FLYING INTO THE BUZZSAW

These days, it takes more guts and brains than ever to be a good reporter. Journalists are operating in an extremely toxic-to-truth environment polluted by official secrecy, business interests, government/business alliances, and corrupt public relations campaigns, waged both inside and outside our government.

In the past couple of years, there has been a spate of books examining who or what is responsible for the problems of American journalism, but *Into the Buzzsaw: Leading Journalists Expose the Myth of a Free Press* distinguishes itself among them all as the most frank and honest book out there. It's the only book in which a group of award-winning journalists and authors actually take you behind the scenes themselves to show you how they did their reporting and how they experienced censorship. No other book so graphically depicts the dangerous landscape in which reporters—particularly investigative reporters working to uncover high-level malfeasance on the part of powerful people or institutions—must operate. The reporters lay bare the "buzzsaw," or powerful system of censorship made up of myriad triggers located everywhere from inside reporters' heads and the offices of newsroom managers to large corporations and government institutions, including the Pentagon and the Oval Office.

In the previous edition, veteran journalist David Hendrix wrote that reporters like *Buzzsaw*'s contributors played a role in society similar to that of canaries in a coal mine: "The songs coal mine canaries sing may become irritating at times, but smart people learn to appreciate their presence and listen for their tunes. The silence of the canaries is a signal that the environment has turned deadly." That's why there is a greater sense of urgency about this edition of *Into the Buzzsaw*. Powerful new voices have joined those of the original group of "canaries" to reveal a news-producing environment that is under more censorship pressure than ever. The venerable Gore Vidal, this book's unwavering champion, has written a brilliant new foreword in his usual fearless yet eloquent voice. In *Buzzsaw*'s lead chapter, CBS's top correspondent, Dan Rather, describes in chilling terms how the pressure to be patriotic compelled him and other journalists to censor themselves. In chapter three, former MSNBC correspondent Ashleigh Banfield speaks frankly about the critical difference between coverage and real journalism and how failing to report all sides of a story, as well as critical stories about what's going on around the world, has created a very dangerous environment of ignorance. And in chapter 2, former FOX Network producer Charles Reina exposes in a stunning impassioned letter to the Poynter Institute* details of how the news billed as "Fair and Balanced" is also a political tool that is shaped daily via an executive memo distributed electronically to FOX's news staff every morning, addressing what stories will be covered and, often, suggesting how they should be covered. Reina explains that "to the newsroom personnel responsible for the channel's daytime programming, The Memo is the bible. If, on any given day, you notice that FOX anchors seem to be trying to drive a particular point home, you can bet The Memo is behind it."

The Memo may strike some as an outrageous development in the newsroom, but it makes good business sense and has probably been a key element in promoting FOX's rapid rise and success in the ratings. The fact is, FOX News targets a large and, until now, underserved, segment of the American population; a segment that has perceived longstanding bias at the other mass media networks. Here's how a veteran investigative reporter for whom I have the utmost respect — and who happens to be a conservative born-again Christian — put it:

---

*The Poynter Institute describes itself as a "school for journalists, future journalists, and teachers of journalists."

"non–FOX News journalists need to understand why FOX is so hugely successful and popular with their biased conservative format. It's not because the news is reported from a conservative view. It certainly is not fair and balanced, for the most part. They are successful because those of us, like me, who are conservative and think we are the guardians of what makes the country great, are elated to see questions asked that we would ask the way we would ask them, and elated to see stories that do not portray conservative Christian values as Nazi ideas redux and liberal nontraditional agendas as being the only policies any sane, clear-thinking person would endorse. I grew to hate, in the last dozen years I was a reporter-editor, the newsroom exchanges and news assignment directives in which the values I held important, and that at least 50 percent of the population we allegedly were serving felt to be important, were trashed, vilified, and considered alien to human logic. If the traditional media, such as CBS, NBC, PBS, CNN, and ABC, ever are going to be considered relevant to the 50 percent of us who feel disenfranchised by most of today's media, the traditionals are going to have to consider us relevant and our ideas, for the most part, worthy. . . . I shake my head when I see conservatives always portrayed as screaming maniacs whose ideas are without merit, and the never-satiated liberal agenda as the enlightened preservation of society. . . . The truth is, each side always needs to question itself more than its opponents."

The "traditional" media have more to worry about than losing their conservative audience to FOX. According to *Guardian* reporter Jason Deans, Americans turned to the BBC in droves for their war news, increasing PBS's audience by 28 percent three weeks after the conflict began. Meanwhile, CBS's nightly news viewership went down 15 percent and ABC's dipped by 6 percent. "Jonathan Howlett, the director of airtime sales at BBC World," wrote Deans, "claimed more viewers were tuning in to the network for its balanced and impartial" reporting. Perhaps the signal here to traditional network chiefs worried about having to go the "FOX" route to make money is that there is a significant audience out there searching for real, relevant, and unvarnished reporting.

If bias in the news is too prevalent, context is too absent. In a new chapter entitled "The War on Terror and the Great Game for Oil: How the Media Missed the Context," investigative reporter and author Charlotte Dennett makes this all too clear. Her authoritative piece, based on almost thirty years of painstaking research, exposes the real context behind the latest war in the Middle East. It contains the kind of sorely needed, in-depth information that was lacking—sometimes intentionally, sometimes not—in prewar (Iraq) reporting. Sins of omission are a big part of censorship, particularly in the current climate. Withholding information that would provide invaluable context and history, explain key aspects of a story, and make the whole situation understandable is much too common these days.

The kind of investigative reporting that Dennett and her husband and coauthor, Gerard Colby, do, literally takes decades to accomplish. They work to shed light on the activities of the most powerful individuals on the planet—members of global family dynasties—who know how to hide their influence and don't take kindly to being scrutinized. Their investigation of the Rockefeller family and its involvement in developing the oil industry became the book *Thy Will Be Done, the Conquest of the Amazon: Nelson Rockefeller and Evangelism in the Age of Oil.* This, along with their follow-up book currently in the works, entitled *The Kingdom and the Power: Oil, the Holocaust, and American Espionage at the Dawn of the Middle East Crisis,* completes what is arguably the most definitive investigative account of the history of the development of the oil industry ever written. You, dear reader, are privileged to get a sneak peek of their next book in Dennett's chapter. In the course of their work, Colby and Dennett have run into several aspects of the "buzzsaw," including one called privishing. The term refers to the methods publishers use to kill a book without an author's knowledge when pressured by a powerful institution or individual to do so. Gerard Colby writes about his personal experience with privishing in a chapter entitled "The Price of Liberty."

A number of chapters in this edition have been updated, and in every case, the news is bad or not good enough. In "The Fox, the Hounds, and the Sacred Cows," Jane Akre writes about how she was fired after refusing to alter to the point of falsifying her investigative piece on the possible dangers of Monsanto Corporation's Bovine Growth Hormone in milk. Her troubles began when Monsanto called FOX to complain about her program. Akre's update on her long, ongoing legal battle with FOX should scare all journalists as well as everyone who depends on the press for information about products that are potentially dangerous or unhealthy. John Kelly's update on CIA activities currently being carried out as part of the War on Terror, as allowed under Section 308 of the Intelligence Authorization Act — a virtual carte blanche for criminal activity — can only be described as the kind of information that stops one cold. It raises serious questions about whether certain ad hoc "offices" and activities are ultimately doing more to perpetuate the War on Terror than to win or end it. It also provides a clear-cut example of the press submitting its reporting to the government for censoring: "Ironically," writes Kelly, "the CIA approved the coverage of its assassinations. This was revealed in a *Washington Post* article that inadvertently disclosed that the *Post* is in the habit of providing the CIA with advance copies of its articles for censorship. 'Provided with a detailed account of the contents of this article,' wrote *Post* reporter Dana Priest, 'US government officials made no request to the *Post* to withhold any of the story's details from publication, as they have sometimes done in other cases involving covert operations.'" In her chapter update, Monika Jensen-Stevenson talks about the latest and most egregious hidden information that she has uncovered about the treatment average American soldiers are currently receiving, even in death. Few journalists have championed America's soldiers for so long and with such determination as Jensen-Stevenson.

If this book is proof of anything, it is proof of the fact that it takes guts to stand up to censorship. I salute those journalists living in the limelight who have spoken out about it, because their voices are heard by many and because they do so knowing there will be consequences. It can't be easy to be an international media star and to have your wrists slapped in front of an entire nation. So thank you Christiane Amanpour and Ashleigh Banfield. And thank you Dan Rather for being so honest in your interview with the BBC. But my deepest gratitude goes to those who are less well known and who not only stood up and spoke out, but also fought long and hard for their stories, making huge sacrifices in the process. Some of them are in this book. Former-DEA-agent-turned-journalist Mike Levine faced death on a number of occasions before becoming a journalist and reporting the ugly truths that he uncovered on the job. Monika Jensen-Stevenson, Gerard Colby, Charlotte Dennett, and John Kelly have dealt with death threats, faced penury, and spent literally decades working on the stories they present here. Yet others pursued stories that led to the demise of their careers, like Gary Webb and Jane Akre. And then there's CBS's Helen Malmgren, who has worked inside the pressure cooker of network television for many years, producing investigative pieces of the highest caliber that have saved lives and made criminals accountable. Her account of the challenges and difficulties of producing a documentary exposing high-level corporate malfeasance—in this case on the part of a large chain of psychiatric hospitals—is riveting. Bob Port's chapter about his fight with the Associated Press to report on the No Gun Ri massacre that took place during the Korean War is a small prose masterpiece that movingly captures his struggles to get the story out, as well as his own sensitive and utterly decent character. After shoving Bob aside for fighting for the story, the AP finally released it—and won a Pulitzer Prize.

Many journalists on less intense tracks regard the breed of reporters in *Buzzsaw* as strange, obsessive creatures with overworked imaginations. For the record, here's what these reporters are really like: generally, they're smarter, more curious, and more enterprising than the average journalist. They are voracious researchers and excellent students of human nature. They are analytical, but like some criminals they investigate, they also have great imaginations and a highly developed reptilian sense. And although it may not seem like it from their behavior in the newsroom, they can connect with, and talk to, anybody—from paragons of evil to living saints—because they actually love people. They can live anywhere and often do. They can handle extreme situations no matter how strange or horrible. And while they're not fearless, they know how to deal with fear and how to work through it. They aren't easily intimidated, and once they've been assigned a story, they want to go after it until they nail it—no matter how long it takes. One of their most important tools is what I'll call their perpetual scanning capacity. This is what looks like "obsession" to others. It's the ability to continue sifting through information and working on a story in your head no matter what you're doing, whether feeding your kids, mowing the lawn, or even sleeping. This process eventually leads to a breakthrough in your understanding, an epiphany of sorts that allows you to see the entire lay of the land that is your story. After that, you know exactly where to find the evidence you've been looking for, and you can predict what the characters in your story will do and say next. That's how you nail it. It's a long, arduous process, but it works every time. Great law enforcement agents understand this; they have the same set of skills and go through the same process. So now I ask you: whom would you rather have in the newsroom covering the big stories in this era of the War on Terror, the reporter who'll go for the information no matter what, or the reporter who'll back down or think twice about asking the tough questions if the wind is blowing in the wrong direction?

I'm investing a great deal of hope in this edition of *Buzzsaw*. I'm hoping that it will get out to more members of the general public who may still not be aware of what's really going on with the information we're all getting. I hope this book will encourage them to think more critically about the news and to look for better sources, thereby sending the message to the current mass media that bad journalism is bad for business. I'm hoping *Buzzsaw* will inspire more journalists to speak out and work against censorship by asking the tough questions when necessary no matter what pressures are brought to bear upon them. I'm hoping more members of the nation's power elite will choose to speak out against corporate and government leaders who use mass media outlets as their mouthpieces or stenographers to lie to the American people. I'm hoping that full-frontal exposure of the crisis in American journalism will spark public demand for, and the creation of, a vibrant and independent press. I'm hoping that in some journalism school somewhere, an academic visionary will be inspired to cut through the cobwebs and politics and begin formulating a curriculum that would provide longer, more rigorous, and more relevant training for future members of US journalism's elite. We need a new corps of ninja journalists, of alley cats with college degrees, schooled in the reptilian arts that are so effectively being used against us now, as well as in traditional academic disciplines. We desperately need critical thinkers and disinformation experts too knowledgeable, too well trained, and too disciplined to fall for lies and misinformation, much less report them. We need more incorruptible warriors like those who tell their stories in this book. We need them now.

CHAPTER I

THE PATRIOT AND THE CENSOR'S NECKLACE
AN INTERVIEW WITH BBC CULTURE CORRESPONDENT MADELEINE HOLT

Lonnie Juli, CBS News

DAN RATHER

Dan Rather is the anchor and managing editor of CBS Evening News *and correspondent for* 60 Minutes II. *During his more than three decades at CBS, Rather has been all over the world and handled some of the most challenging assignments in journalism. He has received virtually every honor in broadcast journalism, including numerous Emmy Awards, a Peabody Award, and citations from critical, scholarly, professional, and charitable organizations. Since he joined CBS in 1962, Rather has held many prestigious positions at the network, including correspondent for, and co-editor of, CBS's award-winning*
documentary unit CBS Reports; *host/reporter for the award-winning newsmagazine show* 48 Hours; *CBS News bureau chief in London and Saigon; and White House correspondent during the Johnson and Nixon administrations. His regular contributions to CBS News Radio include* Dan Rather Reporting, *a weekday broadcast of news and analysis that has been airing since 1981. Rather began his career in journalism in 1950 reporting for the Associated Press and, later, for the United Press International. After that, he reported for several radio stations in Texas, including KSAM in Huntsville, and KTRH in Houston, where he later served as news director. Prior to joining CBS News as chief of its southwest bureau in Dallas, Rather was news director at KHOU-TV, the CBS affiliate in Houston. He is the author of a number of books, including* The American Dream, Deadlines and Datelines, The Camera Never Blinks, *and* The Camera Never Blinks Twice.

Editor's Note: While working in what has been, arguably, the most difficult reporting environment in recent times, CBS's Dan Rather chose to speak out frankly to *BBC Newsnight* correspondent Madeleine Holt about the serious and dangerous constraints that he and his colleagues have experienced in the post-9/11 era. I know of no other working broadcast journalist of Rather's long experience and stature who has been willing to go on the record in such a significant way about these matters.

BBC NEWSNIGHT, MAY 16, 2002

Holt: How much of a challenge professionally has covering September 11 been and the implications of September 11?

Rather: I don't know of any American journalist who doesn't believe that September 11 and what has followed represented the greatest challenge of our journalistic lifetimes. It's certainly true of myself. I've been very lucky and very blessed over the years as a journalist to cover what—I will say and I hope in no self-serving way—is my fair share of these stories, but nothing, nothing, compares with September 11 and what's happened in the wake of it.

Holt: One of the issues that particularly interests us is the issue of access . . . which of course you've spoken about. In your own experience of covering so many administrations over the years . . . could [you] put into perspective how restrictive or otherwise you see this administration has been, and I'm thinking in particular of the Pentagon and getting access to the military side of things.

Rather: The question of access is one that most, if not all, American journalists including myself—I do not except myself from this criticism—has not been asked enough; often enough and deep enough. Let us set aside September 11 and the days that followed in terms of lower Manhattan, the Pentagon, and what is now the hero's field in rural Pennsylvania. Access was extremely limited to the press during the time of September 11 and ever since then. Limited in a way that is unprecedented in American journalism. I do not make that sound as any complaint. This was a unique, horrific situation the likes of which our country has never been through before. So, speaking for myself — but I think it's an opinion shared by many other journalists — there was a full understanding of why access was so limited during that time. For example, you had a police pass, which under all other circumstances would have allowed you to get into certain areas. The police said, and I think rightly so, "It doesn't matter today, you're not going." Now I can't say I liked that, can't say I agreed with it, but I certainly understood it.

In the weeks and months that followed September 11, the question of access became, I think, much more difficult, much more problematic, and more challenging for American journalists, because the federal government began to take an unprecedented attitude about the access of American journalists to the war. [In saying this, I'm] making a division here between what the local and state authorities felt they had to do the day of September 11 and immediately following that, with what has transpired since in the way of the federal government's attitude toward the press and press coverage of the war.

There's never been an American war — small or large — in which access has been so limited as this one. Now what's particularly troubling about this — and the longer we go, the more troubling it is — is that what's being done practically, in real terms, is in direct variance with what the Pentagon's stated policy is. The Pentagon's stated policy is: maximum access and maximum information consistent with national security. That's not only reasonable, I think it's necessary for anybody's military and anybody's federal government during wartime, and I have no argument with that policy. My argument — and I do argue it without apology — is that's not the reality. It's one thing [for the Pentagon] to say, "This is the policy and we're living up to the policy." It's another thing to say that "this is the policy," but without even a wink or a nod, "we're not going to do it."

Holt: So what's going [on] here?

Rather: Well, what's going on to a very large extent, I'm sorry to say, is a belief that the public doesn't need to know. A belief — and let me underscore that I think this is not only erroneous, but dangerous in a society such as ours — that there does not have to be a high degree of communicable trust between the leadership and the led, or, at the very least, that you can manipulate a degree of communicable trust between the leadership and the led, and the way you do that is you just don't let the press in anywhere, and that the public's sense of patriotism will overwhelm any questions about the need for access. Nothing I say to you is more important than the first sentence of what follows: "I take a back seat to no one in my love for this country, in patriotism. I know how corny it might sound to those on the outside, but I would willingly die for the country at a moment's notice and on command of my president under these present circumstances." Having said that, I worry that patriotism run amok will trample the very values that the country seeks to defend. I want to make this as clear as I possibly can. I believe in my marrow that to sustain war for any reasonable amount of time, which we're going to have to do in the War on Terrorism, a high degree of communicable trust between the leadership and the led is not just desirable, it's essential. In a constitutional republic based on the principals of democracy such as ours, you simply cannot sustain warfare without the people at large understanding why we fight, how we fight, and have a sense of accountability to the very top.

Now, let's get down to the practical matter of access in the months that we've had of this War on Terrorism. Limiting access for national security, no argument. Limiting information for national security, no argument. Limiting access, limiting information to cover the backsides of those who are in charge of the war is extremely dangerous and cannot and should not be accepted. And I'm sorry to say, that up to and including the moment of this interview, that overwhelmingly it has been accepted by the American people. And the current administration revels in that, they relish that, and they take refuge in that. But whatever partisan political game it may benefit them, I have no argument about it. But in terms of what's good for the country, a lot of us better start asking stronger, longer questions about it.

Holt: Do you feel that you're the only person who is asking those kinds of questions and would you want other journalists, other news organizations perhaps, to get together and . . . or is that happening, I don't know.

Rather: Well, first of all, I'm not the only person asking these questions about access and information and limiting of same. I'm not even the most articulate or potent voice in American journalism raising the question. As for enlisting the support of others in doing it, my experience has been I have all I can handle to speak for myself, to speak from both my head and heart my experience. What I try to do is think and speak what I believe to be the truth or as close to the truth as I can possibly know. If others agree fine, if they disagree, I'm sorry. I don't want to belabor the point, but I want to come back to the point, that none of us in journalism have asked the questions strongly enough or long enough about this business of limiting access and information for reasons other than national security.

Holt: Do you think in a sense that's because—and you've spoken about this climate of patriotism—that it in some senses seemed to be un-American to be asking tough questions.

Rather: Yes. This is the most dangerous thing for us in journalism. I would argue it's a dangerous thing for anybody anywhere in journalism. But for an American journalist right now not to ask these questions—respectfully and at the same time forcefully and to stay on point because we know, one of things you do in journalism, if someone ducks a question, you need to follow up, keep on asking—it's unpatriotic not to ask questions. It's unpatriotic not to stand up, look them in the eye, and ask them the questions they don't want to hear. They being those who have the responsibility, the ultimate responsibility in a society such as ours of sending our sons and daughters, our husbands, wives—our blood—to face death, to take death. In my position, my view is [that] not to ask the tough questions in this kind of environment is the height of a lack of patriotism. However, there's no question that the patriotism that began to sweep the country—rightfully so the second the awful events of September 11 happened—has contributed to the strength of the country in many important ways, but in this way, it has been a problem for us as a people, as a nation, as a society: there's been a reluctance to ask the tough questions for fear of being seen as unpatriotic. And let me emphasize to you I do not except myself from that criticism.

Holt: Have you yourself felt that pressure both immediately after September 11 and subsequently in the War on Terror?

Rather: Of course I have. And anybody in American journalism who tells you that he or she has not felt this pressure I think is either

kidding themselves or trying to deceive you. I would say in the immediate aftermath of September 11 — on September 11 and in the immediate aftermath — I didn't feel this. This was such a shock to the
system here. Just a terrible thing. I can only speak for myself, but I
know this is widely shared not just among American journalists, but
Americans in general. There was this deep horror [and] mourning
mixed with the deepest and most abiding anger and sense of outrage
that I can remember in my lifetime. And these things were boiling
within oneself. And my own feeling of patriotism ran extremely high
then and has never subsided.

What happened is, as we got away from September 11 — and make
no mistake, it will never, ever be forgotten by me or for that matter by
my American counterparts in journalism and out — but once we
embarked on the war in the very early stages of October, then as the
war progressed, this question arose. We sort of pushed it off to the
side — the question of listen, there's no access, there's no information.
It's not a question of journalists not getting it; it's the public is not getting it. And weeks went by, and one said, "Well, it'll improve."
Months went by. We said, "Well, it'll improve." We understand they
just, they — those being in charge of access and information to the
war— they'll steady themselves [soon]. . . . But now we're talking
about coming up soon a year later, and it hasn't gotten better.

In many ways it's gotten worse. Let me put an asterisk, a footnote
at the bottom of the page. There will be those in the Defense Department and the White House and elsewhere who would argue that
things have gotten better, and in a few minor ways, they have a point.
But the broad overview remains: access to the war is extremely limited, and the fiercer the combat, the more the access is limited. In the
access to information, ditto. And I repeat for emphasis this is a direct
contradiction of the stated policy of maximum access to information
consistent with national security. It doesn't say consistent with protecting some general or secretary, or for that matter the very top of the
command structure, including civilians. It doesn't say anything about
protecting their backsides. It doesn't say anything about this [limited
access] is there if we make a mistake, [so that] we're not [held]
accountable for it. And, I would say that overwhelmingly the limiting
of access to information has much more to do with the determination
to be seen as playing errorlessly, conducting the war errorlessly than
it does with any sense of national security. I recognize there are others

with a contrary point of view, but this is where I stand, and I will stand in no other place about that.

Holt: Could you give me an example of a story or instance where you felt that pressure to not be as tough as you normally would have been?

Rather: Oh boy, the list is so long it's hard to pick any one. What we're talking about here whether one wants to recognize it or not, or call it by its proper name or not, is a form of self-censorship. It starts with a feeling of patriotism within oneself. It carries through with the knowledge that the country as a whole, and for all the right reasons, felt, and continues to feel, this surge of patriotism within themselves. And one finds oneself saying, "I know the right question, but you know what, this is not exactly the right time to ask it." And then the next time, you say to yourself, "You know that question's still there and it's an even better time to ask it. Do you know what, I just don't think it's still the right time." Look, self-censorship is a real and present danger to journalists at every level and on a lot of different kinds of stories. My point is, it's never more important for us to recognize it, to sort of pull it out from within ourselves, to face and to look at it than in time of war because people's lives are at stake and we are asking some of the best among us to be in harm's way. Some have died, more will die. So it gets down to: what's my responsibility as a journalist? We speak of courage and heroism for people in uniform, policemen, firemen, our military people. Well, gently I would say, the world also demands if not courage, certainly something other than cowardice, from those of us who have the responsibility of independent journalism.

Holt: It's a terribly difficult situation to be in, isn't it, for someone like yourself who has had a reputation over the decades for being someone who always asked that tough question? It's something of a dilemma when . . . now more than ever the public must appreciate a news program or an anchor who does ask those tough questions, because now more than ever they need to be asked.

Rather: I appreciate the compliment. . . .
In general, before the war, before September 11, fear ruled every newsroom in the country in some important ways. It was the fear [of] if we don't dumb it down, if we don't tart it up, if we don't go to the trivial

at the expense of the important, you know what, we're not going to be publishing a newspaper or magazine, and we're not going to be on the air; the ratings will eat us up. A more important relative of that fear takes hold in the wake of war. It is, "You know, I know what the right question is, I should bore in and if he or she doesn't answer, I should come back with a follow-up and another follow-up. You know what, I'm not confident the public is going to understand that I see that as patriotic, [rather than] not patriotic." And there is the fear that you will have to pay the price—at the very least that you will be perceived as being unpatriotic. And let us also be candid about one other aspect of this. And this is not an excuse, because I'm not the vice president in charge of making excuses here. I'm seeking to have people understand how the decision-making process works; that those who have a partisan political interest in staying in power or achieving power—the "ins" or the "outs"—there are certain among them who are always prepared that if you don't report the news that they want, in the way they want it, or if you don't pull your punches in the way they want you to pull your punches, that they are determined to make you pay a price, and that is they will certainly hang a sign around you metaphorically [labeling you] with the audience [as] unpatriotic. It's an obscene comparison—I'm not sure I like it—but there was a time in South Africa when people would put flaming tires around people's necks if they dissented, and in some ways the fear is that you'll be necklaced here. You'll have a flaming tire of lack of patriotism put around your neck. Now it's that fear that keeps journalists from asking the toughest of the tough questions and to continue to bore in on the tough questions so often. And again, I am humbled to say, I do not except myself from this criticism.

CHAPTER 2

THE MEMO

Dossi Thayer

CHARLES REINA

Charles Reina has worked in broadcast journalism for more than thirty years as a writer, reporter, editor, and producer. He entered the profession in 1970, working for a series of small-town radio stations in upstate New York, covering local events from politics and government to police matters, criminal trials, and sports. In 1975, Reina joined the Associated Press as a broadcast news writer and editor, eventually covering the media-and-entertainment beat for both broadcast and print wires. In 1982, Reina moved to CBS Radio, where he wrote, edited, and produced newscasts for the network's legendary news team, including Douglas Edwards, Richard C. Hottelet, Marlene Sanders, and Charles Osgood. Reina made the transition to network television in 1984, joining ABC's Good Morning America as a writer and segment producer. Among his personal GMA highlights: on-the-scene coverage of the 1989 San Francisco earthquake and, in 1990, Operation Desert Shield in Saudi Arabia. In 1997, after a brief freelance stint outside "mainstream" network news, Reina signed on with the fledgling FOX News Channel to produce its media criticism show FOX News Watch. Over the next six years he wrote and produced specials as well as edited newsroom copy until he resigned in April 2003.

Editor's Note: The sense of outrage in the letter below written by ex-FOX producer and media critic Charles Reina to Poynteronline's Jim Romenesko[1] is palpable and may inspire skepticism in the minds of

43

those who think damning information is more credible when delivered in a calm, measured manner. Sharri Berg, vice president of news operations for FOX News Channel, responded to the letter by characterizing Reina as a "disgruntled employee," with "an ax to grind." Berg also said that "Mr. Reina's premise about 'the memo' is unfounded. People are proud to work here. They are proud of the product we produce and understand our daily and future goals." No one at FOX has publicly denied the existence of The Memo or the factual content of Reina's missive, which is why I think it is important to read. Beyond his own feelings about certain experiences he had, and things he saw at FOX, Reina exposes a news operation with a clear-cut agenda that is set and managed outside of the newsroom, in corporate executive offices. This, combined with the firsthand accounts of other television journalists in this book, raises serious questions about the future of unfettered reporting on significant issues and events in broadcasting, the most powerful of the mass media outlets.

So Chris Wallace says FOX News Channel is fair and balanced. Well, I guess that settles it. We can all go home now. I mean, so what if Wallace's salary as FOX's newest big-name anchor ends with a whole lot of zeroes? So what if he hasn't spent a day in the FNC [FOX News Channel] newsroom yet?

My advice to the pundits: If you really want to know about bias at FOX, talk to the grunts who work there—the desk assistants, tape editors, writers, researchers, and assorted producers who have to deal with it every day. Ask enough of them what goes on, promise them anonymity, and you'll get the real story.

The fact is, daily life at FNC is all about management politics. I say this having served six years there—as producer of the media criticism show News Watch, as a writer/producer of specials, and (for the last year of my stay) as a newsroom copyeditor. Not once in the twenty-plus years I had worked in broadcast journalism prior to FOX— including lengthy stays at the Associated Press, CBS Radio, and ABC/Good Morning America—did I feel any pressure to toe a management line. But at FOX, if my boss wasn't warning me to "be careful" how I handled the writing of a special about Ronald Reagan ("You know how Roger [FOX News Chairman, Ailes] feels about him."), he was telling me how the environmental special I was to produce should lean ("You can give both sides, but make sure the pro-environmentalists don't get the last word.").

Editorially, the FNC newsroom is under the constant control and vigilance of management. The pressure ranges from subtle to direct. First of all, it's a news network run by one of the most high-profile political operatives of recent times. Everyone there understands that FNC is, to a large extent, "Roger's Revenge" against what he considers a liberal, pro-Democrat media establishment that has shunned him for decades. For the staffers, many of whom are too young to have come up through the ranks of objective journalism, and all of whom are nonunion, with no protections regarding what they can be made to do, there is undue motivation to please the big boss.

Sometimes, this eagerness to serve FOX's ideological interests goes even beyond what management expects. For example, in June of last year [2002], when a California judge ruled the Pledge of Allegiance's "Under God" wording unconstitutional, FNC's newsroom chief ordered the judge's mailing address and phone number put on the screen. The anchor, reading from the TelePrompTer, found himself explaining that FOX was taking this unusual step so viewers could go directly to the judge and get "as much information as possible" about his decision. To their credit, the big bosses recognized that their underling's transparent attempt to serve their political interests might well threaten the judge's physical safety and ordered the offending information removed from the screen as soon as they saw it. A few months later, the same eager-to-please newsroom chief ordered the removal of a graphic quoting UN weapons inspector Hans Blix as saying his team had not yet found WMDs in Iraq. Fortunately, the electronic equipment was quicker on the uptake (and less susceptible to office politics) than the toady and displayed the graphic before his order could be obeyed.

But the roots of the FNC's day-to-day on-air bias are actual and direct. They come in the form of an executive memo distributed electronically each morning, addressing what stories will be covered and, often, suggesting how they should be covered. To the newsroom personnel responsible for the channel's daytime programming, The Memo is the bible. If, on any given day, you notice that the FOX anchors seem to be trying to drive a particular point home, you can bet The Memo is behind it.

The Memo was born with the Bush administration, early in 2001, and, intentionally or not, has ensured that the administration's point of view consistently comes across on FNC. This year, of course, the war in Iraq became a constant subject of The Memo. But along with the obvious—information on who is where and what they'll be covering—there have been subtle hints as to the tone of the anchors' copy. For instance, from the March 20 memo: "There is something utterly incomprehensible about Kofi Annan's remarks in which he allows that his thoughts are 'with the Iraqi people.' One could ask where those thoughts were during the 23 years Saddam Hussein was brutalizing those same Iraqis. Food for thought." Can there be any doubt that the memo was offering not only "food for thought," but a direction for the FNC writers and anchors to go? Especially after describing the UN Secretary General's remarks as "utterly incomprehensible"?

The sad truth is, such subtlety is often all it takes to send FOX's newsroom personnel into action—or inaction, as the case may be. One day this past spring [2003], just after the United States invaded Iraq, The Memo warned us that antiwar protesters would be "whining" about US bombs killing Iraqi civilians, and suggested they could tell that to the families of American soldiers dying there. Editing copy that morning, I was not surprised when an eager young producer killed a correspondent's report on the day's fighting, simply because it included a brief shot of children in an Iraqi hospital.

These are not isolated incidents at FOX News Channel, where virtually no one of authority in the newsroom makes a move unmeasured against management's politics, actual or perceived. At the Fair and Balanced network, everyone knows management's point of view, and, in case they're not sure how to get it on air, The Memo is there to remind them.

NOTE

1. At the Poynteronline Web site, Jim Romenesko is described as a "veteran reporter, editor, and pioneering weblogger." His weblog, ROMENESKO, "provides journalists with brief commentaries about (and links to) articles about journalism or journalists." Poynteronline is the Poynter Institute's Web site and can be found at http://www.poynter.org. On its Web site, the Poynter Institute is described as "a school for journalists, future journalists, and teachers of journalists."

CHAPTER 3

A SHOT MESSENGER'S OBSERVATIONS

Mary Ellen Matthews

ASHLEIGH BANFIELD

Ashleigh Banfield is an international television news correspondent and host who has reported breaking news from across the country and around the globe. For MSNBC, Banfield covered the terrorist attacks of September 11, reporting live from the World Trade Center in New York City. Her work garnered Emmy Award recognition. After eight consecutive days at Ground Zero, Banfield departed for Islamabad, Pakistan, to begin covering the War on Terror. From September 2001 to January 2004, she reported live from Pakistan, Afghanistan, Iran, Iraq, England, Israel (Tel Aviv, West Bank, Gaza), Jordan, Lebanon, Syria, and Saudi Arabia. She anchored several prime-time series, including "A Region in Conflict" and "Ashleigh Banfield: On Location," in which she hosted live programs from locations across the country and around the globe, covering breaking news stories such as the wars in Afghanistan and Iraq, the conflict in Israel, and the abduction of Elizabeth Smart in Salt Lake City. As a correspondent for NBC News, Banfield appeared on The Today Show, NBC Nightly News with Tom Brokaw, *and* Dateline. *While anchoring on MSNBC, Banfield covered stories including the crash of the Concorde on location in France; the 2000 election, traveling with the Bush/Cheney campaign; and the 2000 Summer Olympic Games in Sydney, Australia. Prior to joining MSNBC, Banfield was news anchor for KDFW-TV, the FOX station in Dallas. There she received her first Emmy Award for Best News Anchor for her coverage on "Cadet Killers," as well as a Texas Associated Press Award for Best Series for the controversial "To Serve and Survive." Prior to that, Banfield produced for Canada's CICT-TV in 1992–1993. She was promoted to evening news anchor in 1993. In 1994, she won two IRIS*

awards for Best News Documentary and Best of Festival for her chronicle of the life of a home-
less man. While at CICT-TV, Banfield also freelanced as an associate producer for ABC's
World News Tonight, covering the 1991 Bush/Gorbachev summit in Russia and the 1992
Clinton/Yeltsin summit in Vancouver. From 1989 to 1992, Banfield served as weekend evening
news anchor at CFRN in Edmonton, Alberta. Later, she moved to Winnipeg's CKY station as
a researcher/reporter for their evening news. She began her career in 1988 as a photogra-
pher/researcher/reporter at CJBN in Kenora, Ontario, Canada. She has a bachelor's degree in
political studies and French from Queen's University in Ontario.

Editor's Note: Former MSNBC correspondent Ashleigh Banfield's observations on the triumphs and travesties of reporting on the recent conflicts in the Middle East, her comments about what constitutes real journalism, and her accounts of the personal challenges that she's faced in the current reporting climate are all lucidly articulated in the lecture below, delivered extemporaneously at Kansas State University. Frank appraisals such as this one from a high-profile journalist are rare, and therefore precious. It is unfortunate — and a mistake, I think — that NBC executives chose to construe her comments as an attack on the network. It is puzzling, too, since under NBC's aegis, Banfield was able to provide the kind of exemplary reporting that she discusses in her lecture.

ASHLEIGH BANFIELD'S LANDON LECTURE AT KANSAS STATE UNIVERSITY ON APRIL 24, 2003

The last time I was in Manhattan, Kansas, there were a lot of other stories that were making top headlines, not the least of which were the anniversary of 9/11, the continued hunt for Osama bin Laden, the whereabouts of Elizabeth Smart, and what was to become of Saddam Hussein; and we have some resolution on very few of these stories, but we certainly know at least what Saddam Hussein is not up to these days, and it's leading Iraq.

So I suppose you watch enough television to know that the big TV show is over and that the war is now over essentially — the major combat operations are over anyway, according to the Pentagon and defense officials — but there is so much that is left behind. And I'm not just talking about the most important thing, which is, of course, the leadership of a Middle Eastern country that could possibly become an enormous foothold for American and foreign interests. But also what Americans find themselves deciding upon when it comes to news, and when it comes to coverage, and when it comes to war, and when it comes to what's appropriate and what's not appropriate any longer.

I think we all were very excited about the beginnings of this [Iraq war] conflict in terms of what we could see for the first time on television. The embedded process . . . was something that we've never experienced before, neither as reporters nor as viewers. The kinds of pictures that we were able to see from the front lines in real time on a video phone, and sometimes by a real satellite link-up, was something we'd never seen before and were witness to for the first time.

And there are all sorts of good things that come from that, and there are all sorts of terrible things that come from that. The good things are obvious. This is one more perspective that we all got when it comes to warfare, how it's fought and how tough these soldiers are, what the conditions are like, and what it really looks like when they're firing those M-16s rapidly across a river, or across a bridge, or into a building.

There were a lot of journalists who were skeptical of this embedding process before we all embarked on this kind of news coverage before the campaign. Many thought that this was just another element of propaganda from the American government. I suppose you could look at it that way. It certainly did show the American side of things, because that's where we were shooting from. But it also showed what can go wrong.

It also gave journalists, including Al-Jazeera journalists and Arab television journalists and Arab newspaper journalists, who were also embedded . . . the opportunity to see without any kinds of censorship how these fights were being fought, how these soldiers were behaving, what the civil affairs soldiers were doing, and what the humanitarian assistance really looked like. Was it just a line we were being fed, or were they really on the ground with boxes of water and boxes of food?

So for that element alone, it was a wonderful new arm of access that journalists got to warfare. Perhaps not that new, because we all knew what it looked like in Vietnam and what a disaster that was for the government, but this did put us in a very, very close line of sight to the unfolding disasters.

That said, what didn't you see? You didn't see where those bullets landed. You didn't see what happened when the mortar landed. A puff of smoke is not what a mortar looks like when it explodes, believe me. There are horrors that were completely left out of this war. So was this journalism or was this coverage? There is a grand difference between journalism and coverage, and getting access does not mean you're getting the story, it just means you're getting one more arm or leg of the story. And that's what we got, and it was a glorious, wonderful picture that had a lot of people watching and a lot of advertisers excited about cable news. But it wasn't journalism, because I'm not so sure that we in America are hesitant to do this again, to fight another war, because it looked like a glorious and courageous and successful endeavor, and we got rid of a horrible leader. We got rid of a dictator, we got rid of a monster, but we didn't see what it took to do that.

I can't tell you how bad the civilian casualties were. I saw a couple of pictures. I saw French television pictures. I saw a few things here and there, but to truly understand what war is all about you've got to be on both sides. You've got to be a unilateral, someone who's able to cover from outside of both front lines, which, by the way, is the most dangerous way to cover a war, [and] which is the way most of us covered Afghanistan. There were no front lines, they were all over the place. There were caves, and there were mountains. But we really don't know from this latest venture of the American military what this thing looked like and why perhaps we should never do it again. The other thing is that so many voices were silent in this war. We all know what happened to Susan Sarandon for speaking out, and her husband, and we all know that this is not the way Americans truly want to be. Free speech is a wonderful thing, it's what we fight for, but the minute it's unpalatable, we fight against it for some reason.

That just seems to be a trend of late, and I am worried that it may be a reflection of what the news is and how the news coverage is coming across. This was a success, it was a charge, it took only three weeks. We did wonderful things and we freed the Iraqi people, many of them by the way, who are quite thankless about this. There's got to be a reason for that. And the reason for it is because we don't have a very good image right now overseas, and a lot of Americans aren't quite sure why, given the fact that we sacrificed over a hundred soldiers to give them freedom.

Well, the message before we went in was actually weapons of

mass destruction and eliminating weapons of mass destruction from this regime and eliminating this regime. Conveniently, in the week or two that we were in there, it became very strongly a message of freeing the Iraqi people. That should have been the message early on, in fact, in the six to eight months preceding this campaign, if we were trying to win over the hearts of the Arab world.

That is a very difficult endeavor, and from my travels to the Arab world, we're not doing a very good job of it. What you read in the newspapers and what you see on cable news and what you see on broadcast news networks is nothing like they see over there, especially in a place like Iraq, where all they have access to is a newspaper called *Babel*, if you can believe it. It's really called *Babel*. And it was owned and operated by Uday, who you know now is the crazier of Saddam's sons. And this is the kind of material that they have access to, and it paints us as the great Satan regularly, or at least it used to. I'm sure it's not in production right now.[1] And it's not unlike many of the other newspapers in the Arab world, either. You can't blame these poor sots for not liking us. All *they* know is that we're crusaders. All *they* know is that we're imperialists. All *they* know is that we want their oil. *They* don't know otherwise. And I'll tell you, a lot of the people I spoke with in Afghanistan had never heard of the Twin Towers and most of them couldn't recognize a picture of George Bush.

So you're dealing with populations who don't know better and who are very suspect as to who these new liberators are, because every liberator before has been wreaking havoc upon their lives and their children and their world. So I wasn't the least bit surprised to see these marches and these pilgrimages in the last few days telling the Americans, "Thanks for the freedom to march to Najaf and Karbala, but get out." You know, this wasn't that big of a surprise. I think it may be a surprise, though, to the Pentagon. I'm not sure that they were ready to deal with this many dissenters and this many supporters of an Islamic regime, like next door in Iran.

That will be a very interesting story to follow in the coming weeks and months, as to how this vacuum is filled and how we go about presenting a democracy to these people. If we give them democracy, they will probably ask us to get out, which is exactly what many of them want.

But it's interesting to be able to cover this. There's nothing in the world like being able to cross a green line whenever you want and speak to both sides of a conflict. I can't tell you how horrible and won-derful it is at the same time in the West Bank and Gaza and Israel. There are very few people in this world who can march right across the guarded checkpoints, closed military zones, and talk to Pales-tinians on the same day that they are "embedded" with Israeli troops, and that's something that we get to do on a regular basis.

And I just wish that the leadership of these different entities, ours included, could do the same thing, because they would have an eye-opening experience, horrible and wonderful, all at the same time, and it would give a lot of insight as to how messages are heard and how you can negotiate. Because you cannot negotiate when someone can't hear you or refuses to hear you or can't even understand your lan-guage, and that's clearly what's happening in a lot of places in the world right now. In the West Bank, Gaza, and Israel, there's very little listening and understanding going on. Our language is entirely dif-ferent than theirs, and I don't mean just words. When you hear the word "Hezbollah," you probably think evil, danger, terror right away. [The word] usually connotes fear, terror, [and] some kind of suicide bombing. If you live in the Arab world, "Hezbollah" means Shriner. Hezbollah means charity. Hezbollah means hospitals. Hezbollah means welfare and jobs.

These are not the same organizations we're dealing with. How can you negotiate when you're talking about two entirely different meanings? And until we understand—we don't have to like Hezbollah, we don't have to like their militancy, we don't have to like what they do on the side, but we have to understand that they [Hezbollah supporters] like it, that they like the good things about Hezbollah, and that you can't just paint it with a blanket statement that it's a terrorist organization, because even when it comes to mili-tancy, these people believe that militancy is simply freedom fighting and resistance. You can't argue with that. You can try to negotiate, but you can't say it's wrong flat out.

And that's some of the problems we have in dealing with this war on terror. As a journalist, I'm often ostracized just for saying these mes-sages, just for going on television and saying, "Here's what the leaders of Hezbollah are telling me and here's what the Lebanese are telling me and here's what the Syrians have said about Hezbollah. Here's what they have to say about the Golan Heights." Like it or lump it, don't shoot the messenger, but invariably the messenger gets shot.

We hired somebody on MSNBC recently named Michael Savage.[2] Some of you may know his name already from his radio program. He was so taken aback by my daring to speak with Al-Aqsa Martyrs Brigade about why they do what they do, why they're prepared to sacrifice themselves for what they call a freedom fight and we call terrorism. He was so taken aback that he chose to label me as a slut on the air. And that's not all, as a porn star. And that's not all, as an accomplice to the murder of Jewish children. So these are the ramifications of simply being the messenger in the Arab world.

How can you discuss, how can you solve anything when attacks from a mere radio flak are what America hears on a regular basis, let alone at the government level? I mean, if this kind of attitude is prevailing, forget discussion, forget diplomacy — diplomacy is becoming a bad word.

I'm fascinated to find out how we are going to diplomatically fix what's broken now in Iraq because nobody thinks Jay Garner is going to be a leader for Iraq.[3] They don't want him to be a leader. He says he doesn't want to be a leader, but he sure as heck wants to put a leader in there who is akin with our interests here in America so that we don't have to face this trouble again. Clearly, it's the same kind of idea we had in Afghanistan with Hamid Karzai. You know, they all look at him as a puppet. We look at him as a success story. Again, two different languages being spoken and not enough coverage of that side.

Again, I'm not suggesting support for that side. There are a lot of things that I hate about that side, but there's got to be coverage, there's got to be the journalism, and sometimes that is really missing in our effort to make good TV and good cable news.

When I said the war was over, I kind of mean that in the sense that cards are being pulled from this famous deck now of the fifty-five most wanted, and they're sort of falling out of the deck as quickly as the numbers are falling off the rating chart for the cable news stations. We have plummeted into the basement in the last week. We went from millions of viewers to just a few hundred thousand in the course of a couple of days.

Did our broadcasting change? Did we get boring? Did we all suddenly lose our flair? Did we start using language that people didn't want to hear? No, I think you've just had enough. I think you've seen the story, you've seen how it ended; it ended pretty well in most Americans' view, [so now] it's time to move on.

What's the next big story? Is it Laci Peterson? Because Laci Peterson got a whole lot more minutes' worth of coverage on the cable news channels in the last week than we'd have ever expected just a few days after a regime fell, like Saddam Hussein's.

I don't want to suggest for a minute that we are shallow people, we Americans. At times we are, but I do think that there's a phenomenon of attention deficit disorder when it comes to watching television news and watching stories and then just being finished with them. I think it might come from the saturation we have nowadays. You cannot walk by an airport monitor, you can't walk by most televisions in offices these days, in the public, without it [the television] being [turned] on [to] a cable news channel. And if you're not in front of a TV, you're probably in front of your monitor, where there is Internet news available as well.

You have had more minutes of news on the Iraq war in just the three-week campaign than you likely ever got in the years and years of network news coverage in Vietnam. You were forced to wait for it [Vietnam War news] till six o'clock every night and the likelihood that you got more than about eight minutes of coverage in that half hour show, you probably didn't get a whole lot more than that, and it was about two weeks old, some of that footage, having been shipped back. Now it's real time and it is blanketed to the extent that we could see this one arm of the advance, but not where the bullets landed.

But I think the saturation point is reached faster because you just get so much so fast, so absolutely in real time, that it is time to move on. And that makes our job very difficult, because we tend to leave behind these vacuums that are left uncovered. When was the last time you saw a story about Afghanistan? It's only been a year, you know, since the major combat ended. Operation Anaconda[4] was not more than eleven or twelve months ago, and here we are not touching Afghanistan at all on cable news.

There was just a memorandum that came through saying we're closing the Kabul bureau. The Kabul bureau has only been staffed by one person for the last several months, Maria Faisal. She's Afghan, and she wanted to be there; otherwise, I don't think anyone would have taken that assignment. There's just been no allotment of TV minutes for Afghanistan.

And I am very concerned that the same thing is about to happen with Iraq, because we're going to have another Gary Condit, and we're going to have another JonBenet, and we're going to have another Elizabeth Smart, and here we are in Laci Peterson, and these stories will dominate. They're easy to cover, they're cheap, they're fast, you don't have to send somebody overseas, you don't have to put them up in a hotel that's expensive overseas, and you don't have to set up satellite time overseas. [It's] very cheap to cover domestic news. Domestic news is music news to directors' ears.

But is that what you really need to know? Don't you need to know what our personality is overseas and what the ramifications of these campaigns are? Because we went to Iraq, according to the president, to make sure that we were going to be safe from weapons of mass destruction, that no one would attack us. Well, did everything all of a sudden change? The terror alert went down. All of a sudden everything seems to be better, but I can tell you from living over there, it's not.

There are a lot of people who hate us, and it only takes one man who's crazy enough to strap a bunch of suicide devices onto his body to let us know that he can instill fear in even a place like Manhattan. You know, you're not immune from it. One suicide bomb in a mall in a small town in America can paralyze this country, because every small town will think it's vulnerable, not just New York, not just [Washington] DC, not just L.A. [Los Angeles]—everybody. And we may not be far from that, and I'm desperately depressed that it's come to this, that it's come to American shores in the worst way.

I was under the second tower when it came down in New York City on September 11. I have a real stake in this; I've got two friends whose remains haven't been found yet at the Trade Center. That stays with you for quite a while. It's important that we continue to *want to know* what happens overseas when we leave. It's important to demand coverage of these things. It's important because your safety and your future and your world and your children will depend on this stuff.

If we had paid more attention to Afghanistan in the '80s we might not have had 9/11. If we hadn't left it in such a mess, we might not have had 9/11, and three thousand people would be alive to talk to you today. If we do the same thing in Iraq, it is possible that without you even knowing, a brand-new federation is formed where deals are made in secret because the leadership is not allowed to talk about America in good ways, [because if the leadership did] the street would blow up. Because that's essentially what happens everywhere else in the Arab world right now. You can't talk about making deals and allowing the Americans to use your military bases or you will be out like the shah. Not in the election, of course, but you'd be out like the shah. And most of these people worry about that. I'm very concerned that Iraq may end up in the same way.

There was a report in the *New York Times* a couple of days ago that I read at the Pentagon. It was a report on the ground in Iraq that the Americans were going to have four bases that they would continue to use possibly on a permanent basis inside Iraq, kind of in a star formation, the north, the south, Baghdad, and out west. Nobody was able to actually say what these bases would be used for, whether it was forward operations, whether it was simple access, but it did speak volumes to the Arab world, who said, "You see, we told you the Americans were coming for their imperialistic needs. They need a foothold, they need to control something in central and western Asia to make sure that next door we all come into line."

And these reports about Syria, well, they have been breezed over fairly quickly here, but they are ringing loud still over there. Syria's next. And then Lebanon. And look out Iran.

So whether we think it's plausible or whether the government even has any designs like that, the Arabs all think it's happening and they think it's for religious purposes for the most part. Again, most of them are so uneducated and they have such little access to the media, what they do get is [a] very bad story, and there's no reason why they shouldn't be [as] afraid as they are. They just don't have the luck that we do of open information.

One of the things I wanted to mention [was] about the technology of this war . . . and how that's changed, perhaps not only how the fighters behave, but how we see things. The tanks and the vehicles that are used in the front lines are so high-tech that an artillery engineer can actually pinpoint a target that looks like a tiny stick man on the screen and simply destroy the target without ever seeing a warm body.

Some of the soldiers, according to our embeds, had never seen a dead body throughout the entire three-week campaign. It was like Game Boy. I think that's amazing in two different ways. It makes you a far more successful warrior because you can just barrel right along, but it takes away a lot of what war is all about, which is what I mentioned earlier. The TV technology took that away, too. We couldn't see where the bullets landed. Nobody could see the horrors of this so that we seriously revisit the concept of warfare the next time we have to deal with it.

I think there were a lot of dissenting voices before this war about the horrors of war, but I'm very concerned about this three-week TV show and how it may have changed people's opinions. It was very sanitized.

It had a very brief respite from sanitation when Terry Lloyd was killed and when David Bloom died and when Michael Kelly was killed.[5] We all sort of sat back for a moment and realized, "God, this is ugly. This is hitting us at home right now. This is hitting noncombatants." But that went away quickly, too.

This TV show that we gave you was extraordinarily entertaining, and I really hope that the legacy that it leaves behind is not one that shows war as glorious, because there's nothing more dangerous than a democracy that thinks this is a glorious thing to do.

War is ugly and it's dangerous, and in this world the way we are discussed on the Arab street, it feeds and fuels their hatred and their desire to kill themselves to take out Americans. It's a dangerous thing to propagate.

I hope diplomacy is not dead. I hope that [Secretary of State] Colin Powell at one point would like to continue revisiting the French. I hope that he has success in Syria at some point with [Syria's president] Bashar Assad.

I sure hope we focus on the Middle East, and I sure hope that some kind of peace plan is revisited and attention is paid — American attention is paid — to the plight of the Israelis and the Palestinians on an equal basis and that some kind of resolution is made there, because that is the root of so much of the anger. For right or wrong, it's the selling point of all the dictators and despots and leaders overseas. They use that as a pawn any chance they get. Osama loves to sell the Palestinians' cause. I don't think he cares a hoot about the Palestinians, believe it or not, but he uses it for his cult following to increase his leadership. This is something that we don't understand the power of overseas, and we must. And television has to play a better part in that.

We haven't been back to the West Bank since Operation Defensive Shield[6] last year. It's been a good solid year since we gave you wall-to-wall coverage on what's been going on in the West Bank and Gaza. Hell, they just raided Rafa[7] again. I mean, the Israelis had an incredible raid in Rafa, one of the deadliest in years, but it barely made headlines here.

Again, it is crucial to our security that we are interested in this, because when you are interested, I can respond. If I put this on the air right now, you'll turn it off, and we'll lose our numbers, as we're finding we're losing now, the numbers being so much lower than they were last week.

There is another whole phenomenon that's come about from this war. Many talk about it as the FOX effect, the FOX news effect. I know every one of you has watched it. It's not a dirty little secret. A lot of people describe FOX as having streamers and banners coming out of the television as you're watching it cover a war. But the FOX effect is very concerning to me.

I'm a journalist and I like to be able to tell the story as I see it, and I hate it when someone tells me I'm one-sided. It's the worst I can hear. FOX has taken so many viewers away from CNN and MSNBC, because of their agenda and because of their targeting the market of cable news viewership, that I'm afraid there's not a really big place in cable for news. Cable is for entertainment, as it's turning out, not for news.

I'm hoping that I will have a future in news in cable, but not the way some cable news operators wrap themselves in the American flag and patriotism and go after a certain target demographic, which is very lucrative. You can already see the effects, you can already see the big hires on the other networks, right-wing hires to chase after this effect, and you can already see that flag waving in the corners of those cable news stations where they have exciting American music to go along with their coverage.

Well, all of this has to do with what you've seen on FOX and its successes. So I do urge you to be very discerning as you continue to watch the development of cable news, and it is changing like lightning. Be very discerning because it behooves you like it never did before to watch with a grain of salt and to choose responsibly, and to demand what you should know.

NOTES

1. Before the fall of Saddam Hussein's regime, *Babel* was the number-one newspaper in Iraq, and was controlled by Uday Hussein, Saddam's son, who was killed several weeks after Banfield delivered her lecture.

2. Less than three months after Banfield delivered her lecture at Kansas State University, Michael Savage, whose real name is Michael Alan Weiner, was fired from MSNBC for making antigay remarks to a caller who phoned in on Savage's weekend TV show.

3. After only one month on the job Jay Garner was dismissed as Iraq occupation administrator for the United States, after calling for free elections and publicly supporting allowing the Iraqis to determine their own economic policy instead of accepting a privatization plan that the Bush administration wanted to implement.

4. Operation Anaconda was a massive push against five hundred to one thousand fighters in the Shahi-Kot valley and Arma mountains of eastern Afghanistan. The operation began on March 1, 2002, and ended less than three weeks later.

5. According to Reporters Without Borders, Terry Lloyd was a veteran British war reporter who was working for the British TV network, ITN, when he was killed on March 22, 2003, in gunfire, probably from US-British troops, near Basra. According to Reporters Without Borders, NBC network's David Bloom died on April 6, 2003, of a blood clot in his lung. According to Reporters Without Borders, *Washington Post* columnist Michael Kelly was killed on April 4, 2003, when the Humvee he was traveling in reportedly plunged into a canal while trying to escape Iraqi gunfire.

6. The Internet encyclopedia Wikipedia describes Operation Defensive Shield as "a large-scale military incursion" into the West Bank by Israeli Defense Forces in April 2002 to clear the area of terrorists (http://en.wikipedia .org/wiki/Operation_Defensive_Shield).

7. In late January 2003 (about three months before Banfield's lecture), Israeli forces raided Gaza near the Rafa refugee camp, killing twelve Palestinians and injuring dozens. Located on the border of the Sinai Peninsula, Rafa is one of the most dangerous combat zones in Israel today.

CHAPTER 4

THE WAR ON TERROR AND THE GREAT GAME FOR OIL
HOW THE MEDIA MISSED THE CONTEXT

Gerard Colby

CHARLOTTE DENNETT

An investigative journalist and lawyer, Charlotte Dennett has long personal and professional experience with the Middle East. Born in Beirut, Lebanon, she is the daughter of Daniel C. Dennett, who served in the Middle East with the US State Department, the Office of Strategic Services (OSS), and the Central Intelligence Group (CIG) until his death in a plane crash in 1947. Beginning in 1973, Dennett worked in Lebanon as a reporter for the English Language Middle East Sketch *and the* Beirut Daily Star *until the Lebanese civil war broke out in 1975. She has devoted the greater part —*
almost thirty years — *of her career as an investigative journalist to reporting on the oil industry and the powerful individuals who built and control it. She coauthored with Gerard Colby* Thy Will Be Done: The Conquest of the Amazon: Nelson Rockefeller and Evangelism in the Age of Oil *(HarperCollins, 1995), a meticulously researched investigative history of the Rockefeller family's business activities that took eighteen years to write. For the past ten years, Dennett and Colby have been collaborating on another comprehensive work tentatively entitled* The Kingdom and the Power: Saudi Oil, the Holocaust, and American Espionage at the Dawn of the Middle East Crisis. *This book, which is slated for release in 2006, is based partly on the life of Dennett's father. Ms. Dennett has also written numerous articles, some of which have appeared in the* Middle East, *the* Nation, *the* Los Angeles Times, *the* Philadelphia Inquirer, *and the* American Writer.

Three days after the September 11 disaster, investigative journalist Gerard Colby and I debated whether we should go ahead with our talk at the St. Johnsbury Atheneum in Vermont about our book, *Thy Will Be Done: The Conquest of the Amazon: Nelson Rockefeller and Evangelism in the Age of Oil*. Everyone was so numb with shock and grief that we worried that our assigned topic might be inappropriate. We were planning to present a "bigger picture" of the world based on our investigation of Nelson Rockefeller and the forces of globalization. Our presentation would implicitly criticize American foreign policy.

Our hosts urged us to come anyway. When we arrived, we were surprised to see the room overflowing with people. They needed to talk about what had happened. They were hungry for any insight that we could give them. They were looking for a different perspective, a different context in which to place the 9/11 tragedy. But publicly presenting details on the destructive aspects of the achievements and global activities of a powerful American dynasty — the Rockefellers in this case — is difficult under *any* circumstances, let alone after a foreign terrorist attack.

Nonetheless, we began to talk about Nelson Rockefeller and his brother David, especially since the two men had become eerily relevant to the tragedy of September 11. For what few people in the audience — or for that matter, the United States — realized was that these two powerful Rockefellers had built and financed the World Trade Center. Nelson was governor of New York at the time of its construction. His brother David was chairman of Chase Manhattan bank and the founder of a powerful coalition of business and real estate leaders called the Downtown–Lower Manhattan Association. Lower Manhattan needed revitalizing in the early 1960s, so the Standard Oil heirs combined their formidable resources to create two gigantic monuments to free trade and — as some New Yorkers who had dubbed the Twin Towers "Nelson" and "David" were saying — to themselves. In fact, the Rockefeller brothers were the earliest and most passionate promoters of what eventually became the North American Free Trade Agreement (NAFTA).

It was a terrible irony, I pointed out, that this family which had amassed an unprecedented fortune through oil and had become one of America's most sophisticated and powerful families of the twentieth century, should see the two symbols of its power disintegrate in a matter of minutes, destroyed by terrorists commandeering jetliners fueled by the very source of the family's wealth.

A METHODOLGY OF CONQUEST: FROM THE AMERICAS TO THE MIDDLE EAST

Jerry and I explained how it had taken us eighteen long years to get a bird's-eye view of the Rockefellers' global empire. It wasn't until four years into our investigation of Indian ethnocide and genocide in the Amazon that we discovered how Nelson Rockefeller fit into our story as a major architect of US foreign policy in Latin America. During WWII, President Roosevelt appointed Nelson as Coordinator of Inter-American Affairs. Rockefeller's mission was to rid the South American continent of Axis (primarily German) influence. He carried it out by using extensive contacts among Latin American businessmen and military leaders to build a ranching, mining, and oil empire in the South American heartland that set in motion a process of development that eventually led to the destruction of the Amazon and its people. As we began to see the world from Nelson Rockefeller's overarching perspective, we began to see interconnections among different groups of people working at the ground level—missionaries, anthropologists, health care workers, diplomats, government officials—all involved in separate but related tasks of *development*. But from the perspective of many indigenous peoples, the purpose of their activities was *conquest*. This insight brought into focus a tried-and-true method of development employed all over the world, including in the United States and in the Middle East. We call it a methodology of conquest.

In the American republic, it began with the gradual conquest of the West, eventually extending south into Latin America. Then, as now, missionaries, unwittingly or not, played a vital role. They scouted remote lands for "potentially hostile tribes" and set about pacifying them with the New Testament. "Obey the government," they would tell their wards, citing from Paul's letters to the Romans, "for all authority comes from God." They hoped that the Indians would not resist road-building crews, prospectors, and drillers on their lands. On the secular end of this "soft" counterinsurgency were doctors, anthropologists, and development experts working to win over hearts and minds. The "hard side" of the counterinsurgency kicked in when the Indians fought back. At that point more brutal methods were used, like leaving candy laced with arsenic along riverbeds or dropping blankets infected with smallpox on unsuspecting villages (a tactic first used by Gen. Jeffrey Amherst against Indian tribes in the American northeast). If all else failed, there was military intervention.[1]

As the Rockefellers expanded and diversified their holdings, they increasingly relied on science and technology for innovation and on secular institutions for advice. This led to conflicts with tradition-bound, faith-centered rural communities in the United States and abroad, including the Middle East. In rural America, a major clash called the "Fundamentalist Controversy" erupted in the 1920s. Farmers objected to the Rockefellers' "giant octopus" of economic and cultural modernization (now called globalization) as it extended its tentacles into their schools, their churches, their farms, and their traditions. Small farmers could not afford the expensive machinery or fertilizers used by Rockefeller-allied agribusinesses as they penetrated the American south. Fundamentalist Christian schools, including medical schools, were forced out of business by secular schools funded by the Rockefeller Foundation. Creationism came under scrutiny in the Scopes monkey trial, and even traditional Baptist missionaries who had once been the recipients of Rockefeller largesse saw their funding dry up as the Rockefellers turned to more sophisticated missionary groups like the scientific-sounding Summer Institute of Linguistics to assist in the role of pacification. With all these changes, fundamentalists in the rural heartland never forgave the Rockefellers. Vowing revenge against such "Godless communists," they flocked to the conservative wing of the Republican Party in the 1960s and 1970s and helped defeat Nelson Rockefeller's presidential ambitions. Then they rallied behind Ronald Reagan and later George W. Bush for president. This clash of cultures also happened in the Middle East. In Iran, long before 9/11, a powerful fundamentalist backlash occurred when Ayatollah Khomeini led a revolution in 1979 against the oil-enriched shah of Iran. The shah, David and Nelson Rockefeller's close ally, had tried to modernize his country too quickly, and too abusively, instituting a brutal police state that ultimately failed to contain the violent reactions of rural-based mullahs and their supporters.

Despite the known risks of triggering backlashes, corporate strategists would occasionally admit that they sometimes had little choice but
to make deals with reactionary forces. As Dick Cheney once remarked
during his tenure as CEO of the giant oil contractor Halliburton, "The
Good Lord didn't see fit to put oil and gas only where there are democratically elected regimes friendly to the United States. Occasionally we
have to operate in places where, all things considered, one would not
normally choose to go. But, we go where the business is."[2]

In Afghanistan, Muslim fundamentalists initially obliged American interests — in the 1980s as mercenaries against the Soviet Union
and again in the 1990s as protectors of a possible pipeline route for
Caspian Sea oil and gas. Like Christian fundamentalist missionaries
in Latin America, they engaged in rural pacification, bluntly
explaining their repressive actions as being "necessary to bring the
Afghan people under control." And like their Christian counterparts,
they justified their "restrictions" on people's liberties so that rural
people would learn to "obey the government." For an American oil
company named Unocal, the Taliban's promise to bring stability to
Afghanistan was a good bet for running a secure gas pipeline from the
Caspian Sea to Pakistan through the otherwise war-ridden interior of
Afghanistan. Unocal even invited Taliban officials to Texas in 1997 for
a tour of its oil installations. But relations between the Taliban,
Unocal, and the United States began to sour shortly afterward. First
American feminists raised a hue and cry over the Taliban's repression
of women, creating considerable embarrassment for First Lady
Hillary and President Bill Clinton. Then, in 1998, Osama bin Laden,
who had recently relocated from Saudi Arabia to Afghanistan, created
al Qaeda with the support of the Taliban, who were beginning to
bristle over international condemnations of their human rights
abuses. The bombing of two American embassies in Tanzania and
Kenya (thought to be the work of bin Laden), followed by American
retaliatory bombings in Afghanistan, convinced Unocal to withdraw
from the proposed pipeline deal. Negotiations with the Taliban
resumed when the Bush administration came into office in 2001, but
went sour again in July 2001 when the Taliban refused to turn over bin
Laden despite handsome offers of financial assistance from the
United States. Just as rumors began to fly later that the United States
was seeking alternative partners to the Taliban as well as possible military action against bin Laden, the September 11 attacks occurred.[3]

Here was an extreme case of a fundamentalist backlash against Western-style globalization, triggering sudden changes in the political landscape and creating new dangers for innocent people around the world, including Americans.

Occasionally, even the grand masters of globalization have paid a price in their own blood. Michael Rockefeller, Nelson's son, fell victim to cannibalism in 1961 after his catamaran capsized off the shores of New Guinea, forcing him to swim to shore for help. To his killers, he was just another white-skinned colonialist encroaching on their territory. Michael had come to New Guinea as part of an anthropological expedition sponsored by Harvard and funded by a company that had deep ties to his family. The Freeport Sulphur Company needed social scientists to pave the way to New Guinea's central mountains and a giant outcrop of copper. In one of his last letters home, young Rockefeller deplored the influence of Western culture on New Guinea's coastal Asmat people, who, he wrote, were "beginning to doubt their own culture" and who were being "sucked into a world economy and world culture which insists on economic plenty as a primary ideal." Michael didn't heed warnings that his avid pursuit of peculiar tribal artifacts like elaborately decorated skulls for his father's primitive art collection had begun to revive the old tribal practice of head-hunting, or that his appearance with other white men had provoked an old Asmat tradition of revenge killing.[4] Michael's death pained the Rockefeller family long after the much-publicized tragedy. Forty years after Michael's death, the attack on the World Trade Center no doubt inflicted an equally profound sorrow on the family. How, I wondered at the conclusion of our talk, did David Rockefeller react to the news?

Two months after our talk on Nelson Rockefeller and globalization, we received in the mail the Fall/Winter 2001 edition of *Research Reports*, the Rockefeller Archive Center's quarterly newsletter. The front page featured a picture of the Twin Towers. Inside, the editors had extended an invitation to scholars to read firsthand from original sources about the history of the World Trade Center. Under a section entitled "Globalization" was written: "To the extent that international terrorism must be understood as a reaction to, and to some degree a manifestation of, globalization, the Rockefeller Archive Center is a substantial research resource with material regarding many aspects of international trade, diplomacy, and collaboration." It went on:

These range from (but are not limited to) documentation of the international investment and philanthropic activities of the Rockefeller family; to the service of Nelson A. Rockefeller in five US presidential administrations; to the interest and activity of John D. Rockefeller 3rd in east and south Asia; to the global activities of the Rockefeller Foundation; to the international connections of the Rockefeller University; to the West African, Southeast Asian, and Eastern European programs of the Rockefeller Brothers Fund; and the international research programs of the Social Science Research Council.

The Rockefellers are everywhere. In terms of spreading influence and largesse around the globe, no other family comes close. They are highly sophisticated when it comes to wielding power, and their methods, refined and improved after a century of building global influence, have been widely adopted by other powerful families and corporations. To those of us who have had the privilege of doing research at the Rockefeller Archives, it takes only a week of sifting through this amazing family's personal and financial records to develop a completely different sense of the world.

The fact that we have access to these and other private and public archives, and can use the Freedom of Information Act to obtain sensitive government documents (although the Bush administration is making this much more difficult), reminds us that we still live in a republic.

But *disseminating* this information to the general public, particularly if it is critical of corporate and government power, that's what's *really* difficult, particularly in this age of corporate media conglomeration.

Now, post-9/11, it is even more difficult. The Bush administration has used the formidable power of federal agencies to turn against Muslims, immigrants, dissenters, journalists, and others as it wages its War on Terrorism. Some argue that American democracy as we've known it up to now is also under attack, in part because our current government leaders withhold and/or spin vital information, while attacking those who disagree with them or prove them wrong.

THE MISSING CONTEXT

One result of this is that most Americans still seem lost and confused about the Middle East. Now, three years after 9/11, and as American casualties over there continue to mount, Americans seem no closer to understanding why Muslims "hate us so much" or what's really going on in Iraq.

At every stage of the War on Terror, the mainstream media has been slow to ask probing questions and to fulfill its role as guardian of the Fourth Estate. Media stars like CBS's Dan Rather (who spoke to the BBC) and CNN's Christiane Amanpour mentioned the problem. "I think the press was muzzled and I think the press self-muzzled," Amanpour said to former *Vanity Fair* editor Tina Brown. "All of the entire body politic in my view—whether it's the administration, the intelligence, the journalists, whoever—did not ask enough questions, for instance, about weapons of mass destruction. I mean, it looks like this was disinformation at the highest levels." (CNN Newsgroup president Jim Walton publicly disagreed with Amanpour, saying that her comments "do not reflect the reality of our coverage.")

But there's more to American ignorance than that. Dr. Jan Leestma, a world authority on forensic neuropathology, provided me, quite inadvertently, with the following insight into what ails not just American media, but American culture. I was watching Dr. Leestma on CNN as he described the scene of a crime and then explained how "context is important for any forensic case." He was referring to evidence collected for the sensational murder case involving eight-months-pregnant Laci Peterson, who was beheaded and drowned. It just so happened that Dr. Leestma was being interviewed on the second anniversary of September 11. I was struck at how his comments seemed equally relevant to many of the extraordinary events that led up to and followed the attack on the World Trade Center, most notably the planning and execution of the wars in Afghanistan and Iraq. "Facts in isolation," Dr. Leestma was saying, "lead to all sorts of questions," whereas "facts put in a contextual light" enable the investigator to narrow down the causes.

One of the major shortcomings of mainstream media reporting is the failure to put facts into context. Our schools and universities suffer from this, too. It explains why Americans appear to be hopelessly naive, even dumb. They are neither. They just need context.

Oil context, geographical context, ruling-class context, historical context—all are hidden from the average American. In my experience as a journalist (and I've spent years covering oil, including when I was based in Beirut; as Gerard Colby's coauthor chronicling the hidden history of Nelson Rockefeller's oil, ranching, and banking empire in

Latin America; and as Colby's current coauthor of a forthcoming book about espionage and oil pipelines in the Middle East), few issues are as subject to censorship as oil, especially coverage of who controls it and why it has had such an extraordinary impact on American foreign policy since World War I.[5] So it is no wonder that Americans are ignorant about the Middle East. Control of oil is a national security issue — whether or not we're at war. But there's another overarching reason. Overall, the press does a woeful job of covering powerful individuals and institutions — be they corporate or government. Again, it's no wonder. These powerful entities actively avoid scrutiny and can react fiercely when exposed. But there is an even higher level of power that receives virtually no press coverage. The world's ruling class, comprised of members of family dynasties built over generations, controls vast international resources and wields great influence upon the affairs of nations and the lives of thousands — sometimes millions — of people. These architects of global empires wield enough influence to create circumstances that send nations to war.

The fact is, what's happening now is merely the latest phase of the Great Game for Oil that began not in the 1970s, where most attention seems to be focused, but well over a century ago. It is, and always has been, a deadly game of competition among nations with ambitions of empire. The words of the US ambassador to Turkey during World War II are still relevant today: "Petroleum today constitutes the lifeblood of the industrial world and the most astounding intrigues and devilish ruses are resorted to in order to get hold of new oil resources."[6]

From the 1920s to the 1940s, the primary competitors were the British, the Dutch, the French, the Germans, the Russians and the Americans. Everything's the same today, except that the Chinese, along with the Iranians and the Malaysians, have joined the group, and the United States is playing the most visible role. At the heart of the Great Game is not just oil, but its major commercial arteries to world markets — oil pipelines.

PIPELINE POLITICS

Americans — including those who consider themselves well educated and well informed on world issues — are totally ignorant of this background. The only reason I happen to know it is because my father, one of

America's first master spies in the Middle East, was involved in the Great Game and became one of its first American victims. His mysterious death after a top-secret visit to Saudi Arabia in March 1947 is the subject of a book I'm writing with Jerry Colby that will be published in 2006.

Jerry and I began our investigation by researching what was going on in the Middle East and Saudi Arabia during the month before my father's death. An article in the *New York Times* dated March 2, 1947, turned out to be a great lead. "Pipeline for U.S. Adds to Middle East Issues," ran the headline next to a map showing "A New Pipeline for the Middle East."

By 1950, the article began, "more than one hundred million American dollars will have been laid out across the Arabian and Syrian deserts and the territories of four Middle East countries in the form of a pipeline from Saudi Arabia to the Mediterranean coast." The protection of that investment, the article continued, "and *the military and economic security that it represents* [italics mine] *inevitably* will become one of the prime objectives of American foreign policy in this area, which already has become a pivot of world politics and one of the main focal points of rivalry between East and West." The article continues under the heading "Pipelines and Politics":

> Laying down a pipeline, one of the world's largest and longest, will also mean laying down another major American interest in the Middle East parallel to that of Britain. The Anglo-American partnership, rattled this week by the renewal of fault-finding on the Palestine issue, will be further consolidated or — another possibility — new areas of contention between the two countries will be created. If consolidation occurs, it is not reasonable to assume that other major powers will allow a virtual Anglo-American monopoly of that Middle East oil, the most important commercial alliance ever so established between two countries, to proceed unchallenged.

As I read the article, I realized that several nations — most notably the French and the Russians, and possibly even the British — were not at all happy about the Americans moving in on Saudi Arabia and controlling that pipeline. No less intriguing was the map accompanying the article. It showed not only the proposed route of the Trans-Arabian pipeline, but the route of an earlier pipeline that connected oil in Iraq to two different terminal points on the eastern Mediterranean — one to Tripoli in northern Lebanon and the other to Haifa in

Palestine. In just one article, we had learned that Saudi and Iraqi oil had direct connections, through pipelines, to Palestine and Lebanon, two of the world's most conflict-prone regions.

That led us to investigate the origin of the two earlier Iraqi pipelines to the Mediterranean. It turns out that the British and the French, having won the greatest prize of World War I—the former Ottoman Empire and its Mesopotamian (Iraqi) oil—could not agree on a single terminal point for the pipeline connecting the oil of their newly created Iraq Petroleum Company to markets in Europe. So they split the pipeline into two branches. The northern branch would carry French-controlled oil through the newly created French mandate of Syria and end in Christian-controlled Lebanon, also a French mandate. The southern branch would carry British-controlled oil through the newly created British mandates of Iraq, Jordan, and Palestine to the port of Haifa, which by 1948 would be Jewish controlled.

Later, we learned that Jordan's boundaries were actually drawn to follow the pipeline's rights of way.[7] Germany, which as early as 1901 had identified Mesopotamia as a "lake of petroleum . . . virtually soaked with bitumen, naptha, and gaseous hydrocarbons," was, of course, the big loser, along with its ally Turkey. So much for round one of the Great Global Game: the struggle for the spoils of the Ottoman Empire.

The two branches of the pipeline carrying Iraqi oil to the Mediterranean were completed in 1935. But before their construction, Europeans relied on tankers to carry oil for their industries and war machines. By World War I, tanker transport had become a dangerous enterprise; the British lost twice as much tonnage to German submarines during the first part of that year than during the same period in 1916. Standard Oil of New Jersey lost a total of six tankers, and when the Germans sank the Shell oil tanker *Murex*, they also scored a psychological victory: the *Murex* had been the first tanker to travel through the Suez Canal. It was the brainchild of a Jewish merchant from East London named Marcus Samuel. In 1892, Samuel teamed up with the Rothschilds, one of Europe's most powerful banking families with huge holdings in Russian oil, to get a competitive edge over the Rockefellers' Standard Oil on kerosene sales in Asia. By sending tankers through the Suez Canal, Samuel shaved off four thousand miles of traffic, greatly reducing shipping costs and outbidding the Americans, who still shipped their kerosene in tins carried in ships that went around the Cape of Good Hope.[8]

By 1917 the British and the Americans were staunch wartime allies. Both countries were alarmed by their growing oil shortage. America's ambassador to London sent a desperate cable to Washington in July 1917 warning that "they have lately sunk so many fuel oil ships, that this country may very soon be in a perilous condition— even the Grand Fleet may not have enough fuel. . . . It is a very grave danger." Britain's secretary of state for the colonies sent an equally impassioned appeal to the House of Commons in October. "You may have men, munitions, and money, but if you do not have oil . . . all your other advantages would be of comparatively little value."[9] British oil shortages became so acute that the British government sought to develop, for the first time, an oil policy that saw only one solution to its predicament—more tankers, American tankers. This solved the supply problem, but what about the security of those tankers, especially those loaded with oil from the Middle East?

A NEW LOOK AT THE PROMISED LAND

Here's where some additional context—some geographic and oil baron context—comes into play, putting the Promised Land in a new light. During that same summer of 1917, some of Britain's most powerful Zionist leaders, previously frustrated in their efforts to gain official support for a Jewish home in Palestine, redoubled their efforts by emphasizing Britain's strategic and imperial interests. The Suez Canal, they argued, would be useless if Mesopotamia fell into German hands. The Jews of Palestine had already proven themselves reliable informants on Turkish troop movements. Their string of settlements around Haifa could be similarly useful.[10] On June 19, 1917, Chaim Weizmann, head of the World Zionist Organization and the Jewish Agency for Palestine, along with Lord Rothschild, a strong supporter of Jewish colonization in Palestine, paid a visit to Sir Arthur Balfour, Winston Churchill's successor to the Admiralty and now foreign secretary. Weizmann and Rothschild stated in no uncertain terms that the time had come for His Majesty's government to make a public statement of support for a Jewish home in Palestine. Balfour listened and the rest is history. In November 1917 the British war cabinet approved the famous "Balfour Declaration" upon the recommendation of His Majesty's government, which "favored the establishment in Palestine of a national home for the Jewish people." Prime Minister Churchill would later admit that the so-called Balfour Declaration was based on strategic wartime concerns rather than humanitarian concern for the plight of European Jews. To this day, those strategic concerns have been described as protecting the Suez Canal and Britain's trade routes to India. Balfour's background as former Lord of the Admiralty (British navy) and his concerns about the availability of oil for Britain's war machine in 1916 and 1917 are hardly ever raised by historians, and more often than not, readers are not aware that the historic Balfour Declaration was actually a letter to Lord Rothschild, himself hailing from one of the richest oil families in Europe. The fact that Britain's trade routes from the eastern Mediterranean through the Suez Canal and the Red Sea were also tanker routes has, to my knowledge, never been explored, most likely because Great Britain, like the United States, has been careful to conceal its oil interests under the lid of national security. There are, however, other examples where secrecy was exposed. In 1916, for example, the British and the French divvied up much of the old Ottoman Empire (including Mesopotamia) in what is now known as the Sykes Picot Agreement. At the time, it was all kept secret—until the 1917 Russian Revolution blew it open. The Bolsheviks got their hands on the agreement and leaked it to a reporter from the *Manchester Guardian*. As Philip Knightley, author of *The First Casualty*, reports, "The release of the agreement caused Britain great embarrassment, since she had already promised the Arabs independence in return for raising the Arab Revolt. T. E. Lawrence had to try to explain to the Arabs why the British had double-crossed them."[11] To this day, the 1920 agreement of the Allied Supreme Council that made the dividing up of the Arab world official is referred to as the San Remo Agreement in most history books, although contemporaneous documents refer to it as the *San Remo Agreement on Oil*.

Palestine's importance to British national security would become more apparent, at least within government circles, when Haifa was chosen as the terminal point for the Iraq pipeline. This, too, has received little or no attention by historians.

What historians agree upon is that Britain, bent on controlling her grip on the Middle East, promised the Promised Land to two different peoples during World War I: to the Jews through the Balfour Declaration and to the Arabs in return for their help (under the leadership of the colorful "Lawrence of Arabia") routing the Turks.

Herein lies the crux of the entire Middle East conflict. Its origin is the rivalry between colonial powers whose industry — and war machines — depended on the control of oil. Yet, if you were to browse through the stacks of an American university library and draw from the hundreds of books written on the Arab-Israeli crisis, and if you looked in the indexes of these books, you would be amazed at the dearth of references to oil. That's because our schools and our media tend to focus our attention on individual states. By contrast, oil barons look at a map of the Middle East and see a giant oil operation. As noted earlier, Jordan's borders delineate pipeline rights of way. Iraq and other Gulf States are large oil reservoirs. And Syria, Lebanon, and Israel have served as terminal points for pipelines taking oil to market. Controlling and protecting this huge enterprise is a fundamental reason for the Iraq War and all the other conflicts in which we've engaged in the Middle East over the last century.

AMERICAN INVOLVEMENT IN THE GREAT GAME

Nor can America lay the blame for Middle East conflict solely at the feet of Europe. As early as 1919, Standard Oil president Water Teagle was openly wondering, "if there is any way we can get into the oil producing end of the game in Mesopotamia." By 1920, according to a Gulf Oil official's testimony, the US State Department had called in all oil company executives and "told them to get out and get it [i.e., Mesopotamia's oil]."[12] By 1924, newly elected president Calvin Coolidge declared that "the supremacy of nations may be determined by the possession of available petroleum and its products." According to the *New Republic*, Washington was by that time "wading shoulder-deep in oil. The newspaper correspondents write of nothing else. In the hotels, on the streets, at the dinner tales, the sole subject of discussion is oil. Congress has abandoned all other business."[13]

John D. Rockefeller's Standard Oil of New Jersey ended up getting a share of the Iraq Petroleum Company in return for America's contribution to the war effort. But it was not until World War II, when my father was posted to Lebanon as one of America's top counterintelligence experts for the Office of Strategic Services (OSS), that the Unites States came into its own as a major oil power in the Middle East, thanks to Standard Oil of California's exploration and engineering feats in Saudi Arabia. By then, the War Department (as it was then called), the State Department, and the OSS fully understood that one of the US's primary objectives during the war was "to control the oil at all costs."[14] This control was not just for industry, but also to fuel the modern military machine—a point often forgotten by environmentalists and pacifists as they argue for alternative energy sources as a remedy to dependence on oil. As a US government publication, *World Oil, Fact and Policy*, noted during the height of the war, "World War II is largely a war by and for oil. Petroleum is one of the most important weapons of modern military conflict." Put even more chillingly to members of Congress, the president of the American Petroleum Institute stated in November 1943: "Oil is ammunition. It is a secret behind the secret weapons in this war. . . . We are not floating to victory in this war—we are fighting literally every inch of the way with oil—on land, on and under seven seas, and in the skies. The panorama of millions slaughtered, peoples made destitute, and kingdoms crushed into the earth by mechanized means makes startlingly clear the fact that in this combat oil, more than any other weapon, decides the life or death of civilization."

Much of this documentation is only now coming to light because of the recent declassification of OSS and military records that are now over fifty years old. But some of it lies in the bound volumes of the *Foreign Reports of the United States* (*FRUS*), State Department reports and memos that are filled with official communiqués sent from diplomats stationed in the Middle East to Washington, and can be found in most major American and university libraries. Thus, we can find an introductory paper on the Middle East written in 1947 by an English diplomat, acknowledging that the Middle East is "a vital prize for any power interested in world influence or domination," because control of the world's oil reserves means control of the world economy.[15] John D. Rockefeller, heir to the great Standard Oil fortune, put it slightly differently: whoever controls the oil of the Middle East, he said, controls the destiny of Europe. In 1956 the competition between the British and the Americans for control of Middle Eastern oil had become so intense that the *Wall Street Journal* felt compelled to publish this startling revelation: "In the House of Commons both Conservatives and Socialists rise to contest that much of the unrest in the Middle East is caused by *'rivalry' between American and British oil interests* [italics mine]. Foreign Secretary Selwyn Lloyd stoutly maintains this is not a fact, but party leaders privately concede that most members of Parliament disbelieve him. In conversations with important British oilmen, too, one encounters anti-Aramco (Arabian American Oil Company) sentiment."[16]

What we are witnessing now is phase three of the Great Global Game for Oil. (Incidentally, the founder of Standard Oil, John D. Rockefeller, coined the term Great Game as he struggled in the late nineteenth century to get a monopoly over oil refining and distribution in the United States.) Each major phase has coincided with a world war for the spoils of a defeated empire. Phase one, following the allied victory in World War I, resulted in the defeat of the Ottoman Empire. Control of the planet's most precious oil region, Mesopotamia, was handed over to the British, the French, and, to a lesser degree, the Americans. Phase two was the struggle for British succession during and after World War II, with the United States replacing the greatly weakened British empire as the major oil power in the Middle East, thanks in large part to its hold over Saudi Arabia. Phase three involves the further expansion of US power (with Great Britain, no longer an empire, now playing a subsidiary role) into the Middle East and central Asia after the collapse of the Soviet Russian empire and the resistance to this expansion by the great industrialized nations of France, Germany, Russia, and China.

THE GREAT GAME FOR CENTRAL ASIA

According to testimony by members of the conservative Heritage Foundation before the US House of Representatives in March 1999, the combined oil wealth of the central Asian countries of Azerbaijan, Kazakhstan, Turkmenistan, and Uzbekistan was estimated at fifteen billion barrels of proven oil reserves.[17] The Institute for Afghan Studies estimates that the combined value of the oil and gas reserves in these republics is around $3 trillion.

Secretary of State Colin Powell, speaking about central Asia's oil in February 2002, stated confidently: " The Great Game will not break out again. The area will have continuing presence of US interests in central Asia of a kind that we could not have dreamed of."[18] As Ted Koppel reported, oil-rich Kazakhstan was receiving huge increases in US military aid and had agreed to the installation of military bases, "all in the name of fighting terrorism." In nearby Azerbaijan, the Bush administration lifted sanctions (imposed in 1993 because of its war with neighboring Armenia), "citing the war on terrorism." And US Special Forces were deployed to Georgia to train antiterrorist forces to route out al Qaeda, all in the name of the war on terror."[19]

The War on Terror seems to be best funded and supplied in those regions with great reserves of oil.

Thanks to Ted Koppel's reporting on *Nightline,* as well as to the Internet and a surge of new books by investigative reporters responding to the American public's hunger for information post-9/11, vital information is out there, but you have to look for it.

In his groundbreaking book *Taliban: Militant Islam, Oil, and Fundamentalism in Central Asia,* Ahmad Rashid made sense out of previous American support for the Taliban by documenting America's quest for safe pipeline routes across Afghanistan to connect the oil and gas of the Caspian Sea to markets in Pakistan and India. Policy making in central Asia and the Middle East, Rashid pointed out, "was not being driven by politicians and diplomats but by the secretive oil companies and intelligence services of the regional states."

In 1998, Halliburton's Dick Cheney was doing business with the Taliban of Afghanistan and with central Asian countries (dictatorships euphemistically called "republics") to secure a safe route for Caspian oil.[20]

The United States has also eyed Iran as a possible overland transport route for pipelines connecting Caspian Sea oil to energy hungry markets. Dick Cheney, while still the CEO of Halliburton, remarked that "we find ourselves, American firms, cut out of the action in terms of anything that is being developed with respect to Iran, of course because of the sanctions that prohibited American firms from doing business with Iran."[21] While Iran remained out of the picture because of its radical, hard-to-control fundamentalist mullahs, the Clinton administration pushed for a different route, west of Baku in Azerbaijan through Georgia and across Turkey to a port on the Black Sea. This pipeline route, according to *Nightline,* was "the anchor of national security interests of the United States in central Asia and the Caucuses because that goes to the heart of an American policy goal, that is, the uninterrupted transport of Caspian oil."[22]

George W. Bush, while running for president, told an audience in Boston on October 3, 2000, that "I want to build pipelines to move natural gas. . . . It's an issue I know a lot about. I was a small oil person for a while." Once in office, he appointed so many oil industry executives to his cabinet that the *Oil and Gas Journal* gushed, "From industry's perspective, the casting of the lead roles couldn't be better." Vice President Dick Cheney is probably the best known. Less known to Americans is the fact that Condoleezza Rice, Bush's national security advisor, spent a decade on the board of the oil giant Chevron and was even honored by having a Chevron oil tanker named after her. Her name was removed from the tanker after she assumed office. Bush's top fundraiser and campaign manager, Don Evans, was the CEO of a Colorado-based oil company and a board member of Sharp Drilling, an oil company contractor, before he assumed the position of commerce secretary.

Only three weeks after September 11, I was startled to read in my local *Burlington Free Press* the headline "War Will Be Linked to the Control of Oil." Written by a reporter for the *New York Times* wire service, the article began prophetically: "Beyond American determination to hit back against the perpetrators of the September 11 attacks, beyond the likelihood of longer, drawn out battles producing more civilian casualties in the months and years ahead, the hidden stakes in the war against terrorism can be summed up in a single word: oil. . . . The defense of energy sources [in the Middle East and central Asia] — rather than a simple confrontation between Islam and the West — will be the primary flash point of global conflict for decades to come, say observers in the region." While the reporter's reference to the "defense" of energy sources is subject to debate, this article remains a noteworthy anomaly to most reporting in the mainstream media that tends to steer clear of economic motivations for war.

THE GREAT GAME FOR IRAQ

As for Iraq, it has the second-largest oil reserves next to Saudi Arabia, many of them still untapped in the western provinces. Estimates of Iraq's oil reserves range from 112 billion to 300 billion barrels. Long before the war began, the Bush administration tried to downplay its interests in Iraqi oil. "The only interest the United States has in the region is furthering the cause of peace and stability," spokesperson Ari Fleischer insisted a year ago. He said he "wouldn't even try to start guessing what the military may or may not do" once Iraq's oil fields were liberated from Saddam Hussein. As the world would learn, the US military made a beeline for the oilfields soon after the invasion began, and now an American and former CEO of Shell Oil has been chosen to oversee the Iraqi oil industry.

Before the war, Russia (which Iraq still owes $7 to $10 billion for arms purchases), France, and China were deeply concerned that a new, pro-American regime would rescind their preexisting oil contracts with the Baathist regime. The contracts were supposed to go into effect once sanctions were removed. Within two months of the invasion, Halliburton's contract with the Pentagon to repair damage to Iraq's oilfields was extended to some oil-producing jobs. Whether or not European and Asian oil companies would have their contracts abrogated remained the decision of "the new Iraqi government," according to the US overseer, Phillip J. Carroll.[23] But on the eve of the war, James Akins, a former ambassador to Saudi Arabia, foresaw American oil companies as the "main beneficiaries of this war," even going so far as to denationalize the oil companies and then parceling out Iraqi oil to the American oil companies.[24]

And how will the oil get delivered to market? Through pipelines, of course. And one of the pipeline routes now under study may reopen—or follow the route of—the old Kirkuk-Haifa pipeline that was jointly built in 1935 by American, British, and French oil companies and closed in 1948 during the Israeli War of Independence.

Will the current unrest in Iraq derail the Bush administration's plans? And what of the oil companies? According to journalist Robert Dreyfuss, American oil companies were fretting even before the troops went in. "Executives fear that war could create havoc in the region, turning Arab states against the United States and Western oil companies. On the other hand, should a US invasion of Iraq be successful, they want to be there when the oil is divvied up." Said former US diplomat David Long, "It's greed versus fear."[25]

And so, the Great Game goes on.

THE #1 MOST CENSORED MEDIA STORY OF 2002–2003

Indeed, Project Censored, a program based out of California's Sonoma State University that every year for the past twenty-seven years has identified the twenty-five most censored stories in the US press, selected a game plan for continuing the Great Game as the most censored story of 2002–2003. Entitled "The Neoconservative Plan for Global Dominance," the Project Censored report begins by saying, "Rarely did the press or, especially television, address the possibility that larger strategies might also have driven the decision to invade Iraq." Drawing on the work of five journalists—Neil Mackay, David Armstrong, Robert Dreyfuss, John Pilger, and Paul Rosenberg—the report takes the reader back to the seventies, when the United States was reeling from an energy crisis and was embroiled in a "tug of war over oil" with the Middle East. American military presence in the Gulf was fairly insignificant, the report continues, "and the prospect of seizing control of Arab oil fields was pretty unattainable."

Enter the so-called neoconservatives, Democrats and Republicans who became "influential strategists" in the Defense Department during the Ford, Reagan, and George H. W. Bush presidencies. In 1989, Dick Cheney (currently vice president), Colin Powell (now secretary of state), and Paul Wolfowitz (now deputy secretary of defense) wrote a "Defense Planning Guidance" report "advocating US military dominance around the globe. The plan called for the United States to maintain and grow in military superiority and prevent new rivals from rising up to challenge the United States on the world stage. Using words like 'preemptive' and military 'forward presence,' the plan called for the United States to be dominant over friends and foes alike." The following year, on August 2, 1990, President Bush announced that while the threat of global war had receded, a new "unforeseen threat to national security could come from any angle and from any power." That same day, Iraq invaded Kuwait. Bush responded with Desert Storm.

In 1997, while Clinton was in power, the neocons founded the Project for a New American Century (PNAC) with journalist William Kristol as chairman. In September 2000 the PNAC put out a report entitled "Rebuilding America's Defenses." The report states, "At present the United States faces no global rival. America's grand strategy should aim to preserve and extend this advantageous position as far into the future as possible."

"America's global leadership," the report continues, "and its role as the guarantor of the current great-power peace relies upon the safety of the American homeland; the preservation of a favorable balance of power in Europe, the *Middle East and surrounding energy producing region* [my italics], and East Asia; and the general stability of the international system of nation-states relative to terrorists, organized crime, and other nonstate actors." A section entitled "Repositioning Today's Force" notes that "the United States has for decades sought to play a more permanent role in Gulf regional security. While the unresolved conflict with Iraq provides immediate justification, the need for a substantial American force presence in the Gulf transcends the regime of Saddam Hussein." As for East Asia, the report states: "Raising the US military strength in East Asia is the key to coping with the rise of China to great-power status. It is time to increase the presence of American forces in East Asia." I advise anyone who wants to understand the current administration's present and future foreign policy pursuits to read "Rebuilding America's Defenses."

It would be impossible, in the space allotted, to give a complete analysis of the Bush administration's use of the War on Terror to get its way nationally and internationally as it engages in the Great Game for Oil. Fortunately, though, investigative journalism has survived the PATRIOT Act, Attorney General Ashcroft's Department of Homeland Security, and the quiescence of mainstream media. Foreign journalists have been particularly helpful. Britain's Robert Fisk continues his fearless reporting from Iraq, documenting the local populace's suspicion that oil is the only reason for the war while updating his readers on the progress of Bechtel, Halliburton, and other corporations as they snap up reconstruction contracts. Australian reporter John Pilger recently embarrassed Secretary of State Powell by releasing video footage of an interview Powell had given on February 24, 2001, in which he said, "He (Saddam Hussein) has not developed any significant capability with respect to weapons of mass destruction. He is unable to project conventional power against his neighbors."[26] Pilger has since claimed to have recently uncovered proof that six hours after the September 11 attacks, Defense Secretary Donald Rumsfeld said he wanted to go after Iraq, allegedly saying, "Go Massive. . . . Sweep it all up. Things related and not." Pilger reports that the war in Iraq was set in motion on September 17, 2001, when "Bush signed a paper directing the Pentagon to explore the military options for an attack on Iraq."[27] Most recently, former treasury secretary Paul O'Neil has revealed in his new book, *The Price of Loyalty*, that getting rid of Saddam Hussein was "Topic A" ten days after the inauguration—

eight months before September 11. These revelations give credibility to Phyllis Bennis's warnings before the war. The author of *Before and After: U.S. Foreign Policy and the September 11 Crisis*, Bennis told *Extra!* in a January 2003 interview that "if there's going to be a war, I don't think that it will have anything to do with what the inspectors find or don't find. I think it will have to do with how the Bush administration determines to wage its war for oil and for empire."[28]

The brave warnings of writer Arandhati Roy have also been vindicated. The daughter of a Christian Syrian mother, Roy is a passionate critic of globalization and the current war in Iraq. Two weeks after September 11, she wrote that although the Pentagon's Operation Enduring Freedom was "ostensibly being fought to uphold the American way of life," it would instead "end up undermining it completely. It will spawn more anger and more terror across the world. For ordinary people in America, it will mean lives lived in a climate of sickening uncertainty: Will my child be safe in school? Will there be nerve gas in the subway? Will my love come home tonight?"

Greg Palast (who has an essay in this book) continues to do hard-hitting exposés on the Bush administration's ties to the Saudi royal family, though he is often forced to publish his findings through the BBC and other British outlets, or on the Internet.

Seymour Hersh has published a dramatic series of articles in the *New Yorker* debunking the administration's rationales for its preemptive war in Iraq and later, providing the lurid details of the abuse of Iraqi prisoners at Abu Ghraib.

And Robert Dreyfuss, in an article with Jason Vest entitled the "Lie Factory" in the February 2004 edition of *Mother Jones*, was one of the first journalists to reveal even more about the "close-knit team of idealogues" centered around Dick Cheney who met secretly at the Pentagon in their ad hoc Office of Special Plans. Dreyfuss describes how Cheney, Paul Wolfowitz, and Douglas Feith, a former aide to Richard Perle at the Pentagon in the 1980s, "cherry-picked" raw intelligence from various sources to make their case to Congress and the public for a war in Iraq.

I can understand why professional career agents in the CIA became alarmed over allegations that the president had been misinformed by "faulty intelligence" or that its agents "lacked knowledge" of the Middle East. The members of the Office of Special Plans were bypassing seasoned CIA and State Department analysts because they couldn't be assured that these veterans at deciphering raw data would make the case that they needed. They were right. And now the real experts are in the galling and politically sensitive situation of having to defend themselves.

I know something about the CIA's early history in the Middle East going back to its predecessor, the Office of Strategic Services (OSS) during World War II. The OSS recruited most of its agents among sons of missionaries and university professors (like my father) who had grown up in the area and/or taught in American schools in Beirut, Istanbul, and Cairo. They were well versed in Middle Eastern customs, could speak the different languages fluently, and understood the nuances of religious, tribal, and political affiliations. They were relatively few in number, but over time their numbers grew and so, presumably, did their expertise. Anyone with a modicum of understanding of that part of the world knows that an invasion of an Arab country like Iraq with American forces under flimsy pretexts would cause great upheaval and create lingering instability. My father predicted as much in 1943.

No doubt the Rockefeller family, which because of its enormous stake in Middle Eastern oil has spent decades developing bountiful sources of intelligence there, has been uncomfortable with the turn of events in Iraq. Secretary of State Colin Powell, a self-professed Rockefeller Republican, has kept his foot in the neocons' door no doubt because the stakes for American oil companies in Iraq are huge. But his allies in the State Department have leaked their dissatisfaction over Cheney's "renegade group."[29]

Sen. Jay Rockefeller, vice chair of the US Senate Intelligence Committee and great-grandson of the founder of Standard Oil, led the congressional investigation of 9/11. Rockefeller urged his committee to extend its investigation into the Office of Special Plans. He met regularly with some of the families who lost loved ones at the World Trade Center and has formed a group called Families for a Peaceful Tomorrow. Terry Rockefeller, who lost her sister Laura and was a founder of the group, led a four-person delegation to Iraq before the war, just as the Pentagon was pouring personnel and ships into the Persian Gulf. (Terry Rockefeller denies any family relationship to the more powerful clan with the same last name.) The group went, explained Colleen Kelly, who lost her brother in the World Trade Center attack, "to see the faces of the Iraqi people . . . to learn about their lives. I want to understand that Iraq is not just one more Saddam Hussein, but many, many people, with hopes and dreams and families just like my brother." In a press release issued last summer, they deplored "the cynical use of 9/11 as a reason to invade Iraq and unsubstantiated links made between Iraq and al Qaeda." While somewhat critical of the joint House-Senate committee's work examining the failings in US intelligence, they welcomed its release of a nine-hundred-page document in July 2003, even though "large portions of the text were classified and subsequently deleted from the text by President Bush." The report had been held up for seven months, while political wrangling continued over what portions were to remain classified.[30] Yet for all their frustrations, the families were grateful for the support they had from the senior Democrat on the Senate Intelligence Committee, Sen. Jay Rockefeller. Commenting on the Joint Inquiry's report, Rockefeller scolded the Bush administration for not heeding the warning signs of terrorist attack before 9/11: "At every level—the collection, analysis, and dissemination of intelligence [the administration] fell short. There was a failure to penetrate al Qaeda, a failure to effectively analyze intelligence, and a failure to disseminate information about would-be terrorists."

The Families for a Peaceful Tomorrow also had a role in the creation of an independent commission to investigate 9/11 and insisted that its scope go beyond the actions and inactions of the intelligence community. The families demanded full disclosure. "We remain deeply curious," the organization's July 24, 2003, press release stated, "about the response of the Defense Department to the terrorist attacks, while they were occurring, on the morning of September 11, 2001. And we encourage a vigorous investigation into the business and financial links among Saudi Arabia, the hijackers, and other nations, including our own." The commission took the unprecedented step of subpoenaing the White House for records that would document what the president knew about terrorist threats in the months leading up to 9/11, including daily intelligence reports. "There are a lot of theories about 9/11," its chairman, Thomas H. Kean, said, "and as long as there is any document out there that bears on any of those theories, we're going to leave questions unanswered. And we cannot leave questions unanswered."[31]

A former Republican governor of New Jersey, Kean expressed frustration with White House delays in turning over documents. He even joined a host of independent reporters in openly stating that

George W. Bush knew far more about an imminent terrorist threat than he or his handlers had been willing to say.

And yet the final report, released in late July 2004, merely points to "systemic failures" in intelligence and "lack of imagination" without assigning responsibility to any individuals in the Bush administration. Despite Chairman Kean's promise to leave no questions unanswered, some of the biggest questions about the origins of 9/11, the Bush administration's pathetic response to it, and the subsequent war in Iraq, remain just that: unanswered. A 567-page report hailed by politicians of both parties for its thoroughness and nonpartisan nature floods the reader with details, but leaves out the appropriate context to make a definitive judgment as to who was responsible for arguably the biggest crime to ever hit American shores. Once again, I was reminded of the statements described earlier in this essay by forensic investigator Dr. Jan Leestma: facts in isolation lead to all sorts of questions about a crime, whereas facts put in a contextual light help to narrow down the causes.

Fortunately, this time around more journalists are doing what they are supposed to do: they are probing beyond the 9/11 Commission's postrelease spin for substantive information—or the absence thereof. William Raspberry of the *Washington Post* described the report as a "childlike explanation of what went so tragically wrong nearly three years ago," noting (as a child might say), "the lamp broke" or, as the report put it, the "system failed." Raspberry interviewed Ray McGovern, a twenty-seven-year veteran of the CIA who serves as a spokesman for a group of former agents called Veteran Intelligence Professionals for Sanity that formed on the eve of the second Iraq war. "The whole name of the game is to exculpate anyone in the establishment," McGovern is quoted as saying. " Mistakes were made, but no one is to blame."[32]

Terry McDermott of the *Los Angeles Times* raised other questions: "Who," he asked, "provided the nearly half a million dollars it cost to carry out the [9/11] attack? How could the man who is alleged to have recruited several of the hijack pilots have done this while under the investigation by at least three intelligence services—those of the United States, Germany, and Morocco? Who, if anyone, assisted the hijackers during their time in the United States?"[33]

Author Gail Sheehy, who interviewed 9/11 widows for her book, *Middletown, America*, continues to ask: Where was Donald Rumsfeld—the top Pentagon official who should have been responsible for ordering pilots to shoot down the hijacked planes — on 9/11? "Was the commission comfortable," she asked the commission's vice chair, Lee Hamilton, following the release of the purportedly definitive report, "with the fact that the country's secretary of defense was not in the chain of command or present in the Pentagon's command center until all four suicide hijacked planes were down?" Hamilton, she wrote, was unresponsive: "I'm not going to answer that question," he reportedly said, and he turned away.[34]

Filmmaker Michael Moore, in his own inimitable way, has already made a significant contribution with his *Fahreinheit 9/11*.

In the name of context, I will try to do my part by ending this essay on the subject that started it: the Rockefellers. Sen. Jay Rockefeller was unusually qualified to be the vice chair of the powerful Senate Select Committe on Intelligence and to play a leading role in overseeing the congressional investigation of 9/11. A Democrat with many years of service in the Senate, Rockefeller had gained experience in foreign affairs as a member of the Senate's Foreign Relations Committee, specializing in East Asian and Near Eastern Affairs. But beyond such obvious indicators of his public service, all neatly displayed on the senator's Web site, resides a vast institutional reservoir of knowledge connected with his family's direct participation in globalization, as aptly described by the Rockefeller Archives newsletter mentioned earlier in this essay. Jay (actually John D. Rockefeller IV) is not only the great-grandson of the founder of the Standard Oil fortune, but heir to a long tradition of family involvement in intelligence matters connected with oil, beginning with his great-grandfather receiving secret reports from abroad a century ago from American diplomats — some on the payroll of Standard Oil. Jay's uncle, Nelson Rockefeller, gathered vast amounts of intelligence as Coordinator of Inter-American Affairs during World War II. He became President Eisenhower's special assistant in Cold War Strategy and Psychological Warfare in late 1954, making him privvy to the most secret of CIA covert actions, dubbed "the family jewels." As vice president under Gerald Ford, he chaired the Ford administration's commission on CIA abuses, issuing a report that revealed some abuses and ignored others. He confidently recommended reforms while pledging to clean up an agency beset with scandals emerging out of the Vietnam War.[35] The Senate Committee on Intelligence was actually born at this time, in 1976.

As early as 1951, Nelson recommended the creation of a "superagency" modeled after his coordinators' Office of Inter-American Affairs, only with vast international authority independent of the State Department and other intelligence agencies.[36] He proposed an "Intelligence Czar" to head up this agency, someone of the caliber of, well, Nelson Rockefeller. His idea didn't fly at the time, but now, more than fifty years later, the Commission on 9/11 — a body supported by his nephew Jay, and headed by a liberal "Rockefeller Republican" named Thomas Kean[37] — is making a similar recommendation, pressing Congress — and of course, the leaders of congressional intelligence committees like himself — to approve the creation of a National Intelligence Director with oversight over all the other agencies, some fifteen in number. Why is it needed? Partly to address intelligence ineptitude and facilitate better sharing of information among the different agencies. But there is clearly another objective as well, and that is to monitor — and prevent — the development of rogue groups within the US government capable of steering the nation on foolhardy missions like the war in Iraq. In the tradition of his uncle Nelson, who in 1976 identified then defense secretary Rumsfeld and White House chief of staff Cheney as dangerous rogue elements allied with right-wing ideologues bent on destroying the country (and, incidentally, Nelson Rockefeller's chances for the presidency),[38] Jay Rockefeller has focused the Senate Intelligence Committee on the secret group set up in the Pentagon by Cheney, Rumsfeld, Wolfowitz, and Feith described earlier in this essay. "There's always the question," Rockefeller told NBC's Tim Russert, "that [Douglas Feith] was running a secret intelligence operation that bypassed the entire intelligence community, and the law says you've got to inform the intelligence community of anything that you're doing."[39] Heaven forbid if some of America's most powerful players in the global arena were kept out of the intelligence loop of a renegade group set up deep within the Pentagon. Especially if that group had oil on the mind, and control of Iraqi oil at that.

"My own feeling," Rockefeller told Russert " — and I've felt this a long time — is that there had been a predisposition on the part of the president and his team of some of the people who surrounded him . . . to [say] the time for diplomacy is over. The time for . . . regime change has come in Iraq. The day after 9/11 Donald Rumsfeld was in the White House thinking about what are we going to do about Iraq. And

I think Iraq was on their mind. . . . Iraq is what [the president] wanted, and that's what he got. . . . And in the meantime, we have created, therefore, the lowest standing of the United States in our history around the world."[40]

Ironically, for all his power not even Rockefeller was immune from the buzzsaw of censorship. He and fellow Senate Intelligence Committee Democrats Senators Carl Levin and Richard Durbin complained that the American people were getting only an "incomplete picture" of what actually occurred leading up to the war in Iraq. Though not widely reported in the press, the three senators spelled out their dissenting views at the end of their July 2004 Senate Intelligence Report, strongly suggesting that US intelligence agents had been pressured to produce information that supported the Bush administration's plan to go to war. "The Committee," they noted, "set out to examine ten areas of investigation relating to prewar intelligence on Iraq and we completed only five in this report. The scope of our investigation was divided in a way so as to prevent a complete examination of all the matters within the committee's jurisdiction at one time. The central issue of how intelligence on Iraq was used or misused by administration officials in public statements and reports was relegated to the second phase of the committee's investigation, along with other issues related to the intelligence activities of Pentagon policy officials . . . and the role played by the Iraqi National Congress, led by Ahmad Chalabi, which claims to have passed "raw intelligence" and defector information directly to the Pentagon and the Office of the Vice President. As a result, the Committee's phase one report fails to fully explain the environment of intense pressure in which Intelligence Community officials were asked to render judgments on matters relating to Iraq."[41]

Perhaps it should come as no surprise that this same report, written in part by a Democrat with longstanding family ties to the oil industry, makes no mention of oil, even though the report focuses on a country that has the second-largest proven oil reserves in the world.

Or that the 9/11 Commission Report, chaired by a Republican (Kean) who has served on the board of a powerful oil company (Amerada Hess) puts out a report that barely mentions the subject, even as it tries to chart a "new global strategy" to offset Islamist terrorism in the Middle East.[42]

Or that Sen. Susan Collins, the Republican charged with drafting legislation to overhaul the country's intelligence services as chair of the Governmental Affairs Committee, refuses to conduct hearings on federal contracts awarded to Halliburton, the oil service company once headed by Dick Cheney.[43] American oil interests, in short, continue to escape the radar of official bipartisan investigations.

Still, I am confident that investigative journalists will continue to probe, and that the families who suffered losses from 9/11 and the War in Iraq will keep up the heat on the press and on America's politicians.

As a result of these efforts, the American people are beginning to see the Iraq war in a larger context, one which will enable them to make informed decisions about the direction of US foreign policy and the people leading it.

NOTES

1. See Gerard Colby and Charlotte Dennett, *Thy Will Be Done: The Conquest of the Amazon: Nelson Rockefeller and Evangelism in the Age of Oil* (New York: HarperCollins, 1995). For information on the use of missionaries and secular forces in both hard and soft counterinsurgency, see, for instance, chapter 24, "Deadly Inheritance"; chapter 32, "Poisons of the Amazon"; chapter 33, "The Death of a Continental Revolution"; and chapter 36, "Nation Building through War."

2. Dick Cheney, speech to the Cato Institute, June 23, 1998.

3. Pierre Abramovici, "The U.S. and the Taliban: A Done Deal," *Le Monde Diplomatique*, January 2002.

4. See Colby and Dennett, *Thy Will Be Done*, pp. 363–68.

5. The closest Americans may have come to understanding the identity of the world's "oilagarchs" occurred recently, after Russian president Vladimir Putin arrested Mikhail Khodorkovsy, Russia's richest man and the CEO of its largest oil company. Only then did we learn that Khodorkovsky sits on the advisory board of George H.W. Bush's Carlyle Group, one of the world's largest private equity funds, and that the Russian had been trying to sell some of his vast oil holdings in Yukos oil to Exxon Mobil and Chevron Texaco. But the identities of the top stockholders in America's huge oil companies never get discussed. And rarely do we see even the barest mention of George Bush's family ties, through grandfather Prescott Bush, to Brown Brothers Harriman, a financial giant in banking, transportation, and global oil deals.

6. Ambassador Laurence Steinhardt to Secretary of State Cordell Hull, February 11, 1944. Records of the War Department, National Archives.

7. *Oil across the World: The Saga of Pipelines*. This 1946 publication, which

we found in the National Archives, noted "Our world today has several political states that have been founded and boundaried deliberately as Right of Ways for oil pipelines. These include the Levant States, or the French protectorate of Syria, the hinterlands of Tripoli, which is France's vital Mediterranean terminal for the desert pipelines that lead to the crucial oil pools of Kirkuk, some 700 miles inland in Iraq. Also the onetime British mandated Transjordan, back of the crucial British port of Haifa, the lower Eastern Mediterranean terminal of the same epochal Y of pipeline which carries oil from Kirkuk . . . to the fuel tanks of Britain's merchant ships and the British Navy."

8. Daniel Yergin, *The Prize: The Epic Quest for Oil, Money, and Power* (New York: Simon & Schuster, 1991), p. 66.

9. Ibid., p. 177.

10. Simon Schama, *The Two Rothschilds and the Land of Israel* (New York: Knopf, 1978), p. 205.

11. Philip Knightley, *The First Casualty: From the Crimea to Vietnam: The War Correspondent as Hero, Propagandist, and Myth Maker* (New York: Harcourt Brace Jovanovich, 1975), p. 150.

12. Harvey O'Connor, *World Crisis in Oil* (New York: Monthly Review Press, 1962), p. 306.

13. Yergin, *The Prize*, p. 215.

14. Document released to the author through a Freedom of Information Request.

15. *FRUS* 5 (1947): 569. Cited in Naveez Mosaddeq Ahmed, *The War on Freedom: How and Why America Was Attacked, September 11, 2001* (Brighton, England: Institute for Policy Research and Development, 2004), p. 341.

16. "Aramco, Disputed by British and Arab Interests, Courts Favor in Saudi Arabia and Gains Profits," *Wall Street Journal*, June 28, 1956.

17. Ranjit Devraj, "The Oil behind Bush and Son's Campaigns," *Asia Times Online*, October 6, 2001, http://www.atimes.com.

18. Cited on *Nightline*, April 25, 2002.

19. Ibid.

20. Ibid.

21. Ibid.

22. Ibid.

23. Neela Banerjee, "U.S. Official Treads Carefully in Overseeing Iraq Oil Industry," *New York Times*, May 13, 2003, p. 15.

24. Robert Dreyfuss, "The 30 Year Itch," *Mother Jones* (March/April 2003).

25. Ibid.

26. Paul Mulvey, "Journo Claims Proof of WMD Lies," October 9, 2003, http://www.news.com.au. This Australian-based Internet newsgroup carries articles printed in the *Australian, Herald Sun*, the *Daily Telegraph*, the *Courier-Mail*, and the *Advitiser*.

27. Ibid.

28. Interview with Phyllis Bennis, *Extra!* (January/February 2003): 10.

29. *Insight,* December 9, 2002.

30. "Peaceful Tomorrows Members in Washington, DC, for Release of 9/11 Joint Inquiry Report," Peaceful Tomorrow Email Newsletter, September 2003, http://www. Peacefultomorrows.org.

31. Philip Shenon, "9/11 Commission Could Subpoena Oval Office Files," *New York Times,* October 26, 2003, p. A1.

32. William Raspberry, "Failures of the September 11 Commission," *Washington Post,* July 26, 2004. Elsewhere, McGovern questions "the incongruity of the commission's silence on Iraq, with 140,000 US troops tied down there and terrorists breeding like rabbits. See "Iraq War and Israel Soft-Pedaled in 9/11 Report," posted on http:// July 27, 2004.

33. Terry McDermott, "Questions Persist Despite 9/11 Investigations," *Los Angeles Times,* July 26, 2004, http://www.latimes.com/news/nationworld.

34. Gaily Sheehy, "Who's in Charge Here?" July 22, 2004, http://www .p11citizenswatch.org.

35. See Colby and Dennett, *Thy Will Be Done,* p. 736.

36. Ibid., p. 228.

37. Kean, himself an "oil man," has served as a director of the oil giant Amerada Hess, which at the time of Kean's appointment to head the 9/11 Commission had interests in Azerbaijan in partnership with Saudi Arabia's Delta Oil. (See Nicholas Stein, "Five Degrees of Osama," *Fortune,* January 22, 2003. The former New Jersey governor sits with David Rockefeller Jr. on the advisory board of the GLPW Investment Group Incorporated. See http:// www.glpwgroup.com, financial newsletter, August 2002.

38. Colby and Dennett, *Thy Will Be Done,* pp. 776–79.

39. Transcript of *Meet the Press,* July 11, 2004, http://www.msnbc.com.

40. Ibid.

41. *Report on the US Intelligence Community's Prewar Intelligence Assessment on Iraq* (Washington, DC: GPO, July 2004), p. 449.

42. *The 9/11 Commission Report, Final Report of the National Commission Terrorist Attacks upon the United States* (New York: W. W. Norton, 2004), pp. 362–65.

43. Sheryl Gay Stolberg, "Intelligence Overhaul: Senator Steps in as the Referee in Washington's Turf Battles over Counterterrorism," *New York Times,* August 10, 2004.

CHAPTER 5

THE PRICE OF LIBERTY

GERARD COLBY

Gerard Colby is currently serving as president of the National Writers Union (NWU) while coauthoring a new book entitled The Kingdom and the Power: Oil, the Holocaust, and American Espionage at the Dawn of the Middle East Crisis, *which will be a HarperCollins release. Previously, Colby was national vice president and cochair of the National Book Division for the NWU. His articles have appeared in a variety of national and local periodicals, and he is the author of* Du Pont: Behind the Nylon Curtain *(Prentice-Hall, 1974),* Du Pont Dynasty *(Lyle Stuart, 1984), and coauthor with Charlotte Dennett of* Thy Will Be Done, the Conquest of the Amazon: Nelson Rockefeller and Evangelism in the Age of Oil *(HarperCollins, 1995; HarperPerennial, 1996).*

"Eternal vigilance is the price of liberty."

Wendell Phillips

In the thirty years I have been a freelance investigative journalist, I've seen books suppressed in varying ways, sometimes by the subjects of books, sometimes by publishers, and sometimes by authors succumbing to self-censorship out of fear of repercussions for telling the truth. In the 1970s, a new term came into the vernacular of industry-wise writers: privishing.

According to the sworn testimony in federal court of a twenty-year Viking Press editor, William Decker, the term was used in the industry to describe how publishers killed off books without authors' awareness or consent. Privishing is a portmanteau meaning to privately publish, as opposed to true publishing that is open to the public. It is usually employed in the following context: "We privished the book so that it sank without a trace." The mechanism used is simple: cut off the book's life-support system by reducing the initial print run so that the book "cannot price profitably according to any conceivable formula," refuse to do reprints, drastically slash the book's advertising budget, and all but cancel the promotional tour. The publisher's purpose is to kill off a book that, for one reason or another, is considered "troublesome" or potentially so. This widespread activity must be done secretly because it constitutes a breach of contract, which, if revealed, could subject the publisher to legal liability. In the book-publishing industry's standard contract, the publisher, in return for exclusive rights sold to them by the creator (writer), promises to not simply print the book, but to publish it, including providing an initial print run and promotional and advertising budgets adequate to give the book a fair chance in its given estimated market. Too often, this is not done.

In the "old" days, privishing was usually triggered by quiet interventions against a political book (often a history, social or political study, or biography) by one or more of the book's powerful subjects. Today, privishing has spread beyond political books to any book a publisher may want to kill off for reasons that have little to do with the book's worth. Rather, it has more to do with the way the book-publishing industry's structure has been allowed to evolve into non-publishing conglomerates. Big media corporations have now taken over previously competing publishing houses, and "big box" chain bookstores have pushed small booksellers out of business. What was once secretive because of its political import is now done with impunity under the aegis of bottom-line economics that have little to do with the traditional concepts of a fair marketplace of ideas. Instead of giving books time to build a readership through good reviews and word-of-mouth recommendations, conglomerates and chain bookstores demand quick, high-volume sales and higher profit ratios, thereby shortening the books' lifespans.

I discovered political privishing because my first book, *Du Pont: Behind the Nylon Curtain*, was a victim of the practice. Due to limited space, I can only provide a brief summation of my encounters with privishing. The first happened while I was researching my book in Delaware, the Du Pont family's "Company State" (as Ralph Nader called Du Pont-dominated Delaware). I had just sent out letters to Du Pont family members requesting interviews when out of the blue, a bearded friend of another mutual writer friend showed up at my door. He said his name was Mark Duke and that he was writing a story for *Ramparts* magazine on then-Congressman Pierre ("Pete") du Pont IV's presidential ambitions. One of my writer friends, William Hoffman, vouched for his integrity, so I let him into my home — and into my research files. In fact, according to court records, Duke was an informer found through the services of Richmond Williams, the then-director of the Du Ponts' tax-free family archives, the Eleutherian Mills-Hagley Foundation Historical Library. Williams, in turn, was providing information on me to Du Pont family elders. Moreover, Duke had been contracted to write a book to answer mine, using my own literary agent, Oscar Collier of New York City, as his agent. Collier, obviously because of the ethical conflict involved, kept his relationship with Duke a secret from me. Later, soon after Prentice-Hall successfully privished my book and fired my disillusioned editor for "nonproductivity," they hired Oscar Collier as an editor.

Then there was the Prentice-Hall salesman who, "under orders," leaked the book's unedited manuscript to the Du Pont family. A handwritten index of Du Pont family names that had been specially prepared by someone at Prentice-Hall was attached to the manuscript. The salesman dropped the manuscript and index off at a bookstore in Wilmington, Delaware, that had been previously owned by a Du Pont family member. Another family member, J. Bruce Bredin, picked up the manuscript from the bookstore and delivered it to the Du Pont Company's public affairs department. Public Affairs quickly sent it on to Bredin's brother-in-law, Du Pont Senior Vice President and Director, Irénée du Pont Jr., at the time effectively the family patriarch. After consultations, Irénée flew out of the country to Latin America to inspect Du Pont facilities, leaving the dirty work to Du Pont's public affairs department. A series of phone calls ensued. The first was to Book-of-the-Month Club (BOMC), whose Fortune Book Club had contracted with Prentice-Hall to sell the book. Du Pont Company officials told BOMC officials that family members and their lawyers had found the book "scurrilous and actionable." Duly warned by one of the most powerful corporations in the world, BOMC quickly caved in, canceling the book within twenty-four hours, an unprecedented action in BOMC's history, according to later BOMC testimony.

When BOMC informed Prentice-Hall, their legal counsel, William Daly, called Du Pont to confirm what Du Pont officials had told BOMC. But Du Pont officials, trying to avoid liability, denied they were threatening to sue. At that point, Prentice-Hall's legal division's efforts were undermined when the book's fate was taken over by the editor in chief of Prentice-Hall's trade division, John Kirk, and the president of the trade book division, Peter Grenquist. Kirk and Grenquist cut Prentice-Hall's planned first print run of ten thousand by one-third so that, according to their own documents, the book could not price profitably "according to any conceivable formula." Later, in legal depositions, they claimed that they cut the print run to compensate for the loss of the BOMC print order. The federal trial judge dismissed this claim as bogus, since BOMC was printing its own version, separate from Prentice-Hall's planned ten thousand first print run. Furthermore, instead of calling a press conference to publicly expose the Du Pont Company's interference, Kirk and Grenquist slashed the advertising budget in half. Then they scaled back promotional efforts to a few TV and radio appearances in the two most obvious big-city markets for a book on the Du Ponts, New York and Philadelphia. All this was done in secret. The editor, Bram Cavin, was told to keep the author uninformed.

Two months later, when advance orders for the book were nevertheless building, my editor broke the news to me about Du Pont's interference. He said that John Thompkins, reputedly among *Time* magazine's best investigative journalists, was investigating the case for a story. Thompkins indeed confirmed Du Pont's interference from interviews with Du Pont, Prentice-Hall, and Book-of-the-Month Club officials, and filed his story. Documents later revealed that Robert Lubar, a *Time* magazine editor, was also in touch with Du Pont officials about the book. They had contacted Lubar because they had thought that Time Inc. controlled the Fortune Book Club, the BOMC subsidiary that had picked up the book for sale. For unknown reasons, *Time* killed the story.

The public might never have known about all this had Prentice-

Hall's chief counsel, disgusted with what was happening to the book, not decided to take his file to the *New York Times'* Alden Whitman. But he did, and two weeks after the *New York Times* published a laudatory ("something of a miracle") two-page review of the book in its Sunday Book Section, Whitman's article on Du Pont's interference appeared. He did not disclose, and perhaps did not know, that the *Times* itself had already come under pressure from the Du Pont Company for the review. The *Times'* editor, Max Frankel, had resisted this pressure. Curiously, Whitman's article appeared on the same page the same day that another *Times* article revealed that Du Pont family members had also interfered with the reportage of Delaware's largest daily, the Du Pont family-owned *Wilmington News Journal*, causing a shake-up of its editorial staff.

The *Times* article, while confirming what my editor had told me, could not help the book any more than the rave reviews it was getting. Prentice-Hall's cut in the print run meant there were no books to sell during the crucial Christmas season. Even in those days, book purchasing was increasingly impulsive. In the quarter century since these events, it has been even more driven by publicity rather than word-of-mouth. In the old days, book purchasing was guided by word-of-mouth among readers, which gave a book time to develop an appreciative market. Publishers understood that. Beginning in the 1970s, however, a new book's shelf life was cut shorter and shorter to make way for a flood of highly publicized "celebrity" books with anticipated big sales, huge print runs, and even larger advertising and promotional budgets. Bookstore purchasing was becoming increasingly driven by publicity and the bottom line. Having to compete against this phenomenon is hard enough, but the situation for non-celebrity authors is made even worse if there are no books to sell during an impulse-buying Christmas season. Under such circumstances, the book dies, regardless of how much free publicity the book earns through reviews and news stories.

That is what happened to *Du Pont: Behind the Nylon Curtain*. Worse yet, as one Du Pont family member later recalled, the Du Pont family, after convening a "war council" to discuss what the book might mean for them, sent rented U-Haul-type trucks up to Philadelphia when I was about to appear there for book signings and media appearances. According to this family member, their purpose was to buy up copies to prevent the public from doing likewise. They probably knew that Prentice-Hall would not print more in time to meet the demand. As my agent, Oscar Collier, put it soon after, when I naïvely asked for his help with Prentice-Hall and getting the rights to the book back, "Look, Jerry, the book has had its run." How many secretly privished authors have heard that and blamed themselves, assuming the problem was their writing?

By 1981, I had initiated a federal court suit against Du Pont Company for inducing a breach of contract and against Prentice-Hall for breach of contract. My wife, investigative journalist Charlotte Dennett, and I would work until the wee hours of the mornings before witness depositions. We would go over records subpoenaed from Du Pont, BOMC, and Prentice-Hall to understand what happened to the book and to match documents with questions we had prepared for our attorney's interrogatories of witnesses in New York and Delaware. Although our attorney, William Standard of Rabinowitz, Boudin, and Standard, had lost us our jury trial by failing to simply type in a request for a jury trial on the complaint, all seemed to be progressing well.

Until we found evidence that, despite previously denying that they had known each other, Prentice-Hall's Grenquist and the head of Du Pont's public relations office had served together on a small Eisenhower White House commission sponsored by the American Assembly think tank. We also discovered that before coming to Prentice-Hall, editor in chief John Kirk had worked for two publishers with Central Intelligence Agency ties: the Samuel Walker Publishing Company and the Free Europe Press (the publishing arm of the CIA-funded Radio Free Europe). We found evidence of other Du Pont ties to the intelligence community, including one involving another brother-in-law of Irénée du Pont Jr., who was in touch with the CIA. We even uncovered Prentice-Hall's close business relationship (for business books on tax sheltering) with William Casey, a former Office of Strategic Services officer who had been active with organizations that had received CIA funding. After stints as Nixon's Securities and Exchange Commission chairman and undersecretary of state for economic affairs, Casey had gone on to serve on President Ford's Foreign Intelligence Advisory Board (and was about to become Ronald Reagan's campaign manager and then CIA director). This all suggested the possibility of a network of "old boys" from the intelligence community within the publishing industry (confirmed by the *New York Times* in 1977) who could turn to each other when needed. Our lawyer quickly backed away from probing these "old-boy network" ties, however, when his opponents challenged him during Kirk's deposition, saying they were prepared to complain to the federal judge overseeing the case.

The climax finally came in Wilmington the night before we were scheduled to depose Pierre du Pont, who was by then Governor Pete du Pont of Delaware. At about 3 AM we were awakened in our Wilmington hotel room. Our attorney, William Standard, urgently requested that we come to his room. When we got there, he showed us subpoenaed excerpts of du Pont's diary, surrendered late that night by Pete's lawyer, Edmund Carpenter, another Du Pont family in-law and one of the Delaware Bar Association's most powerful members.

The excerpts proved that in 1974 then-Congressman du Pont had privately been in touch with a local journalist who had filed a complaint with the Delaware News Council in an attempt to prevent the only non-Du Pont-owned daily newspaper in the state, the *Delaware State News*, from serializing the book. The local journalist alleged that the *State News* was deliberately trying to hurt Pete's congressional reelection campaign. The *State News* ran the serialization anyway, and the book became a best-seller in Delaware (although we can't vouch for who actually bought the copies), whereupon the *State News* had its bank loans called, and its editor was packed off to Arizona to edit his family's other newspaper there. At about the same time as this incident, Congressman du Pont had assured the public that he was not concerned about the book.

Now, from his own diary excerpts, we had proof to the contrary. But Standard saw nothing of value in the diary. When we expressed surprise, he told us we owed him $40,000. We were shocked, especially after having paid about that amount for his time only weeks before. I said I didn't think he had called us down to his room in the predawn darkness to tell us he wanted more money. I asked what was the problem. It was then that he confessed that not only did he not want to ask Governor du Pont the questions that we had attached to the diary excerpts, but that he did not believe in the case and never had. He had only taken the case because his partner Leonard Boudin was tied up in another case and asked him to take ours on. I agreed that he should not depose Governor du Pont, and the next day we announced we were postponing the interrogatory.

Thanks to Ralph Nader's recommendation, we got a referral to another New York law firm and ended up hiring Ronald DePetris, a former US Assistant District Attorney who had prosecuted mostly white-collar crime. DePetris was a moderate Republican who believed in the freedom of the press. He had no problems bringing Governor du Pont into a public deposition in Delaware and asking the questions we wanted answered.

The next legal drama, however, proved to be a sad development for investigative journalism's chances to get a fair hearing in American courts. When the case finally went to trial in federal court in downtown New York City, I knew we were in trouble when Irénée du Pont Jr. took the stand and denounced the book before an apparently sympathetic Judge Charles Brieant. (Brieant was our fourth assigned judge. The first two having recused themselves for previously representing Du Pont as lawyers or owning Du Pont stock, and the third judge, a man with a reputation for fairness named Leonard Sands, stepped down shortly before going to trial for unexplained reasons after a year on the case.) Was Irénée upset with the book's telling the story of how his family built the Gunpowder Trust by buying up competitors during the nineteenth century? Or for repeating Secretary of War Newton Baker's denunciation of the family as a "species of outlaws" for overcharging the government and profiteering over $250 million during World War I? Or for reporting how the company helped undermine the 1924 Geneva Disarmament Conference? Or for revealing how it sold munitions to Chinese and South American warlords during the 1920s? Or for quoting Congressional reportage on their smuggling munitions to the Nazis in Cologne in the early 1930s? Or for reporting any of the other revelations of the Senate Munitions Committee? Or for documenting their financing attempts to destroy the New Deal and throw President Roosevelt out of office? Or for citing their profiteering off World War II and the Vietnam War? Or for their efforts to throttle labor union organizing? Or for their support for the Red Scare and witch-hunts of the 1950s while helping to build the hydrogen bomb for the military industrial complex? Or for poisoning the environment or helping to destroy the ozone layer that had previously protected us from global warming?

No, what concerned Irénée du Pont Jr. was his children's possible reactions to statements in the book which raised questions about what happened when the Du Ponts arrived on American soil. My book accurately stated that "accounts differed" over whether the Du Pont family, after having fled the French Revolution for being the king's gunpowder makers and the last nobles to defend the king with drawn swords, had left a gold coin for the meal they had admittedly consumed after breaking into the home of a Rhode Island family. (The unsuspecting family had left their meal waiting for their return from church.) Du Pont acted pained over my raising questions about his family's traditional gold coin story, which had been passed down from one generation of heirs to the next.

But I knew chances for justice were really bad when Judge Brieant suddenly got up from the bench and walked down to Irénée as he was reading a document and reached over to turn on a light for him.

The day before the two-week trial was to end (without any press coverage, I might add, despite press releases), the judge left no doubts about how he would rule in the case. He called lawyers for all sides into his chambers. He told my attorney that he was not going to find a pillar of American society, the Du Ponts, guilty of simply exercising their freedom of speech and expressing their opinion of a book about them. He ignored the fact that Du Pont Company had acted on their behalf and clearly passed on threats of legal action that were unfounded, using legally potent terms documented in the company's own memoranda: "actionable" and "scurrilous." The company's word — despite the company's own memoranda evidence — that no threat of suit was made or intended was good enough for him. Instead, Prentice-Hall, for daring to sign a contract to publish this book, was his target. If Prentice-Hall signed a contract to publish a book, then it had to publish it, not privish it. The message was clear to Prentice-Hall. They offered to settle for an amount that was less than our cost of bringing them to trial, and then only on the proviso that I keep silent.

Keep silent about privishing and what Prentice-Hall had done? I refused, and the trial closed the next day. The judge subsequently found Prentice-Hall liable for breach of contract and awarded me an amount almost equal to what Prentice-Hall had offered. Du Pont, however, was exonerated. Prentice-Hall then appealed, as did we on the Du Pont side of the decision.

Our attorney, being a mild-mannered, honest Republican, was stunned to find the open hostility he encountered from the three-judge federal appeals panel in New York City. Judge Sterry Waterman, an Eisenhower appointee from Vermont, slept through most of the proceedings. Years later, his law clerk during the trial, now a Vermont Supreme Court justice, introduced himself at a bar association dinner in Vermont and graciously apologized to me for the way I had been treated. The second judge was Lawrence Pierce, a former deputy police commissioner for New York City. Pierce had headed up Gov. Nelson Rockefeller's Narcotics Addiction Control Commission, after which President Nixon had rewarded him with a seat on the federal bench and then brought him to the US Foreign Intelligence Surveillance Court. Later, President Reagan nominated Pierce to the federal appeals bench. The third judge was Ralph Winter, then an ultraconservative former fellow of the Du Pont–funded American Enterprise Institute and a former law clerk in Delaware for a judge who had just been charged with suppressing evidence of Du Pont workers suffering from asbestos poisoning. Winter wrote the decision. He found no error of standard of law and no specific error of fact by the lower court, yet he sided with Prentice-Hall. Judge Winter apparently had read enough of the book to see that it contained a great deal of economic and political analysis, minus the usual laudatory commentaries on the Du Pont Company's "better things for better living" success story that appeared in authorized biographies (although it did carry a glowing endorsement from Leon Keyserling, chairman of President Truman's Council of Economic Advisors). Winter concluded—and stated in his opinion—that the book was a "Marxist view of history" that would have no audience among mainstream readers, and that this limited potential readership justified Prentice-Hall's failure to promote the book. Having created a new theory to explain Prentice-Hall's inactions, he substituted for the lower court as fact finder and overturned the lower court's award against Prentice-Hall. All this notwithstanding Prentice-Hall's own sales records and expert testimony to the contrary. Investigative journalism suffered a blow that day. So, in my opinion, did American jurisprudence.

At that point, the office of Reagan's attorney general intervened by reoffering our attorney a position in the Justice Department. He accepted. Broke and desperate for legal representation, we began looking for help. We recognized that Winter, by basing his decision on his political beliefs rather than the lower court's finding of fact, had transformed our original contractual law case into a First Amendment case where an appeals court (i.e., an arm of the government) had stepped beyond federal rules of procedure to squash a book for political reasons. We appealed to the American Civil Liberties Union

(ACLU) for legal help in challenging Winter's position. After prompt-
ing from Harvard's constitutional expert, Professor Lawrence Tribe, the
ACLU took the case to the Supreme Court. "The Court of Appeals, in
clear violation of Rule 52(a) did its own fact-finding," argued the
ACLU. "Such discrimination based on the content of a literary work is
the 'the essence of . . . forbidden censorship' under the First Amendment." But the Rehnquist Court refused to hear the case, and, perhaps
because of Winter's defamatory statements against me, the press
showed little interest in the case's merit as a constitutional issue.

All this should have driven me forever from the wilds of investigating corporate power, but I nevertheless continued pursuing investigative journalism. It is the dirty secret of American journalism that,
but for a few groups like the Fund for Investigative Journalism and
some foundations, there is little institutional financial support for
freelance investigative journalists. But the best kept secret in the
industry is that skin magazines like *Penthouse, Playboy, Gallery,* and
Oui are the best funders of freelance investigative journalism in the
United States—because it sells. The roots of this strange alliance
extend beyond sales to the historical struggle against censorship in
this country.

I was part of the alliance. I wrote investigative pieces about and
interviewed imprisoned boxer Ruben "Hurricane" Carter on his
murder conviction (since overturned) for *Penthouse* magazine, which
helped his case with the public for a new trial. For *Playboy* I interviewed former Green Beret Captain Robert Morasco, who admitted
killing the son-in-law of the president of Saigon's Cholon Bank under
orders from Henry Kissinger's "40 Committee" of the National Security Council. For the venerable North American Newspaper Alliance
(NANA), I investigated the incorporation of national emergency
statutes into normally functioning law, and in Peru, I looked into a
death squad—linked to the ruling military junta—that was stalking
through Lima, the country's capital city. For *In These Times,* journalist
Charlotte Dennett and I investigated links between Brooklyn shore
real estate speculation, offshore oil development, and outbreaks of
arson in a terrified Polish American neighborhood where the local
firehouse was being closed down by the city. Dennett and I went to
South Africa for the *Nation* magazine to investigate South African
troops illegally intervening in the civil war in apartheid Rhodesia
(now, independent Zimbabwe). Two years later, the *Nation* sent us to

cover elections in Zimbabwe. For *Oui* magazine we investigated New York tycoon Daniel K. Ludwig's activities in the Amazon, and for the *Vermont Vanguard*, we looked into the CIA's use of Miskito Indians during the Contra War against Nicaragua and the impact this had had on Puerto Cabezas, Burlington, Vermont's, sister city in Nicaragua. There was also our investigation for first Crown Publishers and then HarperCollins into why America's largest nondenominational missionary organization looked the other way when genocide was being inflicted on Indians in the Amazon and Guatemala.

NANA and *In These Times* didn't print the Peruvian death squad story. Although they paid me, *Playboy* didn't print the Morasco interview either. This led me to focus on writing books because I could publish without encountering prepublication censorship, and the advance on future royalties that I received upon signing a book contract paid for at least a good part of the initial stages of an investigation.

In 1984, New York–area publisher Lyle Stuart, pledging to give the Du Pont book the chance in the marketplace it never had, contacted me and offered a contract for me to write an expanded version. It would concentrate more on an update of the family's activities in both Delaware and in national politics. Stuart had a reputation in the industry as a man who did not bow to threats or deal in censorship and who actually promoted serious books. He had published the best-selling *The Rich and the Super Rich* by veteran financial writer Ferdinand Lundberg, who vouched for Stuart when I called to ask him what he thought. Stuart had also published the aforementioned William Hoffman's *David: Report on a Rockefeller* in the early '70s, a work for which I had provided research and which made number six on *Time* magazine's best-seller list.

This newly expanded edition, entitled *Du Pont Dynasty*, included over three hundred pages of new material on top of the six hundred pages from the 1974 edition. It was scheduled to be published in October 1984. It was published, but not before Prentice-Hall suddenly slapped Stuart with a subpoena in an alleged attempt to recover $12,000 in court expenses from me (curiously, I had not heard from them about this). But when Prentice-Hall lawyers moved into questioning Stuart about trade secrets during his deposition, including what print jobbers he intended to use, and finally asked for a copy of the new *Du Pont Dynasty* manuscript, Stuart's lawyers stopped his deposition. As they rose to leave, they asked who the two men were who had slipped into the room during the questioning. "Du Pont," came their reply; Prentice-Hall lamely explained they thought Du Pont would want to know. Stuart went to *Publishers Weekly* magazine and denounced Prentice-Hall and Du Pont's shenanigans as a "transparent effort" to get a copy of the second manuscript just as they had the first manuscript. He took a full-page ad in the *New York Times*, mentioning the earlier effort to suppress the first edition, and went ahead with publication. At last, I thought, I had a real publisher!

The *New York Times* did not review the three hundred pages of new material in the book, despite revelations of the family's huge contribution to the Reagan presidential campaign, their direct involvement with the CIA in the bombing of Managua International Airport, Elise du Pont's (Pete du Pont's wife) appointment to the Office of Private Enterprise of the Agency for International Development to oversee privatization as the price imposed on poorer nations for US foreign aid, and Pete du Pont's introduction in Delaware of interstate banking and his presidential campaign plans. But I was pleased to see other reviews, almost all favorable. I appeared on the Financial News Network for an interview just as the book appeared in bookstores. After answering questions about Du Pont Company's recent acquisitions of Continental Oil and Consolidated Coal, and the family's interest at the time in diversifying their fortune beyond the chemical company, I was asked about the pressure that had come down against the earlier version a decade before. Happily, I picked up the book to turn to page 637, where, I explained, I had written thirty pages on the suppression of the first book, only to discover those thirty pages were actually missing from the book.

I finished the show as quickly as I could and called home to ask my wife to check the complimentary copies that Stuart had given us. Two books were similarly damaged. Charlotte called Stuart, who said he would check the warehouse's copies. Stuart later got back to us with the bad news: some three thousand copies of the ten thousand first-print run were damaged by the missing pages and could not be sold despite orders coming in. The damage, whether inadvertent or not, had accomplished the same result that Prentice-Hall's cutting their first print run had done for the first book: one-third of the print run was unavailable to book buyers exactly when they wanted to buy. And there was an added boon for Prentice-Hall and Du Pont: the story of the suppression of the first book was itself suppressed.

The only information that Stuart's company would or could provide later was that they had learned that their print jobber allegedly received 80 percent of its business from Prentice-Hall. If Stuart received any compensation from the printer, I saw none of it. The book soon died. The book was not re-released in 1988 when a national market was available as Pete du Pont finally ran for the presidency. Pete did not get the Republican nomination, but he got others to advance his ultraconservative platform in Congress. Reversing the New Deal—long a goal of his family—and the Du Pont Company's efforts to gut environmental legislation that had been passed during the 1970s, became the banner of the Republican Party's right wing. The right wing was led by congressional candidates funded by Newt Gingrich's Government of the People Action Committee (GOPAC). How many voters knew that Pete du Pont had founded GOPAC in the early 1980s to groom promising young right-wing Republican legislators to run for Congress? That GOPAC, whose donors Gingrich had resisted revealing, had been financed by the Du Pont family? Or that the Du Ponts' GOPAC was the major financial force behind the Republican right-wing's "Congressional Revolution" of 1994, the legacy of which we are still living with?

Despite this setback, Charlotte Dennett and I signed up with HarperCollins to write a book on our investigation of Indian genocide in the Amazon and Guatemala. A crucial part of our exposé entailed taking a hard look at the Wycliffe Bible Translators, who are known abroad as the Summer Institute of Linguistics or SIL. This powerful group of more than 5,600 fundamentalist Christian missionaries had worked for years to bring "Bibleless" Indian tribes out of the Amazon jungle and to help local governments end the Indians' resistance to encroachments on their lands and assimilate them into the global cash economy. Trained linguists, Wycliffe's missionaries had earned a successful track record among governments throughout the indigenous world. This record, however, included collaborating with US counterinsurgency operations in Vietnam and with secret CIA/Green Beret wars waged in the Amazon basin during the 1960s. Even more ominous was their silence in the face of the Brazilian military regime's genocidal policies during the 1960s and 1970s and the Green Beret-advised counterinsurgency campaign in the hills of western Guatemala between 1979 and 1987, which resulted in some 200,000 Indians, mostly women and children, being slaughtered and over 400 villages razed.

As a result of its success, Wycliffe became, and still is, America's largest nondenominational missionary organization. They have maintained that funding for their missionaries' expenses comes from church collections, but their own records also showed that operational expenses for their vast infrastructure came from generous donations from Southern and Southwestern corporations, mostly ultraconservative "new wealth" firms in the Bible Belt. Wycliffe has its own air fleet and large "jungle bases" with runways and telecommunications systems. By 1984, its yearly budgets topped $80 million for domestic operations and another $100 million for foreign (SIL) operations. Wycliffe missionaries had access to these vast resources, as well as to sympathetic ears in the State Department and on Capitol Hill, yet they chose to remain silent while genocidal acts and policies were being carried out against the very Indians among whom they were living. This begged the question: Why were the missionaries so silent and unresponsive? Was it because they were blinded by their religious zeal to reach all the Bibleless tribes and thereby fulfill a biblical prophecy to hasten the Second Coming of Christ? Were they compromised by their bilingual education contracts with governments or by corporate backers who might be profiting from the mass displacement of the Indians?

After doing what investigative journalists often do—"follow the money"—we found the answer, an answer that brought our research to an impasse. The money trail didn't lead where we thought it would. We started out researching Wycliffe's Southern and Southwestern backers. But after four years of research, we concluded that it was mostly Northeastern-financed major corporations, corporations with established reputations and long-standing ties to "old wealth" and the US intelligence community, that profited handsomely from Latin American governments driving the Indians off their lands. These lands were rich in oil and mineral deposits and were a prime area for agribusiness and colonization projects (real estate development and speculation).

We switched our focus to the leading political figures in our investigation. By searching through government archives and climbing the rungs of responsibility, we arrived once again at a mountaintop view of power, but one even more spectacular than I had found with the Du Ponts. This time, the ladder of responsibility led us up to Nelson Rockefeller and his quiet investments and activity with American intelligence in Latin America, and then to the Rockefeller family's tax-free archives center at Pocantico, the family's vast estate over-looking the Hudson near Tarrytown, New York.

At this point in our investigation, we noticed that many funding sources that had happily backed us as long as we were investigating Christian fundamentalist missionaries, the CIA, and faceless corporations, suddenly ran dry. Now that we had reached Rockefeller, there was an impasse. We found ourselves facing a difficult choice: go alone, with all that would mean in terms of mounting debt, or throw in the towel and publish what we had, which we knew was not the real story. So we went ahead, driven by our conscience over so monumental an issue as genocide. What really was behind it and the missionaries' complicity of silence?

In 1995, we finally published *Thy Will Be Done, the Conquest of the Amazon: Nelson Rockefeller and Evangelism in the Age of Oil*. We immediately encountered problems with distribution and marketing. Some of the problems had to do with market considerations in an industry that had undergone structural changes since I had last published a book, *Du Pont Dynasty*. Instead of the six months that you could count on in the past to allow word-of-mouth and reviews to build a market for a book, you now had six weeks at most, and in many cases even less. "Big box" retailers like Barnes & Noble and Borders were quickly and constantly sending back huge volumes of unsold books to publishers to gain credit for their bills to these publishers, which had produced too many celebrity books. The publishers found it no longer economical to employ staff to open these crates to sort out the damaged books from those that could fill back orders. Instead, they either shipped the books out again, often to the same "big box" retail stores, to be sold at drastically reduced prices, or they burned them in incinerators adjacent to their warehouses to save warehouse space and inventory taxes.

We also shared in the all-too-frequent experience authors have of not finding our book at retailers in cities we were visiting to lecture, sign books, and appear on media. Of course, here too, we found ourselves struggling to assert our contractual promotional rights. The publisher initially limited our promotional appearances to New York and Washington, DC. When we arranged our own promotional tour as far as Minneapolis, driving our car into the ground in the process, and discovered that our books had not been shipped out as scheduled, we took our evidence from bookstores back to the publisher to press our case for funds for an outside public relations firm.

Although that firm was successful in booking telephoned radio interviews across the country, support from our publisher continued to be sluggish. When a paperback edition was issued (thanks to our editor's efforts), not a cent was spent on advertising for the paperback. When the paperback sold out, rather than print more copies, HarperCollins declared the book "out of stock indefinitely" and refused to print more unless there was a guarantee of five hundred orders. While we worked on getting five hundred orders, the ante was raised to one thousand. When one thousand was reached, the requirement was raised still again to twenty-five hundred.

Additionally, orders for the book were disappearing in the publisher's computers. One order for one thousand copies from a seminary in the Midwest simply disappeared. Another order for two hundred copies from Pierre Laramée, the editor of the North American Congress on Latin America (NACLA), met with the news that the book was out of stock indefinitely and unlikely to be reprinted. Puzzled, he asked how this could be, given the book's excellent reviews. At this point, the sales operator stepped away from the phone, ostensibly to check with a superior, then came back on and said, "This book will never be reprinted!" And hung up.

Statements gathered from these sources were turned over to our editor. The publisher finally agreed to print more copies—but only because we mustered up large orders confirming intended purchases of twenty-five hundred copies. Soon, this print run was declared "out of stock indefinitely," even though Harper's direct mail orders division had to set up a special hotline to meet the demand after we described the book's plight on several radio shows. The hotline disappeared three days after the head of the direct mail orders division excitedly disclosed its existence to Charlotte Dennett. But HarperCollins refused to reprint, stating there were not enough orders to justify printing to demand. Demand not met is demand soon dead. The book died, along with the public's knowledge of the results of eighteen years of investigation and writing. Despite great reviews and acclaim by scholars, within three years of its publication in hardcover and two years after its publication as a HarperPerennial softcover, the book was no longer available for sale to the public. It can now only be found in libraries, despite the fact that we continue to receive requests from academics and the general public for copies.

We continue to write, this time a book on American origins in the

Middle East and the impact of oil pipelines on decision making in the Roosevelt administration regarding the fate of European victims of the Holocaust, the impact of increased Jewish immigration into Palestine, and Soviet encroachments on the Middle East. We are contracted for this book with the same publisher (having signed before *Thy Will Be Done*'s debacle) and are hoping for better results.

But one of the sine qua nons of investigative journalism is libel insurance. Unlike staff journalists, freelance journalists have to take out their own insurance, and premiums can be hefty. In recent years, the National Writers Union, affiliated since 1992 with the United Auto Workers, has had an affordable plan with Lloyd's of London. In 2001, however, Lloyd's began to refuse coverage for precisely those who needed it most: investigative journalists.

So where does all this leave investigative journalism in America today?

Small local newspapers and magazines are usually not able to fund investigations or are unwilling to risk the wrath of business advertisers offended by such "muckraking," as they often derisively call investigative journalism. Large chain newspapers seem mostly content to play to their local markets, even when they have assumed monopolies over those markets. This seems to be the Gannett newspaper chain's strategy. Young journalists are hired with little investigative experience and have fewer local mentors in investigative work. The rapid turnover among reporters does not bode well for gaining the knowledge and contacts needed for good investigative journalism in the mainstream press. The Internet's openness also lends itself to abuses: Rumors posing as stories with no professional standards for sources and corroboration, lower the public's opinion of bona fide journalism. Even this abuse has been used in some quarters to try to justify attempts to censor the Internet or to even challenge freelancers' status as bona fide journalists — in at least one case in California, by a sitting judge.

Hovering over both print and broadcast news media is the looming presence of corporate conglomerates with financial officers increasingly throwing their weight around in publishers' boardrooms. For over a century, freelance journalists in the West have made their living selling their articles and books to different markets. Freelance journalists are now threatened with "all-rights" contracts by which publishers demand all rights to all markets for the same price, including all dramatic rights, all serialization rights, all geographic rights, and all formats, including electronic rights for CD-ROMs and resale to Internet research databanks. I have, as a book contract adviser for the National Writers Union, seen publishers' contracts demanding all rights "throughout the universe" and in "all formats, including those yet to be invented." Writers are being told that unless they surrender all rights, they will not be published at all, effectively subjecting themselves to being blacklisted.

Does this threat by media owners and their financial officers interfering with the content and terms of publishing extend into American newsrooms? Veteran reporters, more than editors, admit it can. In the book publishing industry, owners of conglomerates and their top executives expect profits similar to high-yield cable TV operations (where annual profits of 20 to 30 percent are not uncommon), so they give "bean counters" the edge over editors. In the monumental battle between "the state" (the financial powers-that-be) and "the church" (the editors) in publishing houses traditionally used to an 8 to 11 percent annual return being considered a good year, the state is winning. And celebrity books are pushing out, not paying for, investigative journalism.

Today, corporate publishing, to carry out privishing or to kill stories, does not need the influence of all the CIA assets that the *New York Times* reported in 1977 as being positioned throughout the publishing industry. In this age of corporate globalism, the only rationale needed is that of the "free market." Why should writers, and especially investigative journalists, expect to be spared any more than have small businesses, farmers, workers, entire nations, and even the planet's environment? In this age, writers' organizations across the globe have learned that they are all in the same boat, often facing the same great white sharks.

But what of the long-recognized special role in American journalism of sustaining the free marketplace of ideas so essential for an informed citizenry to keep democracy alive? What of the Founding Fathers' recognition of that role in the special protections and privileges given the press in the Constitution's First Amendment? They are under stress as never before. And never before has Jefferson's dire warning been more urgent for the American people: "Our liberty depends on the freedom of the press, and that cannot be limited without being lost."

SOURCE NOTES

The story of Du Pont Company's actions against *Du Pont: Behind the Nylon Curtain* and the pressure against reportage on the Du Pont family and Du Pont Company brought against the *New York Times*, the *Wilmington News-Journal*, and the *Delaware State News* can be found in *Du Pont Dynasty* (Secaucus, N.J.: Lyle Stuart, 1984), pp. 652–75, with sources on pp. 938–39 (notes 66 to 143). Court transcripts and depositions of witnesses and other exhibits (including internal memoranda of Du Pont, Book-of-the-Month Club, and Prentice-Hall companies) of *Gerard Colby Zilg v. E. I. du Pont de Nemours & Co. and Prentice-Hall Inc.* are on file at the United States District Court for the Southern District of New York in Manhattan, New York City, and at the Second Circuit U.S. Court of Appeals. For the original *New York Times* story on the suppression by Alden Whitman, see *New York Times*, January 21, 1975. For more on the issues of the case, see Robert Sherrill, "The Book That Du Pont Hated," *Nation*, February 14, 1981; Milton Moskowitz, Michael Katz, and Robert Levering, *Everybody's Business, An Almanac: The Irreverent Guide to Corporate America* (New York: Harper & Row, 1980), pp. 604–605; the *Wilmington Morning News*, November 15, 1979; *Philadelphia Daily News*, November 16, 1979; *Wilmington Evening Journal*, January 16, 1981; and "Publishing: Reversal of Ruling Troubles Authors," *New York Times*, September 16, 1983.

For more on privishing, see Gerard Colby, "My Turn," and Charlotte Dennett, "Book Industry Refines Old Suppression Tactic," in *American Writer* (quarterly of the National Writers Union) 3, no. 1 (March 1984); and " 'Privish' and Perish," *Washington Post*, Book World, vol. 13, no. 41, Sunday, October 9, 1983.

For more on the fate of the *Delaware State News*, see Rolf Rykken, "The Lingering Death of the Delaware State News," *Delaware Today* (June 1981) and reporter Jack Croft's letter to the editor in the *Delaware State News*, February 16, 1981.

For more on the *Wilmington News-Journal*, see Christopher Perry, "The Thursday Night Massacre," *Delaware Today* (February 1975); *Wilmington Morning News*, January 4, 6, 7, and 23, 1975; *Wilmington Evening Journal*, December 7, 1974, and January 3, 4, and 8, 1975; *Philadelphia Inquirer*, January 5, 1975; the *Philadelphia Sunday Bulletin*, November 17, 1974, and January 5 and 12, 1975; *Editor and Publisher*, January 11, 1975; and *New York Times*, January 21, 1975.

For the pressure put on Lyle Stuart, Inc., by Prentice-Hall and Du Pont Company, see Leonore Fleischer, "Talk of the Trade," *Publishers Weekly*, July 20, 1984, p. 87.

Finally, with respect to the marketing of *Thy Will Be Done*, the failure to find copies of *Thy Will Be Done* at retailers during our book tour in 1995 was the subject of a letter to our editor at HarperCollins dated July 5, 1995. Other authors have brought to the National Writers Union's Book Division, which I cochair, similar problems with their publishers during book tours. Books not arriving at retailers in time to coincide with an author's promotional appearance in a city is a common problem. What is not common is the disappearance of large orders in a publisher's computer or the refusal of one of its sales operators to take a large order. We presented our editor with written evidence (memorialized in a letter dated April 11, 1997) of an order from a Colorado seminary for one thousand books which had been taken by Harper-Collins's sales department, which nevertheless had not been recorded, the editor confirmed, in HarperCollins's computer. Additionally, the same letter memorializes how a representative of the trade books sales department at HarperCollins had tried to discourage Pierre Laramée from ordering two hundred copies for a promotional campaign for NACLA. The incident was also described by Laramée in a fax to us that we showed our editor.

CHAPTER 6

CRIMES AND SILENCE
THE CIA'S CRIMINAL ACTS
AND THE MEDIA'S SILENCE

Rick Reinhard

JOHN KELLY

John Kelly is first author with Phillip Wearne of Tainting Evidence: Inside the Scandals at the FBI Crime Lab, *which was nominated for a Pulitzer Prize. It is the first, and to date, the only, contemporaneous critical account of the FBI to be published by a mainstream publisher. Kelly is an independent investigative producer. He is the former editor and senior writer for the* National Reporter, *a publication specializing in reporting on the CIA. Kelly has served as associate producer and chief investigator for many documentaries, including* CIA, *a six-part series produced by the BBC, and* The Bureau, *a Channel 4 (England)/WETA-TV (PBS) documentary about the FBI. Kelly is also a former research scientist and chairman of the Intelligence Study Group of the American Political Science Association.*

As we speak, so to speak, or read, the CIA is committing hundreds of extremely serious crimes around the globe in our name and at our expense with nothing to show for it. This is not according to Sy Hersh — the investigative reporter who uncovered the My Lai Massacre — or Amnesty International. This is according to the CIA itself, as reported by the House Intelligence Committee. "The CS (Clandestine Service of the CIA), is the only part of the IC (Intelligence Community), indeed of the government, where hundreds of employees on a daily basis are directed to break extremely serious laws in countries around the world," reads a committee staff study. "A safe estimate is that several hundred times every day (easily one hundred thousand times a year), DO (Directorate of Operations) officers engage in highly illegal activities."[1]

One would think the Cold War never ended.

The report was the first official admission and definition of CIA covert operations as crimes which the committee, without explanation, equated with essential national security operations. In other words, the national security of the United States requires that more than one hundred thousand extremely serious crimes be committed every year. The committee expressed no legal or ethical concerns about these crimes. On the contrary, CIA offenders were portrayed as potential hapless victims of sinister foreign authorities opposed to their lawbreaking. "A typical 28-year-old, GS-11 case officer," reads the study, "has numerous opportunities every week, by poor tradecraft or inattention, to embarrass his country and president and get agents imprisoned or executed."[2]

One would think that one hundred thousand extremely serious crimes a year would be a major story no matter what the CIA's rationale was. At the very least, pundits could have pondered and asked in the press how these crimes serve US national security, particularly since the committee did not bother to do so. Nor did the committee explain the impact the crimes might have on peaceful, diplomatic relations or examine their moral and legal ramifications. In fact, the committee indicated that it did not matter that laws were broken because they were laws of other countries. To claim that our national security requires one hundred thousand crimes a year is a rather stark assertion and operating principle, particularly in a world that increasingly believes the United States acts as if there is one law for America and another for the rest of the world. Beyond that, it would seem that these crimes might actually threaten US national security by making enemies. What nation is going to roll over, play dead, and accept that breaking its laws is axiomatic with US national security?

There was not a single word about any of this even in the alternative press, which was particularly disturbing in light of the nature of the CIA crimes. The report suggested that the CIA's crimes include murder and that "the targets of the CS [Clandestine Service] are increasingly international and transnational and a global presence is increasingly crucial to attack those targets."[3] In other words, we are not simply talking about stealing secrets. We are talking about the CIA committing crimes against humanity with *de facto* impunity and congressional sanctioning.

Other government documents, including CIA reports, show that the CIA's crimes include terrorism, assassination, torture, and systematic violations of human rights. The documents also show that these crimes are part and parcel of deliberate CIA policy (the staff report notes that CIA personnel are "directed" to commit crimes). For instance, an investigation by the president's Intelligence Oversight Board (IOB) conducted in 1996—the same year that the committee staff report was completed—found that in Guatemala "several CIA assets were credibly alleged to have ordered, planned, or participated in serious human rights violations such as assassinations, extra-judicial execution, torture, or kidnapping while they were assets—and that the CIA was contemporaneously aware of many of the allegations."[4]

Also according to the IOB,

> Among the most serious examples of credible allegations against a then-active CIA asset, were those involving an asset who was the subject of allegations that in multiple instances he ordered and planned assassinations of political opponents and extra-judicial killings of criminals, as well as other less specific allegations of unlawful activities. Although some of these allegations were from sources of undetermined or suspect reliability, one was from a source considered credible by the [CIA] station at the time. Another asset was alleged to have planned or to have had prior knowledge of multiple separate assassinations or assassination attempts before and during his asset relationship. A third asset has been alleged to have participated in assassination, extra-judicial killing, and kidnapping during and before his time as an asset.[5]

CIA documents show that the CIA created, trained, and armed death squads in Guatemala as part of its coup and destabilization of the democratically elected government in 1954. These death squads were run by Guatemala's CIA-controlled security services. The IOB reported that, "The human rights records of the Guatemalan security services—the D-2 and the Department of Presidential Security (known informally as 'Archivos,' after one of its predecessor organizations)—were generally known to have been reprehensible by all who were familiar with Guatemala. US policymakers knew of both the CIA's liaison with them and the services' unsavory practices."[6] The IOB added that the CIA considered the security services to be their "partner" and provided "vital" funding even after official US aid had been terminated because of systematic human rights violations.[7] In other words, the CIA carried out its own foreign policy in contravention of official US policy. The IOB also wrote that the CIA had spoken to the security services about human rights, "but egregious violations continued, and some of the station's closest contacts in the security services remained a part of the problem."[8]

According to the IOB, the CIA's assassins and torturers implemented CIA policy, and CIA officers were rewarded and promoted for recruiting as many of these so-called informants as possible, regardless of their criminal records. Contrary to the committee's claim, the IOB found that specific US laws pertaining to the CIA were violated. In Honduras, the CIA's own inspector general reported that paid CIA assets at the highest level created and ran a death squad called Battalion 316 which, according to the Honduran government, murdered at least 184 people.[9] A secret CIA study found that versions of the Guatemalan and Honduran scenarios were replicated throughout Latin America and that more than one thousand informants known as "unsavory characters" were employed around the world. CIA managers themselves were said to have been "startled" by the large numbers of human rights abusers employed as informants.[10]

The House Intelligence Committee's only concern regarding these brutal CIA informants and other CIA offenders was that they might be arrested and prosecuted. The committee did not advise the CIA to cease or even limit its lawlessness. In fact, it said that if the CIA stopped its criminal activities, "the taxpayer would be better off without a CS [Clandestine Service]."[11] It explained neither this assertion nor how crimes protect national security. In response to the committee's concern, the Senate Intelligence Committee proposed a bill that would immunize CIA offenders who violate treaties and international agreements while following orders. This is the Nazi rationale, plain and simple. The bill passed both houses of Congress and was signed into law by President Bill Clinton on December 27, 2000.

The law is Section 308 of the Intelligence Authorization Act for Fiscal Year 2001. It provides that, "No Federal law enacted on or after the date of the enactment of the Intelligence Authorization Act for Fiscal Year

2001 that implements a treaty or other international agreement shall be construed as making unlawful an otherwise lawful and authorized intelligence activity of the United States Government or its employees, or any other person to the extent such other person is carrying out such activity on behalf of, and at the direction of, the United States, unless such Federal law specifically addresses such intelligence activity."[12]

One has to stand back and take a deep breath on that one. Taken literally, it means that the Constitution does not apply to the CIA or any US intelligence personnel, including lowly agent-assassins. Why? Because the Constitution provides that all treaties are the *supreme law of the land*. Not just the law, but the *supreme* law — and no exemptions.

While Section 308 applies to future agreements, if recent history is any indication, the CIA will apply it broadly and retroactively. This would mean exempting itself from all international law. The tragic consequence of such CIA license was seen in the April 2000 shootdown of a plane carrying American missionaries over Peru. The shootdown resulted in the deaths of Veronica Bowers and her seven-month-old daughter, and serious wounds to the pilot. In 1994, in violation of international law, Congress passed a law allowing the CIA to interdict civilian planes suspected as drug carriers and providing immunity from all liability, even for "mistakes." The shootdown in Peru was a CIA-controlled operation. The Senate Intelligence Committee eventually blamed the CIA for it, but there were no repercussions or prosecutions.[13]

While Section 308 applies to treaties and international agreements, it is clear from the record that it covers CIA violations of the laws of other countries as well. According to a report by the Federation of American Scientists, "A congressional staffer said the new provision (S308) was urgently needed, given that the CIA habitually engages in criminal activity abroad."[14] Also an explanation that the intelligence committees provided as to how other countries cannot apply the principle of Section 308 indicates that it covers crimes other than treaty violations. "It (Section 308) is also not meant to suggest," wrote the committees, "that a person violating the laws of the United States may claim any authorization from a foreign government as justification for a violation of a US law, or as a defense in a prosecution for such violations."[15] What's good for the goose, is not good for the gander.

No one is above the law. No one has the right to exempt anyone from the law. Yet the Senate Intelligence Committee, in creating Section 308, claimed on May 4, 2000, that some laws do not apply to the

CIA.[16] This claim parroted former CIA General Counsel Stanley Sporkin's 1987 testimony that some laws "don't have application to the US Government."[17] In other words, the CIA is above the law, and Section 308 was simply turning this fact into an explicit law so that CIA officers, according to the committee, "will not be burdened by the uncertainty that laws never intended to apply to their activities could be so interpreted."[18]

Again, there was not a peep from the media about any of this even though such a story would not have affected corporate sponsorship or profits. I talked about it with Vernon Loeb, who covers the CIA for the *Washington Post*. He agreed that Section 308 was quite disturbing, as was the fact that the intelligence committees held no hearings about the bill. But Loeb wrote nothing about it despite doing several articles about the Intelligence Authorization Act.

Apparently, the intelligence committees felt that *de facto* impunity for committing one hundred thousand crimes a year along with *de jure* impunity for violating treaties just were not enough ammunition for the CIA to do its job protecting national security. So at the same time they were pushing through Section 308, they called for the lifting of all restrictions on hiring and deploying a category of informants commonly known as "unsavory characters," even though these informants carry out assassinations and terrorism for the CIA around the world. The committees recommended that the "aggressive recruitment" of "terrorist informants who have human rights violations in their background" be "one of the highest priorities." "Unquestionably," added the committees, " a robust and effective intelligence effort will, from time to time, require US interaction with extremely dangerous and truly unsavory characters."[19] As usual, the committees did not explain or prove this assertion. Even if it is true, it does not provide a legal or moral justification for hiring human rights violators.

The so-called restrictions the intelligence committees wanted lifted were hardly restrictions at all. They were simply guidelines for hiring informants that then-CIA Director John Deutch instituted after the activities of a particularly "unsavory" informant had been made public. Guatemalan Colonel Julio Alpirez, who had received $40,000 from the CIA, had been directly involved in the murder and torture of Michael Devine, an American innkeeper, and Effrain Bamaca, a guerrilla leader married to American attorney Jennifer Harbury. At the same time, the CIA discovered that more than one thousand such informants were employed around the world. The agency then fired these informants for engaging in the criminal activities they had been hired to carry out. But the CIA did not stop hiring unsavory characters. They simply subjected them to a six-month waiting period. Within months of instituting the guidelines, incoming CIA director George Tenet assured Congress that not a single unsavory applicant had been rejected.[20] Congress then called for the elimination of Deutch's guidelines and the aggressive recruitment of informants. Tenet not only complied, it is very likely that he rehired some of the fired informants. Indeed, as a sign that the good old days of murder and mayhem were back, Tenet awarded the CIA's Distinguished Career Intelligence Medal to Terry Ward. Ward had been fired for his role in the deaths of DeVine, Bamaca, and others.[21]

All of a sudden, "unsavory characters" had been transformed into crucial intelligence sources in the fight against terrorism. The rationale was that it takes one to know one. Or, it takes a terrorist to capture a terrorist. "After all," wrote the committees, "it is an unfortunate fact that individuals with reputable backgrounds rarely yield the key intelligence leads that are critical to the counterterrorist efforts of the United States."[22] Neither the committees nor the CIA presented any proof to support this claim or actual instances. There is no concrete evidence that this has ever been true. In fact, the contrary seems to be the case. The CIA's investigation of the fired one thousand informants revealed that 90 percent of their information was "useless."[23] On the other hand, there is voluminous evidence that the CIA itself uses informants as terrorists.

No one, not even Congress or the president, has the moral or legal authority to deploy known criminals, even if they are key intelligence sources on terrorism. Crimes cannot be authorized or retroactively ratified. It is a contradiction in terms. As the most powerful nation in the world, the United States can do just about whatever it wants. That still does not mean that it has the legal authority to do so. Might still does not make right. Nonetheless, this is precisely what the US government is doing—to the sound of profound silence from the press. There has been no reporting, let alone analysis, of this story. There have not even been questions from the press regarding the rationale for using terrorist informants or how they can be controlled.

As noted, the IOB reported that the CIA's informants were in fact implementors of criminal CIA policies, not intelligence gatherers.

Former ambassador Robert White agrees. He wrote that Manuel Noriega of Panama, Colonel Julio Alpirez of Guatemala, General Gustavo Alvarez Martinez of Honduras, Colonel Nicolas Carranza of El Salvador, and Emmanuel Constant of Haiti, all major human rights abusers, were CIA informants who "enjoyed profitable contractual arrangements with the CIA not because they were particularly important sources of information, but because they served as paid agents of influence who promoted actions or policies favored by the CIA in that country."[24] White reported further that even when the CIA could provide counterterrorist information, it did not. He has written that when he was ambassador to El Salvador, he was under presidential instructions to do everything possible to reduce human rights violations by the military. In 1980, after the assassination of Archbishop Oscar Romero, White directed the CIA chief of station to provide intelligence on violent right-wing leaders and their plans. "With the full backing of headquarters," wrote White, "the station chief refused on the ground that the CIA's mission lay elsewhere."[25] White also wrote that the CIA pursued its own proterrorist policy in Haiti to the point "of hiring a brutish thug and paying him while he persecuted and murdered the supporters of President Aristide."[26]

It was a similar story in Bosnia. According to former State Department official Richard Nuccio, when the CIA was asked to assist in identifying war criminals and terrorists in Bosnia, it refused because it would "undermine its ability to recruit."[27] Nuccio also reported that the CIA carried out its own policy in Guatemala to the point of continuing the terrorism and obstructing US attempts to bring peace there. "The CIA systematically defied US policy to end Guatemala's civil war by refusing to end its ties with torturers in the Guatemala intelligence service," said Nuccio.[28]

Now along with their *de facto* impunity, the CIA's informants are covered by Section 308, which must be seen for what it is: the culmination of the CIA's long-term attempts to obtain statutory exemption from the law along with its self-anointed de facto impunity. This has nothing to do with the CIA's mandate to further national security. No one has shown that the freedom to commit crimes enhances the CIA's ability to protect national security. The CIA has not sought impunity to better carry out its legal mission. It wants to commit crimes and is committing crimes for other reasons and has sought impunity to avoid being prosecuted and stopped from committing those crimes. It is that simple. One can argue as to the true objectives of these crimes, but there is no doubt that they do not serve national security.

The September 11, 2001, terrorist attacks in the United States show that criminal impunity, one hundred thousand extremely serious crimes a year, and the use of terrorists in the guise of informants, have not worked. Even Vincent Cannistraro, former chief of CIA counterterrorism operations has written that, "The catastrophe resulting from the terrorism attacks on the Pentagon and the Twin Towers demonstrates that the United States has made little progress in understanding and deterring the threat from the various fundamentalist extremes."[29] If anything, the CIA's creation and use of terrorists such as the former Afghan rebels has undermined US national security.

The CIA made its first attempt to gain *de jure* impunity on March 1, 1954. On that day, CIA general counsel Lawrence Houston wrote a memorandum of understanding to Deputy Attorney General William Rogers giving the CIA the right to police itself in violation of federal law.[30] Rogers never responded, but the CIA took the memo as a blank check as Houston revealed twenty years later to then-Representative Bella Abzug. Asked whether he thought the memorandum of understanding gave the CIA authority to "give immunity to individuals who happened to work for the CIA for all kinds of crime, including murder," Houston responded, "It could have that effect, yes." "Did it have that effect?" asked Abzug. "In certain cases it did," admitted Houston.[31]

This was the same Lawrence Houston who wrote in 1947, two months after the CIA was established, that, "in our opinion, however, either activity (covert operations and black propaganda) would be an unwarranted extension of the functions authorized in section 102 (d) [paragraphs] (4) and (5). This is based on our understanding of the intent of Congress at the time these provisions were enacted."[32] Houston was responding to an inquiry from CIA director Roscoe Hillenkoetter, who wanted to know whether the CIA could undertake black propaganda (then known as Morale Operations/M.O.) and covert operations (then known as Special Operations/S.O.). Secretary of Defense James Forrestal had requested that the CIA launch covert operations in Europe. Only months before, Forrestal had testified under oath before Congress that the CIA would only coordinate intelligence. It would not even collect intelligence, let alone conduct operations. Houston continued,

A review of debates indicates that Congress was primarily interested in an agency for coordinating intelligence and originally did not propose any overseas collection activities for the CIA. The strong move to provide specifically for such collections overseas was defeated, and as a compromise, sections 102 (d) (4) and (5) were enacted, which permitted the National Security Council to determine the extent of the collection work to be performed by CIA. We do not believe there was any thought in the minds of Congress that the Central Intelligence Agency under this authority would take positive action for subversion and sabotage. A bitter debate at about the same time on the State Department's Foreign Broadcast Information Service tends to confirm our opinion. Further confirmation is found in the brief and off-the-record hearings and appropriations for the CIA [and] unvouchered funds for M.O. (black propaganda) or S.O. (covert operations) work. . . . We believe this would be an unauthorized use of the funds made available to the CIA. It is our conclusion, therefore, that, neither M.O. or S.O. should be undertaken by CIA without previously informing Congress and obtaining its approval of the functions and the expenditure of funds for these purposes.[33]

Speaking of the use of Section 105 as a possible source of authority for covert operations, Houston added, that "Taken out of context and without knowledge of [the act's] history, these sections could bear almost unlimited interpretation."[34] This, of course, is exactly what the National Security Council (NSC) did. In December 1947, the NSC "under the authority of Section 102 (d)(5) of the National Security Act" directed the CIA to undertake a program of covert psychological warfare against the Soviet Union. In June 1948, NSC directive 10/2 cited the same so-called authority and expanded the CIA's covert action programs to include paramilitary operations, economic warfare, and political action programs. These programs were expanded in 1955 by NSC 5412/2, again under the presumed authority of Section 102.

In no uncertain terms, Houston said that the CIA had no authority to conduct any covert operations. He repeated this legal opinion in 1962, singling out the CIA's 1954 coup in Guatemala and invasion at the Bay of Pigs, Cuba, as criminal operations. "There is no specific statutory authority to any agency for the conduct of such activities (covert operations)," wrote Houston. "When the National Security Act of 1947 was enacted in 1947, the consideration of Section 102, which established the Central Intelligence Agency, was restricted 'to the performance of intelligence functions.' The language of paragraph

(5) of section 102 (d), 'to perform such other functions and duties related to intelligence affecting the national security as the National Security Council may from time to time direct,' was intended to be the basis for giving the Agency a charter in the field on clandestine intelligence and counterintelligence."[35]

In other words, all CIA operations have been illegal from the get-go and continue to be since the charter remains unchanged in this regard. It should also be noted that the National Security Council has no legal policy-making authority. CIA general counsel Lawrence Houston admitted in secret that all CIA covert operations were crimes and then proceeded to delegate to the CIA prosecutorial immunity from criminal liability. The CIA did not discover during the course of its operations that crimes were necessary for national security. Quite the opposite. The CIA undertook criminal operations from its inception and then wrapped the flag around them and gave itself immunity.

A 1975 study by the Intelligence Community Coordinating Staff, which included members of the CIA, also found that until 1974, "there was serious doubt that the CIA had authority to engage in covert operations involving the use of political and military force."[36] This means that thousands of CIA "authorized" operations were illegal, and that the deaths and damage resulting from them were unprosecuted crimes against humanity. A report by the ACLU's Center for National Security Studies also concluded "that until the mid-1970s covert operations were conducted without proper authority"; that is, no recognized authority or legal basis.[37]

In 1975, Congress passed the Hughes-Ryan amendment in an attempt to exercise minimal control over the CIA. The law required that the president sign a finding before each covert operation and notify Congress when he did so. The CIA conveniently misconstrued these notifications to Congress to mean that Congress was being informed of, and not objecting to, covert operations. This then, was further misconstrued as legal authorization from Congress to conduct covert operations. The CIA's leaps in logic in these instances are particularly absurd because the purpose of the amendment was to make them more—not less—controllable. To construe the amendment as a process for authorizing covert operations was nothing short of outrageous. The CIA's covert operations have had no legal basis for twenty-seven years—and still do not. Congress acknowledges this every year in its appropriations bill: "The authorization of appropriations by this Act shall not be deemed to constitute authority for the conduct of any intelligence activity which is not otherwise authorized by the Constitution or laws of the United States."[38]

After the Justice Department found Houston's 1954 memo of understanding to be invalid, the CIA continued its attempts to acquire *de jure* immunity from criminal liability. In 1981, CIA director William Casey wrote a letter to Attorney General William French Smith urging that the US criminal code be revised to exempt all CIA employees from criminal liability for any authorized operations.[39] Casey did not even pretend there was a national security need. Three years later, Casey tried to get the CIA exempted from a proposed antiassassination conspiracy bill. Then-deputy assistant attorney general Mark M. Richard testified before Congress that Casey vehemently opposed making assassination conspiracies illegal: "Casey wanted assurances that this proposal would not reach authorized conduct of the agency."[40] The Justice Department obliged Casey by providing the assurances he wanted in a secret letter. But according to Richard, "the agency had taken the position that the letter was not acceptable and that they would only go along with an express provision in the statute exempting authorized intelligence activities."[41]

The Justice Department refused to go along with Casey's demand and instead dropped the antiassassination provision of the bill. In effect, Casey achieved his goal because it was still not illegal to conspire in the United States to assassinate someone overseas. A few months later, Casey himself conspired in Washington to assassinate Sheik Mohammed Fadlallah of Lebanon. No fewer than three death squads were formed to track him down. On March 8, 1985, a car packed with explosives detonated outside of Fadlallah's apartment building, killing eighty innocent people and wounding two hundred. Fadlallah was unscathed. The CIA was not investigated or prosecuted.[42]

Following its failure to obtain written *de jure* immunity for assassinations, the CIA resumed making its own laws through a perverted interpretation and application of "findings." A "finding" refers to the president finding that an individual or group threatens US national security, and that this threat requires CIA attention. Following such a finding, the president signs an order for a CIA response and notifies Congress. As former CIA General Counsel Stanley Sporkin testified before Congress, "A finding is a determination by the President of the

United States that a certain activity in a foreign country, which is undisclosed, is in the interest of national security."[43]

As noted, this does not constitute legal authorization, certainly not the Congressional authorization necessary to make any covert operation legal, particularly since Congress is sometimes not notified and has no veto power over the covert operation. Even if findings conferred authorization, Sporkin revealed that the CIA, not the president, creates findings to fit preordained covert operations and sends the findings to the president as a *fait accompli* for his signature. In five years of writing findings, Sporkin never once talked to President Reagan, not even on the phone. Sporkin also disclosed that an untold number of covert operations had been carried out without findings, and he himself had written a finding for at least one major covert operation after it had been launched. Sporkin, who was the first US judge ever sworn into office at CIA headquarters, added that this finding provided "retroactive ratification"—a concept that has no standing in law.

Even if findings went as they are supposed to, they have no basis in law. Nowhere is it written that the president or the CIA or anyone can unilaterally launch a secret governmental program or operation on the basis of a mystical finding created by the CIA. This process is no more different from, or legal than, the attorney general summarily deciding that school prayers are in the national interest and then providing grants to schools that initiate praying. Again, Lawrence Houston had written as early as 1947 that the CIA had no authority for any operations, period. Later he added that presidents directing the CIA to carry out covert operations (as had happened from time to time) still did not constitute legal authorization, particularly since Congress did not even know about the operations, let alone consent to them. According to Houston, the process was illegal. Creating and signing findings does not legalize the process.

It was clear from Sporkin's testimony that the CIA uses findings to create its own operations and to give them "a legal coloring," as one senator put it.[44] Cloaking covert operations in presidential authority is an illegal smokescreen to begin with because the president by himself has no such authority. In fact, even Congress cannot legally authorize many of the CIA's operations because they are crimes, including crimes against humanity. The Third Reich and Hitler "authorized" Nazi operations. That did not make them legal, and the rest of the world did not treat them as such.

Sporkin's testimony means that the CIA is, in effect, self-authorizing. Using the president as a strawman, he testified that "you can't straitjacket the president. If the president calls in someone and says, 'We've got to move today. Go out and do it.' I think that somebody can be able to go out and do it then later on you do the paperwork. That's what covert operations are; they give the president an opportunity to, through a different regime . . . to do it that way."[45]

Sporkin took this concept a step further and argued that findings allow the president, and through the president the CIA, to legally violate laws. Most, if not all, of the covert operations covered by Sporkin's findings violated serious laws, including the law to notify Congress about any finding. In the finding "authorizing" the arms for hostages, Sporkin himself wrote that the president should not notify Congress. "I do think," he said, "there are instances where you would have non-notification. I think it is built into the statute [requiring the president to notify Congress in advance about covert operations] itself. It's built into the Constitution."[46] In other words, according to Sporkin, a law requiring the CIA to notify Congress in advance about covert operations simultaneously gives the CIA the right not to notify Congress when it chooses, and this right stems from the Constitution.

Regarding violating "general laws," Sporkin said, "you've got to be able, under covert operations, to be able [sic] to do these things [break laws]. I think that an argument could be made that you can override the specific statute by a covert finding. . . . It's in the interest of our country that you can do these things." (Sporkin did not explain why.)[47]

Sporkin was describing the activities of a government of men, not of laws as provided by the Constitution. As long as the decisions to override the law are made by the "right kind of people," it's okay, he concluded: ". . . what I wanted was to make sure that this was being — [that] these requests were coming from the top. . . . These are very important decisions that were being made and they had to be made at the highest levels . . . You don't want a government operating where you have — and I don't want to use the word 'low-level.' . . . But somebody that is beneath a high official . . . making some very, very sensitive kind of decision that could affect the entire country. You wanted to get these [decisions from] . . . the highest levels all the time."[48]

Nowhere did Sporkin indicate the need for the advice or consent of Congress. On the contrary, he made it clear that he and the CIA did not even consider Congress or its elected officials to be sources of authority. The "highest level" sources who Sporkin deemed had the proper authority to make decisions about illegal covert operations included five people: the CIA director, the secretary of defense, the secretary of state, the attorney general, and the national security adviser.[49] Perhaps it was an oversight, but Sporkin did not list the president.

Ironically, a 1975 secret study commissioned by former CIA director William Colby aptly described the use of CIA covert operations as described by Sporkin as an undermining of the Constitution. "Using covert operations to implement foreign policy within the context discussed herein," read the study, "independent of any Congressional grant, affects the equilibrium sought by the framers of the Constitution in providing for the separation of governmental powers. If this authority were recognized as independently existing in the Executive Branch, it would permit the president to secretly 'legislate' foreign policy and then secretly execute it, using covert means in doing so."[50]

This situation, apparently, was not worthy of media coverage. Soon, it may not be possible for the press to cover it. As part of the 2001 Intelligence Authorization Act, Congress passed the first "Official Secrets Act" criminalizing certain press coverage of the CIA. At the last moment, Clinton was embarrassed into vetoing the act. But the CIA said it would go back to the drawing board and continue "crafting" newer versions.

The first Bush administration pushed the legal envelope even further off the charts by reinterpreting Executive Order 12333, which bans CIA assassinations altogether. In fact, an official legal opinion by the US Army judge advocate general reinterpreted the order out of existence with these words: ". . . if the president has determined that the individual(s) in question pose such a threat to US citizens or the national security interests of the United States as to require the use of military force, it would be legally permissible to employ (e.g.) an air strike against that individual or group rather than attempt his, her, or their capture, and [it] would not violate the prohibition against assassination."[51]

Shortly after Executive Order 12333 was reinterpreted, President George Bush signed a secret finding authorizing the CIA and the special forces to conduct an attack on alleged Colombian drug lord Rodriguez Gacha. Instead of capturing him alive, the CIA/Special Forces team, hovering overhead in a helicopter, shot and killed Gacha, his seventeen-year-old son, and five bodyguards as they were fleeing Gacha's compound. According to a published report, the nonassassinations came "in the wake of the new interpretations of laws and executive orders by attorneys from the CIA, Army and the Justice Department that have a collective effect of easing restrictions on operations that may result in the death of foreign nationals." The report added that according to the CIA, deaths resulting from "disruptive activities aimed at narcotics traffickers" are not assassinations "even if a particular individual's death could be [sic] reasonably have been predicted in advance."[52]

These and other efforts to reinterpret the law, along with Casey's actions and Section 308, show that gaining immunity from prosecution is the CIA's long-sought goal. The CIA's activities show exactly why the agency is working so hard to get that immunity. The CIA could then legally establish itself as the arbiter of life itself in the name of national security. It is within this context that one can see the chilling impact of Section 308 and congressional sanctioning of CIA crimes and terrorist informants upon democracy, global security, and the rule of law.

There is something fundamentally wrong with the idea that protecting national security requires exempting the CIA — or any branch of the US government for that matter — from all ethical, legal, and constitutional principles. The world needs to know that this is the institutional operating principle of the CIA, not just a few cowboys or rogue agents, and that the CIA now has the statutory right to carry out all manner of crimes anywhere in the world.

One swallow does not a summer make, but one hundred thousand extremely serious crimes a year makes the CIA a criminal organization. Even if it did not, a suspension of the Constitution exempting the CIA from observing all international treaties and agreements screams for press coverage. So does Congress's sanctioning of CIA crimes against humanity under the well-worn "national security" banner. In fact, there is next to no meaningful coverage ever of the CIA in the mainstream media, let alone analysis. The few exceptions prove the rule, and when they occur, the rest of the media gang up on the exception, side with the CIA, and obliterate the story often before it's published. Case in point: Gary Webb's articles on the CIA's involvement with drugs.

In 1984, I was involved in one such exception. ABC hired me to help produce a story that I had sold about Bishop, Baldwin, Rewald, Dillingham & Wong (BBRD&W), an investment firm in Hawaii that was heavily involved with the CIA. I had earlier provided the same story to BBC's *Newsnight*, which had aired a thirty-five-minute program that included an interview with me. I had also given an interview and worked with CBS on the same story. The story was fully documented, and nobody, including the CIA, was able to disprove the charges. After the CBS program aired, the CIA called CBS and disparaged me but did not counter any charges made in the program.

The ABC show provoked a more brutal response from the CIA. Part of the ABC report charged, based on two videotaped interviews, that the CIA had plotted to assassinate an American, Ron Rewald, the president of BBRD&W. Immediately the lights went out as the CIA demanded a full retraction without providing any counterproof other than their denial. At the center of the uproar was Scott Barnes who said on camera that the CIA had asked him to kill Rewald. The CIA denied any association with Barnes, but later it was uncovered that the CIA had earlier admitted working with him.

The BBC had placed Barnes at the scene of the potential crime. They had documented that Barnes got himself hired as a chaplain's assistant at the Oahu Community Correctional Center in Honolulu where Rewald was imprisoned, awaiting trial for financial fraud. Barnes had written to Rewald as "Reverend Scott Barnes" in an attempt to get close to him. Barnes then became a volunteer at the prison, but quit when he discovered that volunteers could not visit Rewald's section of the prison. He then became a prison guard and visited the local coroner's office posing as a medical student seeking information about toxic drugs. It was at this time that Barnes claimed that the CIA asked him to kill Rewald. He said he refused and fled the island.

The CIA was invited to appear on the ABC program, but declined. After the show aired, CIA officials met with *ABC News* executive David Burke. They were unhappy with it, but presented no evidence to counter the charges made in the program. They did present some newspaper articles critical of Barnes. Nonetheless, Burke was sufficiently impressed "by the vigor with which they made their case" to order an on-air "clarification" in which Peter Jennings acknowledged the CIA's position but stood by the story.[53] But that was not enough for the CIA. Casey then called ABC chairman Leonard H. Goldenson. The call led to three meetings between ABC officials, and, guess who, Stanley Sporkin, CIA general counsel. On November 21, 1984, despite all the documented evidence presented in the program, despite ABC standing by the program in a second broadcast, Peter Jennings reported that ABC could no longer substantiate the charges, and that "We have no reason to doubt the CIA's denial."[54] He presented no evidence supporting the CIA's position.

That same day, the CIA filed a formal complaint, written by Sporkin and signed by CIA director William Casey, with the Federal Communications Commission (FCC) charging that ABC had "deliberately distorted" the news. In the complaint, Casey asked that ABC be stripped of its TV and radio licenses.[55] In January 1985, the FCC dismissed the complaint out of hand, stating that the CIA had not presented sufficient evidence to even launch an inquiry.[56] In February, the CIA filed a second complaint asking for FCC penalties under the "Fairness Doctrine" which requires broadcasters to air at least two sides of "controversial issues of public importance." This complaint was also eventually dismissed. This was the first time in the history of the country that a government agency had formally attacked the press. Yet, there was no uproar.[57]

During this time, Capital Cities Communications was maneuvering to buy ABC. Casey was one of the founders of Cap Cities. He was also chief counsel and board director until 1981, when he became director of the CIA. At the time, he owned some 34,755 shares of stock in Cap Cities, worth about $7.7 million, which he did not place in a blind trust despite his agreement with Congress to do so.[58] The *L.A. Weekly*, which along with the *Village Voice* provided the best coverage of the story, claimed that the CIA's protestations about ABC along with its FCC complaint "had the result of driving down the price of ABC stock in the public market."[59] In fact, in October 1984, the price of ABC's common stock was sixty-seven dollars per share. By November 1, it had dropped to sixty-four dollars, and by the end of the November—shortly after the CIA had filed its FCC complaint—it had dropped to fifty-nine dollars. While the second FCC complaint was still pending, Cap Cities bought ABC for $3.5 billion which was called a "bargain rate" by the trade media.[60]

Besides Casey, two other founders of Cap Cities, Lowell Thomas and Thomas Dewey, had extensive ties to the intelligence community. When Dewey was US attorney in New York, he had a habit of threatening publishers with prosecution if they published books about the CIA. He actually suppressed several such books. Thomas Murphy, Casey's friend and head of Cap Cities, also had long-standing intelligence ties. Before buying ABC, Murphy invited investment guru

Warren Buffett to buy 18 percent of the combined CC/ABC. At the time, Buffett controlled Berkshire Hathaway, then a $2-billion holding company that owned 13 percent of the Washington Post Company, on whose board of directors he sat until the ABC takeover was completed. Buffett was then replaced by Murphy's friend, financier William Ruane. Berkshire Hathaway also owned a large portion of *Time* and *Newsweek*. Once Cap Cities became a network, it sold fifty-three of its cable TV systems to the Washington Post Company.[61] So it is no wonder that none of these publications covered the story. Even if the financial links described above did not exist, it is unlikely they would have covered the story because they have enjoyed unconscionable, collaborative relationships with the CIA for decades. Pulitzer Prize–winner Carl Bernstein (among others) documented this in an October 20, 1977, article he wrote for *Rolling Stone* magazine entitled "The CIA and the Media."

The *L.A. Weekly* speculated that Casey's actions against ABC might have been intended to make ABC less likely to run stories critical of the CIA. I have no absolute proof that there was a connection, but within months, the entire investigative unit was dispersed, and the commentator on the Rewald program was assigned to covering beauty pageants. Needless to say, my contract was not renewed.

UPDATE: SECTION 308 AND THE WAR ON TERROR

I'm not opposed to shooting people, but it ought to be a last resort.
Jeffrey H. Smith/former CIA general counsel

In what humorist Bill Maher would have called a cowardly act, a CIA Predator drone fired a Hellfire missile at a single person, Qaed Salim Sinan al-Harethi, on Sunday, November 3, 2002, in the desert in Marib province in Yemen. There was no attempt to capture. No indictment, trial, evidence, or conviction. No proof he was an al Qaeda leader. It was a simple execution carried out by an agency now notorious for inaccurate, falsified intelligence.

In February 2002, the CIA assassinated three innocent Afghans. The CIA's Predator, thousands of feet above the ground, captured on its camera a group of people greeting a very tall man. It was concluded that the tall man was Osama bin Laden. Minutes later, the group disbanded. Shortly thereafter, the Predator's camera picked up the tall man again, this time emerging from a wooded area with two other men. It was then that the Predator launched a Hellfire missile, killing all three and devastating the area. It turned out that the victims were local men who had been scavenging in the woods for scrap metal.[62]

It appears that then CIA director George Tenet reported this erroneous sighting of bin Laden as an accurate sighting in his written statement to the National Commission on Terrorist Attacks upon the United States. In his statement to the commission (which had documented earlier that Tenet had lied to it on another matter), Tenet wrote of the sighting: "It imaged a tall man dressed in white robes with a physical and operational signature fitting bin Laden. A group of ten people around him were apparently paying their respects for a minute or two."[63] Tenet did not mention that the CIA had launched a missile destroying these innocent people.

In October 1999, the United States bombed a pharmaceutical plant in Khartoum, Sudan, because a CIA report said that it was making nerve gas and that Sudan was an "imminent" threat to US security. It was subsequently proven that the plant was not making nerve gas. A US court later agreed to compensate the victims of the bombing.[64]

In March 2003, then CIA director George Tenet personally informed President Bush that Saddam Hussein and his two sons, Qusay and Uday, were sleeping in a certain residential complex in the suburbs of Baghdad. On March 20, Bush ordered an air strike on the complex, killing and maiming scores of innocent people but not Hussein or his sons. They were not there.[65]

Actually, the original plan was to assassinate fifty top personnel in the Iraqi government, including Hussein and his sons, as a prelude to the invasion. The CIA had prepared a so-called Black List. During the war, the CIA and the Pentagon carried out fifty separate missile attacks to assassinate fifty individuals. These attacks caused the highest civilian casuality rate of the war and did not assassinate a single, targeted individual.

In Yemen, Sinan al-Harethi and five companions, among them American citizen Kamal Derwish, were incinerated alive, denying them burials by their families. The CIA had previously assassinated an unknown number of suspected al Qaeda operatives in Afghanistan, but Sinan al-Harethi was the first one outside of Afghanistan.

The CIA contends that there are al Qaeda operatives in some sixty countries, raising the specter of a worldwide wave of CIA-sponsored killings. Meanwhile, the US press seems to support this practice: "Yemen Strike Not Assassination" was UPI's headline. In its report on the incident, the UPI quoted Suzanne Spalding, an American Bar Association official and former CIA deputy general counsel: "Based on what has been reported in the press, this is viewed as a military action against enemy combatants which would take it out of the realm of assassination. You shoot to kill enemy combatants." Liberal journalist and CIA critic Steven Aftergood, who opposed Section 308, agreed. "I thought that the Yemen strike was necessary and appropriate. . . . The bottom line is these are bad people that need to be stopped, so the mission counts as a success."[66]

Even Derwish's killing didn't give the media pause. "CIA Can Kill Americans in Al-Qaeda" announced one typical headline.[67] Why? Well, George W. Bush said they could. Indeed, his father's administration decreed years earlier: "If the president has determined that the individual(s) in question pose such a threat to US citizens or the national security interests of the United States as to require the use of military force, it would be legally permissible to employ (e.g.) an air strike against the individual or group rather than attempt his, her, or their capture, and [it] would not violate the prohibition against assassination."[68]

The question is, how little or how much constitutes a "threat to US citizens or the national security interests of the United States"? Every US citizen might do well to wonder about the general wording and broad latitude implied in this decree.

The press didn't report when or whether Bush had determined that Qaed Salim Sinan al-Hareth was a threat and whether or not there was any stipulation in Bush's order specifically allowing for the assassination of Americans. But one wire story did mention that "permission to kill Americans is understood instead of specifically designated."[69] The press was supportive even after a secret directive from Secretary of Defense Donald Rumsfeld revealed that "the objective is to capture terrorists for interrogation or, if necessary, to kill them, not simply to arrest them in a law-enforcement exercise."[70]

In the *New Yorker*, Sy Hersh reported that a former high-level intelligence officer told him that "they want to turn these guys into assassins. They want to go on rumors—not facts—and go for the political effect, and that's what the Special Forces Command is afraid of. Rummy is saying that politics is bigger than war, and we need to take guys out for political effect: 'You have to kill Goebbels to get to Hitler.'"[71]

Rumsfeld's ad hoc Office of Special Plans (OSP), which the media describes as an intelligence-analysis operation even though virtually no one in the OSP has anywhere near the experience of top CIA analysts (who themselves are having serious reliability issues), is mandated to provide intelligence to US government assassins, in particular a sinister group known as the Gray Fox. Undersecretary of Defense for Policy Douglas J. Feith and Undersecretary of Defense William J. Luti run the OSP. "Feith and Luti see everybody not 100 percent with them as 100 percent against them," a defense consultant told Hersh. "It's a very Manichean world."

"There are five hundred guys out there you have to kill," added one of Rumsfeld's collaborators." There's no way to sugarcoat it — you just have to kill them. And you can't always be 100 percent sure of the intelligence. Sometimes you have to settle for 95 percent."[72]

Ironically, the CIA approved the coverage of its assassinations. This was revealed in a *Washington Post* article that also inadvertently disclosed that the *Post* is in the habit of providing the CIA with advance copies of its articles for censorship. "Provided with a detailed account of the contents of this article," wrote *Post* reporter Dana Priest, "US government officials made no request to the *Post* to withhold any of the story's details from publication, as they have sometimes done in other cases involving covert operations."[73]

Rounding off the *Post*'s coverage of the CIA was a fireside chat at CIA headquarters with deputy director John McLaughlin, who literally performed magic tricks while talking about the CIA's successes against al Qaeda: "We've captured or killed 75 percent of the senior al Qaeda leaders," he told the *Post*. "We shifted to the offensive dramatically. We are doing things that are arguably precedent-setting. So many of our targets are so small: a suitcase, a person, an apartment building, a room inside an apartment building."[74]

At the end of the interview, then CIA director George Tenet popped into the room. "He does everything," the *Post* reported Tenet saying about McLaughlin as he put his arm around the deputy director's shoulders. "He's a real partner."[75] The *Post* raised no questions about the legality of these operations even though serious questions could and should be asked about breaches of international law. Ironically, Tenet began his directorship by telling a college graduating class that establishing the rule of law was his first priority.

Establishing the rule of law may have been a priority for Tenet, but the fact is that the CIA has been, and is still, practicing criminality to the tune of one hundred thousand extremely serious crimes a year. The CIA and the government have equated these crimes, including assassination and torture, with national security and "legalized" them by enacting Section 308 as well as presidential findings. In this War on Terror era, the CIA not only flouts international law by openly carrying out illegal assassinations in foreign countries, but it even congratulates itself in the press. The press does its part by reporting successes on the front page and failures or corrections that make the agency look bad on back pages. No questions are ever raised about "blowback" or the possible repercussions of all this deadly illegal activity.

After the Sudanese pharmaceutical plant was bombed, Tenet told an audience at Georgetown University: "We were not wrong."[76] The *Washington Post* printed the CIA director's defense on the front page. Four years later, the *Post* reported in a back page that "the agency had been flat out wrong" about the plant.[77] Recently, Tenet returned to the cathedral-like setting of Catholic Georgetown to speak from a pulpit. *Tenet Defends CIA's Analysis of Iraq as Objective, If Flawed* read the *Post*'s banner headline, which was accompanied by a color photo of Tenet pointing an accusatory finger.[78]

The *Post* didn't mention its past flip-flop reporting on Tenet's comments and the CIA's performance. Meanwhile, back in Yemen, a powerful explosion rocked government buildings in Marib province about three weeks after the CIA assassinated Qaed Salim Sinan al-Harethi. Violence begets violence, and now in Yemen, innocent civilians are paying with their lives for al-Harethi's killing. The US media won't be there to cover it.

NOTES

1. House Permanent Select Committee on Intelligence, *IC 21: The Intelligence Community in the 21st Century* (Washington, DC: GPO, April 9, 1996), p. 205.
2. Ibid.
3. Ibid., p. 203
4. Intelligence Oversight Board, *Report on the Guatemalan Review*, June 28, 1996, Anthony S. Harrington, Chairman.
5. Ibid.

6. Ibid.

7. Ibid.

8. Ibid.

9. CIA/Office of Inspector General, *Selected Issues Related to CIA Activities in Honduras in the 1980's* (August 27, 1997): 996-0125-IG.

10. R. Jeffrey Smith, "CIA Drops over 1,000 Informants," *Washington Post*, March 2, 1997, p. A19.

11. Cf. supra, no. 1, p. 205

12. Public Law 106-567, 106th Congress, 114 Stat. 2843 (December 27, 2000), Sec 308, *Applicability to Lawful United States Intelligence Activities of Federal Laws Implementing International Treaties and Agreements.*

13. Alan Sipress and Karen DeYoung, "CIA Failed to Identify Plane Downed in Peru," *Washington Post*, April 24, 2001, pp. A1, A15.

14. Steven Aftergood, "Secrecy and Government Bulletin," *Federation of American Scientists* 84 (June 2000).

15. House Permanent Select Committee on Intelligence, *Intelligence Authorization Act for Fiscal Year 2001*, Conference Report, 106th Congress, 2d Session, Report 106-969 (Washington, DC: GPO, October 11, 2000), p. 45.

16. Senate Select Committee on Intelligence, *Authorizing Appropriations for Fiscal Year 2001 for the Intelligence Activities of the United States Government and Central Intelligence Agency Retirement and Disability System and for other Purposes*, 106th Congress, 2d Session, Report 106-969 (Washington, DC: GPO, May 4, 2000), p. 27.

17. Joint Hearings before the House Select Committee to Investigate Covert Arms Transactions with Iran and the Senate Select Committee on Secret Military Assistance to Iran and the Nicaraguan Opposition, *Iran-Contra Investigation*, 100th Congress, 1st Session, Senate Report No. 100-216, House Report No. 100-433, Testimony of Stanley Sporkin and Presentation by W. Neil Eggleston, June 24, 1987 (Washington, DC: GPO, 1988).

18. Cf. supra, no. 16, p. 27.

19. Cf. supra, no. 15, p. 41.

20. Senate Select Committee on Intelligence, *Nomination of George J. Tenet to be Director of Central Intelligence*, 105th Congress, 1st Session (May 6, 1997): pp. 85–86.

21. Tom Blanton, "Hardly a Distinguished Career," *Washington Post*, March 14, 2000, p. A17.

22. Cf. supra, no. 15, p. 41.

23. Cf. supra, no. 10.

24. Robert E. White, "Call Off the Spies," *Washington Post*, February 7, 1996, p. A19.

25. Ibid.

26. Ibid.

27. Tim Shorrock, *White House Feuding with CIA over Guatemala Killings*, InterPress Service, June 14, 1999.

28. Ibid.

29. Vincent Cannistraro, "Undetected at Home," *Washington Post*, September 12, 2001, p. A31.

30. Memorandum for Deputy Attorney General, Department of Justice, Washington, DC, Subject: Reports of Criminal Violations to the Department of Justice, Lawrence Houston, General Counsel, March 1, 1954.

31. House of Representatives, Subcommittee on Government Information and Individual Rights, Hearings, *Justice Department Handling of Criminal Case Involving CIA Personnel and Claims of National Security*, 94th Congress, 1st Session (Washington, DC: GPO, July 22, 1975), pp. 9–10.

32. CIA general counsel Lawrence Houston to director of Central Intelligence Roscoe Hillenkoetter, September 25, 1947.

33. Ibid.

34. Ibid.

35. CIA general counsel Lawrence Houston to director of Central Intelligence John McCone, January 15, 1962.

36. As cited in Jay Peterzell, "Legal and Constitutional Authority for Covert Operations," *First Principles* (Center for National Security Studies/ACLU) 10, no. 3 (Spring 1985).

37. Ibid.

38. Ibid.

39. Letter to US attorney general William French Smith from CIA director William J. Casey, December 22, 1981.

40. Report of the Congressional Committee Investigating the Iran-Contra Affair, Appendix B, Volume 26, 100th Congress, 1st Session, Senate Report No. 100-216, House Report No. 100-433 (Washington, DC: GPO, March 1, 1988), pp. 10–15.

41. Ibid.

42. Bob Woodward, *Veil: The Secret Wars of the CIA 1981-1987* (New York: Simon & Schuster, 1987).

43. Cf. supra, no. 17.

44. Ibid.

45. Ibid.

46. Ibid.

47. Ibid.

48. Ibid.

49. Ibid.

50. Cf. supra, no. 36.

51. Department of the Army, Office of the Judge Advocate General, Washington, DC 20310/DAJA-IA (27-1a)/Memorandum of Law/Subject: Executive Order 12333 and Assassination, W. Hays Park, Chief, International Law Branch/International Affairs Division.

52. Knut Royce and Peter Eisner, "U.S. Got Gacha," *Newsday*, May 4, 1990, pp. 1, 5.

53. Jim Ridgeway, "Casey at the Bar," *L.A. Weekly*, September 21, 1985, p. 27.

54. Ibid.

55. Ibid.

56. Ibid.

57. Ibid.

58. Andy Boehm, "The Seizing of the American Broadcasting Company," *L.A. Weekly*, February 20–26, 1987, pp. 1–6.

59. Ibid.

60. Ibid.

61. Ibid.

62. Seymour Hersh, "Manhunt," *New Yorker*, December 23 and 30, 2003, pp. 66–74.

63. George Tenet, "Written Statement for the Record of the Director of Central Intelligence, Commission on Terrorist Attacks upon the United States," March 24, 2004, p. 16.

64. Ted Gup, "Imminent Danger at the CIA," *Washington Post*, February 7, 2004, p. A23.

65. Dana Priest, "U.S. Teams Seek to Kill Iraqi Elite," *Washington Post*, March 30, 2003, p. A1.

66. Pamela Hess, "Experts: Yemen Strike Not Assassination," UPI, November 8, 2003.

67. "CIA Can Kill Americans in Al Qaeda," Bloomberg, December 4, 2002.

68. Department of the Army, Office of the Judge Advocate General, Washington, DC 20310/DAJA-IA (27-1a)/Memorandum of Law/Subject Executive Order 12333 and Assassination, W. Hays Park, Chief, International Law Branch/International Affairs Division.

69. Cf. supra, no. 5.

70. Cf. supra, no. 1.

71. Ibid.

72. Ibid.

73. Cf. supra, no. 3.

74. Dana Priest, "The CIA's 'Anonymous' No. 2," *Washington Post*, January 9, 2004, p. A15.

75. Ibid.

76. Gup, "Imminent Danger at the CIA."

77. Ibid.

78. Dana Priest and Walter Pincus, "Tenet Defends CIA's Analysis of Iraq as Objective, If Flawed," *Washington Post*, February 6, 2004, pp. A1, A16.

CHAPTER 7

THE MIGHTY WURLITZER PLAYS ON

Rebecca Miles

GARY WEBB

Webb was an investigative reporter for nineteen years, focusing on government and private-sector corruption and winning more than thirty journalism awards. He was one of six reporters at the San Jose Mercury News *to win a 1990 Pulitzer Prize for general news reporting for a series of stories on northern California's 1989 earthquake. He also received the 1997 Media Hero Award from the 2nd Annual Media & Democracy Congress and in 1996 was named Journalist of the Year by the Bay Area Society of Professional Journalists. In 1994 Webb won the H. L. Mencken Award given by the Free Press Association for a series in the* San Jose Mercury News *on abuses in the state of California's drug asset forfeiture program. And in 1980, Webb won an Investigative Reporters and Editors (IRE) Award for a series that he coauthored at the* Kentucky Post *on organized crime in the coal industry. Prior to 1988, Webb worked as a state House correspondent for the* Cleveland Plain Dealer *and was a reporter for the* San Jose Mercury News *where the* Dark Alliance *series broke in 1996. Months later, Webb was effectively forced out of his job after the* San Jose Mercury News *retracted their support for his story. Most recently, he consulted for the California State Legislature Task Force on Government Oversight.*

f we had met five years ago, you wouldn't have found a more staunch defender of the newspaper industry than me. I'd been working at daily papers for seventeen years at that point, doing no-holds-barred investigative reporting for the bulk of that time. As far as I could tell, the beneficial powers the press theoretically exercised in our society weren't theoretical in the least. They worked.

I wrote stories that accused people and institutions of illegal and unethical activities. The papers I worked for printed them, often unflinchingly, and many times gleefully. After these stories appeared, matters would improve. Crooked politicians got voted from office or were forcibly removed. Corrupt firms were exposed and fined. Sweetheart deals were rescinded, grand juries were empaneled, indictments came down, grafters were bundled off to the big house. Taxpayers saved money. The public interest was served.

It all happened exactly as my journalism-school professors had promised. And my expectations were pretty high. I went to journalism school while Watergate was unfolding, a time when people as distantly connected to newspapering as college professors were puffing out their chests and singing hymns to investigative reporting.

Bottom line: If there was ever a true believer, I was one. My first editor mockingly called me "Woodstein," after the pair of *Washington Post* reporters who broke the Watergate story. More than once I was accused of neglecting my daily reporting duties because I was off "running around with your trench coat flapping in the breeze." But in the end, all the sub rosa trench coat–flapping paid off. The newspaper published a seventeen-part series on organized crime in the American coal industry and won its first national journalism award in half a century. From then on, my editors at that and subsequent newspapers allowed me to work almost exclusively as an investigative reporter.

I had a grand total of one story spiked during my entire reporting career. That's it. One. (And in retrospect it wasn't a very important story either.) Moreover, I had complete freedom to pick my own shots, a freedom my editors wholeheartedly encouraged since it relieved them of the burden of coming up with story ideas. I wrote my stories the way I wanted to write them, without anyone looking over my shoulder or steering me in a certain direction. After the lawyers and editors went over them and satisfied themselves that we had enough facts behind us to stay out of trouble, they printed them, usually on the front page of the Sunday edition, when we had our widest readership.

In seventeen years of doing this, nothing bad had happened to me. I was never fired or threatened with dismissal if I kept looking under rocks. I didn't get any death threats that worried me. I was winning awards, getting raises, lecturing college classes, appearing on TV shows, and judging journalism contests. So how could I possibly agree with people like Noam Chomsky and Ben Bagdikian, who were claiming the system didn't work, that it was steered by powerful special interests and corporations, and existed to protect the power elite? Hell, the system worked just fine, as far as I could tell. It *encouraged* enterprise. It *rewarded* muckraking.

And then I wrote some stories that made me realize how sadly misplaced my bliss had been. The reason I'd enjoyed such smooth sailing for so long hadn't been, as I'd assumed, because I was careful and diligent and good at my job. It turned out to have nothing to do with it. The truth was that, in all those years, I hadn't written anything important enough to suppress.

In 1996, I wrote a series of stories, entitled *Dark Alliance*, that began this way:

> For the better part of a decade, a Bay Area drug ring sold tons of cocaine to the Crips and Bloods street gangs of Los Angeles and funneled millions in drug profits to a Latin American guerrilla army run by the U.S. Central Intelligence Agency, a Mercury News investigation has found.
>
> This drug network opened the first pipeline between Colombia's cocaine cartels and the black neighborhoods of Los Angeles, a city now known as the "crack" capital of the world. The cocaine that flooded in helped spark a crack explosion in urban America — and provided the cash and connections needed for L.A.'s gangs to buy automatic weapons.
>
> It is one of the most bizarre alliances in modern history: the union of a U.S.-backed army attempting to overthrow a revolutionary socialist government and the Uzi-toting "gangstas" of Compton and South Central Los Angeles.

The three-day series was, at its heart, a short historical account of the rise and fall of a drug ring and its impact on black Los Angeles. It attempted to explain how shadowy intelligence agencies, shady drugs and arms dealers, a political scandal, and a long-simmering Latin American civil war had crossed paths in South Central Los Angeles, leaving behind a legacy of crack use. Most important, it challenged the widely held belief that crack use began in African American neighborhoods not for any tangible reason, but mainly because of the kind of people who lived in them. Nobody was forcing them to smoke crack, the argument went, so they only have themselves to blame. They should just say *no*.

That argument never seemed to make much sense to me because drugs don't just appear magically on street corners in black neighborhoods. Even the most rabid hustler in the ghetto can't sell what he doesn't have. If anyone was responsible for the drug problems in a specific area, I thought, it was the people who were bringing the drugs in.

And so *Dark Alliance* was about them—the three cocaine traffickers who supplied the South Central market with literally tons of pure cocaine from the early 1980s to the early 1990s. What made the series so controversial is that two of the traffickers I named were intimately involved with a Nicaraguan paramilitary group known as the Contras, a collection of ex-military men, Cuban exiles, and mercenaries that the CIA was using to destabilize the socialist government of Nicaragua. The series documented direct contact between the drug traffickers who were bringing the cocaine into South Central and the two Nicaraguan CIA agents who were administering the Contra project in Central America. The evidence included sworn testimony from one of the traffickers—now a valued government informant—that one CIA agent specifically instructed them to raise money in California for the Contras. I found a photograph of one of the CIA agents huddled in the kitchen of a house in San Francisco with one of the traffickers and had interviewed the photographer, who confirmed its authenticity. Pretty convincing stuff, we thought.

Over the course of three days, *Dark Alliance* advanced five main arguments: First, that the CIA-created Contras *had* been selling cocaine to finance their activities. This was something the CIA and the major media had dismissed or denied since the mid-1980s, when a few reporters first began writing about Contra drug dealing. Second, that the Contras had sold cocaine in the ghettos of Los Angeles and that their main customer was L.A.'s biggest crack dealer. Third, that elements of the US government knew about this drug ring's activities at the time and did little if anything to stop it. Fourth, that because of the time period and the areas in which it operated, this drug ring played a critical role in fueling and supplying the first mass crack cocaine market in the United States. And fifth, that the profits earned from this crack market allowed the Los Angeles-based Crips and Bloods to expand into other cities and spread crack use to other black urban areas, turning a bad local problem into a bad national problem. This led to panicky federal drug laws that were locking up thousands of small-time black crack dealers for years, but never denting the crack trade.

It wasn't so much a conspiracy that I had outlined as it was a chain reaction—bad ideas compounded by stupid political decisions and rotten historical timing.

Obviously this wasn't the kind of story that a reporter digs up in an afternoon. A Nicaraguan journalist and I had been working on it exclusively for more than a year before it was published. And despite the topic of the story, it had been tedious work. Spanish-language undercover tapes, court records, and newspaper articles were laboriously translated. Interviews had to be arranged in foreign prisons. Documents had to be pried from unwilling federal agencies, or specially declassified by the National Archives. Ex-drug dealers and ex-cops had to be tracked down and persuaded to talk on the record. Chronologies were pieced together from heavily censored government documents and old newspaper stories found scattered in archives from Managua to Miami.

In December 1995, I wrote a lengthy memo to my editors, advising them of what my Nicaraguan colleague and I had found, what I thought the stories would say, and what still needed to be done to wrap them up. It was also to help my editor explain our findings to her bosses, who had not yet signed off on the story, and most of whom had no idea I'd been working on it.

> Two months ago, in an unheard-of response to a Congressional vote, black prison inmates across the country staged simultaneous revolts to protest Congress' refusal to make sentences for crack cocaine the same as for powder cocaine. Both before and after the prison riots, some black leaders were openly suggesting that crack was part of a broad government conspiracy that has imprisoned or killed an entire generation of young black men.
>
> Imagine if they were right. What if the US government was, in fact, involved in dumping cocaine into California—selling it to black

gangs in South Central Los Angeles, for instance—sparking the most destructive drug epidemic in American history?

That's what this series is about.

With the help of recently declassified documents, FBI reports, DEA undercover tapes, secret grand jury transcripts and archival records from both here and abroad, as well as interviews with some of the key participants, we will show how a CIA-linked drug and stolen car network—based in, of all places, the Peninsula—provided weapons and tons of high-grade, dirt cheap cocaine to the very person who spread crack through LA and from there into the hinterlands.

A bizarre—almost fatherly—bond between an elusive CIA operative and an illiterate but brilliant car thief from LA's ghettos touched off a social phenomenon—crack and gang power—that changed our lives in ways that are still to be felt. The day these two men met was literally ground zero for California's crack explosion, and the myriad of calamities that have flowed from it (AIDS, homelessness, etc.).

This is also the story of how an ill-planned and oftentimes irrational foreign policy adventure—the CIA's "secret" war in Nicaragua from 1980 to 1986—boomeranged back to the streets of America, in the long run doing far more damage to us than to our supposed "enemies" in Central America.

For, as this series will show, the dumping of cocaine on LA's street gangs was the "back-end" of a covert effort to arm and equip the CIA's ragtag army of anti-Communist "Contra" guerrillas. While there has long been solid—if largely ignored—evidence of a CIA-Contra-cocaine connection, no one has ever asked the question: "Where did all the cocaine go once it got here?"

Now we know.

Moreover, we have compelling evidence that the kingpins of this Bay Area cocaine ring—men closely connected to the assassinated Nicaraguan dictator Anastasio Somoza and his murderous National Guard—enjoyed a unique relationship with the U.S. government that has continued to this day.

In a meeting to discuss the memo, I recounted for my editors the sorry history of how the Contra-cocaine story had been ridiculed and marginalized by the Washington press corps in the 1980s, and that we could expect similar reactions to this series. If they didn't want to pursue this, now was the time to pull back, before I flew down to Central America and started poking around finding drug dealers to interview. But if we did, we needed to go full-bore on it, and devote the time and space to tell it right. My editors agreed. My story memo made the rounds of the other editors' offices and, as far as I know, no one objected. I was sent to Nicaragua to do additional reporting, and the design team at Mercury Center—the newspaper's online edition —began mapping out a Web page.

At the end of my memo, I'd suggested to my editors that we use the Internet to help us demonstrate the story's soundness and credibility which, based on past stories critical of the CIA, was sure to come under attack by both the government and the press.

> I have proposed to Bob Ryan [director of Mercury Center] that we do a special Merc Center/World Wide Web version of this series. The technology is extant to allow readers to download the series' supporting documentation through links to the actual text. For example, when we are quoting grand jury testimony, a click of the mouse would allow the reader to see and/or download the actual grand jury transcript.
>
> Since this whole subject has such a high unbelievability factor built into it, providing our backup documentation to our readers — and the rest of the world over the Internet—would allow them to judge the evidence for themselves. It will also make it all the more difficult to dismiss our findings as the fantasies of a few drug dealers.
>
> To my knowledge, this has never been attempted before. It would be a great way to showcase Merc Center and, at the same time, use computer technology to set new standards for investigative reporting.

The editors jumped at the idea. From our perch as the newspaper of Silicon Valley, we could see the future the World Wide Web offered. Newspapers were scrambling to figure out a way to make the transition to cyberspace. The *Mercury*'s editors were among the first to do it right, and were looking for new barriers to break. A special Internet version of *Dark Alliance* was created as a high-profile way of advertising the *Mercury*'s Web presence and bringing visitors into the site. Plus, the newspaper could boast (and later did) that it had published the first interactive online exposé in the history of American journalism.

I remember being almost giddy as I sat with Merc Center's editors and graphics designers, picking through the pile of once-classified information we were going to unleash on the world. We had photos, undercover tape recordings, and federal grand jury testimony. In addition, we had interviews with guerrilla leaders, tape-recorded courtroom testimony, confidential FBI and DEA reports, Nicaraguan Supreme Court files, Congressional records, and long-secret documents unearthed during the Iran-Contra investigation. For the first time, any reader with a computer and a sound card could see what we'd found—could actually read it for themselves—and listen in while the story's participants plotted, schemed, and confessed. And they could do it from anywhere in the world, even if they had no idea where San José, California, was.

After four months of writing, rewriting, editing, and reediting, my editors pronounced themselves satisfied and signed off. The first installment of *Dark Alliance* appeared simultaneously on the streets and on the Web on August 18, 1996.

The initial public reaction was dead silence. No one jumped up to deny any of it. Nor did the news media rush to share our discoveries with others. The stories just sat there, as if no one seemed to know what to make of them.

Admittedly, *Dark Alliance* was an unusual story to have appeared in a mainstream daily newspaper, not just for what it said, but for what it was. It wasn't a news story per se; nearly everything I wrote about had happened a dozen years earlier. Because my editors and I had sometimes vehemently disagreed about the scope and nature of the stories during the writing and editing process, the result was a series of compromises, an odd mixture of history lesson, news feature, analysis, and exposé. It was not an uplifting story; it was a sickening one. The bad guys had triumphed and fled the scene unscathed, as often happens in life. And there was very little anyone could do about it now, ten years after the fact.

So, I wasn't really surprised that my journalistic colleagues weren't pounding down the follow-up trail. Hell, I thought it was a strange story myself.

Had it been published even a year or two earlier, it likely would have vanished without a trace at that point. Customarily, if the rest of the nation's editors decide to ignore a particular story, it quickly withers and dies, like a light-starved plant. With the exception of newspapers in Seattle, some small cities in Northern California, and Albuquerque, *Dark Alliance* got the silent treatment big time. No one would touch it.

But no one had counted on the enormous popularity of the Web site. Almost from the moment the series appeared, the Web page was deluged with visitors from all over the world. Students in Denmark were standing in line at their college's computer waiting to read it. E-mails came in from Croatia, Japan, Colombia, Harlem, and Kansas City, dozens of them, day after day. One day we had more than 1.3 million hits. (The site eventually won several awards from computer journalism magazines.)

Once *Dark Alliance* became the talk of the Internet (in large part because of the technical wizardry and sharp graphics of the Web page), talk radio adopted the story and ran with it. For the next two months, I did more than one hundred radio interviews, in which I was asked to sum up what the three-day-long series said in its many thousands of words. Well, I would reply, it said a lot of things. Take your pick. Usually, the questions focused on the CIA's role, and whether I was suggesting a giant CIA conspiracy. We didn't know the CIA's exact role yet, I would say, but we have documents and court testimony showing CIA agents were meeting with these drug traffickers to discuss drug sales and weapons trafficking. And so, figure it out. Did the CIA know or not? The response would come back—So, you're saying that the CIA "targeted" black neighborhoods for crack sales? Where's your evidence of that? And it would go on and on.

There were other distractions as well. Film agents and book agents began calling. One afternoon Paramount Studios whisked me down to have lunch with two of the studio's biggest producers, the men who brought Tom Clancy's CIA novels to the screen, to talk about "film possibilities" for the still-unfolding story. This was about the time I realized the wind speed of the shit storm I had kicked up.

The rumbles the series was causing from black communities was unnerving a lot of people. College students were holding protest rallies in Washington, DC, to demand an official investigation. Residents of South Central marched on city hall and held candlelight vigils. The Los Angeles City Council soon joined the chorus, as did both of California's US senators, the Oakland city council, the mayor of Denver, the Congressional Black Caucus, Jesse Jackson, the NAACP, and at least a half dozen congressional members, mostly African American women whose districts included crack-ridden inner cities. Black civil rights activists were arrested outside the CIA after sealing off the agency's entrance with yellow crime scene tape. The story was developing a political momentum all of its own, and it was happening despite a virtual news blackout from the major media.

Some Washington journalists were alarmed. "Where is the

rebuttal? Why hasn't the media risen in revolt against this story?" fretted former newsman and government flack Bernard Kalb, host of CNN's *Reliable Sources*. Kalb expressed frustration that the story was continuing to get out despite the best efforts of the press to ignore it. "It isn't a story that simply got lost," Kalb complained, during the show, "It, in fact, has resonated and echoed and the question is, Where is the media knocking it down?"

It was an interesting comment because it foretold the way the mainstream press finally did respond to *Dark Alliance*. A revolt by the biggest newspapers in the country, something columnist Alexander Cockburn would later describe in his book *White Out* as "one of the most venomous and factually inane assaults . . . in living memory."

I remember arguing with a producer at a CNN news show shortly before I was to go on the air that I didn't want him asking me to explain "my allegations" because these stories *weren't* my allegations. I was a journalist reporting events that had actually occurred. You could document them, and we had.

"Well, you gotta understand my position," he mumbled. "The CIA isn't admitting it. So we're going to call it an allegation. You can understand that, right?"

"Are you telling me that until the day the CIA confesses to drug trafficking, CNN's position is that these events may not have happened?" I snapped. "What the fuck is that? When did we give the CIA the power to define reality?"

After nearly a month of silence, the CIA responded. It admitted nothing. It was confident that its agents weren't dealing drugs. But to dispel all the rumors and unkind suggestions my series had raised, the agency would have its inspector general take a look into the matter.

The black community greeted this pronouncement with unconcealed contempt. "You think you can come down here and tell us that you're going to investigate yourselves, and expect us to believe something is actually gonna happen?" one woman yelled at CIA director John Deutch, who appeared in Compton, California, in November 1996 to personally promise the city a thorough investigation. "How stupid do you think we are?"

The conservative press and right-wing political organizations were equally hostile to the idea of a CIA-crack investigation, but for different reasons. It meant the story was gaining legitimacy, and might lead to places that supporters of the Reagan and Bush administrations would rather not see it go. John Deutch was blasted on the front page of the *Washington Times* (which had also helped finance the Contras, hosting fundraisers and speaking engagements for Contra leaders while supporting their cause editorially) as a dangerous liberal who was undermining morale at the CIA by even suggesting there might be truth to the stories.

Ultimately, it was public pressure that forced the national newspapers into the fray. Protests were held outside the *Los Angeles Times* building by media watchdogs and citizens groups, who wondered how the *Times* could continue to ignore a story that had such an impact on the city's black neighborhoods. In Washington, black media outlets were ridiculing the *Post* for its silence, considering the importance the story held for most of Washington's citizens.

When the newspapers of record spoke, they spoke in unison. Between October and November, the *Washington Post*, the *New York Times*, and the *Los Angeles Times* published lengthy stories about the CIA drug issue, but spent precious little time exploring the CIA's activities. Instead, my reporting and I became the focus of their scrutiny. After looking into the issue for several weeks, the official conclusion reached by all three papers: Much ado about nothing. No story here. Nothing worth pursuing. The series was "flawed," they contended. How?

Well, there was no evidence the CIA knew anything about it, according to unnamed CIA officials the newspapers spoke to. The drug traffickers we identified as Contras didn't have "official" positions with the organization and didn't really give them all that much drug money. This was according to another CIA agent, Adolfo Calero, the former head of the Contras, and the man whose picture we had just published on the Internet, huddled in a kitchen with one of the Contra drug traffickers. Calero's apparent involvement with the drug operation was never mentioned by any of the papers; his decades-long relationship with the CIA was never mentioned either.

Additionally, it was argued, this quasi-Contra drug ring was small potatoes. One of the Contra traffickers had only sold five tons of cocaine during his entire career, the *Washington Post* sniffed, badly misquoting a DEA report we'd posted on the Web site. According to the *Post*'s analysis, written by a former CIA informant, Walter Pincus, who was then covering the CIA for the *Post*, this drug ring couldn't have made a difference in the crack market because five tons wasn't nearly enough to go around. Eventually, those assertions would be refuted by internal records released by both the CIA and the Justice Department, but at the time they were classified.

"I'm disappointed in the 'what's the big deal' tone running through the *Post*'s critique," *Mercury News* editor Jerry Ceppos complained to the *Post* in a letter it refused to publish. "If the CIA knew about these illegal activities being conducted by its associates, federal law and basic morality required that it notify domestic authorities. It seems to me that this is exactly the kind of story that a newspaper should shine a light on." Ceppos posted a memo on the newsroom bulletin board, stating that the *Mercury News* would continue "to strongly support the conclusions the series drew and will until someone proves them wrong." It was remarkable, Ceppos wrote, that the four *Post* reporters assigned to debunk the series "could not find a single significant factual error."

Privately, though, my editors were getting nervous. Never before had the three biggest papers devoted such energy to kicking the hell out of a story by another newspaper. It simply wasn't done, and it worried them. They began a series of maneuvers designed to deflect or at least stem the criticism from the national media. Five thousand reprints of the series were burned because the CIA logo was used as an illustration. My follow-up stories were required to contain a boilerplate disclaimer that said we were not accusing the CIA of direct knowledge, even though the facts strongly suggested CIA complicity. But those stunts merely fueled the controversy, making it appear as if we were backing away from the story without admitting it.

Ironically, the evidence we were continuing to gather was making the story even stronger. Long-missing police records surfaced. Cops who had tried to investigate the Contra drug ring and were rebuffed came forward. We tracked down one of the Contras who personally delivered drug money to CIA agents, and he identified them by name, on the record. He also confirmed that the amounts he'd carried to Miami and Costa Rica were in the millions. More records were declassified from the Iran-Contra files, showing that contemporaneous knowledge of this drug operation reached the top levels of the CIA's covert operations division, as well as into the DEA and the FBI.

But the attacks from the other newspapers had taken the wind out of my editors' sails. Despite the advances we were making on the story, the criticism continued. We were being "irresponsible" by printing stories suggesting CIA complicity without any admissions or "a smoking gun." The series was now described frequently as "discredited," even though nothing had surfaced showing that any of the facts were incorrect. At my editor's request, I wrote another series following up on the first three parts: a package of four stories to run over two days. They never began to edit them.

Instead, I found myself involved in hours-long conversations with editors that bordered on the surreal.

"How do we know for sure that these drug dealers were the first big ring to start selling crack in South Central?" editor Jonathan Krim pressed me during one such confab. "Isn't it possible there might have been others before them?"

"There *might* have been a lot of things, Jon, but we're only supposed to deal in what we know," I replied. "The crack dealers I interviewed said they were the first. Cops in South Central said they were the first, and that they controlled the entire market. They wrote it in reports that we have. I haven't found anything saying otherwise, not one single name, and neither did the *New York Times*, the *Washington Post* or the *L.A. Times*. So what's the issue here?"

"But how can we say for *sure* they were the first?" Krim persisted. "Isn't it possible there might have been someone else and they never got caught and no one ever knew about them? In that case, your story would be wrong."

I had to take a deep breath to keep from shouting. "If you're asking me whether I accounted for people who might never have existed, the answer is no," I said. "I only considered people with names and faces. I didn't take phantom drug dealers into account."

A few months later, the *Mercury News* officially backed away from *Dark Alliance*, publishing a long column by Jerry Ceppos apologizing for "shortcomings" in the series. While insisting that the paper stood behind its "core findings," we didn't have proof that top CIA officials knew about this, and we didn't have proof that millions of dollars flowed from this drug ring, Ceppos declared, even though we did and weren't printing it. There were gray areas that should have been fleshed out more. Some of the language used could have led to misimpressions. And we "oversimplified" the outbreak of crack in South Central. The *New York Times* hailed Ceppos for setting a brave new standard for dealing with "egregious errors" and splashed his apology on their front page, the first time the series had ever been mentioned there.

I quit the *Mercury News* not too long after that.

When the CIA and Justice Department finished their internal investigations two years later, the classified documents that were released showed just how badly I had fucked up. The CIA's knowledge and involvement had been far greater than I'd ever imagined. The drug ring was even bigger than I had portrayed. The involvement between the CIA agents running the Contras and the drug traffickers was closer than I had written. And DEA agents and officials had protected the traffickers from arrest, something I'd not been allowed to print. The CIA also admitted having direct involvement with about four dozen other drug traffickers or their companies, and that this too had been known and effectively condoned by the CIA's top brass.

In fact, at the start of the Contra war, the CIA and Justice Department had worked out an unusual agreement that permitted the CIA not to have to report allegations of drug trafficking by its agents to the Justice Department. It was a curious loophole in the law, to say the least.

Despite those rather stunning admissions, the internal investigations were portrayed in the press as having uncovered no evidence of *formal* CIA involvement in drug trafficking and no evidence of a conspiracy to send crack to black neighborhoods, which was hardly surprising since I had never said there was. What I *had* written—that individual CIA agents working within the Contras were deeply involved with this drug ring—was either ignored or excised from the CIA's final reports. For instance, the agency's decade-long employment of two Contra commanders—Colonel Enrique Bermudez and Adolfo Calero—was never mentioned in the declassified CIA reports, leaving the false impression that they had no CIA connection. This was a critical omission, since Bermudez and Calero were identified in my series as the CIA agents who had been directly involved with the Contra drug pipeline. Even though their relationship with the agency was a matter of public record, none of the press reports I saw celebrating the CIA's self-absolution bothered to address this gaping hole in the official story. The CIA had investigated itself and cleared itself, and the press was happy to let things stay that way. No independent investigation was done.

The funny thing was, despite all the furor, the facts of the story never changed, except to become more damning. But the perception of them did, and in this case, that is really all that mattered. Once a story became "discredited," the rest of the media shied away from it. *Dark Alliance* was consigned to the dustbin of history, viewed as an

Internet conspiracy theory that had been thoroughly disproved by more responsible news organizations.

Why did it occur? Primarily because the series presented dangerous ideas. It suggested that crimes of state had been committed. If the story was true, it meant the federal government bore some responsibility, however indirect, for the flood of crack that coursed through black neighborhoods in the 1980s. And that is something no government can ever admit to, particularly one that is busily promoting a multibillion-dollar-a-year War on Drugs.

But what of the press? Why did our free and independent media participate in the government's disinformation campaign? It had probably as many reasons as the CIA. The Contra-drug story was something the top papers had dismissed as sheer fantasy only a few years earlier. They had not only been wrong, they had been terribly wrong, and their attitude had actively impeded efforts by citizens groups, journalists, and congressional investigators to bring the issue to national attention, at a time when its disclosure may have done some good. Many of the same reporters who declined to write about Contra drug trafficking in the 1980s — or wrote dismissively about it — were trotted out once again to do damage control.

Second, the *San Jose Mercury News* was not a member of the club that sets the national news agenda, the elite group of big newspapers that decides the important issues of the day, such as which stories get reported and which get ignored. Small regional newspapers aren't invited. But the *Merc* had broken the rules and used the Internet to get in by the back door, leaving the big papers momentarily superfluous and embarrassed, and it forced them to readdress an issue they'd much rather have forgotten. By turning on the *Mercury News*, the big boys were reminding the rest of the flock who really runs the newspaper business, Internet or no Internet, and the extents to which they will go to protect that power, even if it meant rearranging reality to suit them.

Finally, as I discovered while researching the book I eventually wrote about this story, the national news organizations have had a long, disappointing history of playing footsie with the CIA, printing unsubstantiated agency leaks, giving agents journalistic cover, and downplaying or attacking stories and ideas damaging to the agency. I can only speculate as to why this occurs, but I am not naïve enough to believe it is mere coincidence.

The scary thing about this collusion between the press and the powerful is that it works so well. In this case, the government's denials and promises to pursue the truth didn't work. The public didn't accept them, for obvious reasons, and the clamor for an independent investigation continued to grow. But after the government's supposed watchdogs weighed in, public opinion became divided and confused, the movement to force congressional hearings lost steam and, once enough people came to believe the stories were false or exaggerated, the issue could safely be put back at the bottom of the dead-story pile, hopefully never to rise again.

Do we have a free press today? Sure we do. It's free to report all the sex scandals it wants, all the stock market news we can handle, every new health fad that comes down the pike, and every celebrity marriage or divorce that happens. But when it come to the real down and dirty stuff—stories like Tailwind, the October Surprise, the El Mozote massacre, corporate corruption, or CIA involvement in drug trafficking—that's where we begin to see the limits of our "free" press. In today's media environment, sadly, such stories are not even open for discussion.

Back in 1938, when fascism was sweeping Europe, legendary investigative reporter George Seldes observed in his book *The Lords of the Press* that "it *is* possible to fool all the people all the time—when government and press cooperate." Unfortunately, we have reached that point.

CHAPTER 8

MAINSTREAM MEDIA
THE DRUG WAR'S SHILLS

MICHAEL LEVINE

Michael Levine is a twenty-five-year veteran of the Drug Enforcement Administration (DEA) turned whistle-blower, trial consultant, and journalist. Currently, he hosts the popular Expert Witness *radio show on WBAI in New York while working as an expert witness on all matters related to drug trafficking, informants, covert operations, and the use of deadly force for federal and state court cases. He is the author of two best-selling books on his drug war experiences: the* New York Times *best-seller* Deep Cover *and the national bestseller* The Big White Lie. *His articles and interviews on the drug war have been published in numerous national newspapers and magazines, including the* New York Times, *the* Los Angeles Times, USA Today, Esquire, *and the* Journal of Crime. *He has served as a consultant and on-air expert for various national television programs in both Spanish and English, including* 60 Minutes, Crossfire, MacNeil/Lehrer NewsHour, Good Morning America, *and* Contrapunto.

OUTRAGEOUS ACTS: MY PERSONAL EXPERIENCE WITH DRUG-WAR MONTE

Everything you need to know about mainstream media's vital role in perpetuating our nation's three-decade, trillion-dollar War on Drugs—despite overwhelming evidence that it is a fraud— you can learn by watching a three-card monte operation.

Three-card monte is a blatant con game where the dealer lays three cards on a folding table, shows you that one of them is the queen of spades, turns them over, and shuffles them quickly. You're sure you know where the queen is, and you saw a guy before you win easily a couple of times, so you bet your money. If that dopey-looking guy can win, so can you. But incredibly, you've guessed wrong. You lost. You've been taken for a sucker.

The suckers in three-card monte cannot possibly win. It's an obvious and well-known con game, yet as you walk away, you see a whole line of other suckers, eyes gawking, jaws slack, hands deep in their pockets, mesmerized by the show and ready to lay down their money as fast as the dealer can get to them. Why? Because they too saw the dopey-looking guy win. But what they don't know about the dopey-looking guy is that he's a shill.

Shills are the con men (and women) who entice suckers into the phony game by putting on a show intended to convince those watching that the game is honest, that if you keep playing you can actually win. A good shill also helps cover up the operation by distracting the police away from the illegal action. In a court of law where three-card monte dealers are considered crooks and thieves, shills are considered their coconspirators. They are liable to an equal penalty if indicted and found guilty after trial. In the drug-war monte game, mainstream media are the shills.

Media's success as shills is unparalleled in the history of scams, con jobs, and rip-offs and can best be measured by how effectively they continue to sell us a fraud so obvious and so impossible to win that it makes South Bronx gold mine certificates look like a conservative investment.

Here's some of the true history that, thanks to excellent shilling, most of you are unaware of:

When President Nixon first declared war on drugs in 1971, there were fewer than half a million hard-core addicts in the entire nation, most of whom were addicted to heroin. Most of them lived in large inner-city areas, with the greatest number residing in New York City. Only two federal agencies were charged with enforcing drug laws back then—the Federal Bureau of Narcotics and US Customs. These two agencies were greater enemies to each other than to any drug cartel. The total drug war budget was less than $100 million.

Three decades later, despite the expenditure of $1 trillion in federal and state tax dollars, the number of hard-core addicts is shortly expected to exceed five million. Our nation has become the supermarket of the drug world, with a wider variety and bigger supply of drugs at cheaper prices than ever before. The problem now not only affects every town and hamlet on the map, but it is difficult to find a family anywhere that is not somehow affected.

Currently, fifty-five federal and military agencies (that we know of) are involved in federal drug enforcement alone (not counting state and local agencies), while US military troops are invading South and Central American nations under the banner of "drug war." The federal drug war budget alone (not counting state and municipal budgets) is now well over $20 billion a year, and my personal quest to find one individual anywhere in the world who could honestly testify that America's trillion-dollar war on drugs has somehow saved him or her from the white menace has thus far been fruitless.

Do you need a cop to tell you that this is evidence of an overwhelming fraud? If your stockbroker invested your money the way our elected leaders have invested our drug-war monte dollars, you'd have jailed or shot him way before 1972. Yet, the game continues.

Why? Mainstream media, as they did during the Vietnam War, shill us by means of an incessant flow of fill-in-the-blanks bullshit "victory" stories, into believing that drug-war monte is a real war that our leaders intend to win. Media shills, which now include Hollywood and "entertainment" television as well as the publishing industry, are continuously conning us into believing that if—in a fit of sanity—we really tried to end the costly fraud, some unspeakable horror would occur, like Mexican and Colombian drug dealers led by the latest media-created "Pablo Escobar" would invade our insufficiently protected borders to force-feed our kids heroin and cocaine. We might even have to arm the Partnership for a Drug Free America with missiles and rockets.

Unless of course, our kids "Just Say No," as Nancy Reagan's billion-dollar media boondoggle campaign taught them.

And when mainstream media hasn't been directly shilling us into supporting drug-war monte, as they do to this day, they have helped perpetuate it via their censorship, or conscious omission of scandalous events that—had they been reported with the fervor the *Washington Post* showed during the Watergate era—could have brought the whole deadly and costly charade crumbling to the ground three decades ago. I know this firsthand because I personally participated in some of the most significant of these scandalous events either as a federal agent, and/or a court-qualified expert witness, and/or a journalist.

THE VIETNAM WAR

The undercover case that brought me into Southeast Asia during the Vietnam War was the most dangerous of my career, and the source of that danger was not just the dealers. It was the case that first brought me face-to-face with the fact that, like the Vietnam War, the War on Drugs was never intended to be won, and that it was a deadly fraud perpetrated against the people paying for it. It was also the first case that taught me that a runaway, corrupt federal bureaucracy could count on mainstream media to shill for it. Ironically, it began on the Fourth of July (1971).

At the time, President Nixon had recently declared war on drugs. Our political leaders had already begun pimping Americans through media megaphones into believing that our growing drug problem was the fault of evil foreigners and that—other than the Vietnam War—the drug problem was our number-one national security concern. I was a young agent assigned with US Customs' Hard Narcotics Smuggling Unit in New York City. My twenty-five-year-old brother David at that point had been a heroin addict for ten years, and I was a True Believer.

It was on that July 4th day that I arrested John Edward Davidson at JFK International Airport in New York City with three kilos of 99 percent pure white heroin hidden in the false bottom of a Samsonite suitcase, and the investigation known as *U.S.* v. *Liang Sae Tiew et al.* began.[1]

By nightfall, the investigation had brought my team deep inside a desolate swamp on the outskirts of Gainesville, Florida, where a lone trailer was parked at the end of a barely visible trail. During the predawn hours, we raided the trailer and arrested the US-based financier of the smuggling operation, Alan Trupkin, and his heroin-addicted gofer, twenty-two-year-old John Clements (remember this name; we'll see him later). By the following day, I had all the details I needed to destroy one of the biggest heroin import operations on the globe. But there was one major problem to contend with that neither I nor any of the senior officers to whom I reported could have, in our wildest dreams, imagined at the time: the CIA.

Two years earlier, Davidson, stationed with the army in Vietnam, had taken R and R (rest and relaxation) leave in Bangkok. There, he had connected with a Chinese heroin dealer, Liang Sae Tiew, aka Gary. The prices were the cheapest in the world, the supplies unlimited. After Davidson's discharge, all he had to do was smuggle the stuff into the United States, and he and his partners would be rich. Seven trips and twenty-one kilos later, his luck ran out when I arrested him. Now, to do my job in accordance with my training and the very philosophy of the entire War on Drugs, I had to take the next step and go for the source.

One month later I arrived in Bangkok, posing as Davidson's heroin-dealing partner. Within days I made contact with his heroin connections, Gary and someone called "Mr. Geh." At first, my presence in Bangkok was kept secret from the Bureau of Narcotics and Dangerous Drugs, the sworn enemies of US Customs. The war between the two agencies for budget and media coverage had escalated to the level of fist-fighting, arresting each other's informants, and in one instance, came close to a shoot-out. But that's another story. My presence in Bangkok was also kept secret from the Thai police, whose only competition for the most corrupt police force in recorded history—in my experience—came from their Mexican counterparts. The fact was that I was in Thailand illegally. At the time, undercover operations were illegal in most of the world. It was unthinkable that cops would be permitted to commit crimes to catch criminals. I'd already been warned by my own bosses that if the Thai police got wind of me being there to do a drug deal, undercover or otherwise, they would bust my ass and disappear me, and my own country would disavow all knowledge. In short, my butt was way out on a limb, and I knew it, but I did not know the half of my problems.

After a week of hanging out with the dopers, I had managed to convince them that I was the *capo di tutti frutti* of the Mafia hooked into individual mafiosi across the United States, each looking for large quantities of drugs. I was the Main Man. I told them that I needed a new supplier because my previous source, the French Connection, had been busted.

At the time, the largest heroin seizure in history was in the neighborhood of two hundred kilos, part of the original French Connection. I knew the case well; I'd played a small role in it. The two Chinese heroin dealers were as aware of the American market as I was, and they assured me that these amounts were child's play compared to their operation. They had a "factory" in Chiang Mai run by Mr. Geh's uncle that was churning out a couple of hundred kilos a week. What didn't go to the soldiers in Vietnam was going into the veins and brains of American kids. Like my own brother.

I cut a deal: I would buy a kilo of Dragon Brand for $2,500 cash and send it to my US Mafia customers as a sample. I'd then remain in Thailand awaiting their orders. I told Gary and Mr. Geh that I estimated I might need as much as three hundred kilos for the first order. The dopers' price for a three-hundred-kilo load was $2,000 a kilo, or a paltry $600,000. That amount of heroin, at that time, could have met the entire US heroin demand for about two to three weeks. The cost to our nation in death, destruction, and taxes was incalculable; the potential profits to the dopers breathtaking.

French Connection heroin was selling wholesale and delivered in the United States at $20,000 a kilo. The purity of the Dragon Brand heroin I was buying in Asia was as good or better. It was close to 100 percent pure, meaning that you could cut (dilute) the stuff up to fourteen times for the street. The US street price per ounce was $2,000, meaning that a single kilo (forty ounces) of Asian heroin at $2,000 per ounce could theoretically gross $1,120,000. Now just multiply that by three hundred kilos, and your original investment of $600,000 has now yielded more than $300 million.

At the moment I had everything I needed to destroy the operation except for its location, but I knew how to remedy that. I came up with one proviso: before we finalized the deal, I demanded to personally inspect their heroin production facilities, "the factory," in Chiang Mai. If they agreed, I would be one step away from destroying them.

Within days, the two dealers made contact with the factory's owner, Mr. Geh's uncle. He agreed to go forward with the transaction and authorized me to inspect the factory *after* I bought the first sample kilo.

Sitting alone in my room at the Siam Intercontinental that night, I replayed the words of the heroin dealers on a minirecorder. The implications of what I had just learned for our nation, for my own heroin-addicted brother, mixed with the bullshit exhortations of our political leaders, seemed to sink deep inside of me. I felt as if I were playing some hero role in a John Wayne (now Tom Clancy) movie. I was in position to do what our leaders and mainstream media had psyched me up to do: strike at the heart of America's greatest enemies.

I was on a mission from God.

I was a naïve idiot.

Bam! The adrenaline was pumping. I was moving. I made contact with my control officer, Customs Attaché Joe Jenkins. At a predawn meeting, I brought him up to date. He was as excited as I was, but a lot more reserved. I could tell there was something he wasn't telling me, but at that moment I had a pressing need. I was almost broke. I needed cash to maintain my cover as a big-time dope dealer. I needed $2,500 cash to buy the first kilo of heroin. Hell, I didn't even have enough money to pay my hotel bill. I was already receiving notes under my door from the management asking me to bring it up to date.

Jenkins instructed me to meet him later at a girly bar on Sukamvit. By that time he assured me, he'd have headquarters — and more important — embassy approvals for the operation to proceed. And — *most* important — he'd have money.

Late that night I met Jenkins again. As three butt-naked, Oriental doll-women in four-inch spike heels performed a somnambulistic, wriggle-writhe-squat over beer bottles on the bar above us to a Rolling Stones album blasting from monstrous speakers, Jenkins shouted that he had neither approvals nor money. From that point on, things got strange. Very strange.

The suddenly nervous Jenkins, his eyes jerking at every movement in the shadows around us, gave me Kafkaesque, bureaucratic excuses for the delays. He said he needed specific signatures from specific bureaucrats who were, for some reason or other, unavailable. He fed me other bullshit that only a government employee would find normal.

I went back to my room and began stalling both the hotel and the drug dealers. *My people are being cautious; they are sending me a courier. They take no chances.* On and on and on, ad nauseum.

At first, the dopers thought that the caution of "my people" was understandable, even admirable, but when more than a week had passed and the delays continued, I found myself out of excuses and in serious danger. I went back to Jenkins. For the first time in my life I heard myself utter the threat, "I'm going to the press." Jenkins looked at me and just rolled his eyes. He recognized an idiot when he saw one.

Some time before dawn, I was called into the embassy for a meeting with the first CIA officer I'd ever knowingly met. He gave no name, and I didn't ask for one. Jenkins had told me he was CIA, and that was all I needed. The guy was short, stocky, bald, and wearing what I would come to recognize as the typical CIA uniform: a khaki leisure suit. He looked at me with a mixture of bemusement and disdain that I would also learn was typical.

"You're not going to Chiang Mai," he said. "We just lost a man up there. It's dangerous."

"But I'm an undercover," I protested. "Already certified crazy. I didn't take this job to be safe."

Like I said: a naïve idiot.

After not much discussion, the spook looked at his watch and cut the conversation short. "You served in the military, right? (He didn't wait for my answer) Well, our country has other priorities [than the drug war]." He was firm—I was not going to Chiang Mai and that was it. The CIA had made the decision for us—a harbinger of things to come. My instructions were to buy the single kilo of heroin and arrest whomever delivered it. Case closed.

This was years before the CIA would come to be known among Drug Enforcement Administration (DEA) agents assigned overseas as the Criminal Inept Agency and later the Cocaine Import Agency. This was years before anyone with a government job questioned the judgment of the gang that can't spy straight, and years before I would state on my own radio show that the CIA seal at Langley, instead of reading "and the truth shall set you free," ought to read "and the truth shall piss you off."[2]

I'd stumbled into a quick look at an ugly truth that would haunt me for the rest of my life, but at that moment I was not prepared to believe it. I had served three years in the military as an Air Force Sentry Dog Handler—combat-trained military police. I'd been an undercover federal agent for six years. I was a good soldier, trained to follow orders. I believed in the virtue and morality of my leaders. Like the devoted husband who catches his beloved wife exchanging a torrid look with the pizza delivery boy, the truth was too emotionally charged for me to absorb. It was much easier for me to accept that the CIA man knew more than I did and that it was in our national interest for me to simply follow orders.

And that's what I did. I ordered the kilo of heroin and busted the two Chinese dealers on the spot. Back in the United States, I received a Treasury Act Special Award for the first case of its kind, one agent traveling the globe to "destroy" a heroin operation. Another "victory" for the US media shill factory.

For a while I was lost in my own press notices.

But I was no longer the same unquestioning, young undercover agent. My cop instinct nagged at me, told me something was wrong. Within a year I would learn that the Chiang Mai "factory" that the CIA had prevented me from destroying was the source of massive amounts of heroin being smuggled into the United States in the bodies and body bags of GIs killed in Vietnam.[3] All I could do was pray that the CIA knew what it was doing. At that time I rather foolishly believed that they had the best interests of the American people at heart, but how competent were they? And if they weren't competent, to whom do you turn to blow the whistle? Congress? The media?

I was a well-trained, experienced undercover operative who, when in doubt, observed closely and documented what I saw, but took no action—one of the reasons, I believe, that I survived my career. And in the early 1970s, very few were in a better position than I to observe and document the development of drug-war monte.

My unit, the Hard Narcotics Smuggling Squad, was a small group of men (sixteen to twenty) charged with investigating all heroin and cocaine smuggling through the Port of New York, home of the majority of our nation's hard-core drug addicts. By necessity my unit became involved in investigating every major smuggling operation known to law enforcement. We could not avoid witnessing the CIA protecting major drug dealers.

In fact, throughout the Vietnam War, while we documented massive amounts of heroin flooding into the United States from the Golden Triangle (the triangular area formed by northern Thailand, Laos, and Burma), while tens of thousands of our fighting men were coming home addicted, not a single important source in Southeast Asia was ever indicted by US law enforcement. This was no accident. Case after case, like *U.S.* v. *Liang Sae Tiew et al.*, was killed by CIA and State Department intervention and there wasn't a damned thing we could do about it.

It was also during those years that we became aware that the CIA had gone well beyond simply protecting their drug-dealing assets. Agency-owned proprietary airlines like Air America were being used to ferry drugs throughout Southeast Asia, allegedly to support our "allies." (With friends like these . . .) CIA banking operations were used to launder drug money. The CIA was learning the drug business and learning it well.

Those of us on the inside, who were aware of the glaring inconsistencies between drug-war policy as reported through mainstream mass media and what was really going on, were afraid to go to either Congress or the media for help. It seemed impossible that anyone with any knowledge whatsoever of our growing drug problem would not have noticed the absence of enforcement in Southeast Asia. It was just too big, too out in the open. During those years I believe a good journalist could have had many frustrated "inside sources" to quote from, yet no stories appeared.

It was also during the waning years of Vietnam that CIA protection of drug dealers spread to other areas under our watch. As cocaine traffickers grew in economic and political importance in South and Central America, they also grew in importance to the CIA and other covert US agencies.

For example, in 1972, being fluent in Spanish, I was assigned to assist in a major international drug case involving top Panamanian government officials who were using diplomatic passports to smuggle large quantities of heroin and other drugs into the United States. The name Manuel Noriega surfaced prominently in the investigation. Surfacing right behind Noriega was the CIA to protect him from US law enforcement.

After President Nixon declared war on drugs in 1971 and all our political leaders began bleating about how drugs were our number-one national security threat, Congress began to raise our taxes and the drug-war budget on a regular basis that continues to this day. Meanwhile, the CIA and the Department of State were protecting more and more politically powerful drug traffickers around the world: the Mujahedeen in Afghanistan, the Bolivian cocaine cartels, the top levels of the Mexican government, top Panama-based money launderers, the Nicaraguan Contras, right-wing Colombian drug dealers and politicians, and others.[4]

Under US law, protecting drug trafficking was and still is considered Conspiracy to Traffic in Drugs—a felony violation of federal law. President George H. W. Bush once said, "All those who look the other way at drug trafficking are as guilty as the drug dealer."[5] Ironically, not too many years earlier, as the head of the CIA, Mr. Bush had authorized a salary for Manuel Noriega as a CIA asset, while the little dictator was listed in as many as forty DEA computer files as a drug dealer. Seems only fitting that the CIA named its headquarters after Mr. Bush.

In any case, it was clear to us on the inside of international drug enforcement that Congress was either well aware of what was going on, or guilty of terminal ineptitude. It was also clear to us that CIA protection of international narcotics traffickers depended heavily on the active collaboration of the mainstream media as shills.

Media's shill duties, as I experienced them firsthand, were twofold: first, to keep quiet about the gush of drugs that was allowed to flow unimpeded into the United States; second, to divert the public's attention by shilling them into believing the drug war was legitimate by falsely presenting the few trickles we were permitted to interdict as though they were major "victories" when in fact we were doing nothing more than getting rid of the inefficient competitors of CIA assets.

I began to notice the fill-in-the-blanks drug stories. Every week a new "drug baron," or a new drug-corrupted government was—and continues to be—presented as a new "threat" to America's kids. Every case, many of which I took part in, was headlined as "U.S. Authorities Announce Major Blow Against *(fill in the blank)* Drug Cartel." Every country and national leader that the CIA and the State Department wanted to slander (i.e., Castro and Cuba, the Sandinistas, and leftist guerrillas anywhere) was headlined as "U.S. Sources Say *(fill in the blank)* Poses New Narco-Trafficking Threat." Foreign leaders and nations whose images the CIA and the State Department wanted to keep clean (i.e., Manny Noriega for two decades, or Mexico and every one of its presidents since NAFTA) were headlined as "*(fill in the blank)* New Anti-Drug Efforts Win Trust of U.S. Officials."[6]

The media continues to do their shill job well and drug-war monte continues to grow massively, as does our nation's drug problems.

The "Cocaine Coup"

On July 17, 1980, for the first time in history, drug traffickers actually took control of a nation. It was not just any nation; it was Bolivia, at the time the source of virtually 100 percent of the cocaine entering the United States.[7] The "Cocaine Coup" was the bloodiest in Bolivia's history. CIA-recruited mercenaries and drug traffickers—collectively called the "Angels of Death" — unseated Bolivia's democratically elected president, Lidia Gueiler, a leftist (according to the CIA) whom the American government didn't want in power. The drug traffickers also took the opportunity to eliminate their competitors along with all suspected DEA informants so that they could consolidate raw materials and production to meet the United States's skyrocketing demand for cocaine. The result was the creation of what came to be known as *La Corporacion* — The Corporation — in essence, the General Motors or OPEC of cocaine.

Immediately after the coup, cocaine production increased massively, until, in short order, it outstripped supply. This was the true beginning of the cocaine and crack "plague," as the media and hack politicians never tire of calling it. July 17, 1980, is truly a day that should live in infamy along with December 7, 1941. There are few events in history that have caused more and longer-lasting damage to our nation.

What America was never told — despite mainstream media having the information as well as a prime, inside source who was ready to go public with the story — was that the coup was carried out with the aid and participation of Central Intelligence. The source could also testify and prove that, to carry out the coup, the CIA along with the State and Justice departments had to combine forces to protect their drug-dealing assets by destroying a DEA investigation — *U.S. v. Roberto Suarez, et al.* How do I know? I was that inside source.[8]

All the events I am referring to are detailed in my book *The Big White Lie*, a book that, to date, has been virtually ignored by mainstream media — with good reason, as I hope this chapter makes clear. Documentation of the events portrayed in the book was carried out in accordance with accepted techniques and practices of evidence-gathering as taught in each of the four federal law enforcement training academies that I attended. I took precisely the same precautions that I would have taken were I preparing a case for a jury, backing up every assertion with solid evidence in the form of reports and tape-recorded conversations.

The Big White Lie is out of print, but it is available in libraries. I can only urge readers, particularly those in law enforcement and the legal professions, to read the book and judge its evidentiary value for yourselves.

During the months after the Bolivian coup, I watched the massive news coverage with astonishment. Nothing even came close to the true and easily provable events. All of it was accurate in that it frighteningly portrayed the new Bolivian government as one comprised of expatriate Nazis like Klaus Barbie and drug dealers like Roberto Suarez, and reported that the power and influence of the drug economy was much greater than all the US experts had imagined. But the most important fact of all was consistently left out: the coup was CIA-directed and US tax dollars had put these guys in power.

As I detailed in the book, American media's failure to cover what was arguably the most significant event in drug war history was enough to push me over the edge.

I was no hero, believe me. I was an undercover operative who knew well how to play the angles, not someone who took unreasonable chances. But this was not that long after Woodward and Bernstein's concentrated, full-court press attack on the Watergate affair had resulted in real indictments and prison sentences for crimes a lot less serious than what I was about to report. The media still seemed to offer some hope. I could not believe that the failure to accurately cover the Cocaine Coup was intentional. I would provide them with the missing pieces. I was now willing to be the drug war's Deep Throat.

The smoking gun evidence of the CIA's role in the Bolivian coup could be found in the Roberto Suarez case, a complicated DEA covert operation that I had run only two months before the Cocaine Coup. Media shills had trumpeted it as the greatest undercover sting operation in history. Its finale occurred when Bolivian cartel leaders Roberto Gasser and Alfredo Gutierrez were arrested outside a Miami bank after I had paid them $8 million dollars for the then-largest load of cocaine in history. Some of the actual facts of the case were used in the screenplay for the film *Scarface*, with Al Pacino.

What America was never told before my book was published was that within weeks of their headlined arrests, both Gasser and Gutierrez were released from jail. When I learned from my post in Argentina that these two men and their drug cartel were key players in the Cocaine Revolution and that the whole thing was CIA-inspired and supported, I wrote anonymous letters to the *New York Times*, the *Washington Post*, and the *Miami Herald.*

Despite the fact that the letters contained enough information to convince them that I was a highly placed source and could furnish them with information and leads that would quickly and easily bring a true investigative journalist to the truth, nothing happened. Ironically, the only journalists who were at all curious about the sudden disappearance of the case from the news and the DEA's reluctance to talk about it were working for *High Times*, a magazine covering issues having to do with marijuana and psychedelic drugs. They wrote this about the Suarez case:

> The Drug Enforcement Administration will confirm [that the arrests were made] but will go no further. This is curious, because it may have been the all-time great sting operation.[9]

The other messages mainstream media began to deliver with shill-like efficiency were the unquestioned bleatings of politicians, bureaucrats, and "experts" going on about how, as a result of the Cocaine Coup, it was more urgent than ever that more money be budgeted and more federal enforcement agencies and military branches be tasked to fight the War on Drugs. President Carter even mandated the CIA to get involved in fighting drugs.

When this last item hit the news, I ran a little test at the embassy in Buenos Aires, just so that I could say I did it. I asked the CIA station chief to lend me a spy camera to cover an undercover operation I had going in Buenos Aires. "I'm back into the Bolivian cartel," I told him. The spook didn't hesitate or blink an eye when he said he didn't have one single camera available. The CIA was simply not going to help me in any way that might, no matter how remotely, jeopardize their "assets" — "assets" they were using to overthrow, control, intimidate, or influence Latin American governments; "assets" who were funding, through drug trafficking, their own and other CIA-inspired paramilitary operations in the region. Cocaine trafficking was a major source of funding for CIA covert operations. Using drug money instead of funds appropriated from Congress allowed the CIA to operate without having to account to the US government for its actions or expenditures. How then, I wondered, could any international DEA agent who took his job and oath seriously be considered anything but a threat to the CIA? In my Secret Country Report for the year, I described this paradoxical situation in as diplomatic terms as I could muster, pointing out that our policymakers, where the War on Drugs was concerned, seemed at odds with each other. As I expected, I received neither answer nor comment.

Then the "news" story hit that pushed me over the edge, the story that would change my life. Larry Rohter and Steven Strasser of *Newsweek* had just authored a feature piece on the Bolivian Cocaine

Coup that was, in my opinion, the hydrogen bomb of drug-war scare stories. Maybe the greatest drug-war monte story of all time. It detailed how drug money had not only funded the Bolivian Cocaine Coup, but was now funding revolutions around the world. How many of these revolutions, I wondered, were backed by CIA and American taxpayer dollars? But then how, I wondered, could the journalists know the truth unless they had a Deep Throat to steer them straight?

I flew into action without thinking. I should have heeded the words of the CIA chief played by Cliff Robertson in *Three Days of the Condor* — a warning that should be issued to all potential real-life government whistle-blowers. Near the end of the movie, after a CIA employee played by Robert Redford has escaped two hours of agency attempts to kill him to prevent him from blowing the whistle on some typically depraved CIA plot, he is about to enter the front door of a major newspaper. There waiting for him is the head of the CIA, played by Cliff Robertson, who smiles shrewdly and utters the last line of the film: "What makes you think they'll print the story?"

Fade to black.

But my mind was full of Woodwards and Bernsteins. I sat down at my desk in the American embassy and wrote the kind of letter that I never imagined myself ever writing. After fully identifying myself, I detailed on three pages typewritten on official US embassy stationary enough evidence of my charges to feed a wolf pack of investigative journalists. I also expressed my willingness to be a quotable source. I addressed it directly to Strasser and Rohter, care of *Newsweek*. I sent it registered mail, return receipt requested. Within a couple of weeks I got the receipt (which I still have) and waited anxiously to hear from them. Two sleepless weeks later, I was still sitting in my embassy office staring at the phone. Three weeks later, it rang.

It was DEA's Internal Security. They were calling to notify me that I was under investigation. I had been falsely accused of everything from black-marketing and having sex with a married female DEA agent during an undercover assignment to "playing loud rock music on my radio and disturbing other embassy personnel." The investigation into these specious charges would wreak havoc with my life for the next four years.[10] My days as the whistle-blowing diplomat were cut short. I would end up a lot luckier than most high-level government whistle-blowers. I would survive. When push came to shove, I was a well-trained undercover operative with the survival skills of a Bronx roach.

DEA HEADQUARTERS

Back in the "Palace of Suits," I decided that to survive the ongoing and ever-expanding onslaught from Internal Security, I would follow the sage advice of a veteran suit: "A bureaucracy has a short memory. Keep your mouth shut and the suits will forget you even exist." And that's exactly what did happen. To survive, I became a drug-war monte player almost immediately.

On my first day back at DEA headquarters in Washington, DC, assigned to the Cocaine Desk, I fielded a phone call from a wire service journalist. The newsie wanted to know what percentage of drugs being smuggled into the United States were intercepted at the borders. During my undercover negotiations with the Bolivian Cartel, the top cocaine producers in the world at the time, I was told that they factored a less than 1 percent loss at the US borders.[11] Before I could answer, one of the other desk officers overheard the conversation and said, "Tell him 10 percent. That's the [official] number." I repeated the number, and 10 percent was the number published in the story.

It was that easy. The same phony percentage was used over the next two decades without a single so-called journalist ever asking the logical follow-up questions: How can you possibly know you are intercepting 10 percent? Who is doing the calculations? It is interesting to note that the magic number has since been drastically increased and that Hollywood is helping out with the shill job.

I noticed what I recognized as a rigged scene in the hit movie *Traffic*. (It's important to note that the movie was shot with the cooperation and collaboration of the drug-war monte suits). The drug czar, played by Michael Douglas, is visiting a US–Mexico border crossing. He asks a real-life Customs officer (drafted for the movie role) what percentage of drugs is intercepted at the border. The answer, blasted in an unnaturally loud voice, is "48 percent."

Ten percent to 48 percent in little more than twenty years, and there are more drugs on the streets than ever before? An Academy Award–winning movie? If this isn't shilling, I don't know what is.

But you've got to remember dealers and shills have no shame at all. And I suppose you could say that neither did I because, for the next five or so years, I played an active and conscious part in drug-war monte.

OPERATION HUN AND
SOUTH FLORIDA TASK FORCE

I spent much of 1983 shuttling between an undercover assignment on "Operation Hun" and a temporary post as a supervisor in Vice President Bush's South Florida Task Force. Ironically, Operation Hun was aimed at bringing down the same Bolivian drug-trafficking government that the CIA had put into power three years earlier. As I detailed in *The Big White Lie,* the operation, which could have truly been one of the most successful in the DEA's history, was still controlled by the CIA and was ultimately destroyed to hide the fact that protected CIA assets were the guys responsible for producing and distributing almost all the world's cocaine at the time. I can only urge everyone with an interest to read the book as if it were one of my prosecution case reports.

When I wasn't working undercover in Hun, I filled two consecutive assignments in Vice President Bush's task force. My first was watch commander, which basically meant that, during my watch, I was to notify Washington of every drug seizure so that press releases and television appearances could be scheduled for Mr. Bush's first-in-history drug czar, Admiral Murphy. My second task force assignment was as supervisor of Miami airport operations. I had about fourteen to sixteen DEA and Customs agents under my command. Our job was mostly to conduct follow-up investigations of customs drug-smuggling arrests at the airport. The trouble with both jobs and the whole South Florida Task Force concept was that it was all an expensive drug-war monte publicity stunt. A massive shill job.

Vice President Bush and his drug czar, through the ever-reliable media, would shill the public into believing that drug seizures in South Florida had doubled. On any Sunday morning, you couldn't avoid seeing Drug Czar Admiral Murphy—the "Little Admiral," as we used to call him—on two, three, and four popular news shows, waving the drug-war victory flags. The media-driven shilling of the public during this period was relentless. Check it out for yourself. It's easy to research on the Internet. There was only one problem with the claims of drug-war victory: they were pure drug-war monte—bogus and easily disprovable.

The same drug seizures that the DEA, Coast Guard, and Customs were normally making in the South Florida area prior to the task force's existence were now being turned over to the task force and trumpeted as victories, when in reality there were no more seizures than before. What was even more fraudulent, if this was possible, was that the seizures were now being double-counted for congressional budget hearings. Customs would seize one thousand pounds of marijuana and turn it over to the task force. Both the task force and Customs would count the seizures on their yearly statistics for Congress. The media points all went to the vice president's task force. The bill, as always, went to the American taxpayer.

Did the media know the truth and hide it?

I personally tipped off at least a dozen journalists who called for information and I know of other agents who did the same. It would not have taken much investigating to verify what we were saying—no more than a couple of phone calls to the agencies involved. Yet, nothing ever surfaced. Shills don't tell marks anything, do they?

AFGHAN AND CONTRA WARS

While a barrage of media headlines continued to shill America into thinking that Vice President Bush's South Florida Task Force was a valiant and effective drug war effort—the sucker card—the real action that was consciously omitted from news coverage was that some of the biggest drug dealers in the world were funneling drugs directly into the brains and veins of America's children with the protection of the CIA and the State Department. Who were these drug dealers? Namely the Nicaraguan Contras and the Mujahedeen rebels in Afghanistan.

For the entire duration of the Contra war, we in the DEA had documented the Contras—those "heroes" as Ollie North called them—putting at least as much cocaine on American streets as the Medellin cartel. We had also documented the Mujahedeen vying for first place as America's source of heroin. Yet, not a single case of any significance was allowed to go forward to prosecution against either entity. The CIA and the State Department effectively blocked all of them.

The media's shilling and misdirection were both relentless and effective. A particularly galling example: one media poll voted Ollie North one of the "ten most admired" people in the nation despite the fact that his efforts to protect major drug dealers and killers like Honduran army general Bueso-Rosa from prosecution had been well documented by Congress. Astoundingly, North, along with a CIA station chief and a US ambassador, had been banned from entering Costa Rica for running drugs through that democratic nation into the United States (among other crimes). Costa Rica's Nobel Prize–winning president, Oscar Arias, had issued the ban, yet the news barely surfaced in the United States. Now compare this to the Monica Lewinsky coverage.[12]

Even drug-dealing Contra supporters in other countries were being protected. In one glaring case, an associate of mine was sent into Honduras to open a DEA office in Tegucigalpa. Within months he had documented as much as fifty tons of cocaine being smuggled into the United States by Honduran military people who were supporting the Contras. This was enough cocaine to fulfill a third of the US demand. What was the DEA response? They closed the office.[13] The tip-offs—both anonymous and straight out—to journalists continued to fly from sources within the DEA and other agencies, yet not one significant truthful story ever surfaced.

BACK IN THE BIG APPLE— THE DRUG WAR MEDIA CAPITAL

In 1984, I received a hardship transfer back to New York. My fifteen-year-old daughter now had a drug problem. By this time my brother David, a heroin addict for nineteen years, had committed suicide in Miami, leaving a note that said, "I can't stand the drugs anymore." I was going to do whatever it took to save my little girl.

In New York City, I was assigned as the supervisor of an active squad that was constantly being called out to stage raids for television news—CBS, ABC, etc.—all the big players. On a slow news day, the SAC (Special Agent in Charge) would get a call: You guys got anything going down we can put on the eleven o'clock news? We could always come up with something. What was good for their ratings was good for our budget.

During those years, if you linked every doper the media shilled as a member of either the Medellin or Cali cartels, hand in hand, the chain would reach the moon. The cartels were so effectively painted as devils that even the normally levelheaded Mayor Ed Koch called for the bombing of Colombia. Ironically, that's exactly what we're doing now.

I played the game, led the bogus raids, and gave the newsies whatever they needed to sell papers or raise ratings. As an insider, I learned the secret of the drug-war generals' control over the media shills.

Drug stories sold newspapers, got media ratings, and made great shows for the big and little screens. To get "access" to a police agency, to get the "inside story" and "credibility," media executives, producers, and editors have to play the game. They can't broadcast or write an unfriendly story and expect an open door the next day. You don't make a tell-all movie and expect to film it with US government cooperation, do you?

The bottom line is money. No one in the mainstream media has taken an oath to protect anything, although they do protect their jobs. That's not a criticism, just a fact. The Fourth Estate might as well be the Fifth, Sixth, or Seventh Estate — it's all bullshit. For the money, mainstream media could (and can) be counted on to shill the drug-war monte game as if their collective bank accounts depended on it. But this is only part of the media economic story. It gets worse — much worse.

There were a few of us who, in sudden fits of madness or naïveté, did risk our lives and careers to blow the whistle. More often than not we'd find ourselves telling some incredulous Columbia School of Journalism–trained newsie that the current "news" release issued by (*fill-in-the-blank*) drug-war monte agency talking about the "new political hope" in Mexico and/or Colombia and/or (*fill-in-the-blank*) who was going to "clean up" government drug corruption, was just a repeat of the same bullshit story that's been printed every couple of months since the beginning of time. And if they didn't believe us, all they had to do was check their own archives.

We'd tell them that our firsthand experience on the front lines had taught us that as long as Americans bought hundreds of billions of dollars in illegal drugs, there could be no new hope, and that to ignore history and to print or broadcast that bullshit was no different than shilling for three-card monte.

The typical newsie response would be a blank stare. Blank because they didn't have the slightest idea what we were talking about, or the curiosity to research it. Blank, because while they've been trained in sound bites, ellipses, and correct language, they haven't the slightest notion of the history or inner workings of drug-war monte. They don't even know that "conspiracy" is the federal law responsible for the majority of humans in cages. Their editors tell them that whatever "credentialed government spokespeople" say (usually some public affairs officer) *is* the story. They are assigned to be reporters, not investigative journalists.

Meanwhile these encounters leave you, the potential whistle-blower, with a sinking feeling in the pit of your stomach that makes you wish you'd kept your damned mouth shut.

But back then, except for those few fleeting moments of sheer madness, I no longer had the slightest desire to play the Robert Redford role in my own movie. I had a daughter on drugs, a mortgage, and a debt-financed life. The only thing between ruination and me was my job. I had learned the *Three Days of the Condor* lesson well: They most definitely would not print the story.

Then, in 1987, I was once again pushed over the edge. But this time, there would be no turning back.

OPERATION TRIFECTA—*DEEP COVER*

By 1987, as the DEA suit (bureaucrat) had predicted, I'd kept my mouth shut and my "sins" had been forgotten. DEA headquarters was now asking me to play a lead role in a deep cover sting operation that would become the *New York Times* best-selling book, *Deep Cover*.[14]

Posing as a Puerto Rican–Sicilian Mafia chief, I and a small cadre of DEA and Customs undercover agents managed to penetrate the top of the drug world in three countries: Bolivia, Panama, and Mexico. The DEA called it "Operation Trifecta." Customs called it "Operation Saber." Our fictitious little "mafia" managed to make a fifteen-ton cocaine purchase and smuggling deal with the Bolivian drug cartel known as *La Corporacion,* the same group that the CIA had helped take over Bolivia, the same group responsible for most of the cocaine base being processed in Colombia to this day.[15]

Hidden video cameras rolled as I negotiated the price and quantity of the drugs with the cartel's top representatives. The deal done, I sent undercover pilots into the jungles of Bolivia to verify that the cocaine was on the ground and ready for delivery. Then I arranged with top Mexican government officials for military protection of the drug shipments as they transited through Mexico into the United States. Among those with whom I negotiated directly were Colonel

Jaime Carranza, grandson of Mexico's former president Venustiano Carranza, and a bodyguard of Mexico's president-elect at the time, Carlos Salinas de Gortari.

To verify that the Mexican government was keeping its part of the deal, "mafia" representatives (undercovers) were dispatched to Mexico to observe military units preparing our landing field. As part of the deal, my first drug payment—five million dollars in cash—would be made to Remberto Rodriguez, chief money launderer for the Bolivian and Colombian cartels. His operation, as the cartel leaders told me, was protected by then-CIA asset Manuel Noriega. I personally went to Rodriguez's headquarters in Panama City where we made arrangements for the five-million-dollar down payment and shook hands on the deal.

During this harrowing assignment, our team gathered hard evidence in the form of secretly recorded video and audiotapes, firsthand observations, and secret government intelligence reports that clearly indicated that military and staff members of Mexico's incoming president, Carlos Salinas de Gortari, were planning to open the Mexican border for smuggling once Gortari took office and the North American Free Trade Agreement (NAFTA) was passed. We had hard evidence, too, that they had already begun to put their plan into action.

We had also stumbled upon evidence indicating that the corrupt Mexican officials we were negotiating with were also directly involved in training CIA-supported Contras. We uncovered uninvestigated personal links between US government officials (including at least one DEA officer) and corrupt Mexican government officials, some of whom may have been involved in the torture/murder of DEA agent Enrique "Kiki" Camarena and/or its cover-up.

And we had proof that the US paramilitary operation in the Andean Region (then Operation Snowcap, now Plan Colombia and/or the Andean Initiative) was a premeditated fraud on the American people, never intended to have any effect on the supply of drugs from its inception.

As I detailed in *Deep Cover,* once top officials in our government became aware of what we had uncovered, the CIA became involved.[16] We had gone too far and had to be stopped. The top drug dealers, the Panama-based money-laundering operation, and the high-ranking corrupt Mexican government officials that we had snared were effectively protected from prosecution. Operations Trifecta and Saber were destroyed.

Once again, I can only urge the reader of this chapter to read the book and judge it for its factual value, keeping in mind that the information in it was never intended to be a book.

In *Deep Cover*, I detail how all the revelations listed above were first presented to DEA's Internal Affairs in one lengthy memorandum that I entitled "The Memo Bomb." I was hoping—naïvely—that it would end up in the hands of someone in the government with a conscience, some bureaucrat or politician who took his/her oath to defend the Constitution seriously. When I learned that it was going to be covered up, I didn't even consider going to the media. I began writing *Deep Cover*, which was published three months after I retired.

The book made the *New York Times* best-seller list despite being virtually ignored by mainstream media and Congress. What little media coverage it did receive portrayed me as a disgruntled whistle-blower. Why? Because that is what "credentialed government spokespeople" said I was.

DEA and Justice Department officials refused to comment on any of the specifics. Not one single mainstream media journalist undertook to do what my publisher's (Delacorte Press) attorneys had done: conduct a libel reading, or a detailed examination of how I had documented my facts. I was a man whose words in courts across the land were credible enough to convict and sentence thousands to tens of thousands of years in prisons. My book screamed in a loud, clear voice that the drug war was a premeditated fraud, yet no one in the media was interested in investigating the story.

In 1991, Bill Moyers's "Project Censored" called *Deep Cover* one of America's ten most censored stories. Mr. Moyers commented to me while we were taping for a show that he'd heard that *Deep Cover* was the best-read and least-talked-about book between the Washington, DC, beltways. I had already heard the same thing from my own sources inside the DEA and other agencies.

I pointed out to Mr. Moyers that what I found both frightening and depressing about the whole affair was that, despite the fact that a team of US undercover agents had uncovered hard evidence of massive Mexican government drug corruption and involvement in the torture/murder of a DEA agent, our Congress had granted them "cooperating nation" status in the drug war, meaning that they would be rewarded with American taxpayer dollars for their betrayal. I also told Moyers that I was deeply disturbed that despite the book's well-documented revelations showing that Operation Snowcap was a premeditated fraud, Congress was expanding the militarized South American drug war without even making a single inquiry.

All Mr. Moyers could do was shake his head the way a streetwise cop does when he watches the suckers line up to play three-card monte.

Could this have happened if the mainstream media had pursued the facts and leads revealed in *Deep Cover* with the aggressive persistence shown during the Watergate and Monica Lewinsky affairs? I think not. Instead, they averted their collective gazes and have continued the barrage of fill-in-the-blanks, drug-war monte stories. And the suckers continue to watch the show and continue to pay.

MORE THAN TEN YEARS OF JOURNALISM

After retiring and publishing *Deep Cover,* I wrote *Fight Back, How to Take Back Your Neighborhood, Schools and Families from the DRUG DEALERS,*[17] followed by *The Big White Lie* (cowritten with Laura Kavanau-Levine). Whatever I thought I knew about drug-war monte and how to fight it was now in book form, but I still had a lot to learn, only now from the opposite angle.

Beginning with my retirement from the DEA on January 1, 1990, up to this moment, I have been active as a freelance print journalist, media consultant, and on-air drug and crime expert, as well as an expert witness on all matters related to drug trafficking and the use of deadly force for federal and state court cases. Since 1997, I have been the host of *The Expert Witness Radio Show,* which airs on WBAI, 99.5 FM in New York City and around the world via the Internet. The show features interviews with frontline participants in major drug-war monte events and other crime and espionage stories that mainstream media have either misrepresented or consciously ignored.

The screaming need for the show is best illustrated by a program I hosted entitled "100 Years Experience."[18] It was a roundtable discussion with Ralph McGeehee (25 years with CIA), Dennis Dayle (27 years with DEA), Wesley Swearingen (25 years with FBI), and me (25 years with DEA, Customs, Internal Revenue Service Intelligence, and Bureau of Alcohol, Tobacco, and Firearms). All of us had taken part in some of the highest profile events in law enforcement, military, and espionage history. All of us easily agreed that not one of these events

—from the Vietnam War and COINTELPRO (the FBI Counter Intelligence Programs of the 1960s) to the entire War on Drugs—had been reported honestly by mainstream media.

Dennis Dayle, a principal subject in James Mills's best-selling book, *Underground Empire*, stated that the CIA had interfered with and/or destroyed every major international drug-dealing investigation he had ever conducted. You remember seeing that anywhere in the news?

Now, as a journalist, I want to give you details on some of the most important events that I experienced firsthand and the media shilling that went on as they unfolded.

DRUG WAR INVASION OF PANAMA[19]

As I've already said, it was as early as 1971, when I was serving in the US Customs Hard Narcotics Smuggling Unit, that I became personally aware that both US Customs and the Bureau of Narcotics and Dangerous Drugs knew very well that Manuel Noriega was heavily involved in drug trafficking to the United States, and that the CIA—the gang that can't spy straight—was protecting him from prosecution. This wacky little drug dealer, like countless other criminals doing damage to America, was on the CIA payroll. He'd even had lunch with George Bush. The protection had been going on for so long and was so well known that no one in the CIA had bothered to tell DEA agent Danny Moritz and federal prosecutor Richard Gregorie that the dude was off limits.

So the same CIA that didn't know that the Berlin Wall was coming down until the bricks were hitting them on the head, didn't learn that their two-decade, drug-dealing asset Manny "Pineapple Face" Noriega was being indicted until it was too late. Now there was a problem, a problem that only media shills could handle.[20]

On the evening of December 20, 1989, I watched with a mixture of horror and wonder as Noriega's fortress of a home was blown to smithereens along with Chorillo, Panama City's entire inner-city area. It was the opening shot of America's first full-scale, drug-war invasion. Hundreds, perhaps thousands (depending on whom you believe), of Panamanians died. Women, children, and tiny babies were burned, shot, and mutilated by our finest and most advanced weaponry. It was a great opportunity to try out our Stealth bombers and fighter planes. I could not help but be reminded of the Nazi bombing of Guernica, Spain.

I guess the stuff really works.

Twenty-six American soldiers died, many of them shot by friendly fire. All this awesome firepower and death to arrest a man whose drug dealing the CIA had been protecting for almost two decades. How, I wondered, were the drug war generals and the CIA going to hide the truth behind this grotesque atrocity?

Media shills to the rescue. Within months, the media coverage had omitted and obliterated and/or minimized Manuel Noriega's true history and reputation with the CIA and DEA, and had turned the event into a major drug-war "victory." So effective was the media shilling that instead of being indicted as a coconspirator, George Bush enjoyed a massive surge in his popularity ratings. Lee Atwater, the chairman of the Republican Party, called the monstrous atrocity a "political jackpot."

The damage this did to those in law enforcement with a conscience was incalculable. Whatever faith we ever had in media fulfilling its alleged Fourth Estate role was gone.

The "political jackpot" comment was the final straw for me. I had just retired and felt (again, albeit foolishly) relatively safe from retribution, so I began firing off a barrage of articles to every media outlet I could think of. It was a futile attempt from the beginning and I knew it, but I had to try and keep trying. It was only through alternative media and the then-nascent Internet that the truth surfaced, but who paid any attention to that? And as long as alternative media had no affect on the polls, it would have no affect on American politicians.

I was and still am close to many men and women who have spent their lives in law enforcement. All of them, when sitting in comfortable little living rooms after having a couple of drinks, will lower their voices and admit that if any cop had done what those involved with the Noriega cover-up and the subsequent phony invasion had done, they'd have been buried under a federal jail. They'll say the words that no shill journalist would ever print: that anyone who was responsible for that invasion ought to be tried as a war criminal. It was the realization that our silence was the ugliest part of history repeating itself that kept me at my computer trying to out the true Noriega story. But the wall of media shills was impenetrable.

It was after crack addicts killed my son, New York City police sergeant Keith Richard Levine on December 28, 1991, that the *New York Times* published one of my Noriega pieces.[21] I was never sure whether it was my son's very public murder that changed their attitude or the upcoming Clinton-Bush election, but I was grateful, even hopeful.

The Bush-Noriega article — an op ed piece — was a tiny drop in a media tidal wave going the other way, but it made an important point. There was some hope in media. It was not monolithic. While it was, by and large, controlled by easily frightened and manipulated people of little courage, there were editors, producers, and journalists out there who were still willing to risk taking a moral stand against the criminal and/or criminally inept exercise of power.

I was also learning another hard lesson: To force real congressional action against corruption and/or criminal ineptitude at the highest levels of government, one article or one television special is far from enough to combat the ocean of media shills. What's needed is a Watergate/Lewinsky-like wave of investigative journalism. A sprinkling won't work. A sprinkling will only be used to shill us into thinking we really have a free, aggressive media.

RISE IN POLICE DRUG WAR VIOLENCE AFTER PANAMA

It was after the mass murder of women and children in Panama that, as a journalist, I began to notice a distinct increase in the militarization of the drug war in the United States. I noticed a very clear acceptance by our elected "protectors" and the public of an increase in the use of deadly force in the drug war that continues to escalate to this day and affects all aspects of police-community relations.

This could never have happened without mainstream media, television, and Hollywood shilling with bullshit-based, drug-war monte movies like *Clear and Present Danger*, television drug-war specials and programs like *Cops*, and the incessant flow of fill-in-the-blanks drug stories with headlines like "New Threat in Drug Supply Discovered in *(fill in nation of your choice)*"; "New Link in Opium Trail Discovered in *(fill in location of your choice)*"; "The Hunt for *(fill in name)*, New Leader of the *(fill in name)* Cartel"; "Government Sources Alarmed by Increase in Flow of *(fill in drug of choice)*"; "Government Sources Allege Drug Corruption in *(fill in location where the CIA wants to initiate some dan-*

gerous, foolish, and very expensive action)"; and "Startling Rise in Drug Use Predicted by *(fill in name of agency that wants a budget increase)*."[22]

AS AN EXPERT WITNESS

Since my retirement, I've worked as an expert witness for attorneys defending people from the excesses of a drug-war monte game gone wild. I've been directly involved in a continuous flow of atrocities perpetrated on innocent citizens that, thanks to the reliable practice of censorship via omission by mainstream media shills, never get mainstream media exposure.

From my point of view, the use of the word "atrocities" is no hyperbole. As a frontline participant, I've watched the drug war evolve from where, in 1973, DEA agents who raided a premises in Collinsville, Indiana, in honest error were prosecuted for that error in federal court, to where the killing of innocent Americans in their own homes is now not only condoned under the drug-war banner, but actively covered up by drug war generals with the acquiescence of media shills.

Here's an example. Donald Carlson, a Fortune 500 executive in San Diego who couldn't distinguish cocaine from garden mulch, was gunned down in his own home in 1992 by a federal-state, multiagency Drug Enforcement Task Force SWAT team that had conducted a military-style invasion using machine guns and grenades. They were acting on allegations made by a criminal informant who claimed that Mr. Carlson was concealing in his house five thousand pounds of cocaine and four Colombian hit men who had sworn never to be taken alive.

The very gringo Mr. Carlson, despite the drug agents' best efforts to stop his clock, miraculously survived three gunshot wounds. He decided to sue the government. His attorneys hired me to examine the government's reports related to the investigation and to provide an expert opinion—a job I had been trained to do as a DEA inspector of operations. After reviewing more than five thousand pages of government reports, transcripts of interviews, and statements, I came to the conclusion that the government agents had based their probable cause for the search warrant on the uncorroborated words of a street-level criminal informant whom the telephone company did not trust enough to furnish with a telephone. I concluded, citing specific examples from the government's own reports and statements, that the agents and prosecutors were not only criminally negligent, but that they had knowingly violated all of Mr. Carlson's constitutional rights against unlawful search of his home. Then they'd compounded this crime by perjuring themselves in an effort to cover up their misdeeds. My recommendation was, as it would have been had I been doing the job for the Justice Department, that the evidence be put before a federal grand jury with an eye toward a federal indictment of the agents and prosecutors.

Instead of giving US citizens, in the form of a grand jury, the opportunity to review what had actually happened and to make their own decision as to whether the agents and prosecutors deserved to be prosecuted themselves, the United States Attorney, Alan Bersin (a Clinton appointee), called a press conference for the drug war shills.[23] He proclaimed that "the system did fail" but that the agents and prosecutors "had done their job." This proclamation was the "news" that was broadcast as far and wide as mainstream media could reach.

System did fail? What the hell does that mean? Only drug war shills would accept a statement like this at face value, not real journalists.

The bottom line of the whole adventure came soon after I turned in my report. The government settled for $2.7 million in damages to Mr. Carlson, and all government reports were classified.

Classified? How in the hell can these agencies get away with classifying events leading up to the shooting of an American citizen in his own home? I kept waiting for some Woodward or Bernstein to ask the question. It never happened. The media shills did their customary penguin walk, one following the other off the end of a rock, their gazes rigidly pointed away from the truth.

Once again I tried to tell the story through any mainstream media outlet that would listen. The TV newsmagazine program *60 Minutes*, which in my opinion is one of the few remaining hopes in mainstream media, was the only entity interested. The Carlson debacle was run as part of a special called "Informants" during the summer of 1993. Unfortunately, the cover-up was omitted.

Here again, I relearned the lesson that, as much of a media powerhouse as *60 Minutes* is, a single story does not a change in government policy make. As devastating as the "Informant" piece should have been to drug-war monte, it was only another drop against the mighty torrent of mainstream media shilling.

The big question that the Fourth Estate should have been asking was: If our drug warriors and prosecutors could get away with acting so criminally in the case of a Fortune 500 executive, what can the average citizen expect?

Ezekiel Hernandez is the answer. In 1997, the eighteen-year-old high school graduate was gunned down by a marine sniper on "antidrug" patrol while herding his family's goats in his own backyard. The young man probably never knew what hit him since the shot was fired from a distance of more than 250 yards. I couldn't help wondering if they were trying out a new weapon. No one in young Hernandez's McAllen, Texas, community was aware that those odd-moving bushes out on the range nearby were marine snipers in camouflage outfits assigned to patrol the Texas-Mexico border—in direct violation of the Posse Comitatus Act, which prohibits the direct participation of the military in civilian law enforcement.

As a radio journalist who also happens to be a court-qualified expert in the use of deadly force, I began my own investigation of the case, which, in my opinion, was at best a clear-cut case of negligent homicide and/or manslaughter. At worst, it was an execution.

While mainstream media shilled the death of young Ezekiel as an unfortunate but justifiable error, I tried to get a government spokesman to come on my show and explain the government's position on the young man's murder. No one was willing. I watched the media—television, newspapers, and magazines—closely. No government spokesman would field questions on the matter. Only self-serving, vague, and misleading statements were released. Why should the drug war generals explain the murder of an American citizen that occurred during an alleged antidrug action, as long as mainstream media willingly shilled for them?

In this case, like the Carlson case, no government official admitted any wrongdoing. The settlement with the Hernandez family was $1.7 million —significantly less than the very white and still living Mr. Carlson's $2.7 million—but then again, why should that fact interest a shill?[24]

DRUG-WAR MONTE BILLIONS PAID DIRECTLY TO THE SHILLS

A new level of the drug-war monte con game began when President Clinton and Republican House Majority Leader Newt Gingrich raised each other's hands in victory to announce a new billion-dollar, "Say-No-To-Drugs" style ad campaign. The money would be paid directly into the coffers of every Hollywood and mainstream media entity on Wall Street's big board for ads, shows, and articles exhorting Americans to "Just say no." The first $60 million would go to Disney Studios. All the full-page "antidrug" ads you see in the *New York Times* (for instance) are paid for from this taxpayer-funded pot.

I received a tip from an inside person in the upper ranks of government who finds me cheaper than a psychiatrist to talk to and a lot more reliable than anyone in mainstream media. "Fraud," this person said, referring to the legitimacy of the "Say No to Drugs" campaign. "Go get 'em, Mike."[25] So I flew into expert witness investigative action. I mean, get real! Do you think some mainstream media journalist is going to investigate the source of his/her company's millions? Particularly at a time when advertising income is on the decline?

My investigation, buttressed by research that I had done for my book *Fight Back*, revealed that neither the Partnership for a Drug Free America, nor anyone else for that matter, had done any research into the effectiveness of this kind of advertising. In fact, according to psychological studies conducted by neuro-linguistic experts, a growing body of evidence indicated that the ads weren't just ineffective; they actually increased drug use. The creators of the "Just say no" ads used the same slick, highly suggestive Madison Avenue advertising methods normally used to produce powerful ads that sell products. The antidrug ads had an unanticipated effect on teenagers, their target audience. Steven Donziger, policy director for the Partnership for Responsible Drug Information, said that the ads unintentionally encouraged experimentation: "Research shows that the target audience are in a period in their lives where they're open to experimentation and rebellious behavior," he said, adding, "The ads do not speak honestly to adolescents. Many have already experimented. They know when they see ads that demonize the use of illicit drugs . . . that they're not being honest." (*NewsBriefs*, July/August 1998, a publication of the National Drug Strategy Network from 1989 to 2000.)

A lone article in *Brand Week* (April 27, 1998), the highly respected Madison Avenue trade magazine, pointed out that the full amount of taxpayer dollars that the Partnership for a Drug Free America was about to give away was $2 billion, making them the biggest advertisers on Madison Avenue. It called the giveaway "very suspect." My own DEA source pointed out that the $2 billion would have been enough to buy up every coca leaf produced in South America that year. It could have replaced all law enforcement and military operations in effectiveness.

If you put three-card monte dealers and shills in the can for ripping off hundreds of dollars from innocent suckers, what do you think these guys deserve?

CIA DRUG SMUGGLING— THE VENEZUELAN NATIONAL GUARD CASE

What would be the appropriate action of a truly independent mainstream media if, say, the Central Intelligence Agency was caught redhanded actually smuggling as much cocaine into the US as the Medellin cartel, in direct violation of federal law and with no political excuse?

Well, precisely that did happen. Sometime in 1990, US Customs intercepted a ton of cocaine being smuggled through Miami International Airport. A Customs and DEA investigation quickly revealed that the smugglers were the Venezuelan National Guard headed by General Guillen, a CIA "asset" who claimed that he had been operating under CIA orders and protection. The CIA soon admitted, albeit very reluctantly, that this was true. Once again, as in the Noriega case, it seemed that the gang that can't spy straight had failed to notify the DEA and Customs of what they were up to. That would turn out *not* to be the case.

If the CIA is good at anything, it is the complete control of American media. So secure are they in their ability to manipulate media that they even brag about it in their own in-house memos.[26] CIA shills by far outnumber and outclass the drug-war monte variety, but in this case both con games—CIA-monte and drug-war monte—were at grave risk. The CIA Public Information Office, referred to by CIA insiders as "The Mighty Wurlitzer," flew into action. Result: The story appeared nowhere in the media for the next three years.

Example: the *New York Times* actually had the story almost immediately in 1990 and did not print it until 1993. It finally became news that "was fit to print" when the *Times* learned that *60 Minutes* also had the story and was actually going to run it.[27] The *Times* ran the story on Saturday, one day before the *60 Minutes* piece aired. There were, however, serious differences between the *Times* report and the claims aired by *60 Minutes*.

The *Times* piece said:

> No criminal charges have been brought in the matter, which the officials said *appeared to have been a serious accident rather than an intentional conspiracy* [emphasis mine]. But officials say the cocaine wound up being sold on the streets in the United States.

The highlight of the *60 Minutes* piece is when the administrator of the Drug Enforcement Administration, Federal Judge Robert Bonner, tells Mike Wallace, "There is no other way to put it, Mike, [what the CIA did] is *drug smuggling. It's illegal* [emphasis mine]."

Judge Bonner further revealed that his assertion came as a result of a secret joint investigation conducted by the DEA and CIA's internal affairs divisions. As if that weren't enough, Annabelle Grimm, the DEA's agent and country attaché in Venezuela when the incident occurred, was interviewed on camera. She, too, said that the CIA had simply smuggled drugs in violation of lots of US laws.

You don't have to be a police detective to note that there are serious differences in the two reports, or to suspect media shilling in the first degree. The expert witness once again flew into action. I did what I thought a real journalist should do: investigate the story.

Accompanied by my life partner, wife, and cowriter, Laura Kavanau, I flew out to the coast to meet with Grimm, an ex-colleague whose work and forthrightness I had always admired. After speaking with Annabelle, we talked to another DEA officer who was directly involved in the incident.

The sum total of my investigation was that the CIA had not only been smuggling a lot more cocaine — around twenty-seven tons — than the one ton they were caught with, but that the DEA had warned them not to do it, telling them that they were proposing an "intelligence gathering operation" that was not just a wacky idea, but a felony violation of US law punishable by up to life in prison.

The identities of at least two of the CIA personnel who had chosen to ignore the DEA's warning and had gone ahead with the massive smuggling operation had been turned over to the DEA for indictment. But instead of focusing on these criminals, the investigation turned on Annabelle Grimm and others.

As I investigated the incident, I noticed that James Woolsey, the head of the CIA at the time, was appearing on every mainstream media television and radio "news" show that would have him (including National Public Radio), to broadcast the claim that no criminal act had taken place and that the event had all been a "snafu . . . a joint investigation between CIA and DEA that had gone awry."

Woolsey's statement directly contradicted that of Federal Judge Bonner. The overwhelming evidence, my DEA sources assured me, showed that Woolsey, an attorney, was lying and that mainstream media was shilling for him. Any real journalist could have done what I was doing, but none—other than *60 Minutes*—dared. Was there ever a news story more important than one that should have read something like "CIA Betrays Nation—Caught Red-Handed Smuggling More Drugs on U.S. Streets Than the Medellin Cartel," or "Drug War a Trillion $ Fraud?"

The facts behind the case seem to be proof positive that the whole War on Drugs has been the longest-running, deadliest con game in the history of American misgovernment. In the Venezuelan National Guard case, there were top-level, credentialed government spokespeople ready to speak openly, ready to tell a devastating truth about the worst kind of treason possible being committed by the CIA against its own people. Yet no mainstream media entity, other than *60 Minutes*, deemed this news fit to pursue with the same in-depth zeal devoted to investigating the shape of President Clinton's penis.

Censorship by omission? Drug-war monte shilling? I would say so.

Unfortunately for America, my *Expert Witness Show* was among the very few places that this important truth could be heard. I should mention that when I called the Miami US Attorney's office in charge of prosecuting General Guillen and others, I was told that "national security" interests prevented them from providing me with a case status, or any statement whatsoever for that matter.[28]

A fitting postscript for this event: I was recently made aware that John Clements, the twenty-year-old addict "gofer" featured in the Bangkok heroin investigation referred to at the beginning of this chapter, was released from federal prison after serving thirty years. Young Mr. Clements was convicted of "conspiracy" to traffic in heroin for driving a drug dealer to one single meeting to pick up drugs. Of course, the rest of the story is that the media, while ignoring the massive flow of heroin coming into the United States at the hands of CIA assets, had shilled the case to the point where there was no way the kid was going to get anything but the max. Unfortunately I was as guilty as they were.

I can only hope this helps make up for it.

BLACK TUESDAY: THE SHILLING CONTINUES

If what I wrote before has made you see that mainstream media has spent the last three decades shilling the American taxpayer into believing in the efficacy of the War on Drugs when this so-called war is every bit as fraudulent as a game of three-card monte, then here's what you should be asking yourself about what happened on September 11: Did mainstream media also shill for an inept and bumbling FBI and CIA in a campaign to convince Americans that our homeland defense was in the most capable hands possible when, in fact, the Boy Scouts of America might have done a better job? And, did this shilling play a role in making us vulnerable to the events of Black Tuesday?

Hard to believe, right? Well, the fact is — and you can read it for yourself in federal court records — that seven months *before* the first attempt to blow up the World Trade Center in 1993, the FBI had a paid informant named Emad Salem who had infiltrated the bombers and had told the FBI of their plans to blow up the Twin Towers. Without notifying the NYPD or anyone else, an FBI supervisor "fired" Salem, who was making $500 a week for his work. After the bomb went off, the FBI hired Salem back and paid him $1.5 million to help them track down the bombers.

But that's not all the FBI missed. When they finally did catch the actual bomber, Ramzi Yousef (a man trained with CIA funds during the Russia-Afghanistan war), the FBI found information on his personal computer about plans to use hijacked American jetliners as fuel-laden missiles. The FBI ignored this information too.

If at this point you are scratching your head and asking yourself why you haven't heard this story, you can thank mainstream media "coverage" which, for the most part, gave the FBI credit for solving the World Trade Center bombing case. The mainstream media then went on to credit the FBI with solving the Unabomber case when in fact the madman was caught when his own brother turned him in.

Had the media done a professional job of investigating and

192 INTO THE BUZZSAW

reporting the CIA and FBI's amateurish failures, perhaps our elected protectors would have been moved to begin working feverishly on revamping a human intelligence system that appears to be competing with the Three Stooges for our enemies' respect.

Many of the anecdotes and incidents that I've written about in this chapter were taken from events detailed in my nonfiction best-seller, *Deep Cover*, which is subtitled, *The Inside Story of How . . . Infighting, Incompetence, and Subterfuge Lost Us the Biggest Battle of the Drug War*. If you go back to the beginning of this chapter and substitute "World Trade Center" for "Drug War," perhaps you'll come to realize how very dangerous a shill game is being run on us right now.

NOTES

1. Donald Goddard, *Undercover: The Secret Lives of a Federal Agent* (New York: Random House/Times Books, 1988).

2. The *Expert Witness* radio show. WBAI (New York City), KPFK (Los Angeles).

3. *U.S.* v. *Herman Jackson et al.*

4. See Michael Levine, *Deep Cover: The Inside Story of How DEA Infighting, Incompetence, and Subterfuge Lost Us the Biggest Battle of the Drug War* (New York: Delacorte, 1990).

5. Michael Levine, "The Drug War—Fight It at Home," *New York Times*, 16 February 1993, Op-Ed page.

6. A typical example, "Mexico's New Anti-drug Team Wins the Trust of U.S. Officials," was taken from the *New York Times* headlines, July 18, 2001.

7. Testimony of Felix Milian-Rodruiguez, convicted Medellin cartel money launderer, in Executive Session before Kerry committee, June 1986.

8. Michael Levine and Laura Kavanau, *The Big White Lie: The CIA and the Cocaine/Crack Epidemic* (New York: Thunder's Mouth Press, 1993); Levine, *Deep Cover*.

9. Editorial staff, "Cocaine Colonialism: How the Fascists Took Over Bolivia," *High Times* (August 1981).

10. Levine and Kavanau, *The Big White Lie*.

11. Felix Milian-Rodruiguez testimony.

12. Michael Levine, "I Volunteer to Kidnap Ollie North," *Journal of Law & Social Justice* 20 (1993): 1–12.

13. Jonathan Marshall and Peter Dale-Scott, *Cocaine Politics: Drugs, Armies, and the CIA in Central America* (Berkeley: University of California Press, 1991).

14. Levine, *Deep Cover*.

15. Felix Milian-Rodruiguez testimony; Levine and Kavanau, *The Big White Lie*; Levine, *Deep Cover*.

16. Videotapes of our undercover meetings were dispatched directly to the office of then–attorney general Edwin Meese.

17. Michael Levine, *Fight Back: How to Take Back Your Neighborhoods, Schools, and Families from the Drug Dealers* (New York: Dell, 1991).

18. "100 Years Experience," *Expert Witness* radio show, September 17, 1997.

19. *Expert Witness Radio Show*, interview with author David Harris, *Shoot the Moon*, and DEA supervising officer, Ken Kennedy, a participant in the arrest and prosecution of Manual Noriega, May 21, 2001.

20. Ibid.

21. Levine, "The Drug War—Fight It at Home."

22. *Expert Witness* radio show interviews with frontline participants under "Drug War Media Mess."

23. The press conference was held in San Diego, California, in early March 1994, per the Associated Press story, "Feds to Pay for Shooting Man," dated March 3, 1994.

24. "Ezekiel Hernandez Show," broadcast August 1997 on the *Expert Witness* radio show.

25. Articles and audiotapes of shows on the subject of the $2 billion media rip-off may be found on http://www.expertwitnessradio.com.

26. See interviews with Ralph McGeehee, twenty-five-year CIA veteran, on the *Expert Witness* radio show.

27. Tim Weiner, "Venezuelan Anti-drug Unit Sent Ton of Cocaine To US in 1990," *New York Times*, November 20, 1993.

28. The *Expert Witness* radio show, WBAI, New York City and KPFK, Los Angeles, available on audio at http://www.expertwitnessradio.com.

CHAPTER 9

THE SILENCE OF THE LAMBS

AN AMERICAN IN JOURNALISTIC EXILE

M. Richter

GREG PALAST

Greg Palast is the author of the New York Times *best-seller* The Best Democracy Money Can Buy, *an investigative account of fraud and corruption in the highest seats of power. The book is published internationally and has been translated into more than half a dozen languages. Palast's writings have appeared in the* Washington Post, Harper's, *and the* Nation, *as well as in the* Guardian *and* Observer *newspapers of London. He also regularly contributes investigative reports to the BBC's* Newsnight *program. He has won a number of awards, including the ACLU's Freedom of Expression Award for his work in Democracy and Regulation, a National Magazine Award for his writings in* Harper's *magazine, and Salon.com's 2001 "Politics Story of the Year" award, and has been appointed a Trinity College Philosophical Patron. Previous appointees include Oscar Wilde and Jonathan Swift. Palast has spoken and been interviewed widely, including appearing as a guest on* Politically Incorrect *and* C-SPAN's Washington Journal.

Here's how your president was elected:

In the months leading up to the November balloting, Florida governor Jeb Bush and his secretary of state, Katherine Harris, ordered local elections supervisors to purge fifty-eight thousand voters from registries on grounds they were felons not entitled to vote in Florida. As it turns out, only a handful of these voters were felons. The voters on this scrub list were, notably, African American (about 54 percent), and most of the others wrongly barred from voting were white and Hispanic Democrats.

Three weeks after the election, this extraordinary news ran, as it should, on page one of the country's leading paper. Unfortunately, it was in the wrong country: Britain. In the United States, it ran on page zero. The story was not covered on the news pages. It was given big network television coverage. But again, it was on the wrong continent —on BBC television, London.

Was this some off-the-wall story that the Brits misreported? A lawyer for the US Civil Rights Commission called it the first hard evidence of a systematic attempt to disenfranchise black voters; and the commission held dramatic hearings on the evidence.

So why was this story investigated, reported, and broadcast in *Europe*?

I'd like to know the answer. That way I could understand why a southern California hodaddy with a wife and kiddies has to commute to London to tell this and other stories about my country.

The question, *why from Europe?* is best phrased as, How did a hundred thousand American journalists sent to cover the election *fail* to get the vote theft story and print it (and preferably *before* the election)?

Think about all the tales of investigative reporting in this book. They share three things: They are risky, they upset the wisdom of the established order, and they are *very expensive* to produce. Do profit-conscious enterprises, whether media companies or widget firms, *seek* extra costs, extra risk, and the opportunity to be attacked? Not in any business text I've ever read.

But if profit lust is the ultimate problem blocking significant investigative reportage, the more immediate cause of comatose coverage of the election and other issues is what is laughably called America's journalistic culture. If the Rupert Murdochs of the globe are shepherds of the new world order, they owe their success to breeding a flock of docile sheep; snoozy editors and reporters who are content to munch on, digest, and then reprint a diet of press releases and canned stories provided by officials and corporate public relations operations.

Take this story of the list of Florida's faux felons that cost Al Gore the election. Shortly after the British story hit the World Wide Web, I was contacted by a CBS TV network news producer ready to run their own version of the story. The CBS hotshot was happy to pump me for information: names, phone numbers, all the items one needs for a quickie TV story.

I also freely offered up to CBS this information. My first story was about voters falsely accused of felonies; my new story was about those who did in fact serve time, but nevertheless had the right to vote. The office of the governor of Florida, Jeb Bush, brother of the Republican presidential candidate, had illegally ordered the removal of the names of felons from voter rolls — *real felons* — but with the right to vote under Florida law. As a result, *fifty thousand* of these legal voters, almost all Democrats, could not vote.

One problem: I had not quite completed my own investigation on this matter. Therefore CBS *would have to do some actual work*, reviewing documents and law, obtaining statements. The next day I received a call from the producer who said, I'm sorry, but your story didn't hold up. Well, how did the multibillion-dollar CBS network determine this? Why, we called Jeb Bush's office. Oh. And that was it.

I wasn't surprised by this type of investigation. It is, in fact, standard operating procedure for the little lambs of American journalism. One good, slick explanation from a politician or corporate chieftain and it's *case closed*, investigation over. The story ran anyway — on BBC-TV.

Let's understand the pressures on the CBS producer that led her to kill the story on the basis of a denial by the target of the allegations. (Though let's not confuse understanding with forgiveness.) First, the story is difficult to tell in the usual ninety seconds allotted for national reports. The BBC gave me a fourteen-minute slot to explain it.

Second, the story required massive and quick review of documents, hundreds of phone calls and interviews, hardly a winner in the slam-bam-thank-you-ma'am American school of journalism. The BBC gave me *six weeks* to develop the story.

Third, the revelations in the story required a reporter to stand up and say that the big-name politicians, their lawyers, and their PR people were *freaking liars*. It would be much easier, and a heck of a lot cheaper, to wait for the US Civil Rights Commission to do the work, then cover the commission's canned report and press conference. Wait! You've watched *Murphy Brown*, so you think reporters hanker every day to uncover the big scandal. Bull. Remember, *All the President's Men* was so unusual they had to make a movie out of it.

Fourth, investigative reports require taking a chance. Fraudsters and vote-riggers don't reveal all their evidence. And they lie. Make the allegation and you are open to attack or unknown information that may prove you wrong. No one ever lost his job writing canned statements from a press conference.

Meanwhile, back in sunny England . . .

My paper received about two thousand bless-you-Britain-for-telling-us-the-truth-about-our-election letters from United States. Net-heads who were circulating the samizdat presidential elections coverage. I also received a few like this:

> *You pansey [sic] brits seem to think that the average American is as under-educated and stupid as the average British subject. Well comrad [sic], I'm here to tell you . . .*

which ended with some physically unfeasible suggestions of what to do with the Queen.

My editor noticed only one — a letter demanding retraction of my first article on Katherine Harris's phony voter purge — *or else*. It was from Carter-Ruck, a law firm with the reputation as the piranhas of the libel bar in England. They had cornered the market in representing foreign millionaires unhappy about their press. They did not represent the Bush family, but a company that had once employed George H. W. Bush (Bush resigned from this in 1999), a Canadian gold-mining company originally funded by arms dealer Adnan Khashoggi.

You didn't know that Poppy Bush went to work for a Canadian mining company after he left the White House? Of course not — the firm has sued, or threatens to sue, any paper or person who reports on them in ways they find less than flattering.

My reports on the Florida ballot shenanigans first began as a sidebar to this story about the cash flowing into Bush family bank accounts and campaign war chests from firms for which the elder Bush performed favors after leaving the White House.

Who were these Canadian guys who could hire our former president and his Rolodex? If American papers weren't curious, Britons found this stuff fascinating. This Canadian company, Barrick Gold, had purchased a mine, with Bush's apparent help, in Tanzania. I had received information from Africa that in 1996 the previous owner of the mine had allegedly buried alive fifty-some jewelry miners who had refused to leave the property. Sickening stuff, these allegations were also mentioned in a report by Amnesty International, which I cited. I also cited Barrick's denial. Barrick had bought the mine in 1999.

Barrick Gold and its demi-billionaire chairman demanded that my paper retract the *allegations* of killings. They demanded that we print that the *Guardian* newspapers were happy to confirm that no one died at that mine. A Canadian newspaper that had picked up my story already had grabbed their ankles and run that incredible retraction.

In England, there is no defense of repetition. That is, I can't say I accurately reported on the Amnesty allegations; I have to prove that miners were actually buried alive in Tanzania. We called Amnesty, which courageously refused to help, announced it would be silent on advice of lawyers, and allowed the company to state that Amnesty had cleared the company.

I was ready to go along with some kind of apology and retraction, only because I was living on Red Bull, potassium powder, and no sleep, trying to get out the elections story, and I sure as hell didn't need another distraction.

But I had a problem. Our paper encouraged a human rights attorney to go to the Tanzanian mine. He came back with witness statements, *photographs* of a dead exhumed body, and *videotapes* showing bodies being exhumed from the mine pits. His name is Tundu Lissu—and when the company found out about his investigation, they threatened him with a lawsuit as well.

That's when I lost any sense of reason. I hinted that if the *Guardian* fabricated a lie to save a few shekels, I might have a claim against my own paper for defaming me as a journalist. I'd never do it; the threat was nuts (not exactly a career maker), but my paper hesitated about giving in—and got sued by Barrick. It was December. The money clock on legal fees was now ticking, making me the most expensive journalist at the *Guardian* papers.

Meanwhile, back in the United States . . .

Salon.com, the Internet magazine, ran my story on the theft of the elections. It wasn't exactly print, but at least it was American. And now columnists like Bob Herbert of the *New York Times* picked it up, and some radio talk shows too. But still, not one news editor called, not even from the *Washington Post,* with whom the *Guardian* shares material.

From a news view, and the flood of site hits, this was *Salon.com*'s biggest political story ever—and it named part 1 its political story of the year.

But where was part 2? On its Web site and on radio programs, the magazine was announcing part 2 would appear in two days . . . and in two days . . . and in two days . . . and *nothing appeared.* Part 2 exposed how Jeb Bush violated court orders by refusing to register to vote over fifty thousand people who had criminal records in other states. (Florida law bars the vote only to the state's own felons and those in a dozen other states.) The fact that 90 percent of these voters were Democrats should have made it news because this maneuver alone more than accounted for Bush's victory.

I was going crazy: Gore had not yet conceded. The timing of part 2 was crucial. *Where the hell was it?* Finally, the editor told me: the Washington bureau chief (quite a title for *Salon*) had determined that the story didn't check out. You see, we checked with *Jeb Bush's office* and they said . . .

Agh! It was déjà vu all over again.

I called the bureau chieftain himself, who sniffed, I used to work for the *Washington Post,* you know. And the *Post* would *never* run this story.

Well, he had me there. They hadn't, they didn't. Not yet. So God bless America.

Meanwhile, back in sunny England . . .

Bad news. In the middle of trying to get out the word of the theft of the election in Florida, I was about to become the guinea pig, the test case, for an attempt by a multinational corporation to suppress free speech *in the United States* using British libel law.

Here's something I bet you didn't know about Britain: *there is no freedom of the press. There is no First Amendment.* England is one of the few nations on earth without a written guarantee of freedom of speech or press. That's why we Americans celebrate July 4th. Britons don't have freedom of the press, and *they don't want it*—not the public, not the government, and, weirdly, not the editors or the publishers.

This hit me on the head in 1999 when my paper was facing charges under the Official Secrets Act. The *Guardian* had published an innocuous letter by a former MI-5 agent in the Letters to the Editor section. In the United Kingdom, it's a serious violation of the law to pub-lish *anything* by a former agent—even a Christmas card. (The last example is not hypothetical.) *My editor argued with me in favor of the Official Secrets Act, the very law under which he at that moment faced unlimited jail time.* It brought home that Britons are subjects, not citizens.

Lacking a First Amendment, Britain has become the libel suit cap-ital of the world. Stories printed anywhere else draw steep judgments in London. *Guardian* newspapers receive notice of suit or service of suit about three times a day—that's *one thousand libel notices a year*! This creates a whole encyclopedia of off-limits topics, including an admonition from our legal department not to disparage the marriage of Tom Cruise and Nicole Kidman (sent the day *after* they announced their divorce).

Britain's libel law has privatized censorship. No paper could afford to defend all these actions. One excellent reporter, chosen journalist of the year, told me to just sign anything and get out of it. That's just how it's done here. As Floyd Abrams, who defends the *New York Times* in the United States and Europe, explained, the truth alone is not a defense in England. All my photos of dead bodies in Tanzania meant nothing in our case. (Barrick counters that the bodies in the film did not come from their mine site or were not victims of the clearance operation.)

And now the Canadian Goldfingers were about to try something new in the British censorship game: annul the US Bill of Rights. Their legal gambit was brilliant. I have a US-based Web site for Americans who can't otherwise read or view my BBC and *Guardian* stories. The gold mining company held my British newspaper liable for aggra-vated damages for publishing the story *in the United States*. If I did not pull the Bush/Barrick story off my US Web site, my paper would face a ruinous bill.

The legal department begged me to pull not just English versions of the story but my Spanish translation, printed in Bolivia. *¡Caramba!* I resisted.

But Goldfinger was not done. Their lawyers told our paper that I personally would be sued in the United Kingdom over my *American* Web publications of my story—because the Web could be accessed in Britain. The success of this legal theory would further chill US publishers with international sales. Suddenly, instead of the Internet becoming a means of spreading press freedom, the means to break through censor-ship, it would become the electronic highway delivering repression.

And repression was winning. InterPress Services (IPS) of Washington, DC, sent a reporter to Tanzania. They received a note from Barrick that said if the wire service even mentioned the *allegations* of killings, even with Barrick's denial, Barrick would sue. The IPS story never ran. Lawyers told the reporter that there were a couple of newspaper customers in Canada (which inherited British libel laws), and the US-based wire service couldn't chance it. The Internet reach threat was biting.

I chose to fight. In July I issued an alert to human rights groups worldwide. My paper went ballistic: In the United Kingdom, one can't complain about being sued for libel, because under their libel law, a paper is guilty of defamation until it proves itself innocent. Therefore, publicly defending oneself repeats the libel and makes the paper and reporter subject to new damages and court sanctions. Kafka had nothing on the British court system.

Most of my colleagues were sympathetic, but not all. As one noted, any other reporter would have been sacked on the spot. And now my paper was flooded with *thousands* of we-support-your-courage letters.

The pressure was on. And, I'm pleased to say, my editor refused to sign the abject, lying retraction—just fifteen minutes before the court-imposed deadline. Then he sent me this encouraging note: "We are now going to spend hundreds of thousands on some fucking meaningless point you are trying to make. I hope you are happy."

Meanwhile, back in the United States . . .

In February 2001, I took my BBC film crew to Florida, having unearthed a page marked "secret" and "confidential" from the contract between Florida and the company the state had hired to make up the list of names to purge from the voter rolls. Here it was, smoking-gun evidence that the Republican officials knew their operation had knowingly wiped out the voting rights of thousands of innocent voters, most of them African Americans.

(I wondered why not one American news outlet had bothered to obtain these documents, available through Florida's freedom-of-information law. But I did find this in the files: The *Orlando Sentinel* had been suspicious of the conduct of the voter purge before the election. The government e-mail was a gloating message that the *Sentinel* had been thrown off the scent by that brilliant ploy: flat-out official denial and a schmooze job, which the *Sentinel* ran as fact.)

It was February. I took my camera crew into an agreed interview with Jeb Bush's director of the Florida Department of Elections. When I pulled out the confidential sheet, Bush's man ripped off the microphone and did the fifty-yard dash, locking himself in his office, all in front of our cameras. It was killer television and wowed the British viewers. We even ran a confession from the company. Newsworthy for the United States? Apparently not.

My program, *Newsnight*, has a film-trading agreement with *ABC Nightline*, a kind of sister show. Over twenty thousand Net-heads in the United States saw the BBC Webcast, a record; and they banged ABC TV with demands to broadcast the BBC film, or at least report on it.

Instead, *Nightline* sent down its own crew to Florida for a couple of days. They broadcast a report that ballots are complex and blacks are not well educated about voting procedures. The gravamen of the story was *blacks are too freakin' dumb to figure out how to vote*. No mention that in white Leon County, machines automatically kicked back faulty ballots for voter correction; whereas, in very black Gadsden County, the same machines were programmed to eat mismarked ballots. (That was in our story, too.)

Why didn't ABC run the voter purge story? Don't look for some big Republican conspiracy. Remember the three elements of investigative reporting: risk, time, money. Our BBC/*Guardian* stories required all of that, in short supply in American news operations.

Meanwhile, back in sunny England . . .

My paper was again ready to throw me to the dogs. Understandably, they couldn't spend half a million pounds defending a story about a Canadian company in Tanzania, dead bodies or no. But in July, human rights groups bombarded Barrick's Toronto headquarters with petitions demanding they stop trying to censor the story and permit a public inquiry into the alleged killings. And Barrick started to give, getting nervous, offering my paper a (relatively) cheap out.

Would my paper still have to confirm no killings took place? Under the horrific British system, a statement that no one died, read in open court, would have given this factoid the virtual force of law, barring any paper from reporting otherwise.

While Amnesty International's leaders hid under their desks (despite Bianca Jagger's several phone lectures), other groups — Friends of the Earth (Holland), Corner House (UK), and Britain's National

Union of Journalists — took the extraordinary step of intervening in the libel action under a rarely used provision of the law allowing third parties to argue against the settlement of a lawsuit in a manner that could harm the public interest. They presented the judge with evidence of the Tanzanian killings, with a plea to keep the matter open.

Astonishingly, the judge accepted the interveners' position, requiring Barrick to accept that the agreement with the *Observer* did not foreclose allegations of the killings. So that's how it ended: a half-baked apology from my paper and Barrick frustrated, unable to extract a statement that no one died at the mine. Hooray.

Well, half a hooray. I still faced personal ruin. The threat of a lawsuit against a reporter after settling with a paper was not cricket even by English legal traditions. But Barrick told my paper's attorneys that it was still prepared to sue me in the United Kingdom.

Barrick's decision to sue depended, their lawyers said, on my behavior in the United States and Canada.

So I went on the radio in Toronto, where Barrick is headquartered. I talked about Barrick, the Tanzanian mine, and censorship.

As I write, I'm waiting for the writ. My woes are nothing. The Tanzanian papers splashed the story and as a result, lawyer Tundu Lissu is facing charges of sedition there for releasing the videotape.

Meanwhile, back in the United States . . .

My part 2 on the theft of the elections found asylum in that distant journalistic planet not always visible to the naked eye, the *Nation* magazine. Bless them.

In May, the US Civil Rights Commission prepared to report on the election in Florida. They relied heavily on the material uncovered by the BBC for the core of their commission's finding of systematic voter disenfranchisement in Florida. Our documents were their main evidence used in witness cross-examinations.

And then, *mirabile dictu*, the *Washington Post* ran the story of the voter purge on page one, including the part that couldn't stand up for CBS and *Salon*, and even gave me space for a bylined comment. Applause for the *Post*'s courage!

Would I be ungrateful if I suggested otherwise? The *Post* ran the story in June, although they had it at hand seven months earlier while the ballots were still being counted. They waited until they knew the findings of the US Civil Rights Commission Report, so they could fire from behind that big, safe rock of official imprimatur. In other words, the *Post* had the courage to charge out and shoot the wounded.

So there you have it. Take your pick: Work in the United Kingdom where editors are scared of lawsuits, or America, where editors are scared of their own shadows.

And then came September 11 . . .

Journalism is a planet whose inhabitants are rewarded for big mouths and instant answers. On September 11, the vomit of journo-babble began before the World Trade Center towers hit the ground. In the United States, professional hair-do Tom Brokaw was typical. He didn't know who did it, but he knew why: Someone hated these symbols of American capitalism and our spirit of freedom. Across the Atlantic, colleagues at *Guardian* newspapers were just as swift to wag their fingers in print, blaming the attack, as Europeans are accustomed, on the Jews (by way of "Imperial Israel") and gloating that it was about time the Americans learn why everyone hates them.

I spent the day just outside New York, uselessly staring at my laptop, silent and worried sick about my friends on the fifty-second floor of Tower One where I had worked for many years. A simple question nagged at me: not the grandly philosophical *why?* but *how?* How had the FBI, CIA, America's zillion-dollar intelligence apparatus missed this one? Over the next two months, I found a frightening answer: *They were told not to look.*

A group of well-placed sources—not-all-too-savory—spooks and arms dealers—told my BBC team that before September 11 the US government had turned away evidence of Saudi billionaires funding Osama bin Laden's network. Working with the *Guardian* and the National Security News Service of Washington, we got our hands on documents that backed up the story that FBI and CIA investigations had been slowed by the Clinton administration, then killed by Bush Jr.'s when those inquiries might upset Saudi interests.

The story made the top of the news—in Britain. In the United States, one television reporter picked up the report. He was called, he says, by network chiefs, and told to go no further. He didn't. Rick MacArthur, publisher of *Harper's*, asked me why the story did not run in the United States.

Suggested responses welcome.

CHAPTER 10

THE FOX, THE HOUNDS, AND THE SACRED COWS

JANE AKRE

Akre has spent twenty years as a network and local television reporter and anchor for news operations throughout the country. Most recently, she was investigative reporter and anchor for FOX-owned WTVT-TV in Tampa, Florida, where she was wrongfully terminated for refusing to broadcast a story they knew to be false and misleading. Besides anchoring, Akre has been a specialty reporter in the areas of health and medical issues as well as investigative and consumer reporting. She has won numerous awards for her work, including the prestigious Associated Press award for investigative reporting. Akre began her broadcasting career in Albuquerque as a radio news director and moved into TV in 1980 as a weekend anchor for ABC's Tucson affiliate. Later, she accepted a reporter-anchor position at KTVI in St. Louis. For three years she anchored and reported for CNN in Atlanta before moving to a main anchor position in San Francisco. Prior to anchoring in Tampa, Akre was a news anchor for WSVN in Miami.

LIGHTS, CAMERA, ACTION

I t was an unusually cold November night for Florida. The three of us walked shoulder to shoulder, wrapped in our trench coats, the warmth from our breath visibly rising in the cold air. We were in a historic area of downtown Tampa, Ybor City, where Cuban settlers first began rolling the cigars that made Tampa famous. The streets were cobblestone, a fact not lost on my wobbly ankles as my pumps tried to maneuver the curves of the stone.

A lone spotlight shone brightly behind us, silhouetting the three of us as we walked à la *Mod Squad*. Julie, Link, and Pete on the case. Solid.

"All right, that was good; let's try it again."

It was television, or should I say the image of television news. My husband, Steve Wilson, and I were joining WTVT Channel 13, the soon-to-be FOX-owned television station in Tampa and, teamed with the station's consumer reporter, this nighttime stroll was the station's idea of promotion for its hard-hitting team to be known as "The Investigators." The former, longtime CBS affiliate wanted our forty-five-plus-years of broadcasting experience and lured us with promises of a flexible schedule and freedom to investigate stories of our choosing. It all sounded too good to be true.

Our first assignment was to join a film crew, complete with a smoke machine and bright movie lights, to shoot a commercial. In television, image is everything.

(Voice of baritone announcer)

"The Investigators,
Uncovering the Truth!
Getting Results . . .
Protecting You!!!"

The spots started running almost immediately after we were hired in December 1996.

BETA

My photographer, Joel, and I started driving east early one weekend morning in January 1997. We were out to see if we could verify independently what I had been told by those inside the dairy business. Sources were saying that the majority of farmers in Florida and nationwide were injecting their cows with a powerful and controversial growth hormone that forced them to produce more milk. Although approved by the Food and Drug Administration (FDA), scientists around the world remained troubled with as-yet-unanswered questions about the drug's safety for consumers who drink the altered milk.

Besides, my then two-year-old daughter had just discovered and fallen deeply in love with ice cream. Sometimes the best stories come from self-interest.

We spotted a dairy from the car and drove up the gravelly drive. Dairy manager Ken Deaton was as friendly as he could be when we introduced ourselves as a news crew from the FOX station in Tampa. Deaton and a few dairy hands had just begun walking the black-and-white Holsteins into a dark, open-ended barn for their hormone injections. What luck! I thought.

We asked and Deaton did not hesitate to give us permission to take out our Betacam and begin shooting videotape that could become the cornerstone of the news report we were developing.

Each cow jumped as a three-inch-long needle was plunged deeply into her hindquarters. Posilac was the brand name of the product proudly displayed on the syringe and packages that Joel shot along with the name of the drug's maker, Monsanto.

Dairyman Deaton was happy to cooperate further, standing for a lengthy on-camera interview. Later we crouched down in a field and watched as January's cold brought on labor and the birth of two Holsteins, which Joel also recorded.

"Nature's most perfect food," I thought, might be a good beginning of a script describing the scene as the newborn calf Joel named "Beta" teetered on his shaky new legs while finding the first taste of milk.

We were off to a great start!

Little did I know that Beta would soon be shipped off to an early and cruel death at the nearby veal factory. And that this promising story—as well as our own futures in television journalism—would never survive the face-off that was to follow between Steve and me versus Rupert Murdoch's News Corporation and its very deep pockets.

DON'T ASK, DON'T TELL

Monsanto persistently refuses to release sales figures but claims rBGH (or rBST) is the largest-selling dairy animal drug in America. For about a dozen years, the chemical company and its rivals tested the hormone for its effect on animals. rBGH does indeed turn cows into milking machines, forcing virtually every injected animal to give more milk. But high producers almost always have more medical problems, and studies found that hormone-injected animals had more lameness, reproductive disorders, and a painful udder infection called mastitis.[1] To save the ailing cow, farmers almost always treat these infections with the same antibiotics doctors prescribe for humans when *we* and our children are ailing.

Industry studies also found that milk from injected cows was different from nature's version, having higher amounts of a spin-off hormone, insulin-like growth factor-1 (IGF-1).[2]

IGF-1 is widely regarded as one of the most powerful promoters of cell growth in all of nature. After all, it is found primarily in mother's milk, which is supercharged with IGF-1 to spark growth.

But here's a primary concern of scientists around the world: IGF-1 doesn't differentiate between "good cells" and "bad cells" and is known to stimulate the growth of cancerous cells as well. So, will it promote the growth of cancerous cells in those drinking the supercharged milk?

My own research confirmed some truly alarming news for humans consuming milk from treated cows: the longest test for long-term human toxicity, such as cancer, lasted only ninety days on thirty rats.[3]

Ninety days. Thirty rats. And what's worse? Despite Monsanto's assurances that no rat suffered any adverse effects—a claim that apparently convinced the FDA that no further testing of rBGH was required to assure human safety—it was later revealed that about a third of the test rats actually developed cysts and lesions on their thyroids and prostates. Those responses, among others, were enough to prompt safety regulators in Canada to ban rBGH there until more thorough testing proves that the product is safe for humans. (Monsanto, having already convinced American regulators that the product is safe, has little incentive to do further testing and has announced no such plans.)

The Center for Veterinary Medicine (CVM), an arm of the FDA, which approves animal drugs, was charged with oversight of rBGH. Early on, CVM scientist Dr. Richard Burroughs asked too many questions about the lax safety studies required of Monsanto. "The drug review process has become more of an approval process,"[4] he noted before suddenly finding himself "reassigned" to another job within the CVM.

Eventually, Burroughs was fired as a safety watchdog at the FDA, which ultimately gave the green light to Posilac, disregarding the concerns he and others raised. Approval came in November 1993. No withdrawal period was required, no environmental impact statement was needed, and no testing for the possible long-term effects on the health of milk drinkers has been required to this day.

By February 1997 our story was ready to air. It attempted to answer some troubling questions: Why had Monsanto sued two small dairies to prevent them from labeling their milk as coming from cows *not* injected with the drug? Why had two Canadian health regulators claimed, like Richard Burroughs at the FDA, that their jobs were threatened — and then said Monsanto offered them a bribe to give fast-track approval to the drug? Why did Florida supermarkets break their much-publicized promise to consumers that milk in the dairy case would *not* come from hormone-treated cows "until it gained widespread acceptance" among the wary public? And why, in large part because of concerns about human health, was the United States the only major industrialized nation to approve the use of this controversial genetically engineered hormone?[5]

LAWYERED UP

The four-part series took my photographer and me to five states and produced fifty videotapes yielding more than sixteen hours of pictures and sound. Steve was brought in to help produce the piece that was scheduled to run February 24, 1997, during a "sweeps" period.

As most savvy viewers know, advertising rates are set during those ratings periods, so many TV stations try to air their best work at such times to lure as many viewers as possible. (Others resort to sleazy sweeps gimmicks, but that's another book!)

Station managers were so proud of our work that they saturated virtually every Tampa Bay–area radio station with thousands of dollars' worth of ads urging viewers to watch what we'd uncovered about "The Mystery in Your Milk."

But then, our FOX managers' pride turned to panic. Friday evening before the scheduled airdate, Steve and I were called to the news director's office. "Read this," he said, handing us a fax. It was a letter from a New York law firm, Cadwalader, Wickersham & Taft, addressed to Roger Ailes, president of FOX News in New York. It was written on behalf of the firm's client, Monsanto Company, and John Walsh, the lawyer who authored the letter, minced no words.

Walsh charged in a letter that would later become a key piece of evidence in the dispute, that Steve and I had "no scientific competence" to report our story. Monsanto's attorney went on to describe our news reports, which he had ostensibly never seen, as a series of "recklessly made accusations that Monsanto has engaged in fraud, has published lies about food safety, has attempted to bribe government officials in a neighboring country and has been 'buying' favorable opinions about the product or its characteristics from reputable scientists in their respective fields."

He charged that we had conducted ourselves unethically in the field. And to make sure nobody missed the point, the attorney also reminded FOX News' chief that our behavior as investigative journalists was particularly dangerous in the "aftermath of the Food Lion verdict."[6] He was referring, of course, to the then recent case against ABC News that sent a frightening chill through every newsroom in America. The Food Lion verdict showed that even with irrefutable evidence from a hidden camera documenting the doctoring of potentially unsafe food sold to unsuspecting shoppers, a news organization that dares to expose a giant corporation could still lose big in court.

Confronted with these threats, FOX decided to "delay" broadcasting the story, ostensibly to double-check its accuracy. I remember leaving news director Daniel Webster's office but stopping at the door to ask an important question. I had to know whether he had lost faith in us or was frightened by the threat.

"Are you pulling the story because of the letters?" I asked. "Yes," he confirmed in a moment of honesty perhaps not rare for him, but increasingly uncommon in the executive suites of more and more news organizations struggling to maintain profits at virtually any cost these days.

One week later, the station's general manager screened our reports. We were lucky. General Manager Bob Franklin was a former investigative journalist himself. After he found no major problems with the story and we all agreed we could minimize legal risk in the wake of their lawyer's letter by offering Monsanto another interview, a new airdate was set. But Monsanto turned down the interview offer and directed John Walsh to write another threatening letter to Ailes in New York.

This time there was no room for interpretation. Walsh wrote in a letter dated February 28, 1997, that some of the points of the story "clearly contain the elements of defamatory statements which, if repeated in a broadcast, could lead to serious damage to Monsanto and *dire consequences* [italics mine] for FOX News."[7]

Never mind that I carried a milk crate full of documentation to support every word of our proposed broadcast. And never mind that we refuted all claims that we had acted improperly in our newsgathering and reporting. Our story was pulled again.

This time, if not dead, we knew our broadcasts were clearly on life support as FOX's own attorneys and its top-level managers, all of them anxious to avoid a legal challenge or lost advertising revenue, looked for some way to make the whole thing quietly go away.

KILL THE MESSENGER

Our story was pulled shortly after Rupert Murdoch's News Corporation formally closed the $3 billion deal to control WTVT and several other stations he added to his empire in early 1997, making the former Aussie (now a naturalized US citizen) the owner of more American TV stations than anyone else.

And it was not long after our struggle to air an honest report had begun that FOX fired both the news director and the general manager. Put in charge of the newsroom—and presumably the fate of our story—was an assistant news director once quoted as telling a reporter in another newsroom she ran, "This is not the TV news business, this is the entertainment business."

At WTVT, Steve and I were dumbstruck when we heard about her idea to park an empty Ryder truck in front of the Tampa federal building on the anniversary of the Oklahoma City bomb blast—but that was not how we determined Sue Kawalerski's reputation was well earned.

Not long after we arrived, she had somehow decided there was more going on at local health clubs than merely exercise. Jaws dropped all around the table at a meeting of the entire investigative team when Sue suggested maybe one of us could visit a few of the more popular clubs and discreetly scrape the walls and take water samples from the hot tubs. Why? She thought it would be big news if we could discover semen samples that would prove her theory that some club members were involved in illicit sex, exposing other unsuspecting club members to some pretty unsanitary conditions.

And who had FOX chosen to ride herd on journalism leadership of that caliber? The new general manager was brought in from High Point, North Carolina. Dave Boylan had climbed his way into his first general manager's job at the FOX-owned station there and in a few short years had overseen revenue growth that impressed his corporate masters at FOX in Los Angeles. The GM job in Tampa, a big step up, was his payback.

Journalists are often apprehensive about working at stations where the general manager has no experience in journalism and is under constant pressure to protect the bottom line at virtually any cost. Too many times at too many places, such managers view the news as a commodity, not a public service. And when a strong investigative story brings a threat of expensive litigation or the subject of such a report is an advertiser who threatens to cancel and take his ad dollars elsewhere, managers revert to salesmen. They do whatever they feel they must to put the station's interest first, regardless of their obligation to use their broadcast license to serve the public interest.

It was not long after Boylan took over in March that Steve and I scheduled a visit. Perhaps we had an ally who could help get our stalled stories on the air.

We were not completely surprised to find Dave to be "salesman" all the way. Small talk filled our conversation in his glass-enclosed corner office, upstairs, overlooking the station's impressive fountain. A smiling Dave told us his wife collected "accessories" at the many furniture outlets back in High Point. Nice, I thought. Dave seemed sincere when he looked us in the eye and promised to look into the trouble we were having getting our rBGH story on the air. But when we returned a few days later, his strategy seemed clear.

"What would you do if I killed the story, would you tell anyone?" he asked. "Only if they ask," was Steve's response.

Dave started to sweat. Here were two reporters who clearly didn't know how the game was to be played.

He knew the local media writers had heard the radio ads for the milk series, and it wouldn't look good for the station's image if word leaked out that powerful advertisers, backed by lawyers threatening to sue, could actually determine what gets on the six o'clock news —

and what gets swept under the rug. And Dave knew it wouldn't look good for Dave.

To resolve this dilemma, Dave called us into his corner office again a few days later. This time, he was much firmer.

He went on to explain that if we didn't agree to changes that Monsanto and FOX lawyers were insisting upon, we'd be fired for insubordination within forty-eight hours. Steve made it clear that those changes would result in broadcasting what we knew to be false and misleading information to the public. We pleaded with Dave to look for himself at the facts we'd uncovered, many of which conclusively disproved Monsanto's claims, both about its product and about our work to uncover the truth.

We reminded him of the importance of the facts about a basic food most of our viewers consume and feed to their children daily. This was news, we told him. His reply: "We paid $3 billion for these television stations. We'll tell *you* what the news is. The news is what *we* say it is!"

There wasn't much to say after that. "Is this a hill you're both willing to die on?" Dave asked. I could see the disappointment and anger on Steve's face. Before we got up from Dave's plush couch and left his office, Steve was firm but respectful when he made it clear we would neither lie nor distort any part of the story. And if insisting upon an honest report ended up costing us our jobs, Steve told him we'd be obligated to report that kind of misconduct to the Federal Communications Commission.

Forty-eight hours came and went. Dave never called, not until about a week later when he invited us back to lay out *the deal*. We'd be paid full salaries and benefits through the rest of the year in exchange for an agreement that we would drop our ethical objections and broadcast the rBGH story in a way that would not upset Monsanto.

"Will you do the story exactly the way Carolyn wants?" Dave asked. Carolyn Forrest, the FOX attorney based in Atlanta, would have the final say on the exact wording of our report. And after the carefully sanitized version aired, we would be free to do whatever we pleased — as long as we forever kept our mouths shut about the entire episode, Monsanto's influence, the FOX response, *and* we could never ever utter a public word about what we'd learned about the growth hormone.

FOX made it clear we would never be free to report the story for any other news organizations, not for any broadcast or print media, even if they weren't FOX competitors. Never, anywhere, not even at our daughter's PTA could we utter a word about how our milk has changed in what many believe is a dangerous way.

As journalists, Steve and I badly wanted to get the story on the air so the public could make its own judgment. But a buyout, no matter how lucrative for us personally, was out of the question. Neither of us could fathom taking hush money to shut up about a public health issue that absolutely and by any standard deserved to see the light of day.

After asking for and receiving *the deal* [italics mine] in writing, we politely declined the offer—and told Dave we'd decided to just hold onto the written document that laid out his deal.

MEANWHILE, BEHIND THE SCENES

Behind the scenes, Monsanto's threatening letters didn't stop. In January I had interviewed Roger Natzke, a dairy science professor at the University of Florida. Everything had gone well; he'd even given me a guided tour of the "Monsanto Dairy Barn" at the Gainesville dairy school where Posilac had been tested in the mid-1980s. Natzke gave the product a glowing report and admitted he promoted its use to farmers through Florida's taxpayer-supported agriculture extension offices. After spending a few hours with him, Natzke even gave us directions to a good lunch joint.

The professor must have forgotten about our pleasant exchange when he called the station to complain about my reporting techniques, one month *after* the interview. "She's not a reporter" was part of the phone message a secretary took for the assistant news director. The words "St. Simon's Island" were also scrawled on the note.

"What does that mean?" I asked. The assistant news director apparently did not see any connection or conflict in the fact that Natzke admitted that he had just returned from a weekend at the island resort—courtesy of Monsanto.

The pieces of the puzzle behind the Monsanto pressure began falling into place. Natzke's complaint call came the same week as the Monsanto threat letters arrived. And not until months later in the discovery phase of our lawsuit did we learn that a third threat arrived at the station that same week from a local dairyman, Joe Wright.

Wright had spent no more than five minutes on the phone with me the month before in an uneventful conversation about the dairy business. Based on that conversation, he wrote a letter to the station saying, "Ms. Acre's [sic] work is gaining notoriety in our dairy industry. . . . The word is clearly out on the street that Ms. Acre is on a negative campaign based on everyone's assessment of the numerous interviews she has already conducted."

Wright had reached these conclusions after attending the twenty-second Annual Southern Dairy Conference in Atlanta. That little confab was a veritable Who's Who of the dairy industry and apparently, our report was the topic of intense discussion there.

Following the conference, Wright went to Dairy Farmers Incorporated, a dairy industry promotion group, which helped draft his letter of complaint that FOX did not reveal to us at the time.

Also behind the scenes, another group calling itself the Dairy Coalition had launched a much stealthier attack on the story and us. An ad hoc group of dairy and pharmaceutical companies, the Dairy Coalition was formed around the time Posilac was approved by the FDA in 1993. The coalition's job was to help get the good word out about the growth hormone and defend it from any attacks from scientists and consumer groups who insisted more testing was needed.

As we were preparing our case for trial months after we were fired, Steve called the coalition's director, Dick Weiss. Steve said he was a reporter interested in the rBGH story, and what could Weiss tell him about the Dairy Coalition? And what about that rumor that a Tampa TV station had threatened to blow the whistle on the hormone?

Weiss obviously did not make the connection. Instead, he took great pride in bragging that the Dairy Coalition had "snowed the station with piles of paperwork and all sorts of pressure to have that story killed." He laughed like a college kid who had just pulled the best prank in the fraternity.

GETTING THE BOOT

The remainder of 1997, more than eight months, was spent on virtually nothing but this one story. Although they never told us at the time, FOX Television Stations president Mitchell Stern had ordered Carolyn Forrest to "take no risk" with the story. That directive meant cutting out everything that Monsanto, the dairy industry, and even grocers would find offensive and cause for pulling their ads or sparking a lawsuit.

"A risk of cancer?" You don't need to use that word, said company lawers. Instead, call it "human health implications." The credentials of our scientists critical of the Monsanto product? We don't need their credentials, said FOX, just call him a "scientist from Wisconsin." Meanwhile, tell viewers that the FDA reviewed all human health concerns before approving the drug, insisted the assistant news director. The problem with that was that many of the studies were done postapproval, we told her. Do it anyway, she insisted.

FOX threatened us with our jobs every time we resisted the dozens of mandated changes that would sanitize the story, and fill it with lies and distortions. "You'll be charged with insubordination," the general manager threatened, if we didn't do what the lawyers wanted.

In our four decades in the business, Steve and I had never seen a news-editing process that was so incredibly one-sided, and so clearly designed to make the story more palatable to Monsanto.

No case better illustrates why lawyers should never be in charge of the editorial process of reporting the news. Lawyer Carolyn Forrest's mandate was to protect the station against litigation, to "take no risks" that the station would ever have to stand up for the truth in court. Ours was to work, first and foremost, in the public interest to find and broadcast as many facts as we could reasonably report.

Forrest could never understand why we insisted on investigating Monsanto's glowing claims about its product. "While some say this, Monsanto says that" was her approach. Just let the viewers sort it out.

She and a lot of lawyers like her cannot understand the difference between a reporter, especially an investigative reporter, and a stenographer. A reporter's obligation is always to explore the claims made by all voices in any story, critics and proponents alike. If a claim doesn't hold water, we have the obligation to show why not.

But none of that mattered to our friends at FOX who like to boast about news that is "fair and balanced," different than all the others. "We report, you decide" is their motto. During one May phone review of the latest script, after we had faxed her more documentation, Forrest finally leveled with us. "You guys just don't get it. It doesn't matter whether the facts are true. This story just isn't worth a couple of hundred thousand dollars to go up against Monsanto."

So, we suggested, just kill the story. We fully recognize that the employer has the right to set whatever litigation risk level it chooses. In the end, *no story* was preferable to a story that was slanted and distorted. But the lawyers and FOX managers knew killing it would be a "major PR problem," as the local counsel wrote in his notes that also were turned over later during the discovery process. After all, FOX had already spent thousands of dollars on radio ads promoting the series, which were running the weekend before the scheduled airtime. Local newspaper media critics were anxiously awaiting the series. What would the station tell them if the story suddenly disappeared?

So write and rewrite we did. Eighty-three versions of the rBGH story and not one of them was acceptable to FOX lawyers. Instead, what we got was an offer for more hush money. FOX's general manager presented us with an agreement, crafted by FOX counsel, that would give us a full year of our salaries and benefits worth close to $200,000 in no-show "consulting jobs" with the same strings attached: no mention of how FOX covered up the story and no opportunity to ever expose the facts FOX refused to air.

Poor Dave Boylan was so exasperated when we turned down his second hush money offer, he just wagged his head and said, "I don't get it. What is it with you two? I just want people who want to be on TV!" And the sad truth is that today, many newsrooms are full of people like that who call themselves journalists.

At the first window in our contracts, December 2, 1997, we were both finally fired, allegedly for "no cause." But then, an angry-but-gloating Carolyn Forrest wrote a letter spelling out "there were definite reasons" for our dismissals. She went on to characterize our resistance to broadcasting the story as she directed as "unprofessional and inappropriate conduct."

As Steve commented when he read the letter, just what is the "professional and appropriate" response for a reporter when a station directs him or her to deliberately lie on television?

The Forrest letter would prove a major tactical error for FOX and the basis of our lawsuit.

FULL FRONTAL ASSAULT:
OUR TRIAL AGAINST FOX

On April 2, 1998, we filed a lawsuit under the Florida Private Whistle-blowers Act against FOX Television, the first of its kind for any jour-nalist. Under the law, a whistle-blower is any employee, regardless of his profession, who suffers retaliation for refusing to participate in an illegal activity or threatening to report that illegal activity to authorities.

We argued that we were entitled to protection as whistle-blowers because the lies and distortions our employers wanted us to broadcast were not in the public interest and therefore violated the law and reg-ulations of the Federal Communications Commission.

After FOX's local counsel lost two major efforts to have the suit derailed, FOX brass apparently decided they needed bigger, smarter, meaner lawyers. That's when they turned to Bill McDaniels and the Washington, DC, firm of Williams & Connolly, the same firm that Bill Clinton used to help him through Whitewater, Monica Lewinsky, and impeachment. It's the firm that crafted his famous redefinition of the word "is."

Several weeks before the start of the trial, in a scene right out of films like *Class Action*, Williams & Connolly camped out on the top two floors of the Hyatt Regency Hotel, one of the plushest in down-town Tampa. Using more than a dozen lawyers and some of the top firms around the country to help with various pretrial chores, FOX staff lawyers regularly flew back and forth, first class, between Los Angeles and Tampa.

We found ourselves practically living in an old downtown house that served as the offices of my own lawyers, John Chamblee and Tom Johnson. Both of them are extremely competent and well-respected labor and civil rights attorneys who rolled up their sleeves early on, prepared for a fight, and always kept their promise to stand with us no matter who and what the other side kept throwing our way.

Hours of late nights and their well-crafted legal briefs and court-room appearances before three judges eventually allowed us to with-stand all three motions by FOX, which was desperate to have the case thrown out of court without the spectacle of a public trial.

The case FOX had vowed would never go to trial was, after more than a two-year delay that forced us to sell our home and drain our savings, finally going to be heard by six jurors in a Tampa courtroom.

CRAZY LIKE A FOX

The FOX legal strategy was tightly woven from day one and helped by a well-coordinated team effort. Their defense: that we had turned our backs on the story and were using the whistle-blower claim as a "tactic." We missed deadlines, they claimed, and had told managers and lawyers from the first that we were "going to get Monsanto."

I watched as the attack on our competence as reporters softened with time, as it became evident the media conglomerate could be on the hook for defaming our reputations.

The FOX effort, though slick and united, was not flawless. FOX News director, Phil Metlin, told the six-person jury that if he ever learned that a news organization was trying to eliminate risk by using a threatening letter as "a road map" to craft a story, it would "make me want to throw up." Just a few days later, Metlin sat at the defense table with a blank stare when the local FOX counsel took the stand and bragged that he "could edit all risk out of a story" by using threatening letters from the subject (in this case, Monsanto) of the story as "a roadmap" to avoid lawsuits and other trouble for a station. By that, he said on the stand, you knew in advance the subject's hot spots and you could successfully avoid poking the beast. Unfortunately, it's sometimes those hotspots that are precisely the areas that need investigation, whether the subject likes it or not.

Metlin, a likeable but hapless Woody Allen kind of character, also didn't score any points with his bosses or the jurors when he admitted that he never found even a single error in our reporting of the rBGH story and saw no reason why our final version of the story could not have aired.

More than two years had passed since we filed our suit, and our former general manager, Dave Boylan, now had to be flown into town for his testimony. On the eve of the trial, FOX had rewarded him with another precious step up the FOX ladder—promotion to general manager of the FOX-owned station in Los Angeles, the second-biggest station in the group.

Boylan lost his bravado on the stand. He constantly shot quick and nervous smiles at the jurors while repeatedly looking over to the defense team after virtually every answer. During our cross-examination of Boylan, it helped that Steve knew exactly what had transpired during 1997. Earlier in the trial, it had been estimated that lost revenue in advertising from Monsanto ads for Roundup or Nutrasweet could have cost the station about $50,000. FOX bragged that $50,000 was nothing for an organization of its size, but Steve's relentless interrogation of Boylan showed that the actual cost of going up against Monsanto could have been much higher.

"You testified FOX owns twenty-three stations?" Steve asked.

"Yes," Boylan answered.

"Could Monsanto pull advertising off all twenty-three?"

"Yes."

"And the FOX News Channel?"

"Yes."

"And the Sky Channel in Europe?"

"Yes."

"It could extend well beyond $50,000, couldn't it Mr. Boylan?"

"It could," Boylan admitted.

Attorney Bill McDaniels earned the nickname "Thumper" from our team because he made an audible noise with his foot whenever he got nervous. And there was a lot of thumping during the presentation of our case, particularly when Ralph Nader took time from his presidential campaign to serve as an expert witness. Nader is generally recognized as the nation's premier consumer advocate and an expert in the public interest. In our case, we were trying to show the jury that it was not in the public's interest to have broadcasters intentionally distort the news. FOX had tried unsuccessfully, through repeated and desperate objections, to have Nader eliminated as an expert.

On the stand, Nader told the jurors what the FCC has repeatedly said: that it is "a most heinous act" to use the public's airwaves to slant, distort, and falsify the news. "A reporter has a legal duty to act in accordance with the Communications Act of 1934 and in addition to their professional responsibility to be accurate, not to be used as an instrument of deception to the audience," Nader testified.

McDaniels also objected vehemently to Walter Cronkite's inclusion as an expert on our side. "Mr. Cronkite is not an expert in the prebroadcast review of a story," the FOX counsel argued in all seriousness.

I couldn't believe my ears. For thirty years Walter Cronkite was the managing editor of the *CBS Evening News*. During Mr. Cronkite's deposition, McDaniels asked the eighty-three-year-old anchorman whether he was a lawyer and suggested to Cronkite that, unless he was an attorney, he couldn't be an expert in the prebroadcast review of a story.

In his deposition, Cronkite said that every ethical journalist should resist directives that would result in a false or slanted story being broadcast. "He should not go a micro inch toward that sort of thing. That is a violation of every principle of good journalism," Cronkite intoned.

THE RULING

After a five-week trial, the jury awarded me $425,000 but gave nothing to Steve. His last words to jurors in his closing argument, even if they felt his questioning of FOX witnesses was too aggressive in the courtroom—and many times he went for the jugular as well as any trained litigant—were: "Don't take it out on her."

Apparently the jurors listened. In representing himself, Steve realized there were risks, but there was also a lot to gain. His questioning of the defendant in the courtroom and during seventy-three depositions he conducted in five states and the District of Columbia, elicited some of the most damage to their side.

In any event, we view the verdict as a win for us both. Our trial was never about money. It was about a reporter's duty to resist and to blow the whistle loud and strong when he or she is being pressured to lie and distort the news over the public airwaves.

FOX immediately announced that it would appeal. "Your Honor, we just want our good name back," said FOX attorney McDaniels in arguing on two separate posttrial motions that the judge should throw out the jury's verdict.

In what seemed like a final act of desperation, McDaniels seemed to be tossing the entire network's credibility in the garbage by making an argument any legitimate news organization would be embarrassed to voice. The veteran lawyer told the judge, "there is no law, rule or regulation against slanting the news."

The judge denied both motions and allowed the jury's verdict to stand.

Steve planned to appeal as well. In the end, we suspect he received no monetary award because of what seems to have been an erroneous instruction from the judge to the jury. The jurors were told that in order to find for each of us, they had to determine that there was *no other* possible reason each was fired other than the fact that we resisted orders to lie on the air and threatened to blow the whistle to the FCC. Lawyers handling Steve's appeal argued that the standard should be the same as in cases of discrimination, that the discrimination must be an *important* reason, even if not the *only* reason, for an illegal dismissal.

FOX was looking at many years of appeal ahead of it—first to the Second District Court of Appeals in Florida, then on to the Florida Supreme Court, and eventually the US Supreme Court, if it is willing to hear the case.

Meanwhile, I had been out of work since being fired.

WE WIN; FOX SPINS

It was perfect. A television news organization just found guilty of slanting the news, was slanting the news regarding the ruling!

The jury rendered its verdict just after 5 PM Friday, August 18, 2000. FOX's Tampa station, which kept a camera in the courtroom and provided spotty coverage of the trial, ran the news of the verdict at or near the top of its 6 PM broadcast.

The report was a fairly straightforward item announcing to Tampa viewers that the jury had awarded me damages "because the station violated the state's whistleblower law." Anchorwoman Kelly Ring even went on to announce the reason for the verdict in my favor was "because she refused to lie in that report and threatened to tell the FCC about it."

But by 10 PM, the FOX corporate spinmeisters had rewritten the story entirely, crafting a devastatingly embarrassing loss into "good news" for their side.

"Today is a wonderful day for FOX 13, because I think we are completely vindicated on the finding of this jury that we do not distort news, we do not lie about the news, we do not slant the news, we are professionals," said FOX News Director Phil Metlin, looking rather uncomfortable on camera.

Metlin's statement is directly contradicted by the jury's own unanimous verdict so clearly stated on the official Verdict Form for Jane Akre, August 18, 2000. The jurors were asked to rule on this question:

> Do you find that the Plaintiff, Jane Akre, has proven, by the greater weight of the evidence, that the Defendant, through its employees or

agents, terminated her employment or took other retaliatory personnel action against her, because she threatened to disclose to the Federal Communications Commission under oath, in writing, the broadcast of a false, distorted, or slanted news report which she reasonably believed would violate the prohibition against intentional falsification or distortion of the news on television, if it were aired?

The jury's answer: "Yes."

If indeed FOX regarded the jury verdict as "complete vindication," the network would have abandoned its appeals, accepted the verdict, and paid up. But that didn't happen. FOX didn't want to miss a great opportunity to show its other employees what can happen if you mess with Murdoch.

SACRED COWS

You would think that our jury verdict—granting reporters whistleblower protection and finding that a major network had slanted the news, a major network that was now insisting that there was no law against that kind of breach of trust—would spark some interest from the news media itself.

Instead, the silence was deafening.

During our trial, a *New York Times* reporter kept calling asking what would be the best week to come cover the case. We spoke to him after the trial was over to find out why he never showed up. A big story related to the CBS series *Survivor* was breaking at the time, the media writer told us. He was just too busy.

One of the biggest names in investigative reporting for *60 Minutes* sent a producer to spend nearly a week with us in the months preceding our trial. The producer gathered documents to take back to New York, but in the end CBS took a pass. The story was deemed to be "too inside baseball." Our translation: There's an unwritten rule that news organizations seldom turn their critical eye on themselves or even their competitors. The media are the last sacred cows.

A *60 Minutes* producer later called to apologize and offer his support, "We're brothers in journalism," he said.

One might expect a little better from "Florida's Best Newspaper," as the *St. Petersburg Times* calls itself. Its reporter seemed intelligent and fair when she interviewed us after the jury's verdict. Imagine our surprise when we read the part of her story that said, "And the jury did not believe the couple's claim that the station bowed to pressure from Monsanto to alter the news report."

Steve called the reporter to ask how she could have written that we didn't meet the burden of proof in the case we had just won. "I didn't write that," she said, confessing that that paragraph was added later by an editor who did not spend any time in the courtroom and ultimately declined our request to correct and clarify his copy.

One cannot help but wonder what was said behind the scenes, as the same legal firm that frequently represents the *St. Petersburg Times* also represented FOX in the suit we won.

Bad copy takes on a life of its own. When *Reliable Sources*, the CNN program on the media, ran a blurb on the Saturday show following the verdict, the producer substantially repeated the *St. Petersburg Times* version of the story, again reporting the station didn't bow to pressure from Monsanto to alter the news report.

We sent the show's producer the jury instructions and the jury's verdict. Several weeks passed before we heard anything. Finally she got back to us, declining to correct her copy but opening the door to some correction down the road. We're still waiting.

For all the other television stations in Tampa, our trial and the issues it raised was basically a nonevent unworthy of any coverage. No broadcast station in the market (with the exception of the community radio station WMNF, a University of South Florida reporter, and the defendant FOX station that fired us) ever sent a reporter to cover our trial.

Even so, when the verdict was in, the news director at top-rated WFLA Channel 8 did not hesitate adding his two-cent instant analysis in a *St. Petersburg Times* postverdict story headlined, "Verdict Is Not Expected to Affect TV News."

While freely admitting that he "had no first-hand information about the case," WFLA's Dan Bradley nonetheless espoused that ours was merely a case about two reporters' "resistance to vetting." Bradley should know that that conduct can get you immediately fired for insubordination at any television station, so why were we kept on for a full year?

After that article appeared, we offered to have lunch with Bradley. We were eager to avoid the embarrassment for both of us that comes from making irresponsible comments, and we wanted him to know the facts before he blurted out any further opinions. I got a rather curt e-mail in response: "Thank you for sharing your thoughts and comments with me regarding my quotes in the *St. Petersburg Times* article. I have no interest in discussing this any further and see no need to schedule a lunch with you."

St. Petersburg, Florida, is also home to the much-vaunted Poynter Institute for Media Studies. It's a journalism training center and think tank considered a credible resource on and for the media, its motives and inner workings. In 1997 as our battle began, we thought enough of Poynter to schedule a lunch with one of its ethics experts to ask him for some guidance. Could he or Poynter help mediate this situation to some resolution, we asked? We were told the institute has a policy of not getting involved in such situations, especially when the news organization involved is right there in the Tampa Bay area.

Given Poynter's hands-off attitude when we sought assistance there, I was very disappointed to read a posttrial comment by another Poynter "expert," Al Tompkins. Also without a shred of firsthand knowledge of the issues, he jumped at the opportunity to be quoted as concluding ours "was not a watershed case." And when asked what reporters like me and Steve should do when pressed to distort the news, Tompkins told the *St. Petersburg Times*, reporters should "quit" and "walk away."

When Steve called Tompkins and suggested they meet to discuss what really happened, the Poynter fellow said that that would be a great idea; he'd call as soon as he returned from a trip. We never heard another word from him.

Taking an offer of hush money, as we were offered, allowing a news corporation to sanitize and distort a story out of fear or to curry favor, may keep your yolk intact and fuel in the Lexus, but it certainly betrays any reporter's commitment to the public.

We set out to tell Florida consumers the facts that a giant chemical company and a powerful dairy lobby clearly didn't want them to know. That used to be something investigative reporters won awards for. But these days, as we've learned the hard way, it's something you can be fired for whenever a news organization places more value on its bottom line than on honestly delivering the news to its viewers.

Right after we filed our lawsuit in April 1998, we were pleasantly surprised to find that the nation's largest journalism organization, the Society of Professional Journalists (SPJ), was awarding us its prestigious Ethics Award. At the SPJ annual meeting, past president Paul

Brown said that the award was for our "refusing to incorporate false information into an investigative story about bovine growth hormone and then waged [*sic*] a post employment campaign to make sure the record was set straight in this case." We had received the Joe A. Callaway Award for Civic Courage from the Shafeek Nader Trust for the Community Interest, named after the late brother of Ralph and Claire Nader. In awarding the prize, Claire Nader said it was for those individuals who "take a public stance to advance truth and justice, and who challenged prevailing conditions in pursuit of common good."

The Alliance for Democracy honored us for Heroism in Journalism in 1999 and the prestigious Goldman Environmental Prize recognized us as North America's 2001 winners for outstanding environmental achievment in standing up for the truthfulness of the rBGH story. These accolades helped buoy us through some difficult days. The SPJ's 1998 award was particularly gratifying because a group of our own colleagues was standing up to show support. But not for long.

Almost as soon as the news was out, a FOX employee and others affiliated with the local chapter of SPJ, starting writing letters to the ethics committee chairman questioning why the award was given when there was no outcome in our lawsuit.

To his credit, committee chairman Steve Geimann stood up for his decision and quoted the SPJ's code of ethics that says, "deny favored treatment to advertisers and special interests and resist their pressure to influence news coverage." He reminded the critics that the courtroom is not always the best place to find the truth, something any journalist should know.

Geimann may have made his point and fended off the weaker-willed SPJ leaders who didn't want to offend their Tampa chapter, but imagine our surprise when the SPJ's legal defense fund turned us down for a small stipend to help offset the six-figures we owed the lawyers who brought us our victory.

They had turned us down at first because the lawsuit could be construed as an employment dispute and, in any event, our claims had not been proven. But even after the jury ruled in our favor, SPJ offered no further support.

Steve even flew to Columbus, Ohio, to make our case before the group's board of directors at its national conference. When the group's legal fund chairman—Christine Tatum of the *Chicago Tribune*—told her fellow directors, "I don't think we want to be picking a fight with big news organizations over who they hire and fire and why," our fate was sealed. Although we finally got strong support from the Tampa-area directors and others, SPJ's president, president-elect, and others voted us down.

Some board members claimed they were troubled that this was not a First Amendment case but a labor dispute. Surely they knew that the First Amendment does not cover reporters inside a news organization. It is a protection to keep government from restricting a free press. When the press itself is willing to disregard its public trust and individual reporters who are employees stand up to stop it, it will *always* be "a labor dispute."

There are plenty of good journalists working today in places where they are pressured to put good journalism on the back burner of the stove of a fast-cooking corporation bent on maintaining profit margins not to be found in any other industry. We have heard from many of those fine reporters constantly conflicted about how to respond to pressure to slant the news everywhere from local community papers to big-city dailies and television networks.

The choices we made to resist orders to distort the news have proven much easier to make than to live with, but they must come from within the journalism community. How can anyone who calls himself or herself a journalist betray a trust that is the bond between all journalists and the public they serve?

Sadly, we see it being done with greater frequency throughout the so-called mainstream media, by honest people who fear they just cannot stand up and say no without facing the destruction of their careers and their families—and by lots of well-dressed people who just want to be on TV.

YOU GOTTA HAVE FRIENDS

On September 13, 2001, a number of well-known, megamedia companies became FOX's friends in the courtroom, filing an *amicus curiae** brief. The Belo Corporation, Cox Television, Gannett company, Media

---

*According to Merriam-Webster's Collegiate Dictionary, *amicus curiae* refers to a "professional person or organization that is not a party to a particular litigation but that is permitted by the court to advise it in respect to some matter of law that directly affects the case in question."

General, and Post-Newsweek stations, while not active participants in our litigation, added their voices in support of the defense — Rupert Murdoch's News Corporation.

Just what exactly were they supporting? Had anyone from these corporate newsrooms sat in during our trial, covered it for their news outlets, or even debated Steve and me at a journalism conference, I might be able to be convinced that the *issues* of journalism were the basis of this newfound friendship with FOX. But not a single representative from any one of these news organizations made such an effort. Not one of them ever filed a story on our case. Not once did they consult our lawyers. I shouldn't be surprised that this friendship is not about the *news* business, but the news *business.*

Stay out of our newsrooms, the *amici* (friends) argued. The First Amendment gives them the right to control what goes on behind the sacrosanct newsroom doors, they argued. But as they rallied round the flag, these media giants and their Washington, DC–based lobbyists were working vigorously behind the scenes to dismantle any government restrictions they didn't like, such as those limiting the number of television stations one owner can control, equal time for political candidates, and fairness and obscenity standards.

As the *friends* said, nearly forty states have whistle-blower laws, and this case could lead to many more editorial disputes being aired in the courtroom, and that wouldn't be good for business. (Read the *Amicus* brief and others on the www.foxbghsuit.com Web site.)

FOX and its media friends seemed to be ignoring what is getting them in trouble these days. Instead of joining forces to keep reporters in their place, they might fare better if they did a little soulsearching and got behind independent journalism forums where editorial voices, free of commercial concerns, can hear and decide internal disputes while ensuring that the corporations are acting in the public interest. This, in theory, is the FCC's role, but it has been years since that federal agency punished a broadcaster for not acting in the public interest. The FCC now spends most of its time doling out the public's airwaves to private owners who make the most convincing arguments. So, who is watching out for the public interest? Essentially, no one.

It's time for news corporations to take seriously the news end of the news. Maybe then viewers would catch on and start watching again, and reporters wouldn't have to put their jobs on the line and expose the internal workings of a news organization in open court, just to do their jobs properly.

Our competent appeals lawyers, Stuart Markman and Michael Finch, believe that this case will define whistle-blower labor law for private companies and will likely make its way to the Florida Supreme Court. Certainly, FOX will take it there if it loses this first round.

MY FUNNY VALENTINE

It was Valentine's Day 2003. My daughter, Alyx, and I made one of our rare trips from Florida to visit Steve in Detroit. The bitter-cold nine-degree weather felt like a knife cutting through our exposed hands and heads.

Our little family was firmly ensconced in the warmth of Mongolian Barbeque in trendy Royal Oak. We sat down before our bowls of hot vegetables sautéed with the meats, tofu, sauces, and seeds from the buffet. Even Alyx would eat here, which was something of a small miracle.

Steve had a sheepish look on his face. "Do you want to see it now?" he asked. Naturally, I thought, it's Valentine's Day and he's going to hand me a small box with a trinket of his appreciation. All right, I didn't really think that that was likely, but it did occur to me that I *might* think that.

Instead, what I got was news that was nine months in the making. Steve pulled out a document from his coat pocket. The Second District Court of Appeal in Florida had issued its decision that morning while Alyx and I were on a plane. "Cut to the chase," I said, grabbing it, my eyes scanning as fast as I could absorb the words. I turned to the last paragraph on page six—the kicker:

> Accordingly, we reverse the judgment in her favor and remand for entry of a judgment in favor of WTVT. Reversed and remanded.

Reversed and remanded. Reversed and remanded. The victory we fought so hard for had been overturned. The $425,000 the court had ordered FOX to pay us was gone. Gone was the opportunity to collect legal fees from FOX that would have paid our lawyers. And FOX could claim it had its good name back. All because of a technical victory on an obscure point of law.

Remanded meant it would be sent back to the lower court to erase the five weeks of work the jurors had committed to us, to be entered now as a *victory* for FOX. Kelly, Green, and Casanueva — the three wise judges — knew better than six jurors who had listened to the evidence.

What the Second District Court of Appeal decided was that since the FCC's news distortion policy had never been "adopted" as a law, rule, or regulation, there is no protection for news employees who blow the whistle on that gross violation under Florida law:

> While WTVT has raised a number of challenges to the judgment obtained by Akre, we need not address each challenge because we find as a threshold matter that Akre failed to state a claim under the whistle-blower's statute.

The judges took the easy road. And they took nine months to issue an opinion that could have been written in a day if it was so crystal clear. Hanging their robes on the "threshold" issue meant they never had to open the door to the heart of the issue — news distortion by FOX and whether the media conglomerate retaliated against an employee who fought FOX management's efforts to slant, distort, and falsify a story.

What struck me was how disposed the judges appeared toward FOX, evident in how they characterized the torturous editing process:

> Each time the station asked Wilson and Akre to provide supporting documentation for statements in the story or to make changes in the content of the story, the reporters accused the station of attempting to distort the story to favor the manufacturer of BGH.

The opinion was written by Judge Patricia J. Kelly, who was appointed to the Second District Court of Appeal by Gov. Jeb Bush, and who began serving in December of 2001.

And the three-judge panel was very mindful of the effect their ruling could have on other Florida *employers* (remember, the Florida Chamber of Commerce signed on as a Friend of the Court as did five major news organizations):

> Recognizing an uncodified agency policy developed through the adjudicative process as the equivalent of a formally adopted rule is not consistent with this policy, and it would expand the scope of conduct that could subject an employer to liability beyond what Florida's legislature could have contemplated when it enacted the whistle-blower's statute.

My lawyers had argued that there were various ways to adopt a law, rule, or regulation outside of codifying it, publishing it, putting it up for public discussion and then statutorily defining it, and adopting it through the legislative process. In Florida a *policy* that describes the procedure or practice of an agency and is enforceable is, nonetheless, a form of law, and this case was tried under Florida law, not federal, a fine point of the law that eluded Judge Kelly.

Besides, FOX had made the, "law, rule, or regulation," argument at least a half dozen times to avoid trial. Four judges had rejected that argument, and it was rejected each time. Finally, FOX found a sympathetic ear — six of them, actually.

What a slap in the face to the public. You can no longer assume that broadcasters, using your commodity — the airwaves — free of charge, won't lie to you. FOX and its media Friends of the Court are essentially thumbing their collectives noses at the FCC, underscoring the commission's reticence to enforce its own policies, procedures, and rules and begging the question: If the FCC can't regulate broadcasters, who or what can?

BUT WAIT! THERE'S MORE!

A couple of days later, the judges issued the kicker:

BY ORDER OF THE COURT:

Appellant Steve Wilson's motion for attorney's fees is denied.

And on another page:

BY ORDER OF THE COURT:

Appellant's motion for attorney's fees is granted in an amount to be set by the trial court.

There was one of these for each of us. FOX's motion to collect from us attorney's fees that they'd amassed while filing their appeal of my victory, had been granted. Suddenly, the hounds were being chased by the FOX.

We devised a plan with our attorneys. We'd appeal to Judges Green, Kelly, and Casanueva to allow the entire panel of judges in the second district, fourteen in all, to hear the case *en banc*, as it's called. Together, we hoped, they would come to a saner conclusion. If they opted not to do that, we would then ask that our case be certified as one of great public importance and that the Florida Supreme Court be allowed to hear its merits. Our appeal would ask them to consider whether whistle-blowers should ever be saddled with the other side's legal fees.

In the past, the Florida Supreme Court had consistently and liber-ally construed the whistle-blower law in favor of *employees* to give them the widest possible remedy through the courts. Otherwise, it's a dagger through the heart of any potential whistle-blower. Who in their right mind would come forward if there were a possibility that they would have to bear the entire weight of the other side's legal expenses — even if they *won* at trial?

As for the "no law, rule, or regulation against news distortion" issue — going back to the same judges seemed futile. They made their preferences very clear. No veil of ignorance would suddenly lift from their eyes. To pursue it, we'd be throwing good money after bad for an indeterminate period of time.

Just short of Valentine's Day 2004 (they must like this date), Steve got a brief, terse answer:

> Appellant's motions for rehearing, clarification, rehearing en banc and certification of question of great public importance are denied.

Our avenue to get Steve's case before the Florida Supreme Court had been denied. And the court let stand Steve's burden to pay FOX's appel-late fees, which could run into the hundreds of thousands of dollars.

Three weeks later, my ruling said that I should *not* be on the hook for FOX's appeals costs even though my case lacked legal merit, and in direct contradiction to numerous trial judges who let it continue to trial on its merits. But I was denied an opportunity to take the issue of public importance before the Florida Supreme Court.

And the judges cut FOX some slack by lowering the burden it had to meet to eventually collect on trial costs:

> On remand, the trial court will have to make its own determination regarding whether to award trial court attorney's fees to WTVT as the prevailing party. To be entitled to such an award, however, WTVT does not have to demonstrate that Akre's suit was frivolous. No further motions for rehearing will be entertained.

Murdoch's lawyers had spared no expense flying first class to more than seventy depositions, billing at least $525 an hour, staying in the best hotels, hiring trial consultants, and booking the entire top floor of a hotel near our court to prepare for trial. Now, the court said, we could be on the hook for those expenses, too, if the trial judge grants it. What better way to make an example of two former, disgruntled employees?

It took FOX one month to submit its tab. The trial, they said, should cost us $1.5 million. Add in the fees/costs for Steve's appeal, and we are at $1,698,465.92. The ninety-two cents is a nice touch.

HOLD THE PRESSES!

Just as soon as we put one version of this story to bed, there's an update. That's the way it's been for the almost eight years and counting that we've been on the receiving end of a steady stream of painful reminders that we live under a cloud of litigation that shapes our lives everyday.

The latest news comes four years to the day, even to the hour, of my whistle-blower victory in court. At an August 18 2004, hearing, Florida Circuit Judge Vivian Maye decided that Steve and I do not have to pay FOX nearly two million dollars in trial fees. That was the amount FOX requested as "reasonable" reimbursement for the millions it says it spent defending itself from our charges that the "We Report, You Decide" network falsifies the news.

That was good news, but we are not off the hook. Still pending is whether FOX is entitled to about sixty thousand dollars in appellate costs for me and nearly forty thousand dollars in trial level costs for both of us. And the Second District Court of Appeal—the FOX-friendly appellate division that overturned our initial courtroom victory—has decided that Steve absolutely must reimburse his appellate costs and fees of more than one hundred thousand dollars, largely because he lost at trial. The only thing left to mediate is exactly how much.

So let's tally up the cost for practicing good journalism here. We spent hundreds of thousands of dollars to get to trial. We win at trial and then lose in a questionable ruling that any decent news organization should be embarrassed to voice. Then we have to pay the FOX distorter-reporters after eight years of litigation. Then there's all the time spent away from our daughter, career loss from becoming radioactive, loss of future earnings, stress to our fragile relationship, and health problems for Steve.

We did the right thing for the right reason, and I stand by that and all of its implications. But still, I'm outraged. I'm outraged that among journalists there is no outrage. I'm outraged that no journalism organizations came to our side as friends of the court and outraged that journalists continue to be blind to and mute about the implications of this ruling: that journalist whistle-blowers can be saddled with huge costs after winning before a jury, and that there is "no law, rule, or regulation" against news distortion.

HELLO? IS ANYONE HOME?

Do journalists remember why they got into the field? To challenge the status quo, right wrongs, uncover truths hiding in dark places. I know it's not fashionable to get too passionate about anything, but what journalism needs is a good kick in the butt. Ask yourself if you still have any outrage left. Follow it. It might be good for your journalist's soul and remind you who you are. To fail to be outraged at something like this might ultimately be the worst punishment of all. I know I'm just getting started.

Read the decisions at http://www.2dca.com/ by clicking on Opinions; the dates are February 14, 2003, and February 25, 2004, or go to http://www.foxbghsuit.com.

A NOTE ON SOURCES

The story of rBGH began long before I began looking into it in November 1996. For many years, before and after its approval, citizens and scientists have tracked its progress through the system. Monsanto studied the genetically engineered hormone as an animal drug for about a decade, and some of those studies have been made available. The source notes on rBGH studies were among the dozens used to research the original story.

The controversy over rBGH has traveled recently to Canada and the European Union, both of which decided to reject the drug for use in those countries. Numerous articles have been written on the international rejection of rBGH. Since our departure from FOX, Steve and I have conducted an interview with the Health Canada regulators, who spoke of pressure from Monsanto to approve the drug, and Richard Burroughs, formerly of the FDA.

In addition, more than seventy-three depositions taken in preparation for trial yielded some helpful information on what happened to this story within FOX and why. Depositions were conducted on Roger Ailes of FOX News; Dave Boylan, general manager for FOX, now in Los Angeles; Phil Metlin, news director; as well as many FOX employees who were at the station at the time we worked there. In addition, a Monsanto spokesman was deposed as well as several lawyers for FOX, a couple of dairy farmers, and the dairy scientist at the University of Florida. These depositions are part of the court record, and the majority of them have been videotaped. The threatening letters from Monsanto are also part of the public record, attached as Exhibits C and E in the case of *Steve Wilson and Jane Akre* v. *New World Communications of Tampa, Inc., a Florida Corporation d/b/a WTVT Channel 13*, Tampa. FOX 13 is a wholly owned subsidiary of News Corporation.

In this chapter, I mention the Food Lion verdict. It is well known within America's newsrooms for having had an immense, chilling effect on investigative reporting. In this case, producers for ABC News obtained jobs working at deli counters and meat handling areas of Food Lion stores in South Carolina and North Carolina. Viewers of an ABC *PrimeTime Live* program that was broadcast in November 1992, saw hidden camera video of Food Lion employees repackaging and redating fish, grinding expired beef with fresh beef, and applying barbeque sauce to old chicken to mask the smell.

Food Lion sued ABC and was awarded $5.5 million in January 1997, though that was drastically reduced later. In this case, the methods of newsgathering were on trial more than the story. The case was precedent-setting in that Food Lion won without having to prove that the news report in question was false and malicious.

NOTES

1. David S. Kronfeld, "Recombinant Bovine Somatotropin: Ethics of Communication and Animal Welfare," *Swedish Veterinary Journal* (1997); Michael K. Hansen, "Biotechnology and Milk: Benefit or Threat? An Analysis of Issues Related to BGH/BST Use in the Dairy Industry," Mount Vernon,

N.Y., Consumers Union/Consumer Policy Institute, 1990; Freedom of Information Summary, Animal Sciences Division of Monsanto Company, November 1983.

2. Judith C. Juskevich and C. Greg Guyer, "Bovine Growth Hormone Food Safety Evaluation," *Science* 249 (1990): 875–84; "NIH Technology Assessment Conference Statement on Bovine Somatotropin," *Journal of the American Medical Association* 265, no. 11 (1991): 1423–25; William H. Daughaday and David M. Barbano, "Bovine Somatotropin Supplementation of Dairy Cows: Is the Milk Safe?" *Journal of the American Medical Association* 264, no. 8 (1990): 1003–1005; C. G. Prosser et al., "Increased Secretion of Insulin-like Growth Factor-1 into Milk of Cows Treated with Recombinantly Derived Bovine Growth Hormone," *Journal of Dairy Science* 56 (1989): 1726; T. B. Mepham, "Public Health Implications of Bovine Somatotropin Use in Dairying: Siscussion [sic] Paper," *Journal of the Royal Society of Medicine* 85 (December 1992): 736–39; "Residues of Some Veterinary Drugs in Animals and Foods," Monograph prepared by the Fortieth Meeting of the Joint FAO/WHO Expert Committee of Food Additives, Geneva, June 1992; Michael Hansen, "Potential Public Health Impacts of the Use of Recombinant Bovine Somatotropin in Dairy Production," Prepared for a Scientific Review by the Joint Expert Committee of Food Additives, Consumer Policy Institute, September 1997.

3. Samuel S. Epstein, "Unlabeled Milk from Cows Treated with Biosynthetic Growth Hormones: A Case of Regulatory Abdication," *International Journal of Health Sciences* 26, no. 1 (1996): 173–85; Robert Cohen, *Milk the Deadly Poison* (Englewood Cliffs, NJ: Argus, 1997); Final Scientific Report of the Committee for Veterinary Medicinal Products on the application for marketing authorization submitted by the Eli Lilly company, January 1993 (Lilly was planning to market for Monsanto in Europe); Evaluation of Certain Veterinary Drug Residues in Food, FAO/WHO Expert Committee on Food Additives, Geneva, 1993.

4. Richard Burroughs, interview by author, New York, 2000.

5. Patrick Jasperse, "Monsanto Accused of Coercion Fighting 'BGH-free Labels,' " *Milwaukee Journal*, February 1994; Robert Steyer, "BST Has the Mail Moving on Ads, Monsanto Writes Warning Letters," *St. Louis Post-Dispatch*, February 1994; Associated Press, "Hormone to Debut with Debate as the Milk Booster Goes on Sale," *Orlando Sentinel*, February 1994; Letter to dairy farmer Joe Gore from Monsanto's Robert Deaking, US Operations, Monsanto, February 1994.

6. See note on sources.

7. John Walsh letter to Roger Ailes, 21 February 1997, Exhibit C, *Steve Wilson and Jane Akre v. New World Communications of Tampa, Inc., a Florida Corporation d/b/a WTVT Channel 13*, Tampa (a wholly owned subsidiary of News Corporation); John Walsh letter to Roger Ailes, 28 February 1997, Exhibit E in above case.

CHAPTER II

THE STORY NO ONE WANTED TO HEAR

J. ROBERT PORT

Bob Port joined the New York Daily News *as an investigative reporter in July 2000. He has published stories there about garment sweatshops, conflicts of interest among judges, and campaign-finance excesses during Hillary Clinton's senate race. In 1999, he became a senior editor at APBnews.com (All Points Bulletin News), a news Web site covering crime, safety, and justice. His work won an Investigative Reporters and Editors special citation for investigative reporting. In 1995, Port joined the Associated Press (AP) in New York as special assignments editor in charge of a team of national reporters working on investigative projects. He started and supervised the AP investigation of the Korean War massacre that occurred at No Gun Ri in July 1950. His staff's report on No Gun Ri won the Pulitzer Prize for investigative reporting and the George Polk Award for international reporting in 2000. His staff's earlier projects won the AP Managing Editor's award for national enterprise reporting in 1996, 1997, and 1998. Before joining AP, Port worked for twelve years at the* St. Petersburg Times *in Florida, where he led special projects and introduced the newspaper to computer-assisted reporting. His work included stories about illegal gun dealing, inflated payroll-cutting claims by Florida's governor, and teachers with criminal records. He was one of four* Times *reporters who received the Society of Professional Journalists' 1991 National Distinguished Service Award for investigative reporting for a series about abuses in the sealing of criminal records in Florida.*

I n the life of an investigative reporter, at least one who is devoted
to his craft and pursues it for altruistic reasons, there come certain
awful, lonely moments of realization—those rare times when you
stumble upon something you know in your gut, or you think you
know, is not just news, but terribly important news.

You literally tremble when you discover some document you recognize to be a smoking gun. Your hand shakes as you scribble down
quotes from some whistle-blower finally summoning up the nerve to
say what he really knows. You realize people could be hurt seeing the
ugly truth in print, and that you, as the messenger, will probably be
attacked, but you are compelled to tell the story as fairly as you can.
You do this because it is your profession and because you long ago
decided that this pursuit of knowledge, however imperfect, however
unprofitable, is a wiser choice for all of us than secrecy or ignorance.

To keep perspective, you frighten yourself by typesetting a
ninety-point headline in your mind, testing how much power its
words can accurately convey. These moments of realization are like a
head-on highway collision, where your life passes before you. You
imagine in an instant a cascade of consequences your news will likely
set in motion—and whether you still are up to the task.

For me, such a moment came one evening in April 1998, as I
worked late, which I often did then, in my tiny, windowless office—
crammed with spartan steel furniture and buzzing computer
screens—on the fifth floor of the headquarters of the Associated Press
(AP) in New York City's Rockefeller Center. The hundreds who work
there, thanklessly I must say, call it "50 Rock."

The AP is a factory of news that beams an endless stream of words
and pictures by satellite into nearly every newspaper and television
station in America. It has an unmatched reach around the globe. Few
people realize the AP's telecommunications infrastructure carries all
the other major news wires of the United States, too: the *New York
Times* wire, the *Washington Post* wire, Gannett News Service, Knight-
Ridder's wire—even what remains of United Press International
(UPI), the AP's head-to-head competitor that suffered a financial collapse more than a decade ago—all feed their news into the same
"wire." The AP's.

The AP itself is a nonprofit corporation owned by its members,
who are essentially all the news organizations of America. It has

almost nothing in assets, save the computers and telephones its reporters use. Yet with the First Amendment to shield it from the government and UPI out of the picture, it has achieved, in effect, a unique status—that of a constitutionally protected, tax-exempt monopoly. And it wields great power. By deciding what to publish and what to ignore, the AP, perhaps more than any single news outlet, can define what is news. If it speaks loudly enough, it cannot, itself, be ignored.

It also decides what places are newsworthy enough to keep reporters on hand. It is, for instance, today the only Western news-gathering organization with a full-time bureau in Korea.

In New York in 1998, I was the AP's special assignment editor, given the job three years earlier of leading a new team of national writers devoted to investigative projects. I worked for the executive editor, who answered to the AP's president. It was a gritty place to work, with more than its share of petty rivalries, egos, and squabbles. It was a place filled with excellent journalists, but unfortunately for me, it was also a place whose leaders seemed not the least bit interested in the pursuit of investigative reporting for the good of democracy. At the AP, the emphasis is on simple stories and neutrality.

The day before my moment of reckoning at the AP, I had quietly shipped off my investigative team's researcher to the National Archives complex in College Park, Maryland, a gigantic warehouse of mostly military records, to check out a war atrocity claim being pressed—nearly fifty years after the fact—by a couple dozen South Korean citizens. I say "quietly" because I didn't want my bosses to know what I was doing—or what it might likely cost and how long it would take to do it. I assumed they would shut it down. A few days earlier, a local hire, as the AP calls its nonunion foreign laborers overseas, had transmitted an eight hundred-word feature from our bureau in Seoul to the busy International Desk in New York. The writer was Sang-hun Choe (pronounced "Shay"), a young Korean reporter, well thought of and backed up by the editing of a veteran bureau chief, Reid Miller. Tom Wagner in Tokyo, the AP's chief of Asia news, had read the piece, considered it significant and was prepared to devote more resources to it.

Choe described the latest of several futile legal hearings in the saga of a war reparations claim that had remained hidden within South Korea for decades. The claim had begun making local TV news after a newly elected president began to end the suppression of free speech imposed by previous regimes. The French wire service, Agence France-Presse, had noted the case briefly on its wires some months earlier, but the AP had yet to move a word on it. And this story was no trifling matter. It was an accusation from supposed eye-witnesses that US warplanes and US soldiers had deliberately gunned down some four hundred South Korean civilians—women, children, babies, and old men—in the fifth week of the Korean War. The AP's deputy international editor, Kevin Noblet, had given me Choe's copy, with a request: Anything we can do here, meaning within the United States, to confirm this? Noblet was looking for results he might pub-lish within a week or two.

As I sat in my office that evening, my hands trembled as I banged out an answer to a sketchy e-mail from my researcher, Randy Her-schaft. He was at his laptop, working late, too, at the miserable Best Western Motel in College Park, checking-in after a hard day.

His persistence had paid off. "Fax me the thing," I told him. When I saw it, I couldn't believe my eyes.

That day, Herschaft had leafed through dozens of boxes filled with mundane military paperwork from the Korean War, material routinely declassified when it became more than thirty years old, yet never closely studied by anyone—some of it was still bundled in its original brown wrapping and twine as when it was shipped from Japan decades earlier.

There, he found a most remarkable memorandum issued July 27, 1950, by a US Army commander—in the fifth week of the Korean War, the very time when, our South Koreans alleged, US forces had gunned down scores of their fellow villagers.[1] In the memo, Maj. Gen. William Kean, referring to a map that highlighted more than one hundred square miles of central Korea—including the site of the alleged massacre, behind the US front lines—instructed his twenty-fifth Infantry Division thusly: "All civilians seen in this area are to be treated as enemy and action taken accordingly." Herschaft had seen more explicit documents describing similar orders authorizing the shooting of civilians, including a radio message from commanders of the Army's First Cavalry Division recorded as "No refugees to cross the front lines. Fire everyone trying to cross lines. Use discretion in case of women and children."

Herschaft had nailed down another critical fact.

The complaining South Koreans had been surprisingly specific in their accusation. Not just any soldiers, they said, but the Army's First

Cavalry Division had machine-gunned their kin at a railroad bridge on certain dates. In a written denial of their claim, the US Army had been equally specific, saying there was no "evidence to show the US First Cavalry Division was in the area where the shooting allegedly occurred."[2] Well, not so. Herschaft found that units of the First Cavalry Division were all around the area where the shooting had allegedly occurred—and this according to the army's official history from that period of the war, a bound reference book that would be a schoolboy's first stop in checking the day-by-day whereabouts of an army unit during a war.[3]

Could this possibly be, I thought, what it appeared to be?

I knew it would require a massive commitment of time and resources to nail down a worthwhile story, and one suitable for the AP wire. An army division consists of thousands of men, and we had no idea what unit—what regiment, what battalion, or what company— might have veterans who would remember, much less discuss anything. My only reference point for weighing the value of such an effort was the My Lai massacre.

I was forty-three. I had grown up with Vietnam on television constantly. I had watched my cousin, Gerry Coghlan, head off to that undeclared war and then seen his photograph in *Life* magazine on my mother's coffee table. He was carrying the bloodied body of his buddy from the jungle. It affected me. In high school, I had read Seymour Hersh's stories exposing the My Lai massacre—fully a year after it had occurred. To me, Hersh was a war hero. The army was a threat to our national security—more so for trying to keep My Lai secret, than for letting it happen.

Bias has no place in good journalism, but neither does blind patriotism, and I'm not ashamed to acknowledge I make moral judgments as an investigative journalist. The death of the innocent in war is one subject where I believe journalists owe it to their readers to ferret out facts, precisely because the deliberate killing of the innocent is so wrong. I believe the execution of civilians for the convenience of battle, particularly in a war over ideology, as Vietnam was, is especially heinous, inhuman, and evil. It is un-American and Nazi-like. To judge any individual's acts in wartime, particularly those of the lowly foot soldier, is a dangerous game of second-guessing, but massacres, as events, are to be learned from and studied—not hushed up—so that we all might avoid the mistakes of history.

That was my state of mind as I approached this story. If this made me more advocate than journalist—a charge I heard repeatedly in my tenure at the AP—I plead guilty, but I don't think it did. I can write an objective news account. I do admit it, though: I am politically opposed to having soldiers kill babies in secret. Do you know anyone who is in favor of that?

Here, from the forgotten war in Korea, another undeclared Asian conflict, we had more than just Lt. William Calley terminating suspected Viet Cong sympathizers. We had documents reflecting orders to kill civilians, and these orders were issued by generals to thousands of young soldiers in retreat, who would have been expected to unthinkingly obey. I had served a four-year enlistment in the US Air Force, albeit in the peacetime after Vietnam. I knew how the military worked. My God, I thought. What kind of hell was this war in Korea? I had read nothing of this in history class.

I knew we needed to do considerably more reporting, but I don't believe in coincidence, such as secret instructions to shoot refugees having no connection to refugees who independently assert from the opposite side of the planet that they were then shot. And how, I wondered, could the army be so dead wrong in its formal rebuttal to a massacre allegation. Indifference? Negligence? Deception, perhaps? Is there another explanation?

Only a fool, it seemed to me, or someone so biased by loyalty to country—someone who couldn't conceive of the US military doing anything wrong or someone who didn't wish to encourage a discussion of it—would not see this as news: archival evidence that bolstered, even if it did not confirm, a claim of a massacre clung to by South Korean peasants all their lives. We had unearthed documents, inaccessible to historians for decades, showing that entire army divisions were told to kill civilians on sight, an apparent large-scale violation of the law of war. This alone struck me as newsworthy. Those documents were unprecedented pieces of US military history, we would soon learn from a West Point professor who teaches the subject of war crimes to army cadets. And we had the army, confronted with a specific allegation of refugees being shot, publishing a defense that was demonstrably false.

I ask you: If that isn't news, even forty-eight years later, then what is?

I also recalled that it was actually the AP, not Hersh, which first transmitted news of the My Lai incident. A description of the killing was filed to the AP's "B wire," which carries nondeadline news and mostly features. It moved not too long after My Lai occurred. But the news was played down, lacking in detail, and no one particularly noticed it in the crush of other news from Vietnam.

The AP, it seemed to me, had failed in its duty to its readers once before.

I decided to put everything I had — if necessary, every dime left in my $100,000-a-year budget for investigations — and what little staff I could spare into this one story. I decided to pursue the project full bore, to try to answer every question that could practically be answered.

There was one problem: The people who ran the AP. The people I worked for. I knew they would not share my enthusiasm. It turned out to be even worse.

What followed — four months of intense reporting and writing, then more than a year of argument over whether or how to publish the story — became the most frustrating experience of my career.

Some seventeen months later, in September 1999, to its credit, the AP finally published "The Bridge at No Gun Ri." For their efforts, the reporters received the Pulitzer Prize for investigative reporting, the only investigative Pulitzer in AP's history.

Yet before the series had hit the wire, I, the editor who had launched the project, nurtured it, and become its relentless proponent within the AP's executive news staff, found myself out of a job. My position and my department were dissolved. Not sure the AP would ever run the story, I resigned in June 1999. I had been transferred to the AP's communications department. I was demoted to a position that could best be described as chief computer repairman for the newsroom.

What's worse, four years at the AP — with every project I proposed meeting constant internal resistance, even while my staff's work won award after award — had eroded my idealism as an investigative reporter and editor. The AP's president wasn't letting me hire anyone. I had been forced to accept a sad reality of the American news business today: Some of our biggest, most trusted news organizations simply lack the courage, the will, or the leadership to consistently do the work necessary to expose the truth about the most controversial subjects in our world, the AP's belated publication of "No Gun Ri" not withstanding.

The truth is, to publish "The Bridge at No Gun Ri," the AP had to be dragged kicking and screaming every step of the way. Attacks on the story that came later, orchestrated by army veterans with ruffled feathers, have left many people thinking it was somehow made up, when in fact, nothing could be further from the truth.

Armed with intriguing documents, in May 1998, I sent Herschaft and my best reporter, Martha Mendoza, back to the National Archives to comb through every shred of paper available. We obtained military maps from the war, had them copied, and coated the office walls until the Special Assignment Team suite looked like a war room. Radio logs and other records, which recorded dates, times, and coordinates, were used to pinpoint the whereabouts of dozens of different army units. The maps made it clear that one of four army regiments had to be the one at No Gun Ri when any shooting of refugees would have occurred. The unit turned out to be the Seventh Cavalry—the regiment of George Custer and Wounded Knee.

We used veteran groups and eventually unit rosters obtained from the National Archives military personnel records in St. Louis, Missouri, to build a catalog of veterans who might know anything about No Gun Ri. Noblet and the AP's international staff sent Choe searching Korea for more interviews and more details. The international staff tossed in the best reporter and writer it could offer: Charles Hanley, the AP's senior foreign correspondent.

Hanley and Mendoza began phoning veterans cold. Within days they hit upon people who remembered bits and pieces about No Gun Ri. I put them on airplanes to visit anyone who would talk and to question the commanding officers we had located. I wanted face-to-face interviews, and I wanted each reporter to be a separate witness to the others and to what was said. I required interview notes to be typed into a database we all shared. I sent Herschaft to any library that might have anything—the Truman Library in Independence, Missouri, the Army War College in Carlisle, Pennsylvania, and many more trips to College Park. He read every newspaper, magazine, and book from the period he could locate, spending days in front of microfilm machines at the New York Public Library.

It was a massive undertaking. It was beginning to cost a bundle, and yet I was managing to keep the scale of our efforts below my boss' radar. Within a few months, we had burned through more than $30,000 in travel and computer research expenses. So long as any one trip stayed below $5,000, I was authorized to sign off without the executive editor's okay. He seemed to care little about the details of what we were doing.

By late July 1998, we had produced a draft of the main story, with several veterans on the record acknowledging that they had shot hundreds of South Korean refugees at a railroad bridge. Some recalled the orders that no one was to cross the front lines. One machine gunner gave a chilling account of shooting into the crowd. There were, predictably, conflicts in their specific recollections, though on the essential events, they agreed. I gave the draft of the story to my boss, the executive editor, Bill Ahearn. We held a meeting. It quickly grew into an argument.

Ahearn challenged every fact—just what we expected and wanted. But he began to question the nature and the newsworthiness of the subject. Hanley, Ahearn said afterward, was "in love with the story" and could not be trusted. The memories of soldiers would likely never be reliable material for an AP piece, he said. Still, Ahearn was willing to see more.

With nearly each week, another veteran with knowledge of No Gun Ri was located. Experts weighed in. By August, a second, cleaner draft was in Ahearn's hands. He ripped into it. It was too definitive in stating what occurred. He challenged every assertion of anything resembling a massacre. He eventually demanded to review all interview notes, then misinterpreted many of them—statements from soldiers who were nowhere near the shooting, people we had called while searching for people who knew something—to be evidence refuting the story.

I asked to send my two reporters, who by now wanted to see the scene and compare the accounts of soldiers to those of survivors located by Choe, to Korea. It was a trip that would have cost a few thousand dollars at most, money I had in my budget. I thought it prudent. Ahearn refused to allow it.

Mendoza began to lose patience. She had moved to New York to work for me but was finding the cost of living in Brooklyn too high for her husband and two sons. The pay at the AP in New York City is among the worst for journalists there. I begged to get her a raise, something only possible with approval from the AP's president. I got no response. Mendoza asked to transfer to an opening in the AP's San Jose, California, bureau, near her husband's family. I had lost my best reporter.

I was accused of practicing "gotcha journalism." Hanley, the lead writer, was made to revise the No Gun Ri story sixteen times under Ahearn's direction, mostly in ways that played down or obscured what we had found. We were ordered to give the story a feature lead and tone. By Thanksgiving, Ahearn appeared to be stalling, going for weeks at a time avoiding me, not answering e-mails, and not returning telephone calls. When pressed for some word on the story's fate before Christmas 1998, following one stretch of silence, he began yelling at me furiously, accusing me of trying to pressure him into releasing the piece before it was ready.

It became clear to me that he didn't think what we had belonged on the AP wire. Instead he seemed to see it as big trouble.

Through late summer of 1999, newspapers were filled with news of attacks on a Cable News Network (CNN) report on Operation Tailwind. By fall the subject was fodder for journalism trade magazines. The CNN report, meant to launch a new evening news show, had been narrated by Peter Arnett, a former AP correspondent in Vietnam. CNN claimed that Special Forces in Vietnam had used deadly sarin nerve gas in a secret operation to rescue prisoners held in Laos—a stunning revelation, if true. It turned out the story didn't hold up under independent review.

It seemed clear to me that CNN's story was nothing like what we were doing and that its reporting methods fell far short of our own. There were no official documents. Critical sources for CNN were off-the-record. We had startling official documents. I had insisted everything be on the record. None of that mattered. Heads were rolling at CNN. It was time to keep your head down at the AP.

I learned that Ahearn carried ghosts from a war of his own. He'd been an army captain in Vietnam. I asked him if he'd ever killed civilians. Without answering me directly, he described how men would hear a sound at night in a nearby swamp and fire into the darkness, only to find it was a family hunting for frogs to eat. He stared out into the skating rink at Rockefeller Center. I dropped the subject.

After Christmas 1999, I prepared a detailed report with an analysis and summary of our research, including maps and photographs. I attached documents, interview excerpts and the names, birth dates, addresses and telephone numbers of a dozen veterans, plus the names of a dozen Korean survivors speaking about the shooting on the record. I had all but given up. I was weary of trying to explain our investigative effort to editors unwilling or unable to take the time to absorb the complexity and difficulty of the information. I wanted something I could distribute inside the AP—or outside if it came to that—to let others with no prejudice toward our work size it up for themselves. Ahearn said he would give me a decision, but he wanted to consult Lou Boccardi, the president of the AP.

After studying my report, without explanation, Ahearn ordered the story killed. When I appealed to Boccardi, he informed me by e-mail that he agreed with his executive editor's assessment. When I met with him, he summoned Ahearn, who said nothing during a long conversation. Boccardi said he felt the story, as written, belonged in *Rolling Stone* magazine. He said to be suitable for the wire, it needed to lose its prosecutorial tone and be reduced to one story of nine hundred words or less. He said a paragraph needed to be inserted high in the copy describing atrocities committed by North Korea during the war—a subject we had summarized in a sidebar. He said that once reduced to that extent, it wouldn't be much of a story, and he'd be in favor of just dropping it.

"You make these soldiers look like criminals," Boccardi said during the meeting. I had seen it differently. If anything, I thought we had made generals, or perhaps America's Cold War foreign policy in general look criminal—and done so by presenting facts, documents, and the statements of witnesses and experts.

"This is the kind of story," I said, "the *New York Times* would put on its front page."

He was unconvinced. I warned him that his reporters were ready to take their work elsewhere and that this story would eventually come out. He said that if other reporters did the story and hosannas fell upon them, that would be fine with him. I said that if he killed the project, I would not be able to defend his decision. I suggested a solution. Bring in a totally fresh editor, who knows nothing about the subject and who is agreeable to everyone involved, to rework the copy until he, Boccardi, and the reporters reached consensus.

Let's think about it a day was Boccardi's reaction.

It's the last conversation he and I have ever had.

The next day I learned that Jon Wolman, former Washington bureau chief, named by Boccardi the previous fall to be the AP's new managing editor, would take charge of the story. Wolman and I discussed who could be a fresh editor. It took weeks to learn it would be Noblet, who, Wolman announced to me, would rework the project while continuing his duties on the International Desk.

Months of rewriting and rereporting began anew. Reporting to Wolman, Noblet rewrote the main story using the reporters' notes and documents, occasionally asking questions. The reporters were barred from seeing his work until top editors cleared it. Hanley was enraged. When he and Mendoza saw the copy, it told a story they felt made it appear no one was sure what had happened at No Gun Ri. Hanley said it was dishonest and unacceptable. Noblet was caught in the middle. Hanley became a pariah, avoided by management and left to guess for long stretches of time what would happen to his months of work.

I learned my fate. Wolman announced a reorganization of the news staff. His place for me: systems editor. I would be in charge of editing terminals in New York. I had built up considerable skill and a reputation for using computer records in investigative projects, but this seemed dumb. To stay employed, I agreed. I had begun looking for another job in journalism. I resigned a month later.

Leading up to publication, and after, the AP's top managers refused to even speak to Hanley, one of the wire service's most respected reporters worldwide—the author of its 150th anniversary history book—even as they rewrote the words under his byline. Noblet was forced to play intermediary. Hanley would speak to Noblet, who would carry his message to Wolman. Wolman would respond to Hanley's issues through Noblet. Hanley would e-mail or phone Boccardi. Boccardi wouldn't respond. Ahearn was being marginalized as Wolman was groomed to take his place. The atmosphere was surreal, but Hanley pressed relentlessly on.

Every AP bureau chief from Tokyo to Paris knew the AP was sitting on a major story. It became gossip. Hanley was ordered to reinterview anyone who would be quoted with an editor listening in on his conversation—the first time that practice was ever employed in the AP's history. Before publication, Wolman tried to order the AP's Web site to remove images of documents, maps, and videos of interviews that had been produced to bolster a special presentation of the story there. The Web site's editor, Jim Kennedy, refused. The Web version of the story later received Columbia University's Online Journalism Award.

Boccardi, Ahearn, and Wolman had made clear the word "massacre" would be censored from all AP copy—though dozens of newspapers using the story, including the *New York Times*, instinctively turned to that word to write their front-page headlines. Even when government officials, such as Secretary of Defense William Cohen, uttered the word in the context of "massacre" being an allegation, as opposed to a proven fact, the word was banished from the AP wire in connection with No Gun Ri. Soldiers who were there and who called it a massacre saw their quotes left unused. And when the AP ultimately won its Pulitzer, in the wire service's own story announcing its award, Boccardi, a member of the Pulitzer committee himself, personally sat at a news terminal and deleted every occurrence of the word used by the story's writer, who had taken it from the language of the Pulitzer committee's official press release.

In the end, the leadership of the AP could agree with its reporters on only one thing about the No Gun Ri story — the opening phrase of its lead, an artful sentence composed by Noblet that was as telling as he could make it. His words, "it was a story no one wanted to hear," were an intentional double entendre:

"It was a story no one wanted to hear: Early in the Korean War, villagers said, American soldiers machine-gunned hundreds of helpless civilians, under a railroad bridge in the South Korean countryside."

It often occurred to those of us working on this story what a thin thread had even made it possible: the AP's presence in Korea. A young reporter's curiosity. An investigative team ready to handle complicated research using military records. Having the time and the money to undertake in-depth reporting.

Today, there is no Special Assignment Team in New York and no special assignment editor. And what troubles me is this: What other stories like No Gun Ri are waiting out there to be told? And who at the AP will be working hard there to tell them?

NOTES

1. US Army Inspector General, "No Gun Ri Review," US Department of the Army, Washington, DC, January 2001, p. 37.

2. Charles Hanley, Martha Mendoza, and Sang-Hun Choe, "The Bridge at No Gun Ri," Associated Press, New York, September 29, 1999.

3. Roy E. Appleman, *United States Army in the Korean War: South of the Naktong, North to Yalu (June – November 1950)*, (1961; reprint, US Army Center of Military History: Washington, DC, 1992).

CHAPTER 12

VERDICT FIRST, EVIDENCE LATER
THE CASE FOR BOBBY GARWOOD

MONIKA JENSEN-STEVENSON

Monika Jensen-Stevenson is the author of Spite House:
The Last Secret of the War in Vietnam, *which was
optioned by Columbia Pictures, and coauthor of* Kiss the
Boys Goodbye. *A former Emmy-winning producer for
60 Minutes, Jensen-Stevenson has traveled throughout
Southeast Asia as a writer and reporter, lectured widely to
West Point cadets and veterans' organizations, and testi-
fied before the US Senate Select Committee on American
POWs. The Vietnam Veterans Coalition awarded her the
Vietnam Veterans National Medal. She is currently head
of programming for ichannel, Canada's premier digital
public affairs channel.*

W hen in his 1961 farewell speech to the nation Dwight D.
Eisenhower warned of the looming dangers of the military-industrial complex, he left the Fourth Estate out of the equation
and, consequently, out of the national discussion that ensued. Perhaps
he had a premonition that to warn against a military-industrial-*media*
complex would automatically preclude the kind of national discussion he wanted to engender. Even in 1961, an era now fondly
regarded as halcyon, no national discussion of any subject, even one

253

presented by the president, was possible without the participation of powerful media outlets like the *New York Times*. Eisenhower was probably aware that journalists—like most of us—have a great need to see themselves as heroic advocates of truth, the kind envisioned by Thomas Jefferson when he coined the name "Fourth Estate." Such high regard of one's own profession cannot easily absorb reality: that the profession is itself part of a potentially dangerous complex, and that it requires constant vigilance to maintain one's integrity.

Eisenhower warned, "Only an alert and knowledgeable citizenry can compel the proper meshing of the huge industrial and military machinery of defense with our peaceful methods and goals, so that security and liberty may prosper together." Yet he failed to mention how that could be achieved without a completely free and independent press divorced from that military-industrial complex he warned against. After all, his presidency oversaw the Joseph McCarthy debacle when hundreds of lives were destroyed in part because the media failed in its role to check and lend balance to an ego-driven senator who chaired a committee that was running amok. As a producer for CBS's *60 Minutes* during the eighties I was proud—as was the entire news division—that the only reporter with enough clout to "alert the citizenry" to McCarthy's demagoguery and with the integrity to take him on was CBS's own Edward R. Murrow, who had so brilliantly reported on WWII from England. None of us then paid much attention to the fact that Murrow had paid for taking on McCarthy against the wishes of CBS's administration. Afterward, Murrow's position was never again as secure or prominent as it had been before.

McCarthy's intimidation of the media was a harbinger of the future when the press would, with few exceptions, seamlessly mesh with the military-industrial complex Eisenhower warned against: The media leitmotiv, straight from the red queen in *Alice in Wonderland*, "Verdict First, Evidence Later." Less than five years after Eisenhower's speech, reporters would meekly mouth the Warren Commission's findings on JFK's assassination and defame anyone who dared to question those findings. When Oliver Stone, in the late eighties, dared to investigate what reporters should have investigated more than twenty years before, he was accused of being a conspiracy theorist and worse, before the first draft of his JFK screenplay was even completed. The attack on Stone was led by no less an institution than the august *Washington Post*. The press in all its modern manifestations, charged by Thomas Jefferson to keep the citizenry alert and knowledgeable had a new reason for being: itself. As guru Marshall McLuhan so aptly put it, "The medium has become the message."

For me, it was a hard lesson to learn that the medium to which I had dedicated myself often used its tremendous power to destroy ordinary citizens whose only currency was the constitutional guarantee of inalienable rights to life, liberty, and the pursuit of happiness and whose only protection of those rights was the truth made public. No one symbolizes this better than former Marine Private Robert R. Garwood—fourteen years a prisoner of the communist Vietnamese, who was found guilty of collaborating with the enemy in the longest court-martial in US history. I first heard of Garwood in 1979 when I worked for a Canadian news program. Wire reports referred to him as a defector whom the United States government—specifically the Marine Corps—was charging with being a traitor. Because I was an American who had recently moved to Canada, it was a story that interested me immensely, particularly when a few telephone calls to Marine Corps representatives in Washington made it clear that this was a defector who had gone far beyond simply going over to the other side ideologically. The Marine Corps directed me to high-ranking officers who said that Garwood was the first marine in history who had taken up arms against his own countrymen.

I was sorry to have to drop the story because it was not of enough interest to a Canadian audience, but I kept up with American news reports. Massive coverage was given to the court-martial. Out of hundreds of reports, only one report, in the *Daily News* on December 21, 1979, gave me pause. It hinted at "complexities behind the scenes," and went on to describe the case as "filled with moral ambiguities, and much of the testimony in the pre-court martial hearing at Camp Lejeune has been muddled. As a result the public perception seems to be one of confusion, combined with the uneasy feeling that a former POW [Prisoner of War] is being unfairly punished." But even this article like all others tipped the balance toward projecting Garwood as a known traitor when the reporter wrote, ". . . but unlike past cases of collaboration in Korea and Vietnam, which mainly involved propaganda activities, Bob Garwood is charged with having joined the enemy as a rifle carrying guerilla who took direct and hostile action against fellow Americans. As unwanted as the case is, it really can't be dismissed as if the charges, if true, are no more than understandable conduct under the circumstance."

At the end of the court-martial, there seemed no question that Garwood was a monstrous traitor who had been treated fairly and leniently by the government, particularly since he was initially charged with desertion, a crime that carries the death penalty by firing squad. Everything I learned from the media convinced me that desertion charges had been dropped in the interest of healing national wounds left by Vietnam. When I think back on my naïveté then—my fervent belief not only that I worked for a free and independent press, but also that the stars of the medium truly were "the best and the brightest" our country brought forth—I am appalled. My only excuse, to quote Paul McCartney, "But I was so much younger then . . ."

In 1985, while working as a staff producer for CBS's *60 Minutes*, I became interested in Garwood again. He was now speaking publicly about something that had never made the news during his court-martial. The *Wall Street Journal* reported he said that he knew firsthand of other American prisoners in Vietnam long after the war was over. I was surprised when I attended a press conference at the National Press Club in Washington on March 22, 1985, where Garwood spoke briefly: He was supported by Vietnam combat veterans whose war records were, to a man, impeccable.

These veterans told a story vastly different from what was made public during the court-martial and one that was intimately tied to another *60 Minutes* story I was working on—"Dead or Alive?" The title referred to Vietnam POW/MIAs. The résumés of my sources were extraordinary. They included outstanding experts like former head of the Defense Intelligence Agency (DIA) General Eugene Tighe and returned prisoners of war like Captain Red McDaniel, who held the Navy's top award for bravery, had commanded the aircraft carrier *Lexington*, and was, for several years, director of liaison on Capitol Hill for the Navy and Marine Corps. McDaniel's heroism as a prisoner was legendary. With such advocates providing back up, it was hard not to consider the possibility that prisoners (some thirty-five hundred) had in fact been kept by the Vietnamese communists as hostages to make sure that the United States would pay the more than $3 billion in war reparations that Nixon had promised before his fall from grace. Particularly compelling was the fact that of the three hundred prisoners known to be held in Laos by the Pathet Lao, allies of the Vietnamese communists, not one was released for homecoming in 1973.

The big question was, why had the US government declared that all prisoners were returned in 1973, and then four years later officially determined that all but one—"symbolic" MIA Air Force colonel and pilot Charles Shelton—were dead? It boggled the mind that no one in the media asked why all the men on the list, particularly those in Laos, were not returned. Instead of investigating, reporters accepted verbatim the government line that there was no evidence of prisoners being kept behind, certainly no evidence of anyone still alive after 1973.

What the media also missed—or perhaps agreed to keep quiet for what they were told were national security reasons—was the battle going on within intelligence agencies between those, usually old-timers with a military background, who believed in intelligence collected by human beings (HUMINT) whether they were hired spies or volunteers, and those who discounted this as unsavory and unnecessary. The opposition to HUMINT came from those who believed high-tech spying was all that was necessary. Although there was also state-of-the-art, high-tech satellite intelligence on live American POWs in Vietnam, the HUMINT coming in largely from South Vietnamese who had been our allies, was, according to General Tighe (who had made it a priority when he was head of the DIA), nothing short of miraculous. There were numerous sightings of Garwood in the prison camps of Vietnam. One South Vietnamese ally who reported that he had been a prisoner with Garwood for a long period of time was none other than General Lam Van Phat who had been military commander of the Saigon area until the 1975 collapse.

Garwood's return created a huge dilemma for the US government. He was, in fact, proof that the communists had kept prisoners. More important, he was a living symbol of thousands of prisoners who had been declared dead too soon by a government that turned a deaf ear to families, veterans, and, most important, to some intelligence officials who had steadfastly maintained that there was at least enough evidence of live prisoners to keep their status open and make a concerted effort to negotiate for their return. Congress, too, was involved in what some veterans openly called a cover-up. Since 1975, two congressional commissions had formally declared, on the basis of communist assurances, that "there are no more Americans in Vietnam." There were more complicated dimensions to America's deaf-ear policy on POWs left in Vietnam after 1973. Strong intelligence indicated that the Viet Cong had allowed Palestine Liberation Organization (PLO) terrorists to interrogate and torture American prisoners who were left behind. In fact, Garwood maintained that before he was allowed to leave Vietnam, he was interrogated by the PLO and warned of the consequences to himself and his family if he ever spoke about the PLO in Vietnam. This, along with all intelligence on POWs, was considered not credible. General Tighe, loathe to lay blame on anyone in the profession to which he had dedicated his life, attributed this total opposition to any evidence about POWs in Vietnam to "bureaucratic mind-set."

The press too had easily succumbed to "off the record" advisories from the government. Those still concerned about prisoners were described as losers and loonies who couldn't readjust to society, or as distraught widows and others who couldn't face the fact that their loved ones were dead. There was an added factor to why the press belittled anyone who questioned whether the Vietnamese had kept any prisoners.

Many illustrious names in journalism had made their careers reporting either on Watergate or the Vietnam War, and on "the best and the brightest" who ran it. The POW issue was not a scandal like My Lai with an easy target. It was instead, what General Alexander Haig referred to as "a can of worms." Whether filled with hubris or not, most journalists considered it unlikely that with their connections they would have missed a story of such magnitude. No one concerned or knowledgeable about the subject fit in the category of "best and brightest." Instead, they were the ones who had actually fought the war, those described by Clinton cabinet member Donna Shalala as "not the best and the brightest." Most of them were, in fact, enlisted men who had made the military their career. With exceptions like Bernard Fall and Keyes Beach, most journalists who were famous for their war coverage had excelled at stories that exposed the viciousness and excesses of American fighting men. Bobby Garwood was on the top of their list as someone whose deprived background — trailer park upbringing, broken home, mild juvenile delinquency — made it a certainty that he fell into the category of "baby-killing and gook-hunting" soldiers journalists had delighted in exposing during the war. What exacerbated the situation was that even though the worst charges against Garwood had to be dropped for lack of evidence at the court-martial, government spokesmen continued to stir up animosity against him by openly calling him a deserter-traitor and thus someone who could not be believed. The fact that General Eugene Tighe, the intelligence expert, backed up what Garwood said, seemed to escape the notice of journalists. Even when Tighe spoke before congressional committees, he was ignored.

In 1985, in addition to the POW story, I began working on a story about Garwood. At that time, I presented one renowned Pulitzer Prize–winning war journalist/author with the impeccable testimony on missing POWs that General Tighe had given before a congressional committee. He told me, "I have it on very good information that Tighe is in the beginning stages of Alzheimer's." This answer flabbergasted me. I had spent hours talking to General Tighe, as had my researcher, Nellie Lide. We both agreed that he had one of the quickest minds we had ever come across. It would not be long before I began to understand how an influential journalist who had exposed some of the most illegal aspects of President Nixon's administration came to believe such slander.

I had heard of Col. Richard Childress, who was generally known as the government liaison between the National Security Council (NSC) and POW/MIA families as well as the president's advisor. Childress had joined the NSC as what was termed a Southeast Asian Political and Military Affairs Officer in 1961. Since he had no military background, it was generally assumed he worked for the only other government agency that awarded the rank of colonel to some of its employees—the CIA. In what Red McDaniel's wife, Dorothy, considered an abusive telephone call, Childress had accused her husband—one of my sources on the prisoner story—of defying the official line by attacking the concealment of intelligence on prisoners; but not before acknowledging that there were indeed still live POWs in Vietnam.

Now it was my turn. In an effort to get an interview about existing evidence of live prisoners, I had made several fruitless calls to Colonel Childress. After I had locked in Garwood and Tighe for *60 Minutes*, Childress called me at my Washington office. His voice definitely not polite, he demanded, "Are you doing a piece on POWs?" Without waiting for an answer, he proceeded to slander most of the people with whom I had done preliminary interviews. Included was the smear I had already heard from fellow journalists about General Tighe. Since it was none of his business and I was highly suspicious of how he had gotten such precise information about my conversations with potential interviewees, my back was up. He modified his tone slightly and tried another tack: "You could jeopardize the lives of prisoners still over there," he said. If I had any hesitation about doing the story before his call, the shock of this revelation verifying what Garwood had said about other prisoners made me determined to see it through. The conversation ended with the threat that I would do myself no good by continuing with this story.

Despite continuing pressure from intelligence agencies—particularly the National Security Council and the Defense Intelligence Agency—to drop the story, it aired as "Dead or Alive?" in December 1985 thanks in large part to General Tighe's participation. He too had come under tremendous pressure to drop out, just as the network had come under subtle pressure not to interview General Tighe. Correspondents were taken aside by the head of Pentagon covert operations who gave them the definitive spin on the matter of POWs. Even the president of CBS's news division was taken aside at a cocktail party by a prominent former national security advisor. The pressure was subtle and, it was explained, had to do with sensitive matters of national security. CBS administrators were too savvy to believe the smears against an American general who received nothing but the highest praise from his peers in NATO and other allied countries. General Tighe's worldwide reputation as one of the finest intelligence professionals this country has ever produced could not be marred.

Tighe's participation in "Dead or Alive?" insured the program was separately screened by Congress several times after it was aired, triggering the formation of a DIA commission on MIA/POWs chaired by General Tighe. Tighe Commission members included the most knowledgeable professionals in the field, including air ace Gen. Robinson Risner who had been imprisoned for six years in the former French colonial fortress dubbed the "Hanoi Hilton" by his fellow American POWs—mostly pilots—who were held there during the war. The Tighe Commission concluded not only that live prisoners had been left behind, but that there was strong evidence many were still alive. It was immediately classified without public explanation. Its commissioners had advised, among other recommendations, that the DIA hire Garwood to work on the prisoner issue. The suggestion was ignored.

Robert Garwood also appeared in "Dead or Alive?" albeit briefly. Despite my best efforts, I was never able to persuade my superiors to let me do Garwood's full story on television—not even after I got hold of film footage of him in Vietnam that proved his prisoner status. Garwood's court-martial conviction along with continuing government propaganda against him made networks shy away. I would finally write his full story in a book entitled *Spite House: The Last Secret of the War in Vietnam*, published in 1997. General Tighe, by then deceased, provided the road map for me to pursue Garwood's story at the beginning, when I interviewed both men for "Dead or Alive?"

Despite the Tighe Commission recommendation that Garwood be hired by the Pentagon, government policy continued to dictate that only distortions of Garwood's history be made public. Keeping alive the image of Garwood as devil incarnate of the Vietnam War insured no one would pay attention to what he had to report about the men who, like him, were abandoned in Vietnam. To keep this truth from surfacing, in the words of highly decorated Army Major and former Vietnam POW Mark Smith, "Robert Garwood had to become our token sacrificial lamb on the cross of honor and integrity."

When Bobby Garwood returned home in 1979 after fourteen years in communist detention, he was like Rip Van Winkle. His knowledge of American history ended with his capture in 1965, his belief in his country—as the Marine Corps had drilled it into him—unshaken. In 1973, the communists had played Henry Kissinger's statement that all American prisoners from the Vietnam War were now home, over camp loudspeakers. But Garwood fervently believed the communists had deceived the US government. If Washington only knew the truth, it would immediately act on it. It was inconceivable to him that by escaping he had given lie to the government dictum that all prisoners returned in 1973. Worse, for those who had staked their careers on this point and been showered with accolades for bringing about an honorable peace, Garwood knew firsthand that there were others still alive—a lot of others.

As an ordinary grunt, Garwood was probably unique among American prisoners in that he had a formidable natural (untrained) talent for the Vietnamese language. He had used his language and survival skills—learned from a fellow American POW, Special Forces Captain William F. (Ike) Eisenbraun—to survive. Mindful of Ike's advice to stay alive and try to escape at all costs—as long as he did nothing to harm other American POWs—he used, after the war, his talent for fixing machinery of all kinds to repair the broken-down American vehicles scattered all over Vietnam. That had provided him with limited freedom to travel to wherever something needed to be fixed, although never without guards.

Always on the lookout for a way to escape, Garwood used basic

American business savvy to persuade his guards to let him buy a few of the small quantity of Western products available only in hotels frequented by visitors (mostly aid workers) to Vietnam and off-limits to them. With a borrowed white shirt and pants, Garwood passed for a Western aid worker. His guards then traded the soap, cigarettes, or caviar for a tidy profit. Garwood pretended all he wanted in return was an extra ration of cigarettes or food. It was on one of his rare trips to Hanoi that Garwood managed to pass a note to Finnish diplomat Ossi Rahkonen, who passed it directly on to the BBC and Red Cross. Rahkonen did not make the mistake of turning the note over to US authorities, as had previous recipients of Garwood's furtive notes. Those notes were never made public. Rahkonen was also wise in going to the BBC instead of American media. The American media had consistently upheld the US government position that there was not one live American prisoner, or even defector, left in Vietnam.

The BBC report that an American prisoner named Garwood was alive in Vietnam created a huge problem for the politicians and bureaucrats sitting on the prisoner issue. If they were to keep the country convinced Vietnam had returned all live prisoners, Garwood would have to be discredited. He would have to be transformed from heroic survivor of one of the most notorious prison systems in the world into a criminal traitor. People would have to be persuaded that he was more evil than the draft dodgers who had all gotten amnesty; than the pro–North Vietnam US civilians who had openly urged the Vietnamese to shoot down American war planes; and even worse than the Marine Corps colonel who, as a prisoner in the Hanoi Hilton, had collaborated with the enemy in torturing his fellow prisoners. In short, Americans had to be convinced that Garwood voluntarily joined the enemy to fight against other Americans. To make this believable, there had to be every appearance of legality. It had to look like Garwood, the traitor, was given full constitutional rights to defend himself. This could not be done without the full cooperation, witting and unwitting, of the American media. In early 1979, even before Garwood left Vietnam, the government leaked information to key newspapers that a live American defector was sighted in Hanoi.

Government memos from early 1979 in the Jimmy Carter presidential library archives state that "Garwood [claims] that he knows of other Americans who are alive in Vietnam." That information was not leaked to the press although it would have been a simple matter for the press to find out from the BBC that Garwood had contacted Finnish diplomat Rakhonen and then question Rakhonen on just what Garwood had said about himself and about other POWs. Instead, the media, for whatever reason, accepted what the government released on Garwood. "Garwood passed a note with his name and serial number to some western tourists in Hanoi," wrote *Newsweek*, April 2, 1979, "'I want to come home,' he told the tourist." Although *Newsweek* went on to state that Garwood also said he was in a forced labor camp with others, no one believed it. How could an inmate of a forced labor camp contact tourists in Hanoi? Never mind the fact that there were almost no Western tourists in Hanoi at the time. By referring to Garwood solely as a defector, the government had set the stage for Garwood's return. Unchallenged by the press, politicians and bureaucrats managed Garwood's story from that point forward, through the court-martial that would ruin him, and long beyond.

In the process, US officials had to ally themselves with their old enemy, the communist government of Vietnam. Each country needed to prevent the American people from finding out that some American prisoners had been kept by the Vietnamese after the official homecoming in 1973. That the United States had made no effort to get them back had to remain a classified secret. Otherwise, the morale of the armed forces would sink even lower than the all-time low it was at in 1979 — to say nothing of the morale of the American people.

Initially held back by the communists to ensure that the United States would fulfill its secret promise to pay $4.5 billion in reparation monies, by 1979 American POWs had become worthless pawns. They were living ghosts. The United States had not paid the promised monies and had no intention of paying in the future. (President Nixon's letter of February 1, 1973, to Vietnamese Prime Minister Pham Van Dong promising the money was not released until four years later.) To the communists who had never felt obligated to treat prisoners according to Geneva Convention rules, those who survived were useful as slave labor and as a possible embarrassment to the United States. Neither side could have the truth come out without tremendous loss of face and all that it implied. The poverty-stricken Vietnamese, desperate for diplomatic recognition and economic assistance, could not afford to alienate the American people and Western allies. Abandonment of war prisoners was the kind of mistake that could destroy not only careers, but entire political administrations. No amount of effort or money was spared in preventing that from happening.

Garwood's court-martial ended up being the longest in US history. Millions were spent on an investigation that missed — deliberately or otherwise — the most fundamental and easily found truths. Most blatant: Garwood was charged with desertion during the war, a charge that carries the death penalty by firing squad. Yet if anyone had checked his military records, they would have found that he was just days away from the end of his Vietnam tour of duty when he disappeared. It was hardly a time when he would have deserted. Yet that simple fact never made the news until I researched it years later. During the trial, the prosecution put on the stand Lieutenant Colonel John A. Studds and Charles B. Buchta, who had been Garwood's company commander and battalion motor transport officer at the time of his capture. Both men had precise knowledge that Garwood disappeared while on an authorized chauffeuring job, yet they swore under oath that he had not had authorization to leave. Therefore, he must have deserted. When Billy Ray Conley, one of Garwood's fellow drivers at III MAF, Marine Corps tactical headquarters, voluntarily appeared to testify on Garwood's behalf, it never made the papers. He swore that Garwood had in fact been on an authorized mission. That fact was seared in Conley's mind. Hoping to get Garwood's position when Garwood went back to the States, he had been volunteering for some of Garwood's jobs. Garwood's superiors, annoyed that Garwood had his mind somewhere else (he was getting married to his high school sweetheart as soon as he got home), insisted that Garwood do the job. Conley had never forgotten he could have been the one in Garwood's shoes, and he had always made certain to tell Marine Corps investigators the truth.

When desertion charges had to be dropped, no newspaper asked why. No one interviewed Billy Ray Conley. No newspaper questioned whether Buchta and Studds — when they swore under oath that no stone had been left unturned to find out why Garwood had left the base on the day of his capture — had been pressured by the government in some way. Yet the media was consistently careful to note as did the *New Republic* on February 2, 1980, "[although] Garwood faced charges that could lead to his execution . . . the Marine Corps has been scrupulous about due process."

For Garwood's attackers in the government "Live Americans" [were] a "political game" involving the prestige of many high-powered careers. "DIA [Defense Intelligence Agency] and State are playing this game," wrote Michel Oksenberg of the National Security Council (NSC) to National Security Adviser Zbigniew Brezesinski on January 21, 1980. It would be "simply good politics" for Brezesinski to go along with the game, advised Oksenberg. It seems to also have been good politics for reporters.

The game was not one that a Marine Corps private, fourteen-year prisoner of the Vietnamese, without money or powerful friends, could hope to win—or even play. What had sustained Garwood though fourteen years as a prisoner was an almost naïve belief in the goodness of his country, the freedom of the press, and an unwavering belief in his rights as a citizen and soldier. He would have disbelieved it if told that soon after the BBC broadcast, the US State Department made sure that misinformation portions of its interdepartmental and interagency memos were leaked to the press. From the Oksenberg memo: it was "unlikely that PFC Garwood would be free to leave any camp without Vietnamese assistance and . . . it could not be excluded that he had acted at the request or demand of the communist Vietnamese." It was more likely, the State Department argued, "that Vietnam, in its attempts to achieve normalization, was using Garwood as an agent to manipulate the U.S." Other government hacks put a different twist on this when they revealed in the Report to the Assistant Secretary of Defense for Command Control, Communication, and Intelligence, that senior NVS (North Vietnamese Army) officers had told them during bilateral meetings that Hanoi felt "forced to make Garwood leave the country." He had been no good to them. He had been "lazy" and a "troublemaker," not your *ideal prisoner* [italics mine]. No reporter noted this as a brilliant example of what Orwell called "doublespeak."

Garwood's reentry into the free world was carefully orchestrated. He arrived in Bangkok, his first stop after leaving Vietnam, on a French plane. This arrangement, worked out between the United States and Vietnam, gave reporters the impression that Garwood had been free to go or stay in Vietnam. Almost no reporter questioned this even though in 1973 all American prisoners—even known collaborators like the Marine Corps colonel who helped torture his fellow prisoners—had returned on American planes. On arrival, Garwood was kept away from clamoring reporters who nevertheless greeted him with cries of "How do you feel about the Marine Corps calling you a deserter?" Garwood, prevented from answering them by a cordon of military personnel, found the question absurd. So should the reporters asking it. Even elementary research on their part would have established that Garwood was ten days away from the end of his Vietnam tour when he was alleged to have deserted. This begs the question: Were reporters who only a few years before had hunted down every last detail of the Watergate scandal sloppy or simply disinterested in the fate of a low-level grunt whose life hung in the balance?

The media establishment knew that the crime of desertion carries the death penalty. On April 9, 1979, *Time* magazine reported "pending the outcome of the Navy's official investigation, the Marines have tentatively charged Garwood with desertion, soliciting US combat forces to lay down their arms, and unlawful dealing with the enemy. If he is court-martialed on these charges and convicted, he could be sentenced to death."

After desertion charges were dropped because of Billy Ray Conley's testimony, it became increasingly difficult to prove in the courtroom that Garwood had defected and led the enemy in action against his own former comrades. That did not stop the prosecution from putting out a barrage of innuendo to the press and even to Garwood's own attorneys. The prosecutor, Captain Werner Helmer, grabbed every opportunity to take Vaughn Taylor, one of Garwood's attorneys, aside and tell him of Garwood's horrendous record in "harming our troops" in Vietnam. He told Taylor that he had a marine who had been blinded in a Viet Cong attack led by Garwood ready to testify. Helmer claimed the marine could identify Garwood by his voice. Taylor says, "You almost had to believe Helmer knew something the rest of us didn't." Finally, Taylor blew up. The military has a completely open disclosure system. He demanded that Helmer put up or shut up. Helmer's reply: "I don't have anything in particular." Helmer went on to explain that he knew Garwood was guilty because he had studied traitors of history like Benedict Arnold. No one in the media seemed to note that the prosecution had nothing to offer in the way of evidence.

By that time, it had become clear to Garwood that he was involved in a process that, for whatever reason, was unwinnable. He had wanted to take the stand but was talked out of it by his lawyers, who were themselves unsure of what exactly Garwood was guilty of, but were convinced that he was a victim of extreme psychiatric manipulation on the part of Vietnamese communists, and post-traumatic stress disorder. The *Washington Post* reported, "Garwood's attorneys do not deny the substance of the charges." Garwood withdrew into himself, exhausted and resigned to his fate. Only briefly in June 1980 did he think he might have a chance at acquittal because of the unexpected appearance of one potential witness.

Garwood saw newspaper accounts that a defector from Vietnam had given testimony before Congress. Although newspaper photos showed the defector disguised in a motorcycle helmet, Garwood immediately recognized him as Colonel Tran Van Loc, the communist secret-police chief who sat on a five-man tribunal that had determined each prisoner's fate. Of Chinese descent, Tran Van Loc fled Vietnam during the border war that broke out between China and Vietnam in the late seventies. The intelligence he brought with him was so important to the United States that DIA's best Vietnamese language expert and agent, Bob Hyp, was sent to Hong Kong to debrief Van Loc. Garwood never imagined that vindication would come from a former enemy, but the fact that Van Loc had defected to the United States persuaded him that he might be willing to tell the truth about Garwood's prisoner status. Garwood persuaded his lawyers to set up a meeting with Van Loc, despite extreme opposition from the prosecution. The complications of dealing with someone under the witness protection program made such a get-together difficult.

When Van Loc denied knowing Garwood as a prisoner, Vaughn Taylor, Garwood's attorney, lost confidence in defending Garwood on any basis except psychiatric. It would take more than a decade for him to find out that Garwood had not only told the truth, but that Van Loc had been pressured by the government to lie about Garwood. Ten years later, under oath in a deposition for the Senate Select Committee on POWs, Van Loc, questioned by counsel to the committee, described how he had been approached, through the government agency that provided both his protection and livelihood, to meet with a military officer who told him to lie about Bobby Garwood. But by then Garwood's reputation had been so utterly destroyed even Sen. Bob Smith (R–N.H.), the vice chairman of the select committee, could not get the media interested in the truth about Garwood. Nevertheless, Smith ended his opening speech to the committee with these words: "I believe Bobby Garwood." Van Loc's testimony is in the Senate records, and attorney Vaughn Taylor introduced the evidence vindicating Garwood to the Senate Ethics Committee.

Despite suborning the perjury of defector Tran Van Loc and keeping him as well as other witnesses who supported Garwood from testifying, the government had an uphill climb in ridding the public of the uneasy feeling, as the *New York Daily News*—in an exception to what was routinely printed—put it, "that a former POW is being unfairly punished."

Unable to produce any evidence that Garwood had deserted, produced propaganda for the enemy, or acted for the enemy in any way during the war, the prosecution did a complete turnaround, taking the position that Garwood had, in fact, been a prisoner. But their strategy was still character assassination. The charges now were that he had collaborated with the enemy while a prisoner in ways much more abhorrent than his peers. The background of witnesses subpoenaed to testify against Garwood spoke volumes. According to the *Washington Post* (December 29, 1979), "All five of the former POWs who testified against Garwood . . . have acknowledged that they collaborated with their captors . . . [they] did whatever their captors were determined to have them do." Former DIA chief General Eugene Tighe questioned whether that fact gave the prosecution undue leverage in getting them to testify against Garwood. Records of the witnesses' debriefings remain classified to this day, so it is difficult to ascertain just what Garwood's accusers were themselves guilty of. Dr. Edna Hunter, who was chief of the Pentagon's POW unit in 1973 and who at that time interviewed all former prisoners who testified against Garwood, thought the jury should know that every one of his accusers felt guilty about having behaved exactly as Garwood had, or in some cases worse than he had in the prison camp. She pointed out—to reporters on the courthouse steps—that none of Garwood's accusers had so much as mentioned bad behavior on his part during their 1973 debriefings, something they themselves acknowledged during questioning by Garwood's lawyers. Instead, they had talked about suffering they had all endured, Garwood included. Hunter judged none of them, "They were tortured, tricked, and manipulated by the communists."

Hunter wanted badly to testify, but after Garwood's seeming failure to connect with Colonel Tran Van Loc, even his lawyers did not exert themselves in opposing Werner Helmer, the prosecutor, to put her on the stand. Certain that Garwood's mind was so disturbed that he had fabricated his connection with Van Loc, their focus was now on convincing the jury that whatever Garwood had done, he had done under coercive persuasion, that he had been brainwashed and had suffered from bouts of insanity. General Tighe thought the fact that Hunter was not given a chance to testify on Garwood's behalf was a continuation of the kind of manipulation the communists had practiced on Garwood and his accusers; only now the manipulation came from the prosecution.

Unusual allowances were made for the former prisoners who were now Garwood's accusers. In at least one instance, the veteran officer who, arguably, gave the most damaging evidence against Garwood was allowed to substitute a written statement for his sworn testimony into official court-martial records. Missing from court-martial records is a particularly revealing bit of sworn testimony dealing with what many former highly respected prisoners and doctors say amounted to severe physical abuse of Garwood by the enemy. With the help of Marine Corps veterans who at one time had access to complete court-martial records, I was able to obtain the missing testimony for my files. No evidence was ever presented that Garwood was guilty of the kind of collaboration his accusers freely admitted.

On the basis of the evidence brought by his former fellow prisoners who, according to the *Washington Post*, had themselves collaborated, Garwood was found guilty of informing on his comrades, interrogating them on military and other matters, serving as a guard for the VC, and simple assault against a fellow American prisoner. This last damaged him most severely and hurt most deeply. He was condemned before the world of one thing he had never done, harming a fellow prisoner of war.

The accusation came from David Harker, a former fellow prisoner who spoke out strongly for Garwood when Garwood first came home. "Don't Crucify Garwood," one headline quoted him. "If he's guilty, we're all guilty," he told reporters then. But during the court-martial he reported that Garwood had, in prison camp, struck him a blow. "As I recall, " he testified, "he struck me with the back of his hand. I don't know whether it was in a fist or whether it was an open hand that he hit me in the rib. I remember he had a disgusted look on his face. . . . He made the statement, something to the effect that 'you're gonna have to pay for what happened to Russ.'"

Russ Grisset had been Garwood's best friend in the camp, a fellow marine who was beaten to death because he had stolen the camp commander's cat, which was then eaten by Grisset and Garwood's fellow prisoners, including Harker. Garwood, returning from a work detail, came upon the scene after the fatal beating. He was angry with the other prisoners because they had let Russ take the fall instead of sticking together and taking the blame as a group. Going by past experience, Garwood was pretty sure the group would have been punished much less severely than the singled-out Russ. Garwood remembers what the prosecution referred to as a blow as more of a tough shove to get Harker out of the way as he moved toward Russ.

Harker described in detail the brutality of Grisset's beating, but seemed unable to connect Garwood's action with pain and rage felt over what had been done to Russ. Almost sheepishly though, he acknowledged that Garwood's blow neither hurt nor harmed him, but merely surprised him. Years later, working on the *60 Minutes* program, "Dead or Alive?" I asked Harker what made him change his original opinions, "Don't Crucify Garwood," and "He should not be prosecuted because nobody else was." He would only say that he knew Garwood was guilty of other things that never came up in the court-martial, refusing to elaborate. Had the prosecution persuaded him off the record? He did not answer. Was it convenient to have Garwood as a scapegoat so that attention was deflected from what all of his fellow prisoners had done? No answer.

But how was it that the reporters who originally interviewed Harker never went back to search for the answers to these questions? Even Col. R. E. Switzer, the judge of the court-martial, remarked on the apparent injustice done the plaintiff. "We never got at the truth because we never heard Garwood's side of the story," he told me ten years later when I interviewed him for my book *Kiss the Boys Goodbye*.

According to the *New York Daily News* of January 23, 1981, Judge Switzer did hear part of Garwood's story that dealt with other POWs left behind: "a military psychiatrist said on Thursday that Marine PFC R. Garwood told him in October that about 200 . . . POWs are still being held in Vietnam. Navy Captain Benjamin R. Ogburn . . . conducting a court-ordered psychiatric examination on Garwood . . . said Garwood was upset because he was not debriefed in the same manner as other returning POWs. . . . The military judge in the case . . . refused to allow Ogburn's testimony . . . about . . . the alleged retention of Americans in Vietnam, ruling that 'the testimony is irrelevant.'"

"The jurors were not in the courtroom when Ogburn released Garwood's reports about other Americans in Vietnam."

In light of scant evidence against Garwood, the jury came back with a minor but nevertheless punishing verdict. During the time he was given to appeal, Garwood was not to be released by the Marine Corps, but was not to be paid by them either; he was to be reduced to the lowest rank, forfeiting pay and allowances, including $148,000 due to him for fourteen years in prison. There was no money to pay his court-martial lawyers, much less to pay for legal experts to question just how the Marine Corps was able to justify this punishment constitutionally. No one in the media asked the Marine Corps either, just as they had not questioned the constitutionality of Garwood being tried by a military tribunal in the first place when his tour of duty had ended over a decade before.

Like punishment meted out to dissidents in the former Soviet Union, Garwood was turned into a noncitizen in his own country. Suffering from a host of prison-induced illnesses and post-traumatic stress disorder, he received no medical benefits and had no rights as a private citizen of the United States. He did not question it when he was told, incorrectly, that he did not even have the right to vote. As a marine, he was not allowed to find civilian work. He owed hundreds of thousands of dollars in legal bills and began working as a handyman for one of his lawyers to pay him back. All of this made for good investigative journalism. Never was the Fourth Estate more needed to counter the steady stream of government "Newspeak" that glibly justified every constitutional violation in Garwood's case.

In only one instance did the media grant Garwood the kind of massive coverage he might have found useful in bringing to light the injustice committed against him. Early in the court-martial, headlines blazed from every supermarket tabloid: "Garwood Accused of Child Molestation." Garwood easily disproved this charge in court. Uncontested evidence put him hundreds of miles from the scene when the crime was alleged to have been committed. But the fact that he was completely cleared at this trial, which immediately followed the court-martial, was mentioned almost nowhere in the media, and the original tabloid slur festered on. Later, when he married, this deeply and adversely affected his relationship with his in-laws, especially after his first wife died. They told me that such a story simply could not have been concocted. To this day, they do not believe that he was completely vindicated.

After the court-martial, despite the severe restrictions placed on him, Garwood got on with his life. Finally released from the Marine Corps in 1986 when the Supreme Court opted not to hear his appeal, he used his talent to fix things mechanical to make a living. He found the love of his life in wife Cathy Ray, who died in 2000. "God took away fourteen years of my life," he says now, "but he gave them back through Cathy."

Garwood remains committed to other American POWs left in Vietnam. In his quest to bring that information before the public, he had strong support from General Tighe (deceased since 1993), who debriefed him unofficially, assisted by Chris Gugas, the polygraph expert who set up the CIA's polygraph system. That debriefing, full of valuable intelligence that, according to Tighe, could not possibly have been fabricated, shamed the DIA into conducting its own official debriefing. One of Garwood's debriefers was Bob Hyp, the same intelligence expert who had debriefed Colonel Tran Van Loc in Hong Kong. When I was working on my book *Kiss the Boys Goodbye*, Hyp called my editor to say that he would send me documentation that would categorically clear Garwood. I never got the material. Hyp died of a massive heart attack before he could send it. At the end of the debriefing, other DIA professionals let Garwood know in no uncertain terms that he could stay out of trouble with them as long as he kept his mouth shut. "Consider yourself lucky," they said, "you made it back. The others didn't."

The debriefings, which Bob Hyp and General Tighe considered a complete vindication of Garwood, had little impact on government propaganda. Marine Corps textbooks still slandered Garwood as a traitor. The media, disinterested in anything to do with POWs, ignored the debriefings even after they were declassified.

Reporters would briefly show renewed interest in Garwood in the spring of 1993 when, in his capacity as vice chairman of the Senate Select Committee on POWs, Sen. Bob Smith planned a trip to Vietnam. He wanted Garwood to accompany him so that he could verify for himself the accuracy of Garwood's testimony during the debriefings conducted by the DIA. Garwood had described in great detail the location of some of the camps where he was held. That information had been corroborated by evidence brought before the committee. Smith believed other Americans had been held in the same camps. He wanted Garwood to travel with him in a "protected" status provided by the government. But other senators, like former prisoner John McCain, who had never been held in the kind of primitive camp Garwood was held in, were still convinced by false and continuing propaganda that Garwood was convicted of leading the enemy against fellow Americans. McCain did not want to send Garwood "on a vacation to Vietnam." Garwood had to decide whether he would travel with Smith unprotected. General Tighe strongly advised against his going, telling him it was extremely dangerous. He told him that Garwood's captors would have no compunction about having him killed, and the US government was not likely to intervene in the case of a convicted collaborator dying on foreign soil. Senator Smith promised to raise a ruckus if that happened, but was reluctant to press Garwood. He knew the media would not necessarily pick up such a cause.

Against such odds, in early July 1993 Garwood went to Vietnam with Senator Smith. He was determined to help Smith, but he had a private reason for going as well. He wanted to ask the Vietnamese for the remains of his friend and mentor, Ike Eisenbraun, the Special Forces captain who had taught him Vietnamese and how to survive in the horrible conditions that prevailed in the camps. Garwood had buried Ike and burned the gravesite in his memory. In the months before going, he had requested assistance from the United States. Joint Casualty Resolution Center and other appropriate agencies. Both the United States and Vietnamese governments refused to assist him in bringing back Ike's remains. Garwood's efforts got no press coverage.

Even when Senator Smith called a press conference in Bangkok after their return from Vietnam to explain in great detail how Garwood had proven the existence of a prison camp where his former captors said no buildings had ever stood, the press was skeptical, almost hostile to both Garwood and the senator. Smith explained that Garwood had directed the reluctant Vietnamese to an island that, on the surface, seemed bare of signs that anyone had ever lived there. In his DIA debriefings, Garwood had described the precise location of prison buildings, the color of masonry, bricks, and other building materials. The Vietnamese were smug as they led the senator and Vaughn Taylor, Garwood's lawyer, around the empty site. Garwood was left briefly unattended by the usually vigilant Vietnamese security agents who accompanied them when he shouted for Smith to join him. Under some bushes he found a pile of building bricks and rubbish, matching his earlier descriptions precisely. The Vietnamese were in a fury. Smith thought Garwood might not make it out of Vietnam. But the senator's strong presence did keep Garwood protected. Perhaps too, the Vietnamese intuited that the American press would never print Garwood's side of this story.

In fact, most Western reporters uncritically repeated Vietnamese propaganda. Nothing was said about finding evidence of a prison camp. Ho Xuan Dich, director of Vietnam's MIA office, was quoted extensively as saying that Garwood had been a low-ranking Vietnamese officer and that "he had socialized with other Vietnamese officers," and had even been "Dich's own good friend." Dich denied that someone named Eisenbraun had ever existed. Ike's existence was just one more fact American media could easily have found out for themselves by looking at prisoner rolls.

Garwood was approached by Colonel Thai (probably an alias: Thai means war in Vietnamese), the man in charge of American prisoners who had warned him before his release that the US government would never believe he had been a prisoner, and that the Vietnamese had agents all over the United States, including allied PLO informers, who would watch him to make sure he kept his mouth shut. Now Thai came forward and called him friend.

Vaughn Taylor caught Thai and Garwood on camera as Garwood, enraged, pointed his finger at Thai and said, "you tortured my friends." Thai was so furious at this that months later he contradicted Dich, who had said Garwood was a good friend who had regularly socialized with the Vietnamese. During a meeting with Patricia O'Grady-Parsels, the daughter of a missing American pilot, Thai emphasized that Garwood had been a war criminal from the start. He had never allowed himself to be reeducated. He had always had a "bad attitude." He had to be separated from other prisoners so as not to contaminate them. For these reasons, his sentence was not commuted in 1973.

This was the same line some Pentagon staffers had leaked to the press when Garwood first came home, contradicting their own colleagues who said Garwood was an agent of the Vietnamese. More than ten years after Garwood's return from Vietnam, neither his Vietnamese captors nor his own accusers in the Pentagon could keep their stories straight. No one in the media was interested in what O'Grady-Parsels had to say.

Does Garwood's sad experience with America's version of "Newspeak" mean that his message about what happened to the men who still languished in Vietnam's prisons when he left in 1979 has not reached the American people? Surprisingly not. Garwood's true story has somehow made its way across America. Abraham Lincoln said you can't fool all of the people all of the time. Today he might add that even with the media's help, the government can't fool all of the people all of the time.

After my book *Spite House*, telling Garwood's story, came out in 1997, Garwood and I were invited to speak to more than two hundred thousand veterans who were assembled near the Vietnam Memorial on Memorial Day 1998. The veterans and their families traveled—as they did every year—from all parts of the country in motorcycle caravans to commemorate and keep alive the concern for MIA/POWs who had not yet been properly accounted for. The *Washington Post* had featured the veterans as they paraded from the Pentagon parking lot down Independence Avenue and to the wall the previous day. Perhaps for that reason there were network news cameras in the crowd.

Many gathered there in the softly falling rain had at one time believed that Garwood fought with the enemy against them and hated him for it. Some had been disappointed that he did not face a firing squad. But they had educated themselves about the Vietnam War as probably no other American veterans had ever examined their own war. They had done this as brothers, learning from each other's experiences, whether they had been simple grunts, special forces, medics, or generals. They published newsletters in which they reprinted every article that dealt with Vietnam issues from newspapers across the country. They circulated copies of documents like Garwood's debriefing. Some, like Colonel Ted Guy, who as the highest-ranking officer to have been in charge of POWs at the notorious prison camp called "the Plantation," challenged the increasing number of government hacks who, handsomely funded by US intelligence agencies, made careers out of disseminating falsehoods about the war, particularly Garwood's role in it, on Internet Web sites.

When Garwood arrived to speak to the veterans amassed near the Vietnam Memorial, he was embraced by an honor guard of South Vietnamese veterans—some with the rank of general—who had been his prison campmates. As he stepped to the podium and saluted the crowd, it erupted into wild cheers of "Welcome home," and "We love you, Bobby." Garwood, overcome by emotion, continued to salute, unable to speak. The seconds dragged on, the cheering unabated when someone, seeing Garwood struggle to speak, spontaneously came out of the crowd. He was a large man, obviously a veteran because of the large metal hook he had for one arm. He moved next to Garwood, one arm around him, helping to hold him up. Garwood was still unable to speak when a second man came out of the crowd to lend Garwood his arm on the other side. Then a third man joined them. So embraced, Garwood finally began to speak. With his first words, a hush settled over the crowd so completely you could hear a pin drop. Garwood spoke only briefly of the country he loved, the darkness that he knew was not only in his heart but in the hearts of all the veterans, a darkness connected to the brothers they had left behind both dead and alive. Afterward, the three men embraced Garwood as brothers and soldiers embrace.

It was then I noticed the light blue ribbons around the necks of each of the three men who stood with Garwood. Each ribbon held a simple decoration, the American eagle sitting on top of a star, the highest military honor the United States can bestow on a soldier, the Medal of Honor. A clear voice from the crowd said, "Such men do not embrace traitors."

I had been aware of the news cameras rolling throughout this drama. As an old television producer, there was no doubt in my mind that I had witnessed everything one could want for a Memorial Day news story. To make sure the networks that had sent cameras knew the background of what their cameras had recorded, I collared reporters and called old friends in news departments. But nothing appeared on the news programs that night or later.

Even so, what happened on Memorial Day 1998 was a victory for Garwood. Like the dissidents living under the old Soviet regime, thousands of veterans who opened their hearts and minds to Bobby Garwood found the truth against strenuous odds. They continue to keep it alive. It helps Garwood to hold on.

In spite of everything that has happened to him, Garwood considers himself lucky. But what sticks in his craw and still makes his nights unbearable are all those other American prisoners he saw alive long after the war was over, who, for the same reasons of political expediency that destroyed so much of his life, were left behind. He knows that with such a precedent left unchecked, it can happen again and again. In fact, he sees a similar disregard for the grunts who fight in Afghanistan and Iraq and those who keep guard in places like North Korea. He knows that the press will not touch these issues because they are simply not sexy enough and they can be dangerous to important careers.

Stories about soldiers are covered when presidents want to create splendid public relations opportunities for themselves by making surprise landings on aircraft carriers or sneaking visits to the Middle East to share a bite of Thanksgiving turkey with soldiers fighting a guerrilla war. Also covered are stories about the past wartime heroism of attractive presidential candidates, like Sen. John Kerry. But when that same senator, chairing a Senate select committee on POWs, exposed some of the most explosive scandals surrounding that issue, there was no coverage at all. No coverage even though the committee established one undisputable fact: American prisoners were left behind in Vietnam and other countries where we fought secret wars. Only one lone *New York Times* editorial exhorted those who still cared about the ramifications of such a finding to let it be and live in peace. Tell that to the parents who finally have confirmation of what they have known all along: that their sons were alive at the end of the war and were left behind, despite President Nixon's assurance in 1973 that all our American POWs were on their way home. Evidence Senator Kerry's committee collected proved without a doubt that Nixon knew this was not true. Key appointees of the Nixon administration, including former defense secretary and CIA chief James Schlesinger, testified under oath that intelligence data persuaded them that live prisoners had not returned. Schlesinger was asked point blank if he thought that men had been left behind. "I think," he answered, "that I can come to no other conclusion." The mainstream press didn't consider this newsworthy. Only veterans' newsletters and the odd small-town newspaper reported it. What does that say about the media's value system? Reporters were falling all over themselves to get a Watergate scoop, but a scoop about young soldiers abandoned and left to rot in the most cruel prison systems in the world? It was insignificant, even in the light of the Kerry committee findings.

Constitutionally, Congress was meant to be the vehicle for bringing to light and rectifying injustice, particularly as it affects the functioning of bureaucracies that are meant to serve the people. What goes on in the armed forces, particularly during times of war, should be of paramount interest. The Fourth Estate was meant to throw light on the functioning of government and society as a whole. But in the handling of the Vietnam war and the issue of POWs, the government failed miserably, and the press acted as its propagandist and apologist.

Col. Millard S. Peck, the Pentagon's MIA-POW chief in the late eighties, resigned his position in disgust, referring to "official efforts to obfuscate . . . and stall the issue until it dies a natural death." He clearly outlined the problem in testimony before the select committee as well as in a 1991 speech that was well attended by the press. He told the committee that in the late 1980s he had accepted his appointment at the Pentagon with high hopes of helping to resolve the POW issue. He felt there was enough very high-level intelligence showing that there were live prisoners in Vietnam to force the communist government in Hanoi to cooperate. The country was in bad economic shape and desperate to renew diplomatic relations and a trade agreement with the United States. Peck knew that Washington's unshakable position as articulated by Henry Kissinger had always been that "we would never give aid to ransom our prisoners." He resigned when he discovered what this really meant. He believed that Vietnam had not only repeatedly hinted, but had, in fact, put a proposal on the table involving the United States paying four billion dollars through a third country (Canada) and reopening diplomatic relations and establishing trade in exchange for Vietnam returning POWs. Peck eventually began to understand that official US policy with respect to POWs was the exact opposite. Washington was making it clear to the Vietnamese that if they wanted to exchange ambassadors and establish trade relations, they'd better make sure that they didn't return prisoners. Vietnam got the message. There were no more offers to return POWs, and soon diplomatic relations and the all-important trade negotiations resumed. Peck's anger and frustration were made clear when he tacked his letter of resignation to his office door with his wartime bowie knife. There was no press coverage. Not even *Penthouse* magazine did the normally obligatory interview with Colonel Peck, a legendary Green Beret and genuine hero. What did make a few gossip columns around Washington was the unsubstantiated rumor that Colonel Peck dyed his hair.

Perhaps sorriest in the long litany of examples where the press voluntarily — or perhaps under pressure — abrogated its responsibility to cover a story of essential interest to large numbers of Americans was the effort by International Security Affairs to prevent committee staffers from reviewing key POW files. When permission was finally granted to review the files, they had been weeded so thoroughly that not a single paper specifically requested was part of the files. Destroyed were all the documents that listed special codes assigned to airmen during the Vietnam War in case of capture. The codes were to be used by a prisoner to send his own special signal by, for example, writing it with stones or stamping it out on grass so that US satellites could pick it up. In fact, all through the early eighties, satellites recorded a series of such signals in countries like Laos, where it was known that prisoners were being held. Committed members of Congress investigated these, but International Security never released the list of special codes, so no cross-checking could be done. Family members of the missing, veterans, and some in the intelligence bureaucracy had fought a running battle to get at those files so that comparisons could be made with the satellite data. There was great excitement in the POW community when committee staffers were finally given access to these records, only to discover that all files relating to the airmen's codes had been destroyed two years after the war ended. Thus, surviving prisoners who tried to transmit them did so in vain until they died. The government, on the other hand, continued to say until recently that what clearly looked like specialized codes, picked up by satellites over Laos, were "photo anomalies" or "shadows and vegetation." The press showed no interest at all in an issue that was by now twenty years old. When a retired colonel with an intelligence background whose son (also a colonel) was missing in Vietnam received information through an informal network of retired intelligence professionals that his family's old telephone number with area code (from the time his son was a child) had been picked up by satellites, he tried to get the press interested, but to no avail. The phone number was a cry for help, laid out by a specific prisoner using ingenuity to identify himself. The press as a group had been made to believe that the families of the missing simply couldn't accept the tragedy of their loved ones' deaths. In fact, what they couldn't accept was the deliberate deceit and carelessness of a bureaucracy that could arbitrarily destroy lifelines like the specialized codes.

In 1992 a Harvard researcher discovered a top secret Soviet Intelligence document—Quang 1205—recording that just four months before the peace accords were signed, Hanoi was holding twice as many prisoners as it admitted to having and twice as many as it would hand over to the United States. This got some media coverage.

But then the Pentagon issued its version of the document. It was authentic, they admitted, but was "replete with errors, omissions." The Clinton administration declared the document to be false. How could it do otherwise? Quang 1205 was the last thing standing in the way of the US trade embargo against Vietnam, which was lifted a few days after the document was declared to be false. No major news organization was interested in examining the issue further, even though the Pentagon presented no evidence that the document was in any way erroneous and high-ranking defectors from the former Soviet bloc confirmed the information in the document. In fact, if the document did contain "omissions" as claimed by the Pentagon, those omissions had to do with the fact that some US POWs had been shipped from Vietnam to Russia to be used as guinea pigs in experiments that involved amputations and mind-destroying drugs. One of the persons directly involved with shipping those American servicemen from Vietnam to Russia was Warsaw Pact general Jan Sejna, who the Defense Intelligence Agency hired after he defected in the midseventies. When Boris Yeltsin first came to power, he publicly acknowledged that the Soviet Union held American prisoners from as far back as the Korean War and even the Second World War, making it clear that he was willing to release all related records. Washington ignored this. So, except for a brief announcement, did the press. Naturally, Yeltsin mentioned it no more. Only the families of the missing and veterans who continued to care opened a dialogue with Russians, who understood their concerns because they were engaged in a similar search for their sons who had gone missing in Afghanistan. Both sides felt they had more in common with each other than with the bureaucrats in their respective countries who had obfuscated and denied the truth.

The Vietnam War was based on a lie that lives to this day: that Vietnamese torpedo boats attacked the USS *Maddox* in the Gulf of Tonkin. Ultimately, fifty-eight thousand lost their lives because of a trumped-up incident that resulted in one death. At the time of this writing (February 16, 2004), we are once again engaged in a war (Iraq) based on a lie. The lessons have not been learned. Military professionals believe that the president was under the influence of a network of political appointees who, according to recently retired air force colonel Karen Kwiatkowski, operated outside normal structures and practices. A former Pentagon officer and Middle East specialist who once worked in the office of the undersecretary of defense for policy, Kwiatkowski said this network had hijacked key areas of government policy: "Their goal is to perpetuate war to promote abstract global morality through military imperialism, propped up by muscular national socialism at home."

For today's ordinary foot soldiers, modern versions of Bobby Garwood, this does not bode well. But there are other disturbing signs of the government's lack of regard for the average soldier. Take, for example, one of the two letters of decorum issued before the troops left for Iraq: there was to be no display of the American flag in Iraq. Period. Troops were told that they were fighting for the security of their country and that although the flag symbolized the country they were fighting for, the only time that it could be displayed in any way was if they were killed. In that case, the flag could be draped over their coffins. To put this in context, never before in American history were men sent to fight for their country without being able to display in some way the flag they were fighting for. To add insult to injury, since March 2003 a newly enforced military regulation has forbidden taking or distributing images of caskets or body tubes containing the remains of soldiers who died overseas, lest such images disturb the public and remind US citizens of the price they pay to wage war. When Russel Kirk, after almost a year of effort that included filing a Freedom of Information Act request, managed to get 361 such photographs released, government spokesmen cited reasons of privacy for all the secrecy. Privacy? For whom? Certainly not for the nameless and faceless men lying inside the flag-draped "transfer tubes." Trying to hide their sacrifice does make a statement, though.

Anyone who has gone to war knows that intangibles count a great deal, and none count more than the reverence and rituals surrounding the symbol of what soldiers are willing to die for. That is why just before a soldier is buried, attending comrades-in-arms lift the flag off of the coffin and carefully fold it in a proscribed way: blue field with white stars on both sides of a triangle shaped like the cornice worn by George Washington's soldiers. Once folded, the officer in charge holds the triangle with one hand on top and one underneath and carries it to the closest surviving kin. While handing the flag to the soldier's relative, the following words are always uttered: "From a grateful nation."

Families were also disturbed by the fact that troops were dying daily because they were sent to Iraq and Afghanistan with Vietnam-era flak jackets that offered no protection against enemy Kalash-nikovs. Many reservists, who made up the bulk of troops in Iraq, went as long as four months without being paid. In any war, troop morale depends on a clearly scheduled return stateside. Yet troop shortages have meant that many soldiers have seen their return dates post-poned again and again. Many came home from Iraq to head immedi-ately for Afghanistan or South Korea. None were able to spend the usually compulsory time required to update their skills at the national training center at Fort Irwin, California. Nothing, so far, has been done to change this new policy.

The mainstream media, after ten months of war in Iraq, had yet to pick up on such issues even though *Stars and Stripes*, the US armed forces in-house journal, reported early on that soldiers were fed up. Not properly trained for the job they were expected to do, they saw no end in sight for the war and planned not to reenlist. And, reminis-cent of Bobby Garwood, the US government recently blocked modest (one million dollars) reparations to thirty-seven former POWs from the earlier Gulf War, which a US court had ordered to be paid out of Iraqi funds. The fact that American prisoners had even been taken in that war seems to have escaped notice, as has the fact that at least one prisoner of war was being held at the time this essay was written (April 29, 2004). Certainly media coverage was scant. Meanwhile, Defense Secretary Rumsfeld openly ignored international conven-tions involving the Red Cross.

Shades of Vietnam.

CHAPTER 13

INTO THE BUZZSAW

KRISTINA BORJESSON

Judy Schiller

Kristina Borjesson has been an independent producer and writer for more than twenty years. Besides editing Into the Buzzsaw, *she currently works on independent documentary film productions as well as writes and speaks publicly on media issues. Borjesson also produces and cohosts the* Expert Witness *radio show on WBAI in New York City. Prior to that, she produced for CNN's News-Stand magazine shows* (Fortune *and* Entertainment Weekly). *Borjesson joined CNN after working at CBS network, where she won an Emmy and a Murrow award for her investigative reporting on "CBS Reports: Legacy of Shame" with Dan Rather and Randall Pinkston. She was nominated again the following year for producing "CBS Reports: The Last Revolutionary," a film biography of Cuba's Fidel Castro. Borjesson also contributed in-depth, original reporting on the TWA 800 crash to CBS's* Evening News *and developed stories for* 60 Minutes. *Prior to producing for CBS, Borjesson was field producer for "Showdown in Haiti," an Emmy-nominated documentary for PBS's* Frontline. *She produced "Living with Crocodiles" for National Geographic Explorer while developing, acquiring, and distributing programming for the National Geographic Society's Television Division. As series coproducer for* On Television, *Borjesson worked on a thirteen-part series for PBS examining the roles TV plays in American society. Before that, she was director of research/production manager for a PBS film biography of Thomas Merton, the Trappist monk and renowned social critic. Borjesson is an alumna of Columbia University's Graduate School of Journalism.*

Y ou don't choose to have the kind of experience I had while trying to report on the demise of TWA Flight 800. It happens to you. You fall into it. At CBS, I'd recently picked up an Emmy for investigative reporting when I was assigned to investigate the crash. I had no idea that my life would be turned upside down and inside out—that I'd been assigned to walk into what I now call "the buzzsaw."

The buzzsaw is what can rip through you when you try to investigate or expose anything this country's large institutions—be they corporate or government—want kept under wraps. The system fights back with official lies, disinformation, and stonewalling. Your phone starts acting funny. Strange people call you at strange hours to give you strange information. The FBI calls you. Your car is broken into and the thief takes your computer and your reporter's notebook and leaves everything else behind. You feel like you're being followed everywhere you go. You feel like you've been sucked into a game of Dungeons and Dragons. It gets harder and harder to distinguish truth and reality from falsehood and fiction. The sense of fear and paranoia is, at times, overwhelming.

Walk into the buzzsaw and you'll cut right to this layer of reality. You will feel a deep sense of loss and betrayal. A shocking shift in paradigm. Anyone who hasn't experienced it will call you crazy. Those who don't know the truth, or are covering it up, will call you a conspiracy nut. The word "conspiracy" is commonly used now (either as an adjective or part of a phrase) to malign those who raise unpopular questions about sensitive issues. The fact is, conspiracies do exist. There are laws on the books addressing them and Justice Department officials deal with them all the time. However, in the case of the TWA Flight 800 disaster, I don't know of anyone who disagrees with the government's conclusions who describes the official investigation as a conspiracy. Incompetent. A cover-up. These are the descriptions most skeptics use to characterize the official investigation. Not "conspiracy."

WAKE-UP CALL

If TWA 800 hadn't exploded July 17, 1996, on its way to Paris, this book wouldn't have been written. If my executive producer at CBS, Linda Mason, hadn't assigned me to look into the story, you wouldn't be reading this chapter. Trust me, never in a million years did I ever imagine that I'd find myself in my current position as some kind of rebel trying to take on America's journalism establishment. I was reared a member of Haiti's "Morally Repugnant Elite" and educated, for the most part, in private institutions, including Columbia University's Graduate School of Journalism. Not a thing in my frankly elitist background prepared me for this experience.

Looking back, this story was gunning for me from the very beginning.

The night it happened, I'd come home from work around 6:00 PM, totally exhausted. Senior Producer Jamie Stolz and I had been getting ready for the premiere of "CBS Reports: The Last Revolutionary," a biography of Fidel Castro that we'd spent a year producing. It was going to air the following night, July 18, at 9:00 PM The show looked great and had already been critically acclaimed in the press. I couldn't wait to watch it on TV. At home, things were quiet. My husband was already on his way to JFK airport with my eleven-year-old son, who was catching a plane to Paris.

I decided to take a nap. At around 9:45 PM, the phone rang, jarring me out of a sound sleep. At the other end of the line, my neighbor was frantic. Was that my son's plane that just crashed? Her words were like hot oil on my brain. I told her I didn't know and hung up. I started dry heaving. Everything inside me went black.

My son was on Air France, five minutes behind TWA. That night, I cried for hours, out of relief, out of grief for what could have happened to him, and for what did happen to all those passengers on Flight 800.

The next night, my show was preempted by crash coverage.

THE ASSIGNMENT FROM HELL

What I liked about my boss, Linda Mason, was that from the beginning of my tenure at CBS, she was very supportive. Only a few months after I'd been hired, she okayed on short notice an expensive and risky idea I had to go down into Mexico, hook up with a smuggler, and cross the border with a couple of undocumented farm workers. She also spent a lot of money and gave me endless leeway to investigate a brutal crew boss in charge of large groups of undocumented farm workers in several states. But I delivered. The crew boss was busted and our show, "Legacy of Shame," won an Emmy. Then Linda assigned me to deliver Fidel Castro for a film biography, which I did. For three days, Castro gave Dan Rather an unprecedented personal tour of significant sites of the Cuban leader's life.

It was while I was still basking in the golden glow of all kinds of professional praise for the Fidel show that Linda called me down to her office to tell me that she wanted me to look into the crash. The man in charge of the FBI task force assigned to investigate whether criminal activity had caused the incident was already a familiar face on TV. Jim Kallstrom was telling the public barely a week after the crash how confident he was that his task force was going to solve the mystery of TWA 800's demise in no time: "We have a very, very active investigation. We're still getting very good information, so when the day comes, *and I think it will be soon . . . whether it's going to be three or four days or a week* [italics mine] . . . that we decide collectively and based on science and based on good forensic investigation, we will be able to move swiftly, aggressively, and professionally" (*Newshour* transcript, "Sleuthing with Disaster," August 22, 1996).

Later on, senior National Transportation Safety Board (NTSB) investigator Hank Hughes would provide shocking details to a senate judiciary committee about just how "swiftly, aggressively, and professionally" Kallstrom and his men moved for *sixteen months* after Kallstrom made that statement. Meanwhile, there I sat in my little box at CBS, gearing up my own investigation, blithely unaware that I was putting myself on a crash course with Mr. Kallstrom and his crew.

Linda told me that CBS already had reporters out on Long Island whom I could hook up with and that I should go to Washington to talk to correspondent Bob Orr. I flew to Washington and met with Orr, who told me that his high-level government sources in Washington were telling him the crash was caused by a mechanical failure. I didn't say much in response. I told him I was hearing other things and left it at that because it was obvious he trusted his sources.

On a story like this one, I was especially leery of official government sources. I was far more interested in talking to the people actually working at the crash site recovering the debris and investigating the cause. I wanted firsthand information. I wanted to get to the people who were directly involved, people who were not allowed to talk to the press. One of my rules of investigative reporting is: The more sensitive the investigation, the more you avoid "official" sources and the harder you try to get to the firsthand people. Sometimes you have to work with a "cutout," or someone these sources will talk honestly to, because they recognize the person as one of them.

My "cutout" was CBS's law enforcement consultant, Paul Ragonese. A no-bullshit cop from Brooklyn, Paul was on the NYPD's bomb squad and counterterrorism team for six years. He had a wealth of sources dealing directly with the aftermath of the crash—NYPD divers involved in debris recovery, other specially trained NYPD personnel, and even agents on Kallstrom's task force. Here are excerpts from the notes I took when he got back to me after talking to them. For obvious reasons, I'll only identify the sources as being NYPD:

> NYPD: "From day one, there were military guys everywhere on the scene . . . thinks military is involved. Finding absolutely of bomb or missile. He says that the military was doing something twelve miles off the coast of Moriches. The whole thing is screwed up. Just a mess. People running around, touching stuff."

(Altered, tainted, or missing evidence was a hallmark of this investigation, but more on that later on.)

> NYPD: "NYPD divers showed up on Thursday morning, and were given radio instructions by the military not to dive until the military showed up. The NYPD divers waited until Sunday for the military divers from the Explosive Ordnance Division (EOD) from Fort Monmouth to show up . . . military gave NYPD divers orders where to dive."

Paul also secretly met with two high-level members of the FBI task force. The ground rules for the meeting were that they would not offer any information, but would confirm or deny any information Paul ran by them. They confirmed that military exercises were going on in the area that evening and that a drone was part of the exercises.

They also told Paul that they had not yet been given permission (as of October, almost three months after the crash) to "check out" the military.

In an October 18, 1996, memo, Paul, in his inimical, cut-the crap style, drew up a list of unanswered questions that no one else at CBS was asking, among them,

What was a sub hunter doing in the area?

Why was a missile cruise ship on patrol in the area?

Why did the Pentagon deny military presence in the area that night?

Why was the FBI involved from day one when normal procedure is to have the NTSB determine cause?

How do you write off the findings of missile experts who stated what the witnesses saw was consistent with a missile?

How is it that no military personnel that were in the area (P-3 Orion, USS *Normandy*) saw anything when civilians saw a lot?

Shouldn't we question the effectiveness of our defense if two high-tech military units missed something that was in the sky that night?

Paul ended his memo with this: "In any investigation there is an evolution of suspects and scenarios. There is mere suspicion, reasonable suspicion, and finally probable cause. All three scenarios (malfunction, explosive device, missile) cannot all be equal. After three months, one scenario must be the frontrunner. As of now, the malfunction is not logical and I believe never was; the explosive device on the plane is not being supported by the evidence although I believe still very possible, leaving only the missile scenario which includes witnesses which will never go away." Those last six words were prophetic, as even now, the witnesses hang around this officially closed investigation like skeletons that won't stay in the closet.

Besides an endless lineup of the logical sources — eyewitnesses, scientists, law enforcement, medical personnel, airport personnel, etc., I was talking to other reporters. Most journalists hate to share, but on a huge story like this, pooling resources with solid reporters is, I think, a good idea. In his stories, veteran print reporter David Hendrix at *The Press-Enterprise* in Riverside, California, was asking the same questions as I, so I called him. He had some very good military sources who gave him information he was willing to pass along, as well as a few technical experts he was willing to share. David introduced me to cop-turned-journalist Jim Sanders and brought me one step closer to my day of reckoning at CBS.

Like me, Jim Sanders was inadvertently sucked into this story. His wife, Elizabeth, happened to work for TWA training flight attendants and was hearing all kinds of strange rumors. She and her colleagues asked Jim to look into them. Jim eventually hooked up with David Hendrix and a stunning source known to me at the time as

"Hangarman." The only thing I knew about Hangarman was that he was an investigator inside the Calverton hangar (where the remains of Flight 800 were collected) who was so troubled by what he saw going on in there that he started talking to Sanders and smuggling out documents for him to peruse.

Hangarman had smuggled out a copy of the downed plane's debris field that undercut assertions that the center wing tank was the site of the "initiating event" that caused the plane to explode. He'd also sent a copy of the NTSB "Chairman's Briefing/Status Report," dated November 15, 1996, in which Chairman James Hall directs Ron Schleede, deputy director of the NTSB's Office of Aviation Safety, to write a letter for his boss, Bernard Loeb, to sign. The purpose of the letter was eyebrow raising: "The letter will reference," Hall wrote, "the [FAA] technician [not identified by name] who did the analysis resulting in conflicting radar tracks that indicated a missile. It will also inquire why that information was reported to the White House and sent to the FAA Technical Center before the Safety Board was given access to the data." The letter was sent to Mr. David F. Thomas of the FAA's Office of Accident Investigation. It contained a paragraph outlining an interesting sequence of events:

> . . . during the first few hours after the accident, some FAA personnel made a preliminary assessment that recorded ATC [air traffic control] radar data showed primary radar hits that indicated the track of a high-speed target that approached and merged with TWA 800. One of your staff called our office about 0930 on July 8 [sic, the actual date is July 18], 1996 to advise us of the preliminary assessment of the radar data by FAA personnel, suggesting that a missile may have hit TWA 800. This preliminary assessment was passed on to other government officials, including White House officials. After the Safety Board received the ATC radar and reviewed it, it was determined that the preliminary assessment of FAA staff was incorrect.

With that, Bernard Loeb told the FAA that the NTSB's analysis trumped the FAA's. Then came a bit of strong-arming: "We understand that FAA official [sic] now agree [this part is underlined in pen or pencil] with the Safety Board's determination. . . . I would appreciate it if you could verify that all specialists and/or managers involved in the preliminary radar analyses fully agree that there is no evidence within the FAA ATC radar data of a track that would suggest a high-speed target merged with TWA 800." If smoke wasn't coming out of Thomas's ears when he read the part where Loeb tells him to get all the FAA experts to discredit themselves and get in line behind the NTSB's experts, surely he was fuming after reading Loeb's next request: "I would also appreciate an explanation about how the pre-liminary incorrect assessment occurred, so that potential public or media inquiries can be handled in an accurate and consistent manner." So not only did Loeb want Thomas to get his experts to back up the NTSB whether they wanted to or not, he wanted Thomas to provide him with an explanation as to why the FAA experts screwed up, so that Loeb could announce it to the world. In his January 9, 1997, response to Loeb's letter, Thomas refused to roll over completely. He said that he could not confirm that all the FAA personnel involved in the early radar analysis agreed with the NTSB's assessment. On a more conciliatory note, Thomas did say that "The assessment by the FAA Technical Center indicated that the likelihood of a missile was remote," but he qualified this statement by adding, "It must be noted, however, that FAA air traffic radar is designed to detect and monitor aircraft, not high-speed missiles, so any conclusions based on this review must consider the technical limits of the radar."

Network TV coverage of this exchange of letters conveyed the impression that the FAA technician had used bad judgment and flown off the handle too fast when he fired off his memo to the White House. The Loeb/Thomas letters were the prevailing images used. The "missile" part of Loeb's letter was highlighted and excerpted and was followed by the excerpted and highlighted "remote possibility" line in Thomas's response. The coverage bolstered the NTSB's posi-tion and discredited the FAA. Mainstream media wrapped up the whole episode in a nice, neat package, even though any journalist with half-decent instincts could tell there was more digging to be done on the radar issue.

SHIPS—WHAT SHIPS?—IN THE NIGHT

Around the time Sanders was receiving Hangarman's documents, the Pierre Salinger affair broke. A former White House press secretary and network correspondent, Salinger announced to the world on

November 8, 1996, that he'd received documents from French intelligence proving that a US Navy missile had accidentally downed the jetliner. That same day, the FBI's Jim Kallstrom called a press conference to deny Salinger's allegations. When the conference began, he was flanked by Rear Admiral Edward K. Kristensen (the NTSB's Jim Hall was late) and surrounded by a phalanx of other secret service and military personnel. Kallstrom rattled off a prepared speech, and then it was time for questions. A man raised his hand and asked what I thought was a pertinent—and impertinent—question. He wanted to know why the navy was involved in the recovery and investigation while a possible suspect. Kallstrom's response was immediate: "Remove him!" he yelled. Two men leapt over to the questioner and grabbed him by the arms. There was a momentary chill in the air after the guy had been dragged out of the room. Kallstrom, Kristensen, Hall, and their entourage acted as if nothing had happened. There was something very disquieting about the goonish tactics. A dispassionately dismissive response from Kallstrom would have been a more convincing way to tell us that the navy had nothing to do with the disaster. In any case, right then and there, the rest of us had been put on notice to be on our best behavior.

The conference continued. Admiral Kristensen explained that the navy had only two assets in the area that night: a P-3 Orion submarine-hunting plane 80 miles south of the crash and the missile cruiser *Normandy* about 185 miles southwest. He was repeating the Defense Department's statement made moments after the explosion. The admiral was either misinformed or lying. This would become evident as time went on.

Both the P-3 Orion and the *Normandy* were capable of electronically tracking any object that may have hit the plane prior to its exploding. But by alleged unfortunate coincidence, neither did, according to the navy. Admiral Kristensen said at the press conference that at that time, the *Normandy* was conducting "basic engineering casualty control exercises," so the ship's radar was put on low power and couldn't pick up anything past the 150-mile range. Journalist Dave Hendrix scrutinized the *Normandy*'s ship log, which, he reported in *The Press-Enterprise*, "notes every fluctuation on fog, speed, *equipment change* and *on-board exercise*" [italics mine]. The log, Hendrix wrote, "records no exercise or radar reduction that night." Indeed, on that day from noon to midnight the information recorded on the log is routine stuff, like "c.o. [commanding officer] on the bridge," "c.o. off the bridge," and "observed sunset energized nav [navigational] lights." There is absolutely no mention of a "basic engineering casualty control exercise." So again, what we have here is either a lie or a gross oversight on the part of the ship personnel keeping the log and the ship commander who signed off on it. Either prospect is disquieting.

Flight 800 crashed off the coast of Rep. Michael Forbes's (R-NY) district. His constituents called in droves after the disaster, putting intense pressure on him to find out what happened. Forbes told his then–chief of staff, Kelly O'Meara, to look into it. A few weeks after the Kallstrom/Hall/Kristensen press conference, O'Meara met with three FBI agents. She asked them if there had been any submarines in the area when Flight 800 crashed. Their response was to ask her if she had top security clearance. She didn't so they refused to discuss the matter.

Meanwhile, a paper trail of conflicting information flowed into Kelly O'Meara's office from official military sources. In a December 1996 letter to Congressman Forbes, the Navy Department wrote that the P-3 Orion "had flown directly over TWA" [italics mine] just before the explosion and "dropped sonobuoys during a training portion of the flight." In February 1997, the Defense Department's general counsel's office wrote that the P-3 "was flying on a routine training flight *approximately 55 miles southeast of the site*" [italics mine]. Nearly a year after the crash, the general counsel's office reported, "the Navy has confirmed that *there were no submarines* [my italics] in the vicinity of the TWA Flight 800 crash site at the time of the crash. Only two submarines were operating north of the Virginia Capes Operating Area at the time. These *submarines* were operating *approximately 107 and 138* [my italics] miles from the crash site." So, according to official sources, at 185 nautical miles away the *Normandy* was in the vicinity, and at 107 and 138 miles away, respectively, the subs weren't. The same report upgraded the P-3's "routine training flight" to being "en route to operations with the USS *Trepang*," the sub that was 107 miles from the crash site. Later on, it would be discovered that there were more military assets that were much closer. The point here is to show you how information is twisted and turned, how contradictory information is disseminated at different times to create confusion, how lasting misimpressions are manufactured, and how ultimately the truth gets buried under mountains of "information."

O'Meara's most spectacular find with respect to military assets in the immediate area when Flight 800 went down would come around two years later, after she'd been pressured out of her job and had started working as an investigative reporter for the *Washington Time's Insight* magazine. The NTSB had previously released radar information that focused on a 20-nautical-mile circle centered on the crash site. According to O'Meara's September 20, 1999, article for *Insight*, this information "was the basis of the FBI's conclusion that there was little air or naval traffic in the selected area at the time of the crash." But now, O'Meara had received additional radar data from the NTSB which encompassed a larger perimeter. Just outside the 20-mile nautical circle the NTSB had previously released was a stunning sight: ". . . between the perimeters of a 22-nautical-mile circle and a 35 nautical mile circle," O'Meara reported, "a concentration of a large number of radar blips appears to be moving into a well known military warning area closed to civilian and commercial traffic." This warning area, known as W-105, "was activated for military exercises along with several other warning areas along the Atlantic coast," she added. When activated for military use, these areas are off-limits to nonmilitary vessels like commercial and pleasure craft.

Months before O'Meara's article was published, the National Transportation Safety Board's radar analysts had identified the tracks of four surface vessels that were within a *six-mile* radius of the jetliner when it exploded. The closest vessel is now known as the "30-knot track."

In his "Independent Interim Report Regarding Some Anomalies within the Official Crash Investigation of TWA Flight 800," independent investigator and physicist Dr. Tom Stalcup explained why. By the way, Stalcup and his associates were the only independent investigators that NTSB Chairman Jim Hall ever met with (Stalcup told me Hall offered him a job during the meeting on August 22, 2000) to answer questions. In his report, Stalcup wrote,

1. [The 30-knot track was] confirmed a surface vessel by the FBI [Lewis D. Schiliro, acting director in charge, FBI, in a letter to Rep. James Traficant] and NTSB [Radar Data Group Chairman Charlie Pereira, in recorded phone conversation with Tom Stalcup (1998)], it was in the area . . . moments before the debris began to fall. It left the scene at 30 knots (35MPH) rather than assisting with search and rescue. [This is illegal as per maritime law; Federal Code Title 46, Section 2304 "Duty to Provide Assistance at Sea."]

294 INTO THE BUZZSAW

2. Its [the 30-knot track] position just before F800's breakup is consistent with the origin of "flare" type object, which rose from the ocean surface, according to eyewitnesses.

3. Its speed (30 knots) and direction (away from the accident scene and land) are inconsistent with the many citizen mariners who sailed to the area to aid in the search and rescue effort. [The question here is, why was this ship leaving the scene at a fast clip when even citizens in pleasure craft were rushing to the scene?]

4. To date, this vessel has not been identified by the FBI or NTSB as stated in the following letter from Lewis D. Schiliro, Acting Assistant Director in Charge, FBI.

Stalcup goes on to quote Schiliro's response to Rep. James Traficant's question in an April 1998 letter about whether or not the FBI had positively identified all the aircraft and vessels near the flight that evening. Schiliro's response came three months later: "No . . . in January 1997, the FBI first noted the presence of a surface vessel . . . between 25 and 35 knots. . . . Despite extensive efforts, the FBI has been unable to identify this vessel."

After Schiliro wrote to Traficant, Accuracy In Media's Reed Irvine had this phone conversation with FBI task force chief James Kallstrom about the 30-knot track:

Irvine: Hey, the Bureau [FBI] just sent Traficant a letter saying they couldn't identify three vessels that were in the vicinity for privacy reasons — come on.

Kallstrom: Well, yeah. Well, we all know what those were. In fact, I even spoke about those publicly.

Irvine: What were they?

Kallstrom: They were navy vessels that were on classified maneuvers.

Irvine: What about the one that went racing out to sea at 30 knots?

Kallstrom: That was a helicopter.

Irvine: On the surface?

Kallstrom: Well, between you and I, the conventional wisdom was, *although it's probably not totally provable* [emphasis mine], that it was a helicopter.

In one brief "doublespeak" exchange, Kallstrom went from saying the 30-knot track "was a helicopter," to "it's probably not totally provable" that it was a helicopter. Meanwhile, Schiliro, Kallstrom's successor, had already told Congressman Traficant that it was a surface vessel, but that the FBI hadn't figured out what *kind* of vessel it was. It's troubling that these two top dogs in the FBI couldn't get their stories straight. But it's even more disturbing that they couldn't identify the "30-knot track." If they're telling the truth, it says something pretty unsettling about our top law enforcement and military agencies' capabilities. It says that they are incompetent beyond our wildest nightmares and that we are extremely vulnerable to attack. Frankly, I hope they're lying on this one.

Even though the "30-knot track" has still not been identified, Kallstrom has long since assured the American people that no stone has been left unturned. If you ask me, this sure as hell is an unturned stone. In fact, it's been so pointedly ignored that the stone has turned into a boulder in the minds of those paying attention. It should be noted here, too, that O'Meara received the additional radar information almost two years after the NTSB publicly released the original radar data as Exhibit 13A of the "Aircraft Performance Group Chairman's Factual Report" at a hearing in Baltimore. She received it on a disk that, she reported, had "the *complete* [italics mine] database of Exhibit 13A." Here again, it seems that in December 1997 the NTSB used the classic "sin of omission" maneuver to lie to the public about what was out there that night. The radar information released at the Baltimore hearing was cut off right when it got really interesting. This is the kind of stuff that anyone even halfheartedly digging into this story runs into on a regular basis. The lesson here—and I'm going to repeat it over and over in this essay—is that on sensitive stories *you can't trust official sources.*

ALL MISSILES PRESENT AND ACCOUNTED FOR

This is going to be a brief section, but I just had to include it because it shows just how outrageous the lying gets. Shortly after TWA Flight 800's demise, the Pentagon assured the public that all missiles in the US arsenal were accounted for, implying that friendly fire was out of the question. Of course, no one asked how this was done, and done so fast. The answer is it wasn't, and it couldn't have been. There are hundreds of military facilities around the country, and each and every one would have to have been contacted to begin the process. Plus, missiles are constantly being moved around, so even an approximate accounting of the entire arsenal in America would have been difficult. Counting US missiles overseas would have been an even bigger problem. On his way to the crash site on July 17, Jim Kallstrom expressed concern about American missile stocks that weren't accounted for after the Gulf War. And what about all those missiles we gave to the Afghan rebels and then tried to buy back from them — with little or no success? Two months after Flight 800 exploded, the General Accounting Office put out a report entitled "Inventory Management: Vulnerability of Sensitive Defense Material to Theft." Here's part of what's written in the "Results in Brief" section of the report: "Discrepancies still exist between records of the number of missiles and our physical count. Also, the missiles may be vulnerable to insider theft because DOD is not always selecting a representative sample of containers to be opened during maintenance checks. In addition, some facilities are not fully complying with DOD physical security requirements." Gives you a warm, fuzzy feeling, doesn't it? When the Pentagon stepped up to the microphone and announced that all their missiles were present and accounted for, they didn't really mean it. What they were really saying to the public and the press was, "Don't go there."

MINISTERS OF TRUTH

While I was sifting through the reports Paul Ragonese was bringing in from his law enforcement sources on the scene and trying to figure out who was telling the truth and who was lying, Dan Rather was talking to the press about the Salinger situation. Rather told *New York Times* reporter Matthew Purdy that when the story broke, he decided to lead with it "primarily to knock it down." "I'll never cease to be amazed how a rumor takes off like mildew in a damp basement," Rather continued, adding that there was "quite considerable evidence that it didn't happen."

I have a lot of respect for Mr. Rather. He bears the extreme pressure of being CBS New's living logo with great grace for a man of his intensity. When I produced for him, he was quintessentially professional and easy to work with. So I wince when I say this: To my mind, his remarks were out of line. At the time, there was no considerable evidence of any kind, although a large number of eyewitnesses were raising eyebrows about seeing "flare-like" objects going up to meet the plane. Even the FBI was still publicly looking into a possible missile hit. Without a doubt, Salinger's rushing to the press with a statement he couldn't back up was incredibly irresponsible, and he got what he deserved. Rather's comments were just plain inappropriate. When he made them, he (purposely or inadvertently) took off his journalist's hat and became a communications officer for the government. It wouldn't be the last time.

During the first weeks following the Flight 800's demise, there was a great deal of coverage about evidence of a high-pressure explosive force—either a bomb or a missile—causing the jet to blow up. Indeed, the coverage was going in the same direction as the FBI. The *New York Times* was printing headlines like "Jet's Landing Gear Is Said to Provide Evidence of a Bomb," (July 31, 1996), "Fuel Tank's Condition Makes Malfunction Seem Less Likely" (August 14, 1996), and "FBI Says 2 Labs Found Traces of Explosive on TWA Jetliner" (August 24, 1996). But by September, the press was turning around to the new government line, no questions asked. "New Focus on Malfunctions in Inquiry on TWA Crash," read a *New York Times* September 19, 1996, headline.

What's fascinating about this is how the same paper first prints a series of reports talking about hard evidence the investigators have uncovered indicating that a mechanical failure was unlikely—like "traces of explosives in the passenger cabin," "very heavy damage to the landing gear," and "portions of the fuel tank wreckage" being "virtually unscathed"—and then turns around and writes a subsequent story that says, "The investigators acknowledge that they have no evidence pointing to a mechanical malfunction. Rather, they say, the failure to find proof of a bombing, after more than two months, lends indirect credence to another theory..." *Indirect credence to another theory!?* What happened to the traces of explosives, etc., that you reported about earlier?

And that's another huge problem for you, the average citizen seeking good information from your newspaper or TV news broadcast. You probably didn't realize until you read this just how mutable the truth is. You probably didn't know that often what is reported today is the truth, until official sources change it later on. The new truth can be the exact opposite of what was reported before, and it will be reported, no questions asked. What was reported before no longer exists or matters because official sources, our nation's ministers of truth, say it doesn't. Go back and read George Orwell's *1984*. It'll give you goose bumps.

CHAOS AT CALVERTON

While government officials were publicly assuring everyone that the investigation was well in hand and proceeding apace, insiders were saying otherwise. Paul Ragonese's NYPD source's statement, about "people running around touching stuff" at the Calverton hangar where the jetliner was being reconstructed, was later corroborated by an October 28, 1996, document from the Justice Department's Office of Inspector General that investigative reporter John Kelly gave to me. The document contains a transcript of a telephone interview that Inspector Alison Murphy conducted with FBI Examiner Bill Tobin. Tobin talked about a memo he wrote that contained a paragraph about the "hysteria" at Calverton in the first months of the TWA investigation. Tobin told Murphy that he wrote that the NTSB "questioned the behavior of [the FBI's] Explosives Unit Examiner Tom Thurman, because they felt some of his behavior was unscientific and that he had acted inappropriately during parts of the investigation." Tobin described Thurman as "exhibiting storm trooper behavior." "At one point during the investigation," Tobin said to Murphy, "Thurman dug into passenger seats and proceeded to place fragments in pillboxes with no concern for trajectory." (Analyzing and recording the trajectories or directions the fragments came from would help investigators determine what caused the explosion that embedded them in the seats.) Later on, I got even more details about evidence being tainted at Calverton when Kelly O'Meara and I met with an FBI agent who told us that Kallstrom had a posse of agents (including Tom Thurman) who were running around the hangar picking up debris and literally banging it up to make it fit into boxes headed for the FBI lab in Washington. There, the agent told us, this "evidence" was to be used to support Kallstrom's bomb scenario. He also said that agents inside Calverton had taken to calling the FBI task force chief, Jim "It's a Fucking Bomb" Kallstrom. Even more outrageous, the agent told us that FBI agent Ken Maxwell was giving visiting VIPs "missile tours" of the wreckage, ostensibly pointing out evidence of a missile hit.

But back to the altered, tainted, and missing evidence. On the NTSB side, senior investigator Hank Hughes's contemporaneous notes for his May 10, 1999, appearance before a senate judiciary committee hearing on "Administrative Oversight of TWA Flight 800," are even more mind-boggling:

1. ME's [Medical Examiner's] office — [FBI agents at Medical Examiner's office] lacked organization and failed to establish chain of custody on clothing and particulate matter taken from ME staff. Didn't decontaminate same at Calverton.
2. Stowed blood-soaked passenger and crew clothing in refrigerator trailer contrary to universally accepted forensic procedure. Two months into the investigation the refrigerator trailer's refrigeration unit ran out of fuel and the contents of the trailer baked in 90 degree temperature for $2\frac{1}{2}$ days until the trailer was refueled and the refrigerator unit restarted. This resulted in mold cultures growing in the clothing and other potential evidence which had been stored in the trailer.
3. Took seat covers off without documenting where they came from. [In his testimony, Hughes said that "many, many seat covers — there were 430 passenger seats and 21 crew seats — had the seat covers removed and they were commingled in a dumpster. About two months into the investigation, I went to the dumpster with the assistance . . . of an FBI agent . . . and tried to sort out the materials in there. We found, in addition to the seat covers, actually seats that had been missing. . . ."]
4. Didn't x-ray seats in an organized manner. Missed several rows of seats. [Hughes's testimony regarding x-raying and chemical swabbing seats: ". . . my team and I went to great pains to specifically tag the seats . . . that had not been examined. Yet to this day [May 10, 1999], those tags are still there because they have not — the FBI never went back and did a subsequent exam, either by chemical swab or x-ray examination."]
5. Chemical swabbing wasn't done on an on-going basis.
6. Parts were taken from the interior hangar by the FBI without on-scene FBI or NTSB staff being consulted or advised as to what was taken. [Hughes testimony: "Another problem that occurred, and it was recognized about two months into the investigation, was the disappearance of parts from the hangar. . . . We found

that seats were missing and other evidence had been disturbed."] After NTSB complaint was lodged, FBI security caught
two FBI agents in interior hangar in the early morning hours. FBI
installed security cameras and the problem was eliminated.

7. West Coast agent [in his testimony, Hughes identified Ricky
   Hahn as the FBI agent] attempted to flatten pieces of wreckage.
8. Bomb techs did not document evidence in accordance with
   accepted procedures.
9. ERT [Evidence Recovery Team (FBI)] qualification in basic forensics
   very limited. Only four [out of thirty-two] of the ERTs were trained.
10. FBI declined to provide representation on investigative groups.
    [The NTSB's investigation was compartmentalized into a series
    of groups, i.e., the "Witness Group," the "Forensic Pathology/
    Medical Examiners Group," etc. The FBI, according to Hughes,
    did not have representatives in any of these groups. What
    Hughes is saying here is critical because although the NTSB was
    legally mandated to lead the government's investigation unless
    and until the FBI formally declared it a criminal investigation
    (which they never did), the fact is that the FBI took charge and
    controlled access to the most critical evidence. By not providing
    representation on investigative groups, the FBI essentially
    obstructed the NTSB's investigation.]
11. [FBI] Treatment of ATF [Alcohol, Tobacco, and Firearms] was
    unprofessional. Didn't use them [even though explosives inves-
    tigations are ATF's forte].
12. Lack of biohazard training and improper use of equipment.
    Wouldn't let their people [meaning the FBI wouldn't let FBI
    agents] use NTSB equipment.
13. Apparent lack of coordination between FBI bomb tech, lab, and
    agents assigned to investigation.
14. Agents stuck knives and screw [sic, he probably means "screw-
    drivers"] into seat back [sic] which destroyed any chance of tra-
    jectory analysis.
15. FBI took charge of victim recovery but failed to use GPS [Global
    Positioning Satellite] fixes to verify recovery location.
16. An FBI agent, not associated with the activities in Calverton,
    brought an unauthorized psychic into the hangar in September.

Hughes also had this to say about the aforementioned FBI Explosives Unit Manager, Tom Thurman, his group, and what they were
looking for: "Mr. Thurman's group basically got to the scene and when
we started to assemble the parts and catalog them for later reconstruc-

tion, began to do the chemical screening and examination, looking for what they believed was an explosive device, you know, a bomb or a missile. . . . The problem was . . . we [the NTSB investigators] wanted to do it in a systematic organized way. Their job, from what I could see, was more of a shotgun approach. . . . It caused some problems and friction."

Hughes testified that the ratio of "FBI and other folks" to NTSB personnel was about one hundred to one. This, along with the information provided above and the fact that the FBI refused to share its firsthand eyewitness information with the NTSB, should leave no doubt that while the NTSB was, by law, supposed to be in charge of the investigation, it never really was.

One month after his damning testimony before the senate judiciary committee, Hughes provided even more striking evidence of the NTSB's backseat role in the investigation. Committee chairman Sen. Charles Grassley wrote Hughes with one more question on behalf of committee member Sen. Strom Thurmond: Did Hughes talk to his NTSB superiors about the FBI's shenanigans? Hughes's answer was as forthright and brutal as his testimony:

> I saw little positive action taken by the NTSB to address these problems. In my opinion, we (NTSB) had a serious leadership problem during the course of the investigation. One of many examples of this was vice chairman's Robert Francis's absence on a daily basis from all daily investigative progress meetings. . . . I have participated in over 110 major transportation accident investigations while with the NTSB and the TWA 800 investigation is the only one in which the NTSB board member in charge was never available to the investigative staff.

But Hughes didn't stop there: "During the course of the on-scene investigation, which lasted over a 15-plus month period, the NTSB vice chairman in charge of the NTSB investigation not only never showed up for daily investigative progress meetings, he gave away the Safety Board's authority, to [sic] without, to my knowledge, consulting the staff or the headquarters managers. It is easy to see how the FBI just resorted to their usual modus operandi of taking charge even if they didn't know what they were getting into."

The FBI and the NTSB were at loggerheads from day one of the investigation, but the press didn't pay much attention to this crucial detail. There was little cooperation and a lot of compartmentalizing going on. The guys with the guns were really in charge, controlling key evidence, even though legally, they weren't supposed to be.

DAY OF RECKONING

I had started talking to Jim Sanders after David Hendrix introduced us and told Sanders he could trust me. As a result, CBS was the first network to receive a copy of the documents smuggled out of the Calverton hangar. Since my executive producer, Linda Mason, had told me to offer all new information to *CBS Evening News* first, I took the stack of papers consisting of a copy of the debris field and some other documents (including the NTSB "Chairman's Briefing/Status Report" of November 15, 1996) to Northeastern Bureau Chief Bill Felling. I also gave Felling a copy of a lab report Sanders had sent to me which detailed the analysis of red residue found on some of the jetliner's seats. Sanders was soon to become an international figure by announcing that the analysis showed that the elements in the residue were consistent with those in solid rocket missile fuel.

CBS Law Enforcement Consultant Paul Ragonese and I had met with Felling to talk about what we'd uncovered so far. First, there was the fact that an investigator on the inside was leaking documents to Sanders because he felt something fishy was going on. The debris field documents were among them and were interesting because they showed what fell off first and where it landed. Since what is hit first usually falls off first, it raised questions about where the initiating event had occurred. Paul told Felling about his secret meeting with the FBI task force members who had told him that there were military exercises going on out there that night and that a drone had been involved. Felling asked Ragonese if his sources would be willing to come forward. I could practically hear what Ragonese was thinking (What? Is this guy stupid, or what?), but he calmly told Felling that this would not be possible because these guys would not only lose their jobs, but even worse things could happen to them. Meanwhile, Felling didn't seem too interested in the documents I'd handed to him.

When Jim Sanders was ready to go public with his "residue" story, he gave *The Press-Enterprise*, David Hendrix's paper, the print scoop and me the TV scoop. CBS was going to be the first TV network to tell the story of an independent investigator who claimed he'd been given evidence of a missile hitting TWA 800 from "Hangarman," a government investigator inside Calverton.

Since I "got" him, I interviewed Sanders. Sanders has a cheery manner of presenting things, and I couldn't help wondering during the interview if this man realized what he was doing. I remember, too, that an associate producer from my documentary unit had sat in on my interview with Sanders. Afterward, she told me that he gave her the creeps. I was taken aback by her remark but thought that maybe she was put off by the fact that he lacked some kind of title that would make him a more "legitimate" source. Personally, I was feeling a twinge of worry for the guy. To me, it looked like he was headed for big trouble after engaging in what I felt was either an act of courage or of supreme folly. Today, I realize it was an act of courage.

My interview with Sanders was in the can, and the documents he'd given me were on Felling's desk, yet no one at *Evening News* was using the material to put a story together. I couldn't figure out why, and I was getting antsy as other networks were calling him. Out of desperation, I finally did something very politically incorrect in any corporate environment. I burst into a morning meeting of news executives sitting in the glass-encased conference room of the *Evening News* "fishbowl" and demanded to know why we weren't doing a story on Sanders and his documents. At the very least I felt that the fact that an NTSB investigator was smuggling documents out to him was newsworthy. As I stood there in front of a sea of white shirts, someone I didn't recognize looked at me and said, "you think it's a missile, don't you?" "I don't know what the hell it is," I shot back, "but don't you think we should be doing a story that asks a few questions about this guy and his documents?" The silence that followed was deafening. I couldn't believe it. When I'd walked in there, I genuinely thought that there had been some major oversight and that I was helping to correct it at a level where it could be corrected immediately. Their response told me otherwise. I walked out of there feeling like I'd cooked my own goose. As I headed down a hallway back to my office, one of the *Evening News* producers ran after me. She introduced herself and said that she had some good sources who were talking about friendly fire. I don't remember the rest of our conversation because my head was vibrating, but we had a few conversations after that, and it was clear she felt that the issue was worth looking into, but dangerous to a reporter's career. Obviously, she had better survival instincts than I.

Meanwhile, the story was getting very hot and other networks were clamoring for Sanders, so I was forced to give up CBS's exclusive and tell him he could go elsewhere for airtime. Of course, the minute word hit the fishbowl that the other networks were booking Sanders, Felling called me to ask me if I could bring him in again. Controlling my anger, I told him I'd try, but Sanders was already in NBC's clutches. I marched down to the fishbowl, and in front of all the producers yelled out to Felling: "We've lost him to NBC!" He just looked at me and shrugged: "So (as in so what)?" Unfortunately, I couldn't hide my contempt as I turned on my heel and went back to my office.

But CBS could no longer avoid the Sanders story. Felling called and asked me if I could get photographs of the red residue. Sanders FedExed them to me, and I gave them to Felling. That day, I went down to Felling's office to talk to him about the story and remind him of the Sanders interview that we had in the can. As I walked in, Felling was on the phone with David Caravello, a producer in the Washington bureau. Felling signaled me to get on the phone extension to hear what Caravello was saying. I picked up right when an irate Caravello was telling Felling that Sanders wasn't credible and that he wasn't going to give him any airtime. I should have known. Caravello was producing for correspondent Bob Orr who had told me earlier that his top Pentagon contacts had assured him that the US military had nothing to do with TWA 800's demise and that it looked like a mechanical malfunction was responsible.

I couldn't help feeling that Orr was invested in the mechanical malfunction theory because he didn't want to contradict the sources that he depended on to do his job. I couldn't blame him. In the hard and fast TV news business, quick access to top sources is a bottom line.

After hanging up from Caravello, I turned to Felling and told him that I thought the Sanders story should be done with a New York correspondent. For Orr to do a story that might rile his Pentagon sources would, I told Felling, be the equivalent of him "shitting in his own nest." We could run two tracks on this story, I told him, the official Washington track and the New York track that raised more sensitive questions. Felling just looked at me and smiled a weak smile. What I realized later was that there was no way CBS was going to air a story that would rile the Pentagon. Silly me.

CBS used a classic avoidance tactic to keep Sanders off the air while reporting his side of the story. On the *Evening News*, Dan Rather, reading off of a teleprompter, told America about Sanders's allegations. Rather's narration continued while the camera cut to a photo of the residue that Sanders had provided. Then it was time for the FBI's response to the allegations. The FBI's TWA 800 task force chief, James Kallstrom, appeared live. Looming large in a big-screen image, Kallstrom told Dan that the red residue was glue. The fact is, Kallstrom lied to Rather, and Rather bought it hook, line, and sinker. Without one follow-up question, not even one asking how it could be that Sanders was able to get a piece of evidence from the hangar where security was supposed to be so tight, Rather thanked Kallstrom and moved on to the next story.

Shortly thereafter, Sanders wanted to know if I wanted a sample of the seat foam with residue on it so CBS could have it tested and report the results. He still trusted me, and I still hadn't given up on the network, so I told him that I'd ask around and get back to him. I called Felling and asked him if *CBS Evening News* was interested. He told me he'd get back to me. He called back and said no. Given my previous dealings with him, I wasn't surprised, so I didn't ask why. I went up to *60 Minutes* (I was already developing some stories for them) and offered it to Senior Producer Josh Howard. I warned him that a federal grand jury had been convened to deal with legal transgressions connected to the TWA 800 investigation, including evidence being "stolen" (which is how the feds viewed the residue samples sent to Sanders) from the hangar. Howard wasn't fazed. "We've dealt with grand juries before," he said. I was elated. In the world of news, *60 Minutes*, I told him, was the "last broadcast with balls."

With Howard's permission (which he more recently told me he didn't recall giving to me, although he does recall getting the sample) in hand, I called Sanders, and he FedExed the sample to me. The minute it arrived I took it to Howard's office and put it in his desk for safekeeping until I could locate a lab. A couple of days later, my beeper went off. I dialed the phone number indicated. It was my executive producer, Linda Mason. She sounded a little rattled. She said the FBI wanted to talk to me about some stolen evidence and that she told them I didn't have any. "Linda, we need to talk," I said.

In her office, I told Linda about the sample in Howard's desk. I told her that I'd given it to him after Felling had declined to take it. She told me that Felling had spoken to CBS's lawyer, Jonathan Sternberg, and he had advised against accepting it. Felling hadn't said a word to me about consulting with CBS counsel, but I wasn't surprised he'd kept that information to himself. We weren't exactly on the friendliest terms. I won't go into the rest of my conversation with Linda because she asked me to keep it confidential. She sent me up to see Sternberg, who told me that the government's lawyer, Valerie Caproni, was anxious to have me testify before her grand jury in Brooklyn about what I knew about Sanders's inside source, "Hangarman." The government was desperate to find out who he was. I had no idea who Hangarman was, although I would have given my right arm to know (although not for the purpose of telling the feds). Sanders had refused to tell me. Sternberg managed to convince Caproni that I wasn't the canary she was looking for. Linda arranged to return the sample to the feds, where it disappeared forever. I was deeply disappointed.

So just what was that red residue? To this day, I can't say for certain. But I can say this: physicist Tom Stalcup oversaw the same test on the glue named by the feds (after soaking it in sea water from the same area where the jetliner went down) that Sanders performed on the residue. The results are clearly different: the glue—a specific 3M-brand adhesive (Scotch Grip 1357)—contains no silicon (a common solid rocket fuel ingredient), while Sanders's sample contains 15 percent silicon. The 3M adhesive contains only trace amounts of calcium (the pyrotechnic that provides the burn when mixed with oxygen-providing perchlorate)—0.0220, while Sanders's sample contains 12 percent calcium. The 3M adhesive contains trace amounts of aluminum (aluminum powder fuels rockets)—0.0065, while Sanders's sample contains 2.8 percent aluminum. Other elements found in Sanders's sample were undetected in the 3M adhesive.

With the comparative test results in hand, Dr. Stalcup called the National Transportation Safety Board to inform them of his results. He spoke directly with their scientist in charge of chemical testing, Dr. Merrit Birky. Dr. Birky said he had not compared the adhesive with Sanders's sample because if they didn't match, "Well, you're not going to put the thing to bed." When Stalcup told me about this conversation, I couldn't help thinking about how the American public had not only paid for the investigation of TWA 800, but for the cover-up, too.

One final note about the residue and explosives: NTSB investigator aka "Hangarman," Terrell Stacey, told Sanders that the residue was found on seats in rows seventeen through nineteen. Interestingly, these rows were among the rows (fifteen through twenty-five) where the FBI admitted that traces of explosives PETN and RDX had been found. The FBI tried to explain away the explosives findings with a lie covered with a veneer of truth. They said that most likely those explosives were deposited there from a "spill" during a bomb-sniffing exercise carried out on the 747 when it was parked at the St. Louis airport a little more than a month before Flight 800's demise. Indeed, the 747 that was to become Flight 800 was parked at that airport. The lie here is that the bomb-sniffing exercise took place in the 747 that was Flight 800. Officer Herman Burnett of the St. Louis Police Department carried out the exercise in an empty TWA 747 jetliner. He told the FBI that he began the exercise at 11:45 AM and that it took him about another half hour—until 12:15 PM—to conduct the exercise and then take the dog and explosives off the plane. Burnett didn't note the tail number of the jetliner he had used, but according to TWA's records, the 747 at the St. Louis airport with the same tail number (17119) as the future TWA 800, left its gate at 12:35 PM with more than four hundred passengers on board. Big question: How do you load four hundred–plus passengers and crew along with their bags and food on an aircraft in just twenty minutes?

CBS: HASTA LA VISTA

A few weeks after the FBI's visit to CBS, I received my walking papers. I'd been expecting them. The unexpected had occurred earlier, when the institutional buzzsaw that kills sensitive stories and eventually comes after the journalists trying to tell them had been revealed to me.

Law enforcement consultant Paul Ragonese eventually got his walking papers, too. Bill Felling's farewell comment to Ragonese was, "You and Kristina were wrong about TWA 800." Ragonese was replaced by none other than the FBI's TWA 800 task force chief, James Kallstrom.

Sometimes I wonder if Mr. Caravello ever thinks about his assessment of Jim Sanders as an uncredible source. By the time CBS had become aware of him, Sanders had penetrated the investigation more deeply than any other reporter in America. The feds came down hard on him for it too. They illegally obtained his e-mails from AOL and then dragged his wife (because she had contacted NTSB investigator Terrell Stacey for her husband on a couple of occasions) and him to court, hanging threats of long prison sentences over their heads for coercing Stacey into sending Sanders the residue sample. The residue was evidence "stolen" from a federal investigation, and Stacey, who had nabbed it, wasn't the guilty one, it was that evil Sanders guy and his crafty wife who had cajoled him into taking it. Stacey testified against Sanders.

All journalists should take very careful note of what happened to James Sanders and his wife. If it could happen to them, it could happen to you and your spouse or loved one.

After leaving CBS, I wanted nothing more to do with TWA 800. I wasn't sure I wanted to have anything more to do with journalism either. But my phone was ringing off the hook. Reporters — from *Current Affair* to the BBC — wanted to talk to me about what happened at CBS. I refused to talk about that, but I did invite one Japanese journalist to come to my house and review my documents because he seemed genuinely interested in investigating the crash. While sifting through my papers, Yoichiro Kawai kept telling me that I should contact Congressman Mike Forbes's chief of staff, Kelly O'Meara. I kept smiling and saying yes, but thinking that I'd be damned if I was going to call some government flak to "share." From where I was sitting, the government was doing a great job of keeping a lid on any real information about TWA 800. A few days after Yoichiro's visit, Kelly O'Meara called me.

TOURING CALVERTON WITH CHIEF OF STAFF KELLY O'MEARA

A seventeen-year veteran of Capitol Hill, Kelly O'Meara was just recovering from a decade-long investigation of the suspicious "suicide" of a young US Marine in El Salvador when TWA 800 exploded in the sky. Years of fighting with the military to get to the truth of what really happened to the young soldier had finally culminated in the government changing the cause of death from "suicide" to "undeterminable." Then suddenly, Congressman Forbes (R-NY) charged Chief of Staff O'Meara with looking into the crash.

Way before we met, she was raising the same questions I'd been asking. After a long conversation on the phone, we decided to meet to compare notes. We invited *The Press-Enterprise*'s David Hendrix to join us. O'Meara, Hendrix, and I spent many hours in Congressman Forbes's office pouring over the hundreds of documents we'd gathered in the course of our respective investigations. While we had documented evidence of official lies being disseminated to the general public about the investigation, the "smoking gun" remained elusive.

Although deeply shaken by my experience at CBS, I had been sucked right back into TWA 800. When O'Meara invited me to accompany her and Diana Weir (Forbes's chief of staff on Long Island) to visit some of the areas that were key to the investigation, I agreed to go along. After visiting the Moriches Coast Guard Station, we went to the Calverton hangar. O'Meara told me to wait in the car while she and Weir went inside for a tour. But then Weir suggested that we ask if it would be all right for me to go along. I walked in, presented my passport, signed in as Weir's guest, and off I went. I had no press credentials at the time.

Inside the hangar, the FBI's Ken Maxwell met us and took us to a small room for a briefing before the tour. As he spoke, both O'Meara and I noticed something interesting on the wall behind us. There on a triangulation map of the area where the jetliner exploded, was a spot identified as "possible missile launch site."

Calverton hangar is enormous. One area, called the "bone yard," was a huge hallway containing pile after pile of debris. Looking at this seemingly endless line of stacked-up metal, my thought was that it must have taken a very powerful force to fragment the plane into so many small pieces. While examining the reconstructed interior with its rows and rows of mangled seats, O'Meara and I noticed another interesting thing: some rows were missing. Among them was row seventeen. According to "Hangarman," or NTSB investigator Terrell Stacey, the seats in that row were covered with the mysterious red residue that he'd sent to Sanders.

During the tour, I tried to keep my mouth shut, but my curiosity got the better of me, and I asked a few questions. While examining the reconstruction, I made a comment about the center wing tank that, I think, made Maxwell realize that I had more than just a passing interest in the mock-up. Right then, he excused himself. When he came back, the tour was cut short.

Two days later, FBI agent Joe Valiquette called O'Meara. "You know," He said, "Mr. Kallstrom is very upset that that woman was in the hangar and he is going to be calling the Congressman about this incident." Kallstrom told *Deadly Departure* author Christine Negroni, "I was furious. Here we were trying to cooperate with the congressional people and one of the staff members would bring someone from a news organization into the hangar."

I guess Kallstrom forgot that I wasn't from a news organization. According to Diana Weir, when Kallstrom spoke to Forbes, the FBI task force chief mentioned that he had a "huge file" on me. I sent FOIA (Freedom of Information Act) requests to the FBI, CIA, navy, and everyone else I could think of to get my own copy of that voluminous file. I was curious to know just how evil I was in Mr. Kallstrom's eyes. Everyone, including the FBI, wrote back saying they had nothing on me.

Kallstrom's talk with Forbes triggered the end of O'Meara's seventeen-year career on Capitol Hill. She'd become a political liability while doing the job he'd asked her to do. O'Meara, who knows the ins and outs of government like the back of her hand, who possesses investigative skills superior to those of most veteran reporters, is now an investigative journalist.

INTERBODY IMPLOSION

The most gruesome and fascinating bit of information O'Meara and I uncovered during our investigation came to light while talking to Suffolk County Medical Examiner Dr. Charles Wetli. He had told us that an extremely high-pressure, forward-moving force had ripped through the cabin, turning the air deadly with flying objects: "It was like a machine-gun nest in there," he said. He showed us some slides, including one of a piece of bone embedded in fuselage, like an arrow shot into a tree. He told us that many bodies were completely riddled with bits and pieces of wire, fuselage, and other objects. These were painstakingly removed and handed right over to FBI agents standing at the autopsy tables.

Then Wetli told us about something that belongs on *Ripley's Believe It or Not*: interbody implosion. Every body that came into the morgue was identified by DNA. During the course of this process, it was discovered that two bodies that had come in two weeks apart shared the same DNA—a virtual impossibility. Further research revealed that they were a husband and wife who had been sitting next to each other when the aircraft exploded with such intensity that their flesh was fused together. Since he'd never seen anything like it before, Wetli had to coin a new term for it: interbody implosion. The question to ask here is, Would an explosion in the center wing fuel tank sparked by a short circuit create such an extreme-pressure environment?

GETTING STONED

My phone started acting funny after I came home from CBS. On certain calls, I'd hear all kinds of clicks. Sometimes I'd be talking and the line would just go dead. I tried to keep my paranoia under control, but I did call Bell Atlantic to ask them to check for a wiretap. They never got back to me. After a while, I settled into a liberating, what-the-hell-I've-nothing-to-hide mindset.

After O'Meara left Forbes's office under duress, we decided to write a book about our experiences with TWA 800. It was the summer of 1997. The book's working title was *Unauthorized Access*. We were nervous about doing it, but we shared a strong sense of outrage. We went to a number of publishing houses for pitch meetings, and several editors wanted it. Our literary agent, Sandra Martin, set up an auction so they could fight for it. The morning of the auction, one by one, the editors called up to back out. Sandra said she's had editors not show up for auctions and then call later to say that they couldn't get the advance money or give some other reason. "But I never had them call and say I can't participate in the auction—and give no reason, just say, 'I can't participate,'" she said.

Summer folded into fall, and on the day before Halloween, my family and I moved to La Crescenta, California, right outside of Los Angeles. I spent months working odd jobs, including working on an ABC special, *Sex with Cindy Crawford*, a stint that paid well but marked the lowest point of my producing career.

Then, out of the clear blue sky, I was dragged back through the looking glass into the TWA 800 story. Tom McMahon, an award-winning, ex-network producer who has his own production company in Los Angeles, called to set up a meeting to talk to me about doing a segment on TWA 800 for a series pilot he was producing for Oliver

Stone. Stone wasn't really interested in TWA, McMahon said, but McMahon wanted me to write up a pitch to submit to him. By this time, I was soul-tired of TWA. I was tired of trying to get the story out, tired of all the weirdness, tired of fighting the powers-that-be. "Tired, Tired, Tired," to quote comedian Chris Rock. But McMahon was really excited about it. So, I asked him, "What makes you think that this segment will ever see the light of day?" I'll never forget his reply: "Consider this a rip in reality," he said.

Like most Americans, Stone had no idea about all the shenanigans going on behind the scenes of the TWA 800 investigation. Kelly O'Meara and I wrote up a pitch. Stone okayed it. So we headed to New York to start producing the segment.

It was then that the most bizarre incident I've experienced to date with this story occurred. O'Meara and I had driven up to New York from Washington in her car. We had arrived late at night and parked on the street right in front the building we were staying in. We decided to take out our bags and leave everything else in the trunk.

"Everything else" included our TWA documents, O'Meara's computer, a movie camera, a tool chest, and some tennis rackets.

The next morning, we went to the car, and O'Meara opened the trunk. Everything was there, except for the TWA 800 documents and O'Meara's computer. The trunk lock itself looked untouched and worked perfectly. Yes, ladies and gentlemen, these things do happen in the United States of America. I would never have believed it if I hadn't experienced it myself. As I read some random notes that O'Meara wrote up about this episode, I actually smile. She has a certain righteous fierceness about her that, combined with her superior reporting skills, makes her a great journalist: "I'm sitting in the police station in Manhattan," she wrote, "and the only thing I can think of is to make sure that woman types up on that report that they stole my TWA documents." I have to confess before moving on that Kelly and I had no one but ourselves to blame for the theft. We had broken a cardinal rule of journalism: never, ever let your most important documents out of your sight. Fortunately, we had followed a second cardinal rule: we had made backup copies of these documents and squirreled them away in various places—just in case.

Our story for Oliver Stone was going to be an investigation of the investigation; our independent investigation of the official investigation. Since some of the most troubling issues surrounding the official investigation had to do with the eyewitnesses, we decided that the centerpiece of our segment would be a huge eyewitness shoot that would take place in an airplane hangar. We'd gather as many eyewitnesses as we could find and bring them together in a sort of town meeting to talk about what they'd seen and how the authorities had dealt with the information they provided. In a couple of weeks' time, we'd gathered more than thirty eyewitnesses, found some local production help, and were closing in on a hangar. Then we got a call from Los Angeles.

It was Tom McMahon calling to tell us to stand down. The shoot would have to be postponed. There was a problem with ABC.

This was a little discouraging as it took a lot of convincing to get so many eyewitnesses to agree to go on camera. As we waited for word to move again, the buzzsaw kicked into high gear. It began with a "Periscope" piece in *Newsweek* entitled "Stone's Take":

> The theory that TWA Flight 800 was brought down by a missile may be widely discredited, but it won't die. The latest conspiracy crank to delve into the mysterious crash is none other than film director Oliver Stone. His production company is preparing a one-hour, prime-time "reality" special called "Oliver Stone's Declassified" for ABC's entertainment division, including a segment on the missile theory. But not everyone at ABC is thrilled with the project. Like most mainstream media, *ABC News* has reported federal investigators' conclusion that the crash was caused by a mechanical malfunction. Says an ABC News spokeswoman: "We are confident that this program will be clearly identified as Oliver Stone's point of view."

I immediately called Tom McMahon and asked if anyone from *Newsweek* had called over there to ask what we were doing on TWA 800. He said no. I told Tom that I had a bad feeling about the "Periscope" piece, and that I was fairly sure that this was an opening salvo, and that in a few weeks' time, there'd be a barrage of press on our show. Then, I fired off a letter to Michael Kramer at the now-defunct media watchdog magazine *Brill's Content*:

> Dear Mr. Kramer:
>
> In all my many years of reading *Newsweek*, I've never been aware of any "planted" stories but I think I've found one on page six of the October 19, 1998, issue. The brief Periscope piece entitled "Stone's Take" (a copy

of which is enclosed) caught my eye because I am producing the segment on TWA 800 for Oliver Stone's "Declassified" show.

For the record and edification of the Periscope reporter who wrote "Stone's Take," Mr. Stone isn't delving into the TWA 800 crash, I am. I was hired to do the story because I am an award-winning investigative producer and I've spent more than two years following the story. I don't know who told Periscope that my segment is about the "missile theory," but I didn't and it isn't. And to the *ABC News* spokesperson who expressed her confidence that "this program will be clearly identified as Oliver Stone's point of view," I have this to say: I don't give a damn what Oliver Stone's point of view on TWA 800 is and I'm sure that's just fine with him. I wasn't hired to do a piece from his point of view, I was hired to do a solidly reported segment based on the more than two years my associate producer and I have spent looking into this story.

With the cooperation of ABC News, a Periscope reporter has written a piece discrediting "Declassified" and the TWA story before the show has even been filmed. In effect, Periscope has telegraphed to *Newsweek*'s large readership that "Declassified" couldn't possibly have any merit as a serious investigative program because "conspiracy crank" Oliver Stone is in charge. Periscope and ABC News may have succeeded in the short run. Ultimately, Stone's show will stand or fall on its own merit.

I may be wrong, but it looks to me like ABC [News] is upset (and scared too, maybe) about the fact that a hardcore investigative show is being produced outside of their purview. They should be. But "Stone's Take" is a nasty little bit of mouthpiece journalism and Periscope should be ashamed.

Kristina Borjesson

The only thing I was wrong about was the timing of the press barrage. It came much earlier than I expected, virtually on the heels of the "Periscope" piece. *Time* magazine's "The Conspiracy Channel?" and "Casting the First Stone but Not Airing It" said it all about mainstream media's "balanced" view of "Declassified." "The Conspiracy Channel?" starts off like this: "Which would you rather watch: a responsible and balanced *ABC News* report about the tragic but accidental crash of TWA flight 800 or a stylish *X-Files*-like show exposing the bastards who blew her out of the sky, narrated by conspiracy auteur Oliver Stone?" Here's a note to John Cloud, Jeffrey Ressner, and William Tynan who worked on this piece: Even today, years after you put your piece together, government investigators *still claim they don't know what happened* to TWA 800. Their best *guess* is that an electrical short circuit ignited fumes in the fuel tank, but they admit they have no conclusive evidence to back this up. So, what information did you have proving that the crash was "accidental"? What information did you have showing that Stone was going to "expose the bastards who blew her out of the sky"? Just how much did you know before you cobbled together your witty little piece?

In his November 7, 1998, piece in the *New York Post* entitled "Oliver Stone's Take on Flt. 800 Yanked by ABC," reporter Don Kaplan quotes a network news source saying, "ABC has such a strong news brand, and people might confuse the Oliver Stone special with a news special." No they wouldn't. The Oliver Stone special would have been much harder hitting than anything allowed on a regular news special (I know, I've worked on network documentaries). And that, I think, was the real problem. Imagine ABC's entertainment division coming up with a more journalistically sound, harder-hitting newsmagazine show than ABC's news division—or any other network news division—would ever dare to put on. Aye, now there would be a rub.

The *New York Times*'s Lawrie Mifflin also weighed in: "ABC Says It Is Dropping Plans for Stone Special on Flight 800." Mifflin reported that ABC decided to kill the show after some "ABC journalists had expressed dismay to their superiors about the proposed program. . . . Fearing that viewers would perceive it as an *ABC News* report, ABC has reported that the missile theories are groundless." Later on in the article, Mifflin writes, "The National Transportation Safety Board, the Federal Bureau of Investigation and the *Central Intelligence Agency* [italics mine] have all said there is no evidence to support the theory that the crash was caused by a missile or missiles." The CIA? What mandate did they ever have to be involved in the investigation? They did, however, put together an animation for the FBI that was completely discredited by the eyewitnesses whose testimony the CIA claimed to have used to create it (more on that later).

Without a doubt, the coverage of "Declassified's" death was, with few exceptions, a propaganda juggernaut that made it clear that anyone who didn't believe the government's officials or the journalists who unquestioningly reported what the officials said was a conspiracy nut. This, of course, is the old "marginalization" routine. If you don't go along with the party line, you're shoved into the margins and eventually out of the picture.

"Declassified" had been approved and in the works for six months when O'Meara and I were called out of the field. The show was canceled within three or four days after we were told to stand down. In that brief period, agents were called and the deal was off and settlements were made. Negotiations to revive the show would not be considered, end of story. Oliver Stone said it was one of the worst things that had ever happened to him in his professional life. The big question here was: Where did the pressure come from? From ABC's news division that had invested in the mechanical theory and was afraid "Declassified" might make them look bad? Stone told me that the pitch for "Declassified," described the prospective series as an edgy investigative magazine show that would make *60 Minutes* pale in comparison. I could see why ABC's news division would try to kill it. And what about the FBI and the NTSB? The FBI in particular had a real "thing" about denying the public access to information about the eyewitnesses.

THOSE DAMNED EYEWITNESSES

The FBI's "thing" about the eyewitnesses was first apparent at the National Transportation Safety Board's public hearings held on December 8, 1997, in Baltimore, Maryland. Days before the hearing, James Kallstrom wrote to NTSB Chairman James Hall to ask that information on the eyewitnesses and the red residue found on the seats not be discussed at the hearing. Hall complied with Kallstrom's request. Now, I don't know about you, but a letter asking that these specific items be omitted from the roster would send me digging deeper in precisely those two areas. Sometimes, in a sensitive investigation, if you pay attention, you'll find that if you're told not to bother looking somewhere, it is exactly where you should look. If you're told something isn't important, go check it out because it might be very important.

Paul Ragonese once said during a conversation we were having about the eyewitnesses that standard operating procedure for a law enforcement officer arriving on the scene of a crime or accident is to ask everybody in sight, "Did anybody see anything?" In the case of Flight 800, hundreds of people saw something and they reported what they saw to the FBI. Ultimately, over six hundred witnesses spoke to FBI agents. But the FBI and the NTSB did everything they could to diminish the importance of eyewitness testimony. Perhaps the most startling effort the FBI made in this regard was to commission the CIA to create an animated sequence that would convince the public that what the eyewitnesses said they saw was actually an optical illusion.

The CIA animation was based largely on the testimonies of eye-witnesses Dwight Brumley and Mike Wire. Although the eyewitnesses said they saw a "flare-like" object *rising* from the ocean surface to meet the jetliner, the video's narrator said in so many words that what they actually saw was jet fuel streaming *down* from the crippled craft after it had exploded. Mike Wire is a Vietnam veteran who was working on a bridge on the south shore of Long Island at the time of the disaster. He had this to say after reviewing the video: "The animation didn't match anything that I had seen in no way, but I just figured well, let's just be quiet about it 'cause they're still investigating and it could be a story they could correct later on.'" Dwight Brumley was an active-duty master-chief in the US Navy flying on US Air Flight 217 in the crash site area right before and during the time TWA 800 occurred. He was looking out his window when the tragedy occurred. He didn't think the animation was accurate either: "For them to put that flare moving from my left to right is completely — it's almost perpendicular to the path that I observed. . . . What they're animating as a flare doesn't even get close to what I saw, not even close. There's no way that was headed east, northeast." Do you suppose Lawrie Mifflin at the *New York Times*, who mentioned the CIA as a credible source debunking the missile theory, ever picked up her phone to ask these eyewitnesses about the credibility of the CIA's animation that was based on their testimonies?

Brumley and Wire's assessments matched those of other eyewitnesses on Long Island who viewed the CIA video and were certain that what they had seen that night was ascending, not "streaming down." Local businessman Richard Goss, who was sitting on the porch of the West Hampton Yacht Club at the time, called the video "a joke." Retiree Paul Runyan was standing in his yard: "What I saw was going up from the surface . . . like a rising flare." Suzanne McConnell, a nurse, was watching from her back porch: "If it was something from the plane, it would be going down, but this was clearly going up." Darrell Miron is a carpenter and graphic artist: "I seen that video and I did not enjoy watching it because I did not see that that night. There's no way physically possible that that happened. . . . It started low and went up. The streak of light caused something in the sky to explode. I don't call it a missile because it's their job to tell me what it is. I seen a streak of light heading up and something happened to the point where that plane was. . . ."

Miron was also among those eyewitnesses who were struck by the FBI's less than enthusiastic response to receiving the information they wanted to provide. "It was rather odd . . . when the FBI came to my house and talked to me," said Miron, "because it seemed to me that they were more interested in what I knew rather than what I seen. . . . I offered to create a graphic animation of what I seen, exactly. They didn't want me to go there. They told me no, do not do that. I thought that was odd."

Perhaps even more odd was James Kallstrom's attempt to legitimize the CIA video by telling victims' family members that the eyewitnesses had reviewed it before it was released and found it to be credible. That was in late 1997. Almost a year later, in an interview with Dr. Tom Stalcup, chairman of the Flight 800 Independent Researchers Organization (FIRO), Kallstrom admitted that the eyewitnesses had *not* screened the CIA video prior to its release.

Under FIRO's aegis, Dr. Stalcup compiled a comprehensive statistical analysis of the government's eyewitness information and put it in a report entitled "Review of the Official TWA Flight 800 Witness Reports." Very interesting information emerged from Dr. Stalcup's number-crunching. For instance, 94 percent of the eyewitnesses who saw a streak of light early enough to note its origin, said it rose from the ocean's surface. Of the 134 witnesses who provided information related to the rising streak's trajectory, 116 are *inconsistent* with the official (CIA video) explanation for the streak. "Most reject the official scenario," the report says, "because Flight 800 in crippled flight didn't originate at the surface [and] Flight 800 was never ascending straight up."

In another FIRO report, Dr. Stalcup writes: "It was stated that 'the witness reports were the first and only evidence or indication of a missile attack.' This is factually false." Then he goes on to list the other possible evidence/indications of a missile attack:

> PETN and RDX (explosives used in missiles) were found in the wreckage. The NTSB has not conclusively determined the sources of these explosives [remember the FBI trying to throw the public off the trail with the dog-sniffing story?] and their detection anywhere on the wreckage is indicative of a possible missile attack.

FAA radar detected high-speed (Mach 2) targets apparently exiting Flight 800 immediately after the initiating event. The targets are also indicative of a possible missile attack.

The "localized re-crystallization of portions of the rear spar" cannot be explained by the official breakup sequence. The re-crystallization of metal is indicative of a missile attack.

The last time official investigators publicly discussed the eyewitnesses was during a brief period at the tail end of a legally mandated — per the Government in the Sunshine Act — public hearing that the NTSB held in late August 2000 to inform the public of their final findings. I attended the hearing and believe me, the government's officials did everything in their power to avoid any sunshine on the eyewitness issue. They spent long periods of time discussing issues like the dangers of lint on wires — which seemed like a deliberate exercise in navel-gazing for the purposes of taking up time and avoiding the real issues. On the second and final day of the hearing, toward its very end, the board members finally got around to addressing the eyewitnesses, albeit only briefly. This alone tells you how loath they were to publicly discuss this part of the investigation. They had good reason. The fact is, that of all the 670 eyewitnesses the FBI tracked down, the NTSB only spoke to about a dozen of them, according to NTSB Witness Group Chairman, Dr. David Mayer. At the hearing, a brief presentation was followed by a trivial question and answer period that was marked by one board member suggesting that some eyewitnesses who reported seeing an ascending object had been drunk at the time. The whole hearing felt rigged, with no dissenting voices allowed. Conspicuously absent, for example, was a representative from the International Association of Machinists and Aerospace Workers (IAMAW) who disagreed with the NTSB's final conclusion about the cause of TWA 800's demise. The IAMAW concluded that the initiating event occurred not in the center wing tank but on the left side of the aircraft's exterior: "a high pressure event breached the fuselage and the fuselage unzipped due to the event. . . . The explosion [in the center wing tank] was a result of this event."

The eyewitnesses have been and are still the 900-pound gorilla in the middle of the room, *because there are so damned many of them.*

BOTTOMFEEDERS VERSUS BACKBITERS

During my tenures at CBS and CNN, I rarely ran into a producer working on a very sensitive story. If I had to tell you why, I'd say this: Getting a job at a network is hard enough because the competition is brutal, but keeping it—especially since there's no job security and your contract comes up for renewal every two or four years—is a skill that requires as much political savvy as journalistic talent. There's no point in looking for trouble or hard work by pitching a tough story. Network producing is an all-consuming job. The hours are horrendous. Investigative pieces in particular can wreak havoc on your mind, body, and family.

On a story like TWA 800, as you saw with my experience at CBS, you can become a pariah among your colleagues as well as with government investigators if you persist with your politically incorrect investigation. But what's interesting about TWA 800 is the number of independent investigators who are, even to this day, working hard to get to the bottom of this disaster. This has angered government investigators. James Kallstrom, who, as the Haitian expression goes, doesn't keep his "tongue in his pocket," seemed particularly upset by Oliver Stone's efforts: "The real facts are glossed over by the likes of Mr. Stone and others who spend their life bottom-feeding in those small, dark crevices of doubt and hypocrisy," he told the Associated Press's Pat Milton. Kallstrom was implying that independent investigators are "bottom-feeders" out to make a buck at the expense of the victims' families, who require our silence to achieve peace of mind and closure.

I don't know of one independent investigator or journalist who has made big bucks pursuing the truth in this matter. On the contrary, it is a tough row to hoe financially speaking. As for the families' peace of mind, I think Kallstrom implying that we should drop it for their sakes redefines the term "manipulative." With all due respect to the families, what about the peace of mind of all the living who get on planes every day to fly off the coast of Long Island?

Even worse, from my point of view, are those I call "the backbiters." They are the journalists who gratuitously attack other journalists working the unpopular sides of a story. I'm going to name names here because I find this practice insidious and a real discredit to our profession.

After leaving CBS, I felt that the best policy was to keep my mouth shut about what happened. I didn't really want to continue looking into the story, much less become the story. When the *New York Observer*'s Philip Weiss called me for an interview, I told him off the record about what I'd experienced and then refused to say anything for public consumption. He asked me if I minded if he spoke to the people at *60 Minutes*, and I told him to do as he pleased because I had no right to tell him whom he could and couldn't talk to. The senior producer of *60 Minutes*, Josh Howard, told Weiss that my "official relationship with CBS ended" before I had pitched the TWA story. Then he went on to say this about the proposal I submitted to him for a story on TWA Flight 800: "It sounded kind of wacky, and we said, 'No thanks.'" First, here's the "wacky proposal" or "blue sheet" (as it's called inside the network) that I submitted to Howard on March 18, 1997:

TWA 800: TROUBLE INSIDE THE INVESTIGATION

A retired cop turned journalist is on the run, wanted by the FBI for "stealing" evidence. The FBI seizes a copy of FAA radar tapes from a retired pilot who claims he got them from a source inside the investigation. A grand jury is convened for what appears to be an unprecedented purpose—investigating leaks within the TWA investigation. Meanwhile, crash investigators called to the Hill have little progress to report; the NTSB's Dr. Bernard Loeb saying that there was evidence consistent with the plane being struck by a missile fragment only seemed to add to the confusion. At the same hearing, Representative Frank Wolf said, "the credibility of the U.S. government could be tarnished if this thing goes on much longer."

Indeed. So what is going on? What's going on between the FBI and the NTSB? Why are people inside the investigation leaking documents, forensic evidence, and key information to the press, including CBS's law enforcement consultant, Paul Ragonese, who secretly met with two members of the task force? Is Jim Sanders, now hiding from the FBI after announcing that the red substance he received from a source inside the investigation was fuel exhaust from a missile, a publicity-seeking flake or a credible journalist with an incredibly good source? Will the congressional subcommittee inquiries help or hurt the investigation?

60 Minutes focuses on the drama behind the scenes of this unprecedented investigation and looks for clues to the ultimate question: What really happened to TWA 800?

Now isn't that just the "wackiest" thing you've ever read?

As I mentioned before, Josh did not say "no thanks." If he had, the

FBI would never have come calling at CBS. Also, my official relationship with CBS ended when they gave me notice. Prior to that, I was working on a month-to-month basis as my contract had ended and there was no documentary to assign me to at *CBS Reports*. During that time, as Josh Howard may have forgotten (and I have the memos to prove it), I was developing several stories for *60 Minutes*, including one on child soldiers, another on former SAC commander General Lee Butler, and another on Korean alien smugglers. CBS correspondent Bob Orr also took his best shot across my bow. In his interview with Philip Weiss for the *New York Observer*, Orr said that he was "never impressed by Ms. Borjesson," and then posed these rhetorical questions: "What was her level of access and expertise, and who did she talk to? Who were her sources? One, and he was alarmingly thin." I spoke to Bob Orr once and only briefly. He never asked me about my sources, "level of access," or "expertise." His assumption that I only had one source on this story was, to put it mildly, incorrect.

Besides misspelling my name (that would be Kristina with a K, Ms. Negroni, not a CH) Christine Negroni, an ex-CNN reporter and author of *Deadly Departure*, a book about the Flight 800 disaster, incorrectly described what happened with Sanders's sample when it reached CBS and then went on to incorrectly state that the reason *The Press-Enterprise*'s David Hendrix and I had "much information in common," was because we were staying in touch with Kelly O'Meara. I didn't meet O'Meara until *after* I'd left CBS. I had no idea that we'd uncovered similar information until I met her later on. Negroni, who seems to have had liberal access to James Kallstrom, quotes him implying that O'Meara was pushing "a conspiracy thing" in Congressman Forbes's office: "I was aware from people around the investigation that Forbes's office was part of this whole conspiracy thing to some degree. . . . A lot of people were concerned and puzzled by what his office was doing. I didn't know how much he was doing and how much was happening by some strong person [he's talking about O'Meara here] with a lot of leeway in his office." In the last paragraph of this chapter, Negroni writes that O'Meara and I had "convinced" Oliver Stone that "the investigation of Flight 800 was worth another look." As you read earlier, we didn't "convince" Stone of anything. Stone's producer, Tom McMahon, approached me and asked for a pitch. If anything, he had to convince me to wrap my arms around the TWA 800 tar baby one more time.

In all fairness to Negroni, I refused to talk to her, but that's no excuse for not getting her facts straight.

The most puzzling attack on O'Meara came from a highly respected *Washington Post* reporter, Howard Kurtz. She had recently received new radar information from the National Transporation Safety Board, so she asked for and was granted an interview with the NTSB's Peter Goelz and Bernie Loeb. Shortly thereafter, on August 23, 1999, Howard Kurtz wrote the following in the *Post*'s Style section:

UNFRIENDLY FIRE

Peter Goelz, Managing Director of the NTSB was taken aback when he was interviewed by a reporter for *Insight* magazine, the *Washington Times'* sister publication. He says Kelly O'Meara was "extraordinarily antagonistic." O'Meara was questioning Goelz about secret government radar reports that she said showed plenty of activity nearby on the day in 1996 that TWA Flight 800 crashed. The government says it found no evidence to support theories that a missile downed the plane. Goelz quickly realized he knew O'Meara from previous incarnations. She had pursued the missile theory while working as chief of staff to Representative Michael Forbes, then a New York Republican who had questioned whether there had been a terrorist on the plane, and she had worked on an Oliver Stone docu-drama about TWA 800 that the filmmaker was preparing for ABC before the project was cancelled. "She really believes that the U.S. Navy shot this thing and that there was a fleet of warships," Goelz says. O'Meara did not return calls, but *Insight* Managing Editor Paul Rodriguez called her previous jobs irrelevant. "She has working knowledge of an issue, it's like saying someone who worked as a tax accountant has a bias towards tax accountancy. If anyone has questions about her bias, wait until they see a printed product finished. It's just carping about an aggressive reporter."

Goelz had contacted Kurtz within an hour of the interview, which was tape-recorded and leaves no doubt as to who raised the conspiracy issue (it wasn't O'Meara). Kurtz ran his piece within forty-eight hours of the interview—days before O'Meara completed the article she was working on.

I have several questions and comments about Kurtz's piece. First of all, I can't figure out what is newsworthy about it. If a reporter being aggressive is big news, then we should be seeing articles like this everywhere all the time. Most reporters are pushy, whether they're asking the right questions or not. It's clear that Goelz got in touch with Kurtz to write the article. Could it be that this high-caliber journalist stooped so low as to write a piece the sole purpose of which was to make another journalist look bad?

Kurtz writes about O'Meara's "previous incarnations" as if they were big minuses in her current career. O'Meara's long experience with the TWA 800 story was the reason she managed to get the additional radar information in the first place. I disagree with Rodriguez that her previous jobs were irrelevant. Her previous jobs were utterly pertinent to covering the TWA story. (Why do you think CBS hired James Kallstrom as their law enforcement consultant after he retired from the FBI's TWA 800 task force? Same difference.) She had more documentation on, and experience with, this story than ten regular reporters. I can't help feeling that Goelz used Kurtz to publicly bite back at her. Also, one correction, Mr. Kurtz: The Oliver Stone piece was not a docu-drama; it was a straight-up newsmagazine piece.

This concludes the *Enquirer* segment of this essay, but please, don't let the gossipy, backbiting tone distract you from the main point: Don't let official sources use you as a mouthpiece to attack a fellow journalist—or anyone else for that matter. As Ted Koppel put it, "Aspire to decency. Practice civility toward one another. Admire and emulate ethical behavior wherever you find it."

PLUS ÇA CHANGE, PLUS C'EST LA MÊME CHOSE (THE MORE THINGS CHANGE, THE MORE THEY STAY THE SAME)

On July 17, 2001, five years almost to the hour that TWA Flight 800 blew up off the coast of Long Island, New York, on its way to Paris, I sat down to begin writing the first draft of this chapter. A few minutes into my efforts, I received notice that the government's TWA 800 damage-control buzzsaw was still firmly in place.

The notice came in the form of an e-mail from Emmy-winning documentary film producer Jack Cashill. Lawyer Greta Van Susteren of O. J. Simpson fame had invited Cashill to appear on her 7:30 PM CNN show, *The Point,* to talk about *Silenced,* Cashill's recently released investigative documentary on the official investigation into the TWA 800 crash.

Cashill's e-mail arrived at 5:45 PM, a little less than two hours before he was to go on the show:

> Just got the call I was half expecting. CNN cancelled. No one from the NTSB [National Transportation Safety Board], FBI, etc. will do the show with me. CNN says that I can't do the show myself because that would not be 'responsible journalism.' The NTSB folks, however, may appear by themselves. That is 'responsible journalism.' The producer and Greta Van Susteren are furious. Not their fault. This came from the top. Yesterday, when this was set up, there was [sic] no conditions put on it. They told me I probably would do it alone. The standards for responsible journalism seem to have changed over night. . . . If you ever needed a textbook case of what is wrong with the media, this is it.

I put in a call to Cashill's contact on Van Susteren's show to confirm what he wrote in his e-mail. Her voice mail picked up. I left a message, but she didn't call back. I finally spoke to someone who said that they'd been deluged with calls on this matter and that all calls had to be referred to CNN's public relations department. I told this person that I didn't want to play that game, that I just wanted to run Cashill's e-mail by someone over there to check its accuracy. The person agreed to talk to me as an unidentified source.

The person told me that the show's executive producer made the decision not to allow Cashill to go on alone. "We had no idea we were going to run into this problem," the source said. Then the source told me that the NTSB's Jim Hall and Peter Goelz both refused to appear on the show with Cashill, and that Hall would be going on alone. Then why, I asked, if it's not "responsible journalism" for Cashill to go on alone, is it "responsible journalism" for Jim Hall to go on alone? Because, said the source, Hall is a *"legitimate news guest."* Then, slightly defensively, the source quickly added this about Cashill: "Lots of people warned us about this guy."

The "legitimate news guest"—as opposed to what in this case—the "illegitimate news guest?" In cases of stories dealing with sensitive issues or exposing high-level corporate or government malfeasance, legitimate news guests are often official spokespeople with big titles who deliberately do one of two things when facing the press. They deliberately mislead or outright lie to the reporter. Or, they simply don't address your question but instead talk a lot and say nothing (this is a favorite with politicians) until their time — or yours — runs out.

What I have to say to a reporter or correspondent who accepts at face value anything an "official" source or a "legitimate news guest" has to say about a sensitive issue or an explosive event like TWA 800 is simple: Don't do it. Whether you're a big network's ten-million-dollar man or some Podunk paper's ten-thousand-a-year cub reporter, you can bet your booties that your "legitimate news guest" from the FBI or the NTSB or Congress or even the White House is going to lie to you at some point. Far too often, legitimate news guests are invited on shows where the correspondent's producers simply haven't done their homework. The results, in terms of meeting basic journalistic standards of conveying the truth, are disastrous.

Van Susteren's chat with Jim Hall is an example. I'm going to deconstruct her encounter with him on her program and show you why. I'll begin with the introduction she read (she may or may not have written it by herself), which was very politically correct and downright biased:

> At first, people suspected that a bomb went off on the plane. But a painstaking search brought up most of the shattered pieces of the 747 for investigators to reconstruct. Their conclusion: an electrical spark probably ignited vapors in the jet's empty fuel tank, vapors caused by the heat of air conditioning units located just under the tank. Just two months ago, the government ordered airlines and plane manufacturers to change the way fuel tanks are designed, repaired, and operated.

Here's how I read the subtext in Van Susteren's introduction: investigators worked their butts off (that's the "painstaking search" part) and finally concluded — although they can't prove it (that's what the word "probably" tells you) — that an electrical spark caused the plane to explode. And, they're doing something about it (albeit belatedly).

Next comes the intro's grabber, the sensational part that's supposed to make you want to hear what the legitimate news guest — former NTSB Chairman Jim Hall — has to say:

> Is that the end of the story? And what about the conspiracy theorists who keep insisting the jet actually was shot down?

Now she's telling you to think that anyone who doesn't buy the government's unproven theory, anyone who thinks the jet may have been shot down, is a "conspiracy theorist." Tacitly attached to the term "conspiracy theorist" are all kinds of other nouns and adjectives like "goofball," "nutcake," "bottomfeeder" (Jim Kallstrom's personal favorite), "crazy," and so on. Using insulting and false labels to marginalize dissenting or politically incorrect voices is a ploy that government and corporations as well as the press use on a daily basis.

Van Susteren cuts right to the chase after her intro. She asks Jim Hall a straight yes or no question: "Jim, can you say with one hundred percent certainty that the people who think that this was shot down — this flight was shot down, that they are wrong?"

Jim responds with the classic don't-answer-the-question-just-talk-a lot-and-say-nothing ploy. He goes on for over a minute (an eternity in TV time) about the victims and the investigation, and as he moves to a higher level of inanity by talking about how this "accident" is comparable to that of a Delta jetliner downed by wind shear in that they are both tragedies that have resulted in "great advances in aviation safety," Van Susteren interrupts him:

"Then does that mean, Jim, that you are one hundred percent certain that these — that the *conspiracists* [emphasis mine] who some say that they saw a white light traveling skyward, uh, zigzagging, disappearing and then an orange ball of fire — can you say with one hundred percent certainty that they're wrong?"

There she goes with that "conspiracist" stuff again. But this time, Van Susteren gets credit for being the dog that won't let go of a bone.

Hall's second response, particularly on the heels of his first long-winded answer, tells me that he is trying to avoid outright lying. He succeeds with a Bill Clintonesque semantic maneuver that would get him off the hook in a court of law (Hall has a law degree). The average viewer probably didn't pick up on it, but Van Susteren, who is a lawyer, probably did: "Greta, *in my mind* [emphasis mine]," Hall says, "with one hundred percent certainty, our investigators based on the facts that they developed, uh, uh, they are wrong, they are incorrect." The subtext here is that by using the words "in my mind" Hall is only conveying a personal opinion, not an objective certainty. He's doing this to avoid stating as a fact that his investigators are right and the "conspiracists" wrong. "In my mind" is followed by "with one hundred percent certainty," creating a strong impression of factuality when again, he's only conveying a personal opinion.

This unquestioning, uncritical, soapbox-providing, ersatz journalism has got to stop. This censorship via disinviting dissenting voices—in this case, an award-winning reporter—who have dug around and unearthed evidence that official sources don't want aired on a mass medium is not just shameful, it's downright dangerous.

RAISON D'ÊTRE

If ever there were a time when disseminating disinformation via official sources, when uncritical, uninformed, and inane reporting were dangerous, it's now. On September 11, 2001, the most amazing act of terrorism ever seen on this planet occurred, triggering a war and other deadly military operations overseas and a climate of fear and restricted freedom here. Information about our government's activities here and abroad with respect to the "War on Terrorism" is being tightly controlled. We have reached a point in the history of our nation where our leaders speak openly and often about controlling our access to information and protecting the truth with lies. Even more chilling, we've been told to "watch" what we say and do. In such a climate, reporters must be astute and creative to get to the truth and get it out. While great caution must be taken not to report anything that would jeopardize those out there putting their lives on the line for us, we have to be careful not to allow ourselves to be completely led by the nose either. Now, more than ever, we need a critical press willing to *dig deep* and cut the stenographer-to-official-sources act. Beyond that, news consumers and reporters should look for respected foreign print and broadcast news. Foreign reporters aren't subject to the same constraints as America's journalists when reporting on sensitive American affairs.

One final word about "official sources": I've had plenty of negative things to say about them, but I do want to add here that they don't always lie. Nonetheless, the press should follow the Ronald Reagan lesson plan for dealing with sources that may or may not be honest. Like Ronald Reagan with the Soviets, the press often has no choice but to deal with official sources. Reagan had to communicate, negotiate, and even break bread with Mikhail Gorbachev. But when it came to accepting his word at face value about the size and makeup of the Soviet arsenal, Reagan smiled his thousand-watt smile and said these now-famous words: "Trust, but verify." The subtext here is, I'm not just going to trust you, I'm going to check out everything you say.

So, *trust but verify*. Hang that on your walls in big bold letters, dear up-and-coming colleagues and all those who have forgotten the "verify" part. In my view, journalists are this nation's last line of defense for keeping all of us from becoming a nation of expendable cockroaches. This, I believe, is our real raison d'être.

CHAPTER 14

COAL MINE CANARIES

DAVID E. HENDRIX

Courtesy Carlos Puma

Hendrix has been a print journalist for thirty-eight years, divided almost evenly between reporting and editing. He retired from the full-time news profession in June 2002 at The Press-Enterprise *in Riverside, California, where he served in various reporting and editing position for eighteen years. While there, he earned national and international recognition for his investigative and deadline stories about the crash of TWA Flight 800, US anti- and counterterrorism training and programs, missing Vietnam War servicemen, the illegal transfer of surplus military aircraft to private aerial firefighting contractors,* and natural disasters. He also has been an expert witness in court and before the US Senate, and has provided evidence to Congress members and staff. Today, he reports and writes part time for the rural southwest Oregon newspaper the South County News *and is writing novels based on historical events.*

I t's impossible not to get angry. At least, it's impossible for me.

Nothing can excuse the scam perpetrated on the relatives and loved ones of the 230 people killed when TWA Flight 800 exploded off

New York's Long Island and rained bodies and debris into the Atlantic Ocean more than two miles below.

Nor can anything excuse the deception perpetrated on the American public and world by bogus elements of the so-called investigation into the July 17, 1996, disaster.

Nor can most members of the media be excused for becoming blind, unthinking guardians of untruth and deception dished out by some US officials and agents involved in the "investigation" of the Boeing 747 jumbo jet's breakup and its cause.

We journalists are not supposed to get angry. We get trained to not let our emotions get in the way of our alleged unquenchable search for the truth. But, despite our illusions about ourselves and Hollywood's major misrepresentations about us, we are human.

Maybe we need to be more conscious of our humanity.

But this essay isn't about my feelings. It's about a disaster that remains unsolved and continues to haunt people. The essay also is about good journalists and investigators who were fired or prosecuted because they did not submit to official pronouncements and editorial decisions based on bias rather than fact. This essay also is about what journalists can do when goaded by gutsy editors more interested in evidence than spin.

It's also a case study of what people can get away with when the guard dog becomes a lap dog. Everybody is victimized when that happens.

I'll start at the beginning. The trail is littered with heartache, lies, presidential politics, timidity, and heroics.

You judge the evidence.

Not all news organizations are created equal. I was fortunate to work for *The Press-Enterprise* in Riverside, California. East of Los Angeles and Orange counties, Riverside County is a long, narrow strip of Southern California that begins about fourteen miles from the Pacific Ocean and extends to the Colorado River. Most of the county is desert, but it is home for aerospace workers, thousands of active and retired military servicemen and women, and Hollywood's elite who enjoy life in Palm Springs.

At the time Flight 800's deadly fireball lit up the night sky in mid-1996, the *P-E* was an aggressively independent, family-owned newspaper with a daily circulation of about 160,000 homes and businesses.

When the news and pictures of Flight 800's dead passengers and debris filled TV screens, we, like others, assumed the explosion could well be terrorist based. After all, the 1996 Olympics were only a week away in Atlanta, Georgia, terrorists had a habit of blowing up and shooting down airliners, a radical Islamic group had used a huge truck bomb to try to topple one of the World Trade Center towers three years earlier, and Ramzi Yousef was standing trial in New York City for a plot to blow up about a dozen airliners at the same time over the Pacific. And a lot of people in the Mideast didn't like us because of America's support of Israel and because of the 1991 Gulf War.

No wonder the Joint Terrorism Task Force, a special mix of FBI and New York City police, immediately began investigating Flight 800's destruction.

Coincidently, the morning after the aerial explosion I met with Jim Sanders in rural Riverside County. His wife, Liz, was a TWA training supervisor, and she and Jim knew many of the fifty-two TWA people killed in the crash. Liz had worked the Paris flight many times.

A friend, ex-cop, and freelance investigative journalist Jim Sanders and I were keeping a long-standing appointment with an intelligence source to discuss secret US-Vietnam negotiations in 1985 for live American servicemen still being held prisoner of war in Southeast Asia.

Sanders and I had worked the POW issue independently for more than a decade, and our pursuits frequently crossed paths. He and another journalist colleague, Mark Sauter, wrote two scholarly books about US POWs missing from all American wars in the twentieth century, and I had written dozens of stories about the same subject. The Senate Select Committee on POW/MIA Affairs subpoenaed each of us in 1993 to be expert witnesses about POW issues.

Jim and I did our interview, but the Flight 800 issue promptly took over Jim's and Liz's lives. TWA officials called Liz that morning and told her to return to St. Louis and New York to deal with the disaster's aftermath. We parted, believing it would be no time until investigators determined the cause of Flight 800's crash.

None of us had the slightest idea we would be involved in that investigation. In my case, the crash was three thousand miles away and didn't affect Riverside County. I was working on stories about the illegal transfer of US military aircraft to private aerial-firefighting contractors and wanted to get into the middle of the Gulf War Syndrome issue; Jim was working on an explosive POW-related book.

But this business is like the food chain: small fish lead to bigger ones, which lead to even bigger. Good cop reporters eventually run across corruption involving people bigger than the corner drug dealer. Maybe it's the dealer's law enforcement suppliers.

Years of chasing POW and other military-related stories had led me through many corridors and uncovered legal and illegal activity connected to US defense agencies, contractors, and intelligence organizations. Along the way, I picked up good inside sources who fought the illegal activities.

If you do a good job, they remember. They sometimes call when least expected.

One such source had helped me immeasurably in the series about the illegal transfer of the military cargo aircraft. I had never quoted him in a story. Until his call about three weeks after the Flight 800 crash, his role simply was as a trusted, proven guide.

"You need to look into the TWA Flight 800 crash," he told me. "You'll find that it was a case of friendly fire."

If I hadn't known him, I would have thought him delusional. There had been some speculation about such a thing, much of it unsubstantiated on the Internet, but most people still believed a terrorist bomb or missile brought down the jumbo jet. Actually, some of my other aviation sources and I thought Flight 800 might have been the victim of metal fatigue catching up with an aging Boeing 747-100. I had considered doing a story about that possibility.

I really didn't want this call. I was in the midst of a rare extra day off and halfway through mowing my lawn on a hot August afternoon. And after thirty years in the business, I knew these types of allegations never end in a nice, neat package. I didn't need another years-long story with no discernable ending.

I asked him how he knew Flight 800 was a friendly fire casualty. He said some navy colleagues, men who supervised and monitored military and civilian air communications along the East Coast, told him. They were on duty the night of July 17 and heard the military communications on the "FOX Trot line," as it was called. My source said it was a training exercise gone awry. The scenario included a drug plane being shot down, but somebody accidentally launched a missile and Flight 800 became an actual target. They heard somebody say, "Get the ships out of here."

"How trustworthy are these people?" I asked.

"Very," he said. He had worked with them when he used to supervise the scheduling of the military operating areas, or MOAs as the training zones are known. I hadn't known that much about his navy career and knew nothing about the MOAs. He gave me some more details, and we ended the phone conversation.

Damn! This wasn't my expertise, and I was almost sure we wouldn't get into TWA 800. The incident had happened on the other side of the continent, and the FBI had the case well in hand, or so it appeared from news accounts. Besides, it was my day off. I stood at my kitchen counter and pondered calling my boss or pretending the phone exchange hadn't happened.

But this source had never been wrong before. He sometimes tipped me to government decisions two weeks before they were announced. And he knew the gigantic nature of what he had told me now. I could envision the story about the exercises breaking three or four weeks downstream and me telling my editors that I had known the story a month earlier but hadn't told them.

So I called my boss, Metro Editor Norm Bell, just to be on the record, and told him who called. To my surprise, Norm told me to come in and work the story for a couple of hours and see where it led. I reminded him I would be on overtime. He told me the company could afford it, especially if it turned out to be good.

I spent a couple of hours and then a couple of days. And then a couple of months and then several years. We found two major problems: outright deception within the investigation and a seeming predisposition by national media to accept whatever top officials "leaked" out. As a doctor friend of mine says, it sounds like journalism by urology: the biggest leaker wins.

I've had reporters tell me that they had no choice but to accept what they were handed: they could not educate themselves about the intricacies of fuel volatility, aerodynamics, military exercises, or the difference between rocket fuel and glue. That's not true. It just takes time and resources.

Actually, I had no idea where to begin. No other major stories or series we had done matched this. And the bodies, wreckage, and evidence were three thousand miles away.

The first thing I did was perform what I call the "Chicken Little" test. If somebody says the sky is falling, the first thing I must do is determine if a sky exists. No sky? Then it can't be falling. There is a sky? Has it the properties to fall, or has it ever fallen before? If so, where, when, and under what circumstances? And so on, step by step.

I had to find out first about those military operating areas. Where were they?

My source told me to go to the local airport to buy East Coast aviation maps, on which I would find the military operating areas outlined. Their number and proximity to shore amazed my editors and me. Flight 800, and all other aircraft headed up the East Coast or to and from Europe, had only about a twelve-mile corridor in which to operate. It certainly created a narrow target zone for potential terrorists. Flight 800's wreckage and the bodies inside rained down on the outskirts of Military Operating Area W-106.

The "W" stands for "Warning." The aviation maps admonish pilots: "Warning: National Defense Operating Area. Operations hazardous to the flight of aircraft conducted within this area."

OK, so there was a sky. But that still didn't prove a chunk of it had fallen. No matter how good my source was previously, this was a new subject, and his information had to be proved or disproved. Other than him, I had no real contacts. His people didn't want to talk, afraid they might jeopardize their jobs. Ninety-one percent of the world's whistle-blowers face immediate job security problems.

So I read everything I could find about the crash and began calling official agencies. I anticipated ridicule and didn't expect anybody to say, "Oh, yeah, we shot the plane down." I wasn't disappointed.

I called more than a dozen official agencies, told them the story about the alleged exercise and accident, and asked them what they knew. Nada. Nothing. Zilch. Additionally, navy, FBI, coast guard, New York Air National Guard, and Federal Aviation Administration representatives said that no military or any other type of operations or training exercises were scheduled or unscheduled near where Flight 800 went down or in the area the night of July 17, 1996.

These are what I call "on-the-record" statements. The public information officers, the type I usually got passed to because I wasn't with the *New York Times* or *Washington Post*, usually know only what they're told. They take my questions, ask others who are authorized to speak, and then pass the responses back to me. I know this. But it's important to build this official record. Sometimes they're told the truth. Many times they're not.

"No friendly fire. No exercises, so how could there be?" everybody responded. My source was outnumbered 13–1. I was ready to tell my bosses "no story" when an unrelated call from Jim Sanders, my POW-hunting colleague, changed that. Jim was following up on a story each of us was pursuing about the secret postwar return of some of the American POWs.

Jim and I hadn't talked since the day after Flight 800's crash, when his wife was recalled to St. Louis, so I told him I was working the disaster story. That's odd, he said, because he was, too. Some TWA employees, aware that he was an investigative journalist and ex-cop, asked if he would look into the crash.

Several TWA employees were part of the National Transportation Safety Board's (NBSB) investigative teams and were sharing some of their intimate information. Some of the TWA investigators had even worked on or flown the specific Boeing 747 that exploded. Jim told me that friendly fire was among the possibilities being discussed. I told him about the call from my source. Jim's source was totally different, so I called his, who told me about the friendly fire rumors.

My original source's information was better than rumor but hadn't been proved. The TWA rumors were connected to people inside the accident investigation but unsubstantiated. Rumors by definition are general talk not based on definite knowledge. Gossip. That doesn't mean the information is true, false, or unfounded; it means that the speaker is spreading someone else's information.

My boss told me to put everything into story form and see what it looked like. I did. It looked like a story that reported interesting rumors surrounding a major investigation. Nothing substantiated. No first-person account.

One of my cardinal rules is to try to keep my sources separated if they don't know each other. Source A's confirmation of source B's information is not confirmation if A got it from B. If A and B both got it from C, it certainly is not independent confirmation. I know of one intelligence agency in which a person at one desk would call a specific reporter, "leak" information to her, and a person at the next desk would "verify" or "confirm" the information when she called him. That's not confirmation—that's manipulation of a naive reporter.

Anyway, my boss, Norm Bell, passed the completed story to our managing editor, Mel Opotowsky, a journalist of great integrity and national standing who has no fear of man, God, or beast. Mel looked at the piece, thought it interesting, but without a hook for us to use to run it. Bank it in the computer, he said. Something might come along for us to use the information.

A story did break that said faint traces of explosives found on Flight 800 cabin debris, thought initially to point to a bomb or missile, could be residue left on the plane from a June 10, 1996, exercise for a bomb-detection dog in St. Louis. That disclosure seemed to take a lot of punch out of national reporting that looked at a bomb or missile as a possible cause of the deaths of 230 people.

Nobody examined the bomb-sniffing exercise to see if it were true. That proved to be a grievous error for everybody—victims' families, investigators, journalists, and the nation. I'll discuss that later.

I continued poking for some authentication that military-style exercises near Long Island had occurred the night Flight 800 went down. My original source told me to push the FAA for its July 17, 1996, flight controller logs, which would tell the status of the northeastern MOAs.

On Sunday, August 25, 1996, Mel called me at home. He said that a *New York Times* story for Monday might be the piece in which to sandwich my reporting about the friendly fire rumor. The *Times* story was about Long Island photographer Linda Kabot, whose July 17 snapshot at a political fundraiser returned with a strange object in the background sky. The cigar-shaped object looked like it might have something fiery coming out of one end. Was it a missile? A drone? The FBI had taken the negatives and photos, except for one held by the photo lab, and hadn't returned them or disclosed test results.

Could an abbreviated version of my piece insert into the *Times* story? Sure. "Beyond Linda Kabot's photo, a related rumor about the TWA crash keeps making the rounds," our insert began. "It does not involve terrorists, but a supposed exercise that went awry involving units of the coast guard, Customs, Drug Enforcement Agency, and Air National Guard operating in the vast restricted military practice area off the Long Island shore."

The insert included additional information, and concluded:

"But according to federal officials, there are some major holes in the story:

- There was no exercise that night.
- The air space was available for civilian use.
- The nonmilitary agencies don't even have anti-aircraft guns, let alone missiles.
- And there is no national plan to shoot down drug smugglers' planes."

(Actually, I didn't find out until much later that a quick-response multination NATO naval flotilla had just returned to the East Coast in July 1996 after spending time off South America helping track suspected drug-smuggling aircraft with the ships' radar. And on April 20, 2001, a Peruvian air force pilot shot down a civilian airplane being tracked by a CIA-sponsored surveillance aircraft. The downed plane, suspected of being a drug flight, turned out to be a US missionary and his family. The incidents do not prove Flight 800 was a victim of friendly fire; they do, however, prove that US assets help track suspected drug aircraft and include the use of deadly force.)

I read the rumor story in Monday morning's paper with everybody else and figured that was the end of *The Press-Enterprise*'s involvement in the Flight 800 case.

I was so wrong.

The next day, an FAA source faxed me the flight controllers' logs I had sought for weeks. They proved to the world that I had been lied to, often and frequently.

A large area within twelve miles of where Flight 800 exploded not only was active, off-limits to nonmilitary aircraft, and considered dangerous to civilian air traffic, but another large area normally off-limits to the military had been reserved for navy operations. The navy P-3 Orion antisubmarine aircraft that was almost over Flight 800 at the time the jetliner exploded was headed for the special zone for a hide-and-seek game with the nuclear submarine USS *Trepang*.

I showed the logs and map to my editors. I can still see us, checking the FAA documents against the aviation maps. We kept asking the same question, over and over: Why were we lied to?

The three FAA pages did not, and still don't, prove a missile shot down Flight 800 or that US equipment was involved in the disaster. But it answered one of my Chicken Little questions: Were military operating areas near TWA 800 "hot" at the time it exploded, and were there exercises scheduled in them? Yes.

The flow of information accelerated for several weeks. We learned that at least one US sub, and maybe two, was relatively close to the disaster site. I say "relatively" because the FBI and navy said the two navy assets closest to Flight 800 were the nonlethal P-3 and the guided missile cruiser USS *Normandy* 185 miles south.

Well, that was patently false. It took almost two years, but we proved through the navy's own information that, minimally, three or more subs, a patrol plane, and aircraft carrier exercises were between Flight 800 and the *Normandy*.

And the *Normandy*, according to official navy records and statements, was in four different places at the time of the crash, ranging from 185 miles to 290 miles south. The southernmost site adds more subs, a guided missile frigate, aircraft carrier, and carrier jets to the pool of military units operating in the area that US investigators proclaimed to be in the "vicinity of the crash" and void of exercises.

(Many people argue that if a US military asset launched a missile that struck Flight 800, men and women serving aboard the plane or ship would blow the whistle. As a reminder, thousands of American servicemen fought in or bombed Laos without disclosing the secret war in that nation between 1965 and 1975. As for Flight 800, no news organization was permitted to interview crewmembers of the P-3, *Normandy*, the submarines operating in the area, or other ships the navy and FBI refused to identify. Navy officials continually rebuffed attempts to interview crewmembers, even to have them say they were not involved. Many navy officials told me the FBI would not permit any such interviews. One ship's weapons crewmember recently contacted said he reported detecting a radar "lock-on," such as that created by a missile launcher, from an unidentified source about the time Flight 800 went down. He said he was told by his superior not to tell crash investigators.)

Radar data the NTSB released for its December 1997 hearings, almost eighteen months after the Flight 800 incident and our story, revealed four other mystery tracks "consistent with the speed of a boat" within three to six miles of the jumbo jet's course at the time of its midair breakup. None returned to offer any assistance.

The names of the four vessels remain undisclosed to this day. The FBI says it has no idea what the closest vessel was. A memo released under our Freedom of Information Act (FOIA) request quotes a navy captain at the Pentagon as telling an Atlantic Fleet officer to keep the names of three merchant ships that could have been close to Flight 800 "in-house Navy for the time being." The ships were never publicly identified, nor were many others that were ultimately disclosed as being near the crash. The question is whether they could have been a platform off which a missile was fired.

But we didn't know in September 1996 to what extent the official record had been falsified, only that it had.

If there were nothing to cover up, why was there a cover-up?

I called the FBI's New York office, which was handling the investigation, and asked if the bureau wanted a copy of the FAA documents that contradicted agency and navy statements about no nearby military exercises. "No," I was told. "We have all the information we need." I called the navy and then the Department of Defense to ask about the discrepancies. Their representatives said the FBI had forbidden them to say anything about Flight 800–related issues.

I beg your pardon? The FBI had forbidden the navy and Department of Defense?

In thirty years of covering military issues, some even more significant than this, I had never heard such a thing. Defense agencies always bristled at the suggestion that they couldn't handle their own issues. In this case, they appeared eager to hide behind the FBI.

One navy spokesman finally told me he was forbidden to answer questions on the phone about anything related to Flight 800 issues. But, he said, if the same questions were submitted as part of a FOIA request, I could get the answers. I recognized the officer's response for the gift it was and immediately submitted a request with thirty-seven questions. It took months to get the invaluable documents in response.

Because we had no sources inside the Pentagon, Mel turned to one of his former reporters, Knut Royce of *Newsday*. We fed Knut the FAA documents, and he got some responses, which he fed us. They were very different from what was being printed elsewhere, and one navy official confirmed a P-3 versus sub operation.

"This had to be a command-and-control exercise or exercise to qualify somebody to do something or whatever," a retired senior Pentagon officer said. The "whatever" could range from missions with the army's Special Forces to exercises with a foreign navy's submarine.

Said one Navy official:

Keep this on background. Submariners get freaked out when you talk about what they're doing. We have no subs with surface-to-air missiles. But there's nothing to say that if you're on a littoral [shoreline] operation with Special Forces you couldn't put Stingers [shoulder-launched missiles] on them. The Russians had worked with a rocket system on their subs because one of the things that scared them to death was our anti-submarine helos [helicopters]. They always wanted a way of last resort to fire back.

We ran our story Friday, October 4, complete with a map-graphic and the responses Knut got for us. Our lead:

> On the night TWA Flight 800 exploded in midair, nearby military training areas covering thousands of square miles were assigned to exercises deemed potentially dangerous to civilian aircraft, Navy and federal aviation records reveal.
>
> Solid clues as to what caused the July 17 disaster continue to elude investigators. Officials say a missile, bomb, or mechanical failure probably caused the crash. And unsubstantiated rumors persist that the plane was brought down by "friendly fire."
>
> Details of what was happening in the active military training areas remain an official secret more than two months after the nation's second worst air crash killed 230 people. But government records contradict weeks of official denials that any significant amount of military activity was scheduled the night of July 17.

A sidebar described the narrow corridor Flight 800's crew had to use because of the scheduled exercises.

The stories were to be transmitted to the Associated Press for worldwide distribution Thursday night, but our computer link didn't work. Therefore, the stories didn't get the attention they deserved.

Some of our readers, however, contacted other publications, and our information began circulating. The chief US correspondent for the French magazine *Paris Match* called, and I sent him the FAA documents and a copy of our map-graphic. *Paris Match* printed their version and credited *The Press-Enterprise.*

Almost simultaneously, I was invited to fly to Washington, DC. Remember, it was a presidential election year.

An ex-CIA agent, a World Health Organization official, and others told my editor and me that important congressmen "from both sides of the aisle" felt that US officials were covering up something about the crash but didn't know what and didn't know which questions to ask.

Could I quickly come to Washington, at their expense, and tell the congressmen or their staff members the questions they needed to ask crash investigators? They, then, would make the inquiries and give the answers to us first.

It wouldn't be my first trip to DC as an expert witness or to respond to a request to discuss with congressional investigators what wasn't being asked in major inquiries. Our stories about American

servicemen still missing from the Vietnam War, alleged drug trafficking by US officials, and illegal use of surplus military aircraft had
resulted in trips to the capital or investigators making trips to my
Riverside home.

As in the other issues, our stories in *The Press-Enterprise* turned up
information that other media had missed or appeared to be uninter-
ested in pursuing. Our editors had proved themselves before by
printing stories other newspapers sometimes ran from and then
sniped at.

I sometimes felt like a coal mine canary, the bird that miners use
to detect poisonous gas. If the bird suddenly quits chirping and drops
dead, the miners know they have to get out fast. Singing solo in such
conditions can be lonely and frightening, but singing is preferable to
silence. Miners learn to listen for the canary — or its silence.

My editors and I decided to accept the invitation to DC. What
could we lose? The upside was better than the downside. On October
24, 1996, I flew to Washington.

As soon as I met my escort at Ronald Reagan National Airport, I
knew we had been used. The young man meeting me at the gate introduced himself as a driver for the Bob Dole for President organization.
It was just past midnight, eleven days before the 1996 presidential
election. The polls showed Dole faring badly.

I was not there to be somebody's eleventh-hour bid to win a presidential election, and I doubted the driver was taking me to Clinton
Reelection Committee headquarters for a joint conference.

It was about 1:00 AM when I was checked into the Hyatt Regency
Washington, room 716. I didn't care about the hour. Somebody was
going to be awakened. I called the go-betweens and told them that if
the meeting were taking place at Dole campaign headquarters I
wouldn't attend and I would write a story about the one-sided ren-
dezvous. The meeting was switched to a law firm's conference room,
where, at about 10:00 AM, I met the ex-CIA Mideast station agent and
Bob Dole's chief of policy, Richard Fore. My chauffeur was the wife of
an aide to Sen. Bob Smith of New Hampshire.

So much for "both sides of the aisle." I decided to give them a
copy of our October 4 story, the list of questions I asked the navy to
respond to, and left.

Fore said it was too late to affect the election anyway.

The trip to Washington produced nothing tangible.

In November 1996, days after Clinton defeated Dole for the presidency, ex–Kennedy White House press chief Pierre Salinger entered the Flight 800 mix. He cited the *Paris Match* story about the military activity and said a document that intelligence agents gave him stated Flight 800 was the victim of friendly fire. The "document" turned out to be a copy of an Internet-distributed assertion that a US ship accidentally downed Flight 800. I had seen the Internet printout weeks earlier and determined it to be unreliable.

In response, navy spokesman Rear Adm. Edward Kristensen, who was directing salvage operations, said in a national press conference that the P-3 and the *Normandy* 185 miles south were "the only two assets that the Navy had operating off the East Coast . . . in the vicinity of the TWA 800 crash site."

How many times would that response go unchallenged?

I persuaded my editors that we should not get involved in Salinger's allegations but should stick with our own investigating. I have nothing against Mr. Salinger; I just felt he might not be receiving the best advice.

Within the investigation, officials were shifting toward pinning the explosion on some type of undiscovered mechanical failure. Only 15,000 to 20,000 pounds of the approximately 370,000-pound airplane remained on the Atlantic Ocean's floor. No other major media seemed to have picked up on or to have been investigating the misstatements about military activity. And quite honestly, just because the government was prevaricating about that issue did not prove "friendly fire."

But it did keep us searching. If I find my dog dead of gunshot wounds at my neighbor's fence, that doesn't prove he killed it. However, if my neighbor said he was gone that weekend but really was home with his gun club, it makes me wonder.

At times, I felt our voice to be the only one challenging the official chorus. The only canary in the coal mine. Thankfully, I found others. Several paid a dear price for their independence. Kristina Borjesson, then an independent producer with *CBS Reports*, also was developing stories for *60 Minutes*. She called me from New York. She got my number from *Paris Match*. She had won an Emmy for investigative reporting that she'd done for *Legacy of Shame*, a CBS documentary about migrant farm workers. Borjesson said she was concerned about the general media's seemingly blind acceptance of the government's take on Flight 800. Her law enforcement sources were providing different views from inside the investigation, talking about missile and explosives evidence that wasn't getting proper consideration and about the FBI's inordinate grip on other agencies.

She said her executive producer had assigned her to look into the crash and share anything she uncovered with *CBS Nightly News* first and then any other CBS show that might be interested. Borjesson said she was concerned that her reporting was not going to go anywhere at *CBS Nightly News* because it contradicted the information a Washington correspondent was getting from Pentagon sources, who were saying the crash was caused by a mechanical failure.

I was alternately pleased and concerned: pleased that a journalist at the national level was critically reviewing the investigative process but concerned that people in a major news outlet seemed worried about upsetting the establishment.

Whom were we trying to keep honest?

I also connected with reporters or publishers of newsmagazines and aviation industry publications who were concerned about government misstatements or pieces that didn't fit mechanical failure as a cause.

In early 1997, I got another call from Jim Sanders. A major source within the investigation had supplied him with documents showing how Flight 800 debris landed in the ocean. Officials had said for months that the debris pattern would point to the cause of the crash.

Jim used a computer spreadsheet program to collate the information and found the plane had unraveled right to left just behind the wing front. An NTSB metallurgy study suggested that the plane was falling apart before the center fuel tank exploded. Critical pieces inside the tank seemed to be burned *after* the plane began disintegrating, not before.

I sent a copy of the metallurgy study, with its graphics, to a long-time source who is an aviation expert and crash investigator. I asked him to read the report and tell me what he thought, without my influencing him. He said that the information told him that the plane was falling apart before the fuel tank exploded. He especially was interested in drawings that showed unexplained gouges on the plane's exterior, at just about the right wing front. The gouges were covered with soot deposited after the gouges were made. The aluminum skin, which began peeling when the aircraft was breached, also stressed inward at this point. All this led the expert to conclude that something bumped into the aircraft before it began falling apart. (The gouges also were in the area where traces of explosive chemicals were found on the aircraft's exterior, but the metallurgy report did not deal with such issues.) The FAA had told the White House hours after the explosion that radar seemed to indicate a high-speed object was closing in on Flight 800 seconds before the disaster; NTSB officials wanted the FAA to recant, but FAA officials refused.

And then there was the red residue.

After the computer work revealed a clear, narrow path of initial destruction through the plane, with three consecutive rows of seats among the first debris streaming out of the crippled airplane, Jim's source looked at the debris and said the recovered seatbacks for all those rows had a red substance on them. The source removed two small pieces of the substance-laden fabric and mailed them to Jim, who had one tested for contents. Meanwhile, alerted by Jim that he had this material, I scouted for people who could tell me what solid fuel for rockets might contain. Clanging inside my brain was what my original retired navy source had told me just before my trip to Washington: Have somebody check debris for evidence of solid fuel for rockets; if an inert missile passed through the fuselage, it would leave a chemical trail of fuel exhaust. I learned from experts that solid fuel for missiles is a rather basic recipe of explosive ingredients mixed in differing proportions, depending on the speed and distance you want the object propelled, as well as its size and weight. A rubber-based bonding agent keeps the fuel components from separating. Solid fuel for rockets, when ignited, generates a continuing, controlled explosion. Cars are moved by the energy from controlled explosions inside the engine block.

Until Jim got the pieces of red-encrusted fabric, four media outlets, all bigger than *The Press-Enterprise*, were interested in presenting his information. Two bailed after he got the material. They expressed concern about the legality of his having the fabric. I was afraid that Kristina Borjesson and CBS would present vital information before I could, but the ball bounced into my court; Jim contacted me, asked if we could present his evidence, and I talked to my editors.

Jim flew from Virginia, where he lived, to California and presented his information, including results of an independent lab test of the red substance's contents. A genuine rocket scientist told me the ingredients and proportions were consistent with solid fuel for missiles. I had the other expert's opinion that the metallurgy report showed the plane began unraveling before fuel-air vapors ignited in the center tank. A separate set of color graphics showed that only two seats and passengers' bodies in the forward part of the aircraft had burn marks. If the fuel tank explosion and fire ignited the disaster, where were the burn marks on the bodies and cabin interior closest to the first flames?

My editors decided the public had a right to the information Jim had acquired. They assigned another reporter to help me, and we began writing, while our graphics department turned information into understandable visual explanations. I had two long phone interviews with Jim's inside source who had provided the documents and material.

On March 7, 1997, I called the New York office of James Kallstrom, the assistant FBI director who was leading the bureau's investigation into Flight 800. It was the first time I got through to him, personally. I told him the evidence we had, including the lab report about the red residue.

"There is a red residue trail, but it has no connection to a missile," he told me. "I'm not going to get into it. There's a logical explanation, but I'm not going to get into it."

Had he told us what he thought it was, we could have postponed publication, handled that question in about two days, and provided information that could have helped the FBI and NTSB. But he didn't tell us, so we couldn't tell him. The FBI had refused our offer of information before and now they refused again.

We had wanted to publish our stories on Saturday, March 8, 1997, but several problems prevented us from doing so. I was still writing, and my bosses wanted to edit the copy calmly, not in a rush. Additionally, Pierre Salinger's colleague Mike Sommer wanted us to review and print excerpts of their fifty-eight-page essay that contended the navy accidentally shot down Flight 800. Sommer offered us exclusive US publication rights of purported radar images that showed some unidentified high-speed object intersecting Flight 800's path if we printed some of the essay. The earliest he could get the package to us from Paris was Saturday morning our time. We waited, read the material, and decided to print our own information and not hitch ourselves to Salinger's wagon.

We published our package for the morning of Monday, March 10. I faxed copies to the NTSB and Kallstrom's office, as soon as the first papers came off the press late Sunday night, and we sent electronic copies to the Associated Press, which we had alerted beforehand.

The story exploded around the world.

"New evidence, much of it distilled from FBI and National Transportation Safety Board documents, points to a missile as the cause of last July's crash of TWA Flight 800," the lead story began. I wish I could take credit for such a succinct lead, but my metro editor, Norm Bell, bailed me out of my legalistic drafts and distilled it into readable English.

The stories, graphics, color photo of Jim's mottled-red fabric, and large bold-faced headlines made an incredible package. We even shoved the index off the front page for the first time in anybody's memory. I went home a tired but satisfied reporter.

At 3:00 AM I bolted upright in bed, gripped by a terrible panic. Dreadful questions reverberated inside my head: What makes you think you're right? What makes you think you have what it takes to do this story? What makes you think you know more than other reporters? What makes you think you haven't dragged your newspaper over a cliff, a fall from which it and you will never recover?

The fact that I had prayed a lot wouldn't sway a jury. Sweat seeped from each pore. In my mind, I went over each story and fact, line by line. We not only had double-checked, we had triple, if not quadruple-checked. We had not taken Jim at his word. We checked the information independently and ensured the documents were genuine. I had checked the debris recovery chart against latitude-longitude maps to ensure the aircraft parts were recovered where Jim said they were. I had found independent analysts who had no connection to Jim.

Finally settled in my mind, I went back to sleep, thankful for the extra hour my bosses had given me because of the late nights.

Nothing in my previous thirty years of journalism prepared me for that Monday morning I walked into work. Phones rang incessantly, and news assistants could hardly keep up with the messages.

Our stories were being reported worldwide. Radio and TV newscasts led with our reports. Call slips from at least four dozen news outlets, including talk shows and some European media organizations, were on my desk. Mel Opotowsky, my managing editor, had taken some of the more important ones and responded to them, especially ones that required an official *Press-Enterprise* spokesman. It was heady stuff, just like out of a movie, but scary. This was real. We were smack in the middle of one of the biggest stories around.

We decided I would continue with the story, and Mel would handle the media inquiries. We wanted the focus to remain on the information, not the newspaper and/or me. We weren't the story; the story was the story. That may sound simplistic, but it was an important decision and invaluable lesson. I can't imagine what would have happened had I dissipated myself by responding to the media frenzy or trying to justify the stories we did.

Other media organizations wanted our information, but none of the majors I know of began their own really independent inquiry to determine if what the government was telling them was true, except for Borjesson. The *Village Voice* began carrying challenging stories by freelance writer Robert Davey, but almost all others threw the information overboard when the FBI said the red residue was adhesive, aka glue. The other media took the FBI's pronouncement as gospel, and thereafter many viewed Sanders as a fraud. Even columnists at my own newspaper ridiculed Jim and me and began sniping at our stories. One eventually told me he was embarrassed to work at the same newspaper as I. *Et tu, Brutus?*

Glue?

Kallstrom told me where to go Monday morning. He said Jim had used a good lab but that "the boys" used to handling such stories back East would have asked what else the red stuff might have been and made that inquiry before printing such a story. Well, I had asked him that question three days earlier, but he said he wouldn't tell me, so that took care of asking him. But Monday he was conciliatory, telling me that he knew I was a sincere, honest reporter who had been led astray. I avoided the argument. Knowing when to accept an offer, I asked what I ought to look for, and he told me I might consider whether the red residue was adhesive from 3M Corporation.

I thanked him, called 3M, and talked to their lead expert. I read him the ingredients and proportions of the red stuff, and he said most of the same elements were in adhesive but in much smaller proportions. Also, with rubber bonding agents being part of solid fuel for rockets, some adhesive would show up anyway.

Jim had one piece of red-encrusted fabric left, which he wanted a media organization to have tested independently. NBC's *Dateline* turned down the opportunity, but Borjesson was interested. He shipped the evidence to her, but the FBI discovered *60 Minutes* had the fabric, and CBS turned it over to officials at the FBI's request. CBS let Borjesson go a few weeks later.

Nine months later, at its December 1997 Baltimore hearings on the

Flight 800 crash, the NTSB released a report that said the "red residue" was 3M's "Scotch Grip 1357 High Performance Contact Adhesive." For some reason, the report didn't point out that Scotch Grip 1357 is green, not red.

I pressed the NTSB and finally got to interview Henry Hughes, who supervised the agency's analysis of cabin debris, including seats. He told me that tests the FBI did were of glue used to form the plastic inset into which lap trays are stored when not in use. That glue was not red residue; it was glue. The red residue was something else.

The day after our March 10, 1997, story, a House of Representatives committee happened to be having a hearing about the NTSB's budget. Congressmen asked about the residue. NTSB representatives said they had ordered their own tests of the reddish substance. Because the NTSB didn't have its own laboratory to conduct the test, the agency asked the National Aeronautics and Space Administration (NASA) to analyze the material.

Who better than NASA to see if the material was glue or exhaust from solid fuel for rockets? At least, that's the logical assumption. But the assumption became a smoke screen.

It was that NASA report that was released in Baltimore. But the NASA chemist did not say that the red residue he tested was the same material tested by Jim Sanders. The chemist said it was impossible for him to determine if the product he tested was the same that was used on the 747 seats of Flight 800. He told me in August 1998 that the test he was instructed to conduct determined that 1357 was present in the samples he was given but that "there was other material in there."

"At no time was I asked to analyze for or determine the presence of materials which may also be found in solid rocket fuel," the analyst said for our August 10, 1998, story, more than two years after the plane exploded off Long Island. He told me that there were tests that could have conclusively proved whether the red residue was missile fuel or not, but that the NTSB had prohibited any such tests.

We faxed the story, before we printed it, to the NASA chemist to ensure we had quoted him accurately and in context, because of the story's significance: given the opportunity to determine if the red residue was consistent with solid fuel for rockets, the NTSB said no. It was like testing a dead man's blood for caffeine and refusing to test for strychnine.

To ensure that we weren't missing something, we ordered a

gallon of 3M's Scotch Grip 1357 High Performance Contact Adhesive. The green liquid is highly volatile. We asked a private laboratory in Phoenix to do a comparison test of Jim Sander's report, the NASA report, and 1357. We asked a professor at California State University, San Bernardino, to do the same. Each said that the red residue had something more than 1357 in it, if indeed the adhesive were present.

The university professor went an extra step. She burned the green glue to see if it turned red. It turned brown, not red. Besides, the seats off which the red residue was taken were not burned. Green glue is green.

The red residue is only indicative of how uninvestigative critical elements of the "investigation" became. It also demonstrates how wedded most reporters and editors are to official pronouncements. Because the FBI said the red residue was glue (without mentioning the glue was green), most reporters and editors took the edict as gospel and did no independent investigating. Why would FBI and NTSB officials lie? I don't know. They didn't tell me. But any news organization could have, and should have, done the testing we did.

We did more stories than just the red residue piece, of course. Because of our attention to detail, our growing reputation for investigating the investigators, and our looking for evidence instead of just quotes, many people who saw flaws in the official inquiries came looking for us or were sent our way.

For instance, ex–Air National Guard helicopter pilot Maj. Frederick Meyer decided to break his silence because he heard the NTSB talking about pinning the explosion on some unknown spark igniting heated fuel in the center fuel tank—never mind that physical evidence said the plane was breaking up before the fuel tank blew up.

Meyer was one of two pilots in an Air National Guard helicopter who saw streaks headed toward the jumbo jet before it exploded. Meyer is a Vietnam veteran and experienced at watching missiles explode in midair. He said what he saw was military ordnance exploding near Flight 800 before the plane burst into a fireball. He took his story to congressional investigator Kelly O'Meara, who directed him to me. O'Meara later was pressured to resign after she angered FBI officials by challenging the official investigation. She worked for Rep. Michael Forbes (R-NY), off whose district Flight 800's victims and debris fell into the ocean. O'Meara, Borjesson, and I spent the 1997 Fourth of July congressional break in Forbes's office looking at documents that proved the FBI and navy were being untruthful.

"I'm not a professor with a PhD in explosion watching, I'm an eye-witness," Meyer told me two weeks after my DC visit. "I know what I saw. I saw an ordnance explosion. And whatever I saw, the explosion of the fuel was not the initiator of the event. It was one of the results. Something happened before that which was the initiator of the disaster."

The NTSB, at the FBI's request, refused to let eyewitnesses testify at its Flight 800 hearings. How could they? They would have rebutted FBI and NTSB conclusions that there was no evidence a missile or bomb brought down the plane. Those hundreds of people, including Meyer, who saw streaks headed toward the plane were deluded, officials decided.

Our August 10, 1998, story about the NASA scientist's report and comments turned out to be my last for the newspaper about TWA Flight 800, although I later did a chapter for Jim Sanders's book, *Altered Evidence*. He wrote it, the second of his three books about the TWA 800 crash, after a Brooklyn federal grand jury indicted him and his wife on charges of conspiring to steal pieces of debris (two small pieces of residue-coated seat fabric) from an airplane crash. A jury convicted them in federal court after the judge ruled Jim and Liz could not argue that they had received the evidence as part of a First Amendment–protected journalistic investigation.

Jim's attorney wanted to subpoena me to testify that Sanders's inside source, whom we dubbed Hangarman, provided information freely and of his own volition. I had interviewed Hangarman, who was TWA's lead 747 pilot, after he agreed. The night before Flight 800's explosion he had flown that plane to New York from Europe, and he shared information with me openly, although he did not want to be identified in our story. We did not publish his name. Because of his unique position, he had access to much of the investigation's information and documents. The US Attorney's office had wanted Hangarman's identity and pressured Jim and Liz to provide it. They refused, citing First Amendment rights and laws protecting journalists. When federal officials determined Hangarman's identity was Terrel Stacey, they pressured Stacey to provide information they could use to prosecute the Sanderses. Jim and Liz had angered federal officials by refusing to turn over a confidential source, so the federal officials decided to punish them using an obscure law intended to protect sensitive material critical to crash investigations, not investigators who were hiding evidence.

I did not want to get on the witness stand because I had many other confidential sources whose futures would be jeopardized for telling the truth if their identities were known. We could not be sure that I wouldn't be asked about other sources once I began talking about Hangarman. Under a compromise, I wound up providing Jim's attorney notes of my interview with Hangarman, and they were used to counter the government's contention that the Sanderses coerced Stacey into providing them material from the investigation.

The Press-Enterprise wound up paying $20,000 in attorney fees to keep me off the stand and thereby protect other confidential sources. Protecting freedom of the press is not free.

Jim and Liz were not permitted to argue that Jim was a journalist and that the First Amendment or other laws that protect journalists protected his actions. Liz was prosecuted because she knew Hangarman and talked to him twice about her husband's efforts. They were convicted, but the federal judge sentenced them to probation and public service, refusing the prosecution's desire to have them imprisoned. Their appeals were denied, and the Supreme Court refused to review their case. No major media organization came to their defense, although they did more to turn the spotlight on deceptive investigative practices than anybody. Jim and Liz have spent hundreds of thousands of dollars defending themselves and their right to investigate investigators.

They since have filed a federal suit against the US government and specific federal investigators and agents, including the FBI's lead investigator, James Kallstrom. The Sanderses assert the government illegally stole Jim's journalistic work product without a warrant, as required by law, and that Kallstrom and others conspired to violate their civil rights. Liz was forced to retire without benefits from TWA and now works for a small airline. Jim is still writing investigative books. Their civil suit, as of this writing, is pending in front of the same federal judge who heard their criminal case.

I've recently been told by my ex–executive editor that the reason *Press-Enterprise* editors pulled the plug on my Flight 800 stories was because the newspaper was short-handed and I was too valuable to continue pursuing a story whose end was nowhere in sight and whose resolution was in doubt.

I suppose I should be thrilled I was considered that valuable. I have another theory. The two editors who licensed me to do the scores of

Flight 800 stories we did were no longer at the *Press-Enterprise*. Norm Bell was reassigned as projects editor and then left for another newspaper; Mel Opotowsky retired. My new editors did not have the background or investment in the Flight 800 stories I had done. They were new coaches, and I was operating under an old game plan. They had a new vision and wanted to use my talents for more regional issues.

I'm proud of my publisher and editors for having the guts to print stories no other outlet seemed interested in pursuing. We had, with the government's own words, proved many untruths or misstatements government investigators and officials made about the nation's second deadliest accident.

Counting my salary, my editors' salaries when they were working Flight 800 issues, staff support, $20,000 in attorneys' fees to keep me off the witness stand in the criminal court case, trips to the East Coast, and other expenses, *The Press-Enterprise* probably spent at least $250,000 to $300,000 covering the story. Maybe more. It's a rough estimate and is no small sum. But I think they quit one story too soon.

The story I had when I was called off had to do with the bomb-detection exercise the FAA said was conducted in St. Louis on June 10, 1996, aboard Boeing 747 No. 17119. A few weeks later that jetliner became the ill-fated TWA Flight 800 aircraft.

A month after the jetliner's destruction, the FBI used that alleged June 10 exercise to explain away the traces of PETN and RDX that crash field tests found on exterior and interior parts of 17119's fuselage. PETN and RDX are compounds found within explosives. PETN is more common, while RDX, at the time of the crash, was manufactured only for the US military.

The FBI, in a letter to then representative James Traficant (D-OH), gave its account of the police officer's bomb-detection exercise, with his dog, aboard 17119. The officer hid several types of explosives in the airplane's passenger sections and asked his dog to find the samples, which it did. The exercise aboard the empty plane ended at noon, the FBI said. The police officer did not follow usual protocol by having a training officer observe and didn't log the tail number of the airplane because he wasn't required to, the FBI said.

That story had more holes than traditional Swiss cheese.

Company records reveal that 17119 backed away from the terminal at 12:35 PM, late on its trip to Hawaii with more than four hundred passengers. With the help of Kay Pennington, an invaluable researcher for many of my stories, I traced the pilot and copilot of that June 10 flight. I talked to them. They said there's no way the plane could have been empty and available at the time the FBI report says the bomb-detection exercise took place. The cockpit crew for a 747 board the aircraft at least an hour before takeoff, if not earlier. Flight attendants arrive in the cabin even earlier because passengers begin boarding at least forty-five minutes before scheduled take-off, which was 11:45 AM. Galley and other support staff are on the plane even earlier. Never, said the pilot and copilot, in their twenty-plus-year careers, did a bomb-detection exercise ever delay one of their flights, and they never interrupted an exercise in progress.

So, based on a report about an impossible inspection, the FBI explained away evidence of explosive residue found inside and outside Flight 800.

Records show that a second Boeing 747 was empty and parked exactly opposite plane 17119 in St. Louis the morning of the alleged bomb-sniffing exercise. It was plane 17117, Flight 800's sister, and didn't depart for New York until more than an hour after 17119 left for Hawaii. That other plane had plenty of time for a bomb exercise. But it was never tested.

No other journalist had the story. We got it because I had to rely on rank-and-file sources and evidence, not high-placed "leaks" and "press releases," thank goodness.

Officials still haven't found the cause of Flight 800's demise. Or if they know, they're not saying. The official explanation is that some unknown spark probably entered the center fuel tank some unknown way and ignited a volatile fuel-air mixture that exploded and began a cataclysmic disintegration of the 747.

The case is not over. Physicists and engineers who say evidence does not support government conclusions, or who want access to evidence the CIA, the FBI, and the NTSB refuse to share, have filed suits to get information kept out of public reach. Except for the *Albuquerque Journal*, a few small newspapers, and Internet publications, no media are reporting these important events.

For instance, retired engineer and pilot Ray Lahr filed suit in federal court in Los Angeles to force the CIA, the FBI, and the NTSB to provide information and calculations the agencies used to assert that Flight 800 climbed more than three thousand feet after the explosion decapitated the plane's nose, about eighty thousand pounds of aircraft. The issue is important because the FBI, using the CIA's analysis, and the NTSB concluded that hundreds of witnesses, including military veterans, did not see a missile streaking toward Flight 800 before the midair explosion. The agencies' officials said that what the witnesses saw was flaming fuel from the crippled airliner as it soared upward after the hypothetical mechanical initiating event.

"I don't believe the zoom climb ever happened," Lahr said. "Boeing provided before-and-after data to the NTSB, and it was published in the accident report. Eighty thousand pounds of nose and cockpit were blown off. This shifted the center of gravity far aft and generated about six million foot-pounds of nose-up torque. The aircraft immediately pitched up and stalled.

"The wing probably failed right then since its center box structure had been blown apart," Lahr continued. "But using Boeing's data, I calculated that even if the wing had held together, the most the plane could have climbed is a few hundred feet, not the 3,200 feet claimed by the CIA. That is why I want the data and calculations that were used to produce the CIA and NTSB videos."

The CIA and the NTSB do not want the information released. They said it contains information proprietary to Boeing. What is proprietary about whether an airplane that loses eighty thousand pounds in front can soar upward more than three thousand feet? Isn't it more important to determine whether eyewitnesses really saw burning fuel or a missile trail? What's to fight?

On the East Coast, engineer Graeme Sephton is suing the FBI to get the forensic evidence about hundreds of foreign objects the FBI seized from the bodies of the crash victims during their autopsies. It's not a macabre foray into highly personal and private domains. The evidence never was shared with the coroner nor requested by the NTSB.

Sephton, who works at the University of Massachusetts, said he realized that "unlike other evidence collected from the bottom of the Atlantic, the foreign body evidence is definitive because there is no chain-of-custody ambiguity. It cannot readily be explained away."

Sephton filed his FOIA request in 1998 and is still fighting the FBI for the results.

It's important to review the government's pronouncements in the TWA Flight 800 case. They said:

- No nearby military exercises were being conducted when Flight 800 went down. Not true.

- No military assets were in the area other than a P-3 and the USS *Normandy*. Not true.
- There was no evidence of missiles or explosives. Not true.
- The debris had no evidence of explosives. Not true.
- The explosive residue found on the plane's interior (and exterior, evidently) is explained by an earlier search-dog exercise. Not true.
- Tests say red residue is adhesive and not consistent with solid fuel for missiles. Not true. (The adhesive is green, and the NASA scientist conducting NTSB tests said he was not permitted to test for the red residue's origin).
- The FBI and the military identified all ships and planes in the area. Not true.
- The decapitated 747 "zoom climbed" more than three thousand feet after the forward eighty thousand pounds of fuselage fell off. Impossible.
- The NTSB does not know what caused the center fuel tank to explode. True.
- The NTSB has no idea what all the FBI knows. True.

Okay. And the reason we should believe everything these investigators tell us is . . . ?

Other than Robert Davey for the *Village Voice* and Kelly Patricia O'Meara for *Insight* magazine, few regular newspapers continued to challenge the government's official reports about Flight 800's death. Kelly, a respected congressional aide and researcher for eighteen years on the Hill before she turned journalist, provided invaluable assistance to me while she was working for Representative Forbes.

One last observation before I close with some insights about journalism today. It troubles me how government agencies meddled with news outlets in this story and how some of the nation's biggest media organizations let it happen.

Case no. I:

A navy official called my then-publisher, Marcia McQuern, in November 1997 and told her the Flight 800 story was over because Pierre Salinger was quitting the active hunt for a cause. Therefore, the officer said, there was no reason to respond to my inquiries about certain navy equipment. Marcia, a respected reporter and editor before being appointed my newspaper's chief executive, told the officer that we were not directed by Salinger's actions, we would determine whether we had a story or not, and that the navy's function was to provide us the information to which we legally were entitled. None of us had ever experienced such a call before. We ultimately got the information and used it for stories.

Case no. 2:

Kristina Borjesson and Kelly O'Meara contracted with a California production company to produce a program hosted by Oliver Stone for ABC Entertainment that would include interviews with Flight 800 witnesses, whose testimony the FBI asked the NTSB to exclude from its December 1997 public hearings. Stone is famous — or infamous — for his movie that portrays a conspiracy to assassinate President Kennedy. After officials objected to ABC, the ABC News Division asked that the program be scuttled, arguing that viewers would get mixed up seeing a news-style program produced by the entertainment side. The truth is, every network's news department should have interviewed the witnesses years ago and presented a program with their information. The networks all dutifully carried the government's opinion that the witnesses didn't see what they saw. The American public is smart enough to separate fact from fiction. That's why the US Constitution still requires jurors to be drawn from the general population.

Case no. 3:

After O'Meara resigned from Representative Forbes's staff, she became an investigative reporter for the *Washington Times' Insight* magazine. She took along her insider's knowledge of the mistruth the government presented in the Flight 800 investigation. Eventually, she asked for and obtained a copy of hours of radar tracks before and after the crash and extending beyond the limited scope officials provided the public. A careful, independent analysis showed more ships and aircraft in the area at the time of the event than even I was aware of. I was envious of her findings but glad they landed in the hands of someone with her knowledge and tenacity. Of course, she took her findings to the NTSB before she did a story and asked officials there to explain. Basically, they said the information wasn't saying what it said. When she left, they called the rival *Washington Post* and said a conspiracy theorist reporter, once connected with Oliver Stone, was going to publish a misguided story about ships and aircraft near TWA Flight 800. Well, Kelly wasn't a conspiracy theorist, but she did uncover government cover-ups, and the information about which she was reporting was information federal agencies compiled. The *Post* published the hit piece, generated by a government agency that's commissioned to get all the information to the public, not cover it up.

What does all this mean? What has it taught me, and what should it teach you, as a reader, and maybe as a journalist? What have I learned after almost forty years in this profession?

In the American system, when judges like the NTSB or the FBI are granted the authority to also serve as jurors, they decide whether some type of evidence is insufficient or not. It therefore becomes officially insufficient, no matter how much information is generated to the contrary. An official pronouncement of insufficiency does not make it actually so, but the edict remains official and is repeated as gospel for decades—maybe forever. Because an official says it is so doesn't make it so. Think about it.

Journalists, with insufficient time or desire to pursue a story for years on end, take the quickest way out: They recite the official record and depend on pronouncements or "leaks" from bureaucrats who helped draft the official record or have a stake in the official edict. Reporting only what they or the official records say is not journalism in its best form. It simply is reporting—reporting what officials want you to repeat.

I think journalism in its best form is striving to find the truth, not just what somebody says is the truth. Sometimes you begin with the latter to find the former. You must be inquisitive, not just nosey.

When the government source or institution is the accused, it all too often has the authority to determine what constitutes evidence against itself. It's fortunate most criminals don't have that same right.

Whatever editors are convinced of is what the readers will read or the public will hear or see. A reporter can know everything in the world, but without some editor's authorization somewhere, the story remains in the reporter's brain. The reporter can be brilliant and the editor superior, but in a disagreement, editors have the last word.

I have over- and underreacted as a reporter and editor. The public loses when that happens. An editor must ensure that he or she makes the reporter prove the story. But editors also must ensure they do not bend or kill stories to meet their own prejudices or hold the bar so high that no amount of proof will meet the test.

Editors have the power of life and death. Reporters have the power of truth and deceit. Together they are incredible, quarrelsome rescuers or uncomprehending assassins of reality.

In a story with no apparent end in sight, make hay while the sun shines. Do the stories while you can. Editors, don't let reporters loaf when they should be getting that next chapter completed. Reporters, don't mistakenly believe you will be on the story forever. Readers, demand the next installment. Tell the media outlet what interests you. The economy will change or editors will change, and the story may become nothing but history.

Reporters must approach *each* story as an explorer entering uncharted territory. More inviting, maybe, they should approach each story as if it were a lover whose body is being explored for the first time. Such a sense will leave the reporter interested and attentive to each detail, eager to learn more.

Each story, no matter how small, affects somebody, somewhere. A reporter had better be ready to back up what he prints or speaks or shows. In Turlock, California, when high school athletes didn't like stories I wrote, they found out where I lived and egged my car.

I believe that journalism, a profession I consider one step below being a minister for God, is corrupted in America. I didn't say corrupt; I said corrupted, and we are the most probable perpetrators. That's tragic. Because once an investigator is seduced by and depends on the group he or she sets off to expose, the investigator, intentionally or not, becomes part of a cover-up. Anybody waiting for an honest report is deceived.

The rush for a figurative romantic success has too many journalists — reporters and editors — sleeping with anybody at an official level who will talk. The differences between a prostitute and call girl are location and price, but a john is still a john. Too many journalists have turned into johns.

Just because you read it in a big paper or see it on network TV doesn't make it so. The same holds true for small outlets and the Internet. But, conversely, it doesn't necessarily mean the information isn't so. Ask yourself, "What evidence (not opinion) are they providing?"

Be skeptical of people—including reporters. They—we—all have our axes to grind and other people's oxen to gore.

Reporters, as with most people and energy forces, usually follow the path of least resistance. That means that you can lead many reporters where you want them to go by opening the door through which you want them to go.

A leak from a source is not a leak: it is information the source wants to give you to lead you up a certain path. It's up to you to be wary of the path and determine if integrity or duplicity is waiting as a reward. If it's the latter, what are you going to do when you find out that you've been used to hoodwink the audience? Reporting a spokesman's comments is not reporting; it's becoming the spokesman's spokesman. Don't believe everything you're handed, especially by a friend. Triple-check it before you use it, and remain skeptical to the end.

Don't expect to be loved at the end of a story, especially if it takes a long time to develop or goes against the grain. Editors will begrudge the extended time you're taking to prove or disprove something, and colleagues will think you're trying to create some type of privileged job.

Government owes us a truthful explanation of events. In reality, we are the government, but people by and large have abdicated power and responsibility in return for safety, security, and convenience. Let leaders lie to us and cheat as long as we have food, money, and pleasure. Let somebody else take care of our children and parents so we don't have to be burdened with the responsibilities.

When the watchdog is asleep, it becomes the burglar's tool.

Who owns your loyalty: the public or your sources?

Newsday, which did yeoman's work early on about Flight 800's demise, won the Pulitzer Prize for its reporting about the disaster. One of the team's reporters told me at the NTSB's crash hearings in Baltimore that journalists really prefer at least one other media representative to echo a reporter's findings.

"No reporter likes to be out on a limb alone," the reporter said. "Well, nobody except maybe you."

I laughed because it's true. I would have preferred some other "mainstream" media outlet to be reporting separately what I was finding. It's lonely being alone, and I have awakened more than once with panic attacks like the one I described. But I consider the reporter's observation as one of the greatest compliments I've received.

A commentator once said about Winston Churchill, "When he found he was alone on an issue, he didn't mind the company." I wish I always had that sense of purpose.

The songs coal mine canaries sing may become irritating at times, but smart people learn to appreciate their presence and listen for the tunes. The silence of the canaries is a signal that the environment has turned deadly.

CHAPTER 15

WHEN BLACK
BECOMES WHITE

PHILIP WEISS

Philip Weiss is a journalist and a novelist. He is the author of American Taboo, *a nonfiction account of a murder in the Peace Corps in 1976 (HarperCollins). He has been a columnist for the* New York Observer *as well as a contributor to the* New York Times Magazine, Harper's, *and* Esquire. *He has also reported for the* Philadelphia Daily News *and two Minneapolis weeklies.*

My journalistic training was pretty classic. When I was in college, Seymour Hersh came to visit the school paper (where I lived), slouching against a counter in a cheap suit, to tell a group of young writers how he'd run up his credit cards tracking down the witnesses to the My Lai massacre. We gazed at him reverently. A couple of years later, I worked at a daily newspaper in Philadelphia, and the reporter at the next desk and I wrote a letter to legendary newsman Harrison Salisbury to ask him whether we would ever get an opportunity as good as the Pentagon Papers story. Salisbury wrote back. "Every reporter who dedicates himself will get great stories," he advised, "just work at your craft."

Back then that meant midnight to eight, working out of police headquarters and rushing out on major crimes. One night the overnight guy on the desk chewed me out for failing to report in which leg a murder suspect was shot when a cop brought him down in a subway tunnel—hey kid, right leg or left leg?

At that time the journalistic culture was already changing. Newsrooms were beginning to look more and more like insurance offices. Computers were crowding out the old Facit and Royal manuals. The hardboiled reporters at my paper complained about the SYJs—Serious Young Journalists—who were coming on to the job; kids like me, from Ivy League schools, who were of a better class than the old reporters. SYJs didn't have a pint of whiskey in the desk drawer, they saw themselves as godlike bearers of accurate information.

In the old culture you weren't allowed to take yourself too seriously. You were union. "Newspapers are classified as manufacturing," an older reporter told me one day. You identified with cops and with the clerks at City Council, and you were duty-bound to cheat on your expenses and hit the Pen and Pencil bar when you finished a day's work.

All that was going by the boards, and back then, a writer intent on serious work, I was happy to see it go. Now I'm not so sure. Today's mainstream journalistic culture is a lot more responsible than my newspaper was just twenty years ago. I'm still embarrassed by some of the statements my paper made without checking them out very closely. Libel law and professionalism have made reporting a lot more accurate.

But we've paid quite a price for that professionalism. When I started, reporters didn't identify with lawyers or city councilmen; they identified with the middle class, and with underlings. Being aggressive and contemptuous of authority were valued attributes. Today those sorts of attitudes strike people in the profession as unseemly and vaguely dangerous.

The change is more than cultural, it's also structural. In the information age, the media are far more influential than newspapers were when the rewrite guys were sipping whiskey. A couple of classmates I knew in journalism at Harvard are now more powerful than many senators. That idea would have boggled our minds years ago. Then there were a thousand newspapers that didn't care all that much what other newspapers were saying. Even the *Washington Post* was just another voice. Television was still finding itself. No small group of outlets could ever function as the political agenda-setters that a relatively small group of outlets is today. Globalization had not yet integrated our economy with Japan's.

Today the big media corporations are Atlases of the international economy, whether the news people like it or not. News executives have one eye on the stock price. This new role has made them temperamentally conservative, sober, and afraid of deep controversy. As a result it's just not the same being a reporter.

My focus here will be my experience in the '90s, but the war against terrorism has solidified the trend I describe. Of course, any administration in wartime will attempt to control information. But in the present war, the reporter's duties seem more burdensome than ever: to not just bring back the good news from the battle front, but to affirm the free market values of the West, which Islamic fundamentalists reject. Even if you enjoy those values and think they're worth fighting for—as I do—you have to marvel at the ways in which various issues make it into the agenda, or don't make it. The discussion of some unsettling questions will be highly circumscribed, for instance: Is our culture shallow and materialistic? Is American policy in the Middle East evenhanded or unfair? What can be done to address these sorts of inequities?

I believe that discussions of these questions at dinner tables are likely to be far freer than the public discussion—that the American people have become more interesting than the mainstream media. It's the loss of professional freedom that I regret.

My own realization of the cultural change came, dramatically, in the middle '90s, when a very responsible magazine I work for now and then sent me out to Arkansas to try and figure out why so many people hated Bill Clinton so much. It was a liberal magazine, by and large. The editors (and I) had voted for Clinton (in 1992 anyway). Probably, I was meant to be writing a "reported essay" about how backward backwoods America was, about the ways that Bill Clinton had threatened traditional ideas of manhood by supporting gays in the military and having a modern marriage with Hillary Rodham Clinton. And yes, I think there's some truth to that analysis.

Duly, I visited the White House first, and amid the spellbinding architecture of the Old Executive Office Building, met with a young aide in the White House counsel's office who handed me a thick report showing how everyone who was saying hateful things about Clinton was frothing at the mouth, getting heard on the Internet, and their claims were ultimately making it into the legitimate press. "Communications Stream of Conspiracy Commerce," was the report's weird title. Before long that report would become a scandal, but not, I'm embarrassed to admit, because I understood how disgraceful it was.

I got out to Arkansas a few days later, just before the election in 1996, and soon met a woman named Linda Ives. After I'd spent five minutes with her, I knew she was no lunatic. Her son was one of the two "boys on the tracks." He and a buddy had been killed when they wandered in on a drug operation outside Little Rock. The killers had tried to disguise their handiwork by laying the boys' bodies on railroad tracks, to be run over by a freight train. It was just a small-town crime, except that the killers had been able to count upon some measure of political protection. The state medical examiner, appointed by Bill Clinton, had blatantly helped frustrate justice in the case, by ruling that the boys had committed suicide by smoking dope and laying on the tracks. When his judgment was at last revoked and the cases treated as murders, several witnesses to a local grand jury were rubbed out, and no one was ever charged in any of the widening circle of violence. It went beyond the county. "This goes deep," a relative of one of the executed witnesses told me one night sitting in his car. He declined to go public. Linda Ives had been fighting for justice for years without a hearing from anyone in power. She was deeply alienated. (This story has been fully explored and related by Mara Leveritt in her book, *The Boys on the Tracks*.)

I saw other cases that had the same atmosphere of sinister corruption and blind supposition. You knew something was wrong, but you didn't know who exactly was responsible. As a writer who cares about the legitimacy and accountability of authority, I was curious to learn more. Meantime, I felt I could make a strong case about Arkansas political culture: it was not particularly democratic, a one-party state where authorities turned a blind eye to local abuses. As an ambitious machine politician trying to institute marginal reforms, Bill Clinton had a passive but complicit role in these practices. Meanwhile, the abuses had—legitimately, I felt—fostered hatred for Clinton among working-class, white right-wingers.

My editors were completely incurious. They didn't want to open the box. It wasn't so much that they were liberals who'd voted for the guy. It was that they were uncomfortable even raising such questions about authority. I remember one of them saying, "There's no way to fact-check any of this." What he meant was there was no way to say for sure who was right, or what was true. And he was right. It did not appear, at the outset anyway, that there was any sure way to establish the truth. By printing the claims, the only thing you could be sure you were doing was raising serious questions about the president's integrity.

The alternative was to dismiss the claims by mocking the sources. My editors wanted to go that route. I couldn't bring myself to do it. I'd met these people, and believed some of them. My editors and I ended up printing a compromise that was a botch. The most revealing thing about the episode was how paralyzed my editors were. They couldn't even hear the information. It was too unsettling.

For instance, one of the stories involved a blustering and aggressive man named Jerry Parks. Parks had served as head of security at Clinton campaign headquarters in Little Rock during the '92 campaign and then a year later, in September 1993, had been gunned down mob-style on the streets of Little Rock. His son Gary told me (and his widow Jane made the claim elsewhere) that Jerry Parks had been killed because he had information about Clinton's sexual activities, which he was threatening to peddle. (And this was at the very time that the state troopers were about to go forward with assertions about Clinton's behavior.)

I never cared much about Clinton's sex life. I'm a child of the '70s, and relished all that I could partake of the sexual revolution. Clinton's sex life was never that interesting to me. But I respected the rights of others to talk about that stuff if they wanted. And in the end, the real story, for me, was the Clinton team's efforts to suppress those who knew and cared about his sex life. I never cared what Monica did with her thong and Bill did with his tongue. The scandal was important because it demonstrated the atmosphere of vague threat and character assassination that soon cloaked anyone who objected to the way the president dealt with women.

My editors couldn't have cared less about Jerry Parks. Their response was to throw up their hands and say Gary Parks was crazy. I'd met him a couple times and was pretty sure he wasn't crazy. In my view, his story deserved investigation by journalists as much as a third-rate burglary at the Watergate carried out by a motley crew on the right had deserved further investigation in 1972.

The mainstream press completely ignored the Parks story. But you could find loose talk about Jerry Parks all over the Internet. There was free speech on the Internet, maybe too much free speech. Irresponsible speech. But to the exact same degree as the Internet was wild, the corporate media were cautious. They would do nothing to rock the boat.

Once during that same period, a big editor sighed to me that he had too much power. He was nostalgic for the spirit of free expression that had gotten him into the business in the first place. Now he commanded as much power as any congressman—through his publication—and as much as he enjoyed it (who doesn't like a little power, who doesn't aspire to influence?), he knew that he had lost a basic freedom, to say what came to his head.

I have sympathy for friends who work in the corporate media. It's a terrible burden to be setting the agenda. They have to mull their statements carefully before they speak. They didn't ask for that power. The world changed right under them in the last twenty years. The American political parties atrophied; their power to select candidates was taken over by television. Media companies became big players in the new economy. And these changes have affected the way any well-paid reporter treats an open microphone or a blank screen. Issues like globalization and the integrity of high officials are not issues on which a reporter is allowed to be dispassionate, or casual.

In late 1993, a financial newsletter behaved casually about such things when it reported a rumor that a Democratic senator was of the belief that the late White House lawyer Vince Foster had not died as it was asserted he had, by his own hand in Fort Marcy Park. The report had a dramatic effect. The markets were reported to have slid sharply on the rumor.

This was the information age at work; this was the "synergy" that had been so buzzed. The media came to understand, in an unspoken and instinctual way (as opposed to a policy that anyone had to spell out), that certain types of stories were dangerous even to talk about, stories that suggested that our leaders were not telling us the truth about important questions.

I remember describing to an editor at my mainstream publication some of the questions surrounding Vince Foster's death. He cut the conversation off. "Listen, Vince Foster killed himself in Fort Marcy

Park," he said, as if he had been there. Of course he hadn't been there. He didn't know that that was true any more than I knew the alternative to be true. But I had legitimate questions, and he was not able to hear them. On this matter, the official version could not be reexamined. And especially after a Mike Wallace report on *60 Minutes* declared (shakily) that the Foster skeptics were loonytunes, it wasn't.

Compare this culture for a moment with the 1970s culture of the *Washington Post*, the paper that took on a president. It goes without saying that the defiance of Richard Nixon was a special moment in American history. It wasn't just Katherine Graham's bravery or Woodward and Bernstein's persistence that brought Nixon down. The smell of cordite was in the air those days. Nixon was weird. Vietnam and the Kennedy and King assassinations had produced a revolutionary upheaval in our awareness and values. People were smoking dope in newsrooms (believe me).

Just the same, the *Washington Post* experienced a sharp drop in its stock price when it took on Nixon. And yet it did so anyway. Katherine Graham resolved to weather the Wall Street storm.

Would any publication display such sangfroid today? I think it is extremely doubtful. The corporate media are just too big, and dependent on too many backers, their editors too answerable to business executives, and their reports too integrated into the economy, for them to be able to go out on a wing and a prayer, as Woodward and Bernstein did initially (they had nothing hard, they had some sharp questions), and investigate the legitimacy of the powers-that-be.

Now consider a lesser contemporary scandal than Watergate, but one that certainly approaches the perimeters of power: the strong pattern of suppression of evidence by the FBI over the last ten years, from Ruby Ridge, Idaho, to Waco to Oklahoma City. It would be hard to find an organization more rife with doubtful official behavior. Yet none of these hammer blows was initiated by the mainstream media. The questions have resulted from a right-winger's lawsuit, from a right-winger's movie, even from an FBI internal investigation.

Where are the journalistic birddogs? Why haven't these scandals sown dragon's teeth in the mouths of the media? Why hasn't anyone in the corporate media called for radical reform?

It simply won't happen. The reporters are making too much money and have too much invested in the stock market to possess the inclination to raise fundamental questions about the government's exercise of power. It's sociological. Reporters do not think of themselves as irreverent characters from the movie *The Front Page,* let alone Tom Paine raining invective on his masters. They are the new masters; they understand themselves, accurately, to be winners in the global economy. When a high government spokesman comes out to address them — often a spokesman who has been in the media, or will be — they feel an Ivy League identification with him, certainly more identification than they do with ordinary Americans, who generally make far less than the reporters do and are not as interested in power.

I see the early '90s as a turning point. The shift in journalistic temperament is best shown by the sharply different coverage of third-party candidates Ross Perot, in 1992, and Ralph Nader, in 2000. Perot, who I think is a true maniac, got endless coverage for his wacky ideas. He was all over the front pages of the big papers. The *New York Times* even ran two profiles of his vice presidential candidate, James Stockdale, in which Stockdale went on about his war experiences, his taste for the Greek philosopher Epictetus, and so forth.

Now name Ralph Nader's vice presidential candidate. Chances are you can't. (It was Winona LaDuke.) I'd be hard pressed to find an occasion when the *Times* even mentioned her, let alone told us what she liked to read.

It is unquestionable that Perot's stunning 19 percent in the polls in 1992 was media-aided, while Nader's 3 percent in 2000 was beaten-down by the media. Perot was a wonderful character who also had something to say, and when he came along, the media were still a little bit freewheeling and could still take delight in a maniac. They were as surprised as anyone that he polled nearly one in five votes. Eight years later, Ralph Nader (a maniac in his own right, in my opinion, but more cerebral and serious than Perot) took on some of the same issues (from a different point of view of course), and while his groundswell was not as significant as Perot's, his ideas were virtually shut out by the media.

I'm not suggesting a conspiracy. Over eight years, stability had become a much greater value to the media. They worked for big corporations and had a bias when it came to Nader's anticorporate ideas. Those ideas seemed foolish to the reporters. They were incapable of giving him a full hearing.

This sort of conservativism has invaded even public television (which draws support from the likes of Archer-Daniels-Midland). Jim Lehrer officiated at the debates that sidelined Ralph Nader in fall

2000. Whatever mathematical rationalization any organization wants to offer for leaving Nader out, he was without a doubt the most important dissenting voice in the presidential fray. And one has to ask, what is the role of public television in the discourse? Is it to include or exclude alternative views? (This is, after all, the same Jim Lehrer who, somewhat uncomfortably, asked Bill Clinton about Monica Lewinsky in an interview at the beginning of 1998, was lied to by Bill Clinton, and never addressed that lie publicly, even as he was later decorated by Bill Clinton with the National Humanities Medal.)

Public broadcasting is now virtually indistinguishable in its concerns and attitudes from the mainstream liberal media (the *Washington Post*, the *New York Times*). Reporters who work for National Public Radio (NPR) often go on to be hired by the prestigious corporate media, intermingling their worlds. Veteran NPR star Susan Stamberg was, as of summer 2001, airing interviews of actors on network television shows. It was the same sort of in-depth celebrity stuff that you might find in the *Post*'s Style section. What is public media's raison d'être?

A more telling example is Terence Smith, of the *News Hour*. He is a former reporter for the *New York Times*. In the summer of 2000 he opened a segment about the government's report on the crash of TWA 800 by saying, provocatively, that the government's findings (that most probably a spark from an unknown source ignited fuel vapors in the jetliner's center wing fuel tank, causing it to explode) were "controversial." But in the ensuing dialogue, which involved a couple of members of the mainstream press, there was no hint at all of why Smith had called the report "controversial," no exploration of that controversy whatsoever. Smith was obviously terrified of even lifting the carpet on such a discussion. Not that he was above teasing his segment by using a provocative term. His comment was not merely a bait and switch, or a moment of intellectual dishonesty (though it was both those things). It was deeply revealing of the ways of the mainstream press. They know that something is going on out there, that government is being sharply criticized. They hear the rumble, on the Internet, on independent radio, and in the alternative media. But they disbelieve it, and they are simply powerless to provide a forum for that criticism.

What the critics suggest, sometimes compellingly, is that government will lie to its people about important matters. And that is, right now anyway, too fundamental a criticism for the mainstream to entertain.

That night on the *Jim Lehrer News Hour*, the two reporters discussing TWA 800 went on and on about the government version of the crash. They passed on what government spokesmen had said as gospel. They were completely incapable of acknowledging, let alone assessing, the harshly different view of that crash that is held widely in the alternative media, and indeed among the citizens of southern Long Island, near where the crash occurred.

I first learned about the alternative view of the crash at a forum conducted in 1998 by the right-wing group Accuracy In Media at the Army-Navy Club in Washington. A beefy and homespun former navy aviator named Bill Donaldson gave a rambling talk about his personal investigation of the matter. He had brought along videotapes of himself heating jet fuel in a crab pot on his backyard barbecue, then trying to make the fuel ignite, unsuccessfully, in an emulation of a center wing tank explosion. More important, Donaldson brought audiotapes of several interviews he'd done with eyewitnesses. The eyewitnesses sounded calm and sane, and each of them said that he had seen a flare-like streak go up from the surface of the sea, followed after some seconds by a fireball in the sky. These simple and assured statements contradicted the official version of the crash, for they suggested strongly that a missile had struck the plane.

Intrigued, I decided to meet some of these eyewitnesses myself, and not Donaldson's. I went to the community of Center Moriches and began looking for people who had seen the crash. I spoke to half a dozen. What I found — and what many other reporters found, before and after me — was that there existed a large group of people who had seen something that the government later saw very differently. Indeed, these people felt misrepresented by the government version and insulted by the cartoon enactment of the crash that the CIA had produced, without talking to a single one of them.

A cartoon enactment of the crash produced by the CIA — did you read that right? You did. In the '70s, a CIA-produced animation would have elicited only astonishment, anger, and mockery. The culture of the press held government if not in contempt, in some great distrust, and if the CIA, of all faithless outfits, extruded a film purporting to show what ordinary people had seen one night, without talking to any of those people (the CIA based its cartoon on FBI witness reports), everyone would have picked up a stone.

And this is what is so perplexing: Today, the CIA has in fact been stoned and ridiculed for this video enactment, so ridiculed that the gov-

ernment has withdrawn the video as part of its evidence. Yet this process
— the debunking of a government statement, and the government heeding the debunkers — has taken place completely outside the mainstream
media, which embraced the cartoon. That debunking process took place
on the Internet and among the community of TWA 800 skeptics.

These skeptics have been influential. They have had a sort of
power. The CIA cartoon (with its absurd claim that the plane rose
three thousand feet after breaking apart) is on the trash heap of history. The clear aim of the National Transportation Safety Board's hearings and reports has been to pacify or neutralize those skeptics. But
you would never know it from the mainstream media, which simply
regurgitates the official version, while nervously mentioning a "controversy" it is afraid to go into.

I'm not trying to advance the missile theory here (although clearly
I support that theory as the best explanation of what happened on
July 17, 1996). My goal is to describe the conduct of the establishment
press when someone puts forward a serious challenge to government
integrity. They just can't hear it.

After I went to Long Island and talked to eyewitnesses, I went
back to some big editors to discuss what I had heard. It was astounding to me that in the shadow of the media capital of the United States,
you had a burgeoning Roswell, New Mexico — a community that completely distrusted the government version on an important question
and believed an alternative theory. I wanted to write an article about
this clash of realities.

My editors weren't interested, just as all the other mainstream
media have never been interested in this question. It is, again, simply
too at odds with their understanding of the world; it suggests that the
government would lie flatly about an important matter. The mainstream media's response has been to behave as if the skeptics either
don't exist, or they're crazy (e.g., Greta Van Susteren on CNN referring to these people as "conspiracists").

Whether right or wrong, the TWA 800 skeptics come from a fairly
broad spectrum of people who have opposable thumbs, who you
would think should have a hearing. There are the scores of eyewitnesses, some of whom have a military background and presumably
know what they are talking about. There are right-leaning and left-
leaning organizations, from Accuracy In Media to Donaldson's group
of retired aviators among the hawks to the Flight Eight Hundred

Research Organization, which is chiefly academics, many on the left. There are diverse publications, from the *Village Voice* to Riverside, California's *The Press-Enterprise* to *Insight* magazine in Washington, DC, to *Dan's Papers* on Long Island. In the aviation industry, there are many retired TWA employees and an aircraft workers' union that was a party to the official investigation that have questioned the findings. The French press has been sometimes contemptuous of the American government version. And I haven't even gotten to the Internet.

The questions these people raise are not trivial. For instance, they have pointed out that James Kallstrom, then of the FBI, said, vehemently, at a press conference in 1997, that every boat in the area of the crash had been identified. Subsequently, government radar data was released showing that the boat closest to the crash had never been identified and had sped away from the area at more than thirty knots an hour.

What do you do with such a troubling set of facts? It is not as if anyone in the mainstream media has seriously considered these issues and come up with a good answer. Opposing theories of the Kennedy assassination got a lot more attention than these skeptics. The mainstream media's response has been a dull one—to solemnly and stoically report the government's assertions, over and over. They simply cannot entertain the possibility that the government has lied to them.

They seem to identify with the government experts. Indeed, Jim Kallstrom, who misrepresented the facts on the boats when he was working for the FBI, later was hired by CBS.

I have many friends among the mainstreamers, and I have sympathy for them. Their hands are tied. Their organizations are just too powerful. In decades past, musings about the Kennedy assassination never threatened to upset the apple cart. The same cannot be said for such considerations by an agenda-setting corporation today.

Wondering about what really happened to TWA 800 on, say, ABC would have serious consequences. It would represent a powerful accusation that people could not ignore—as they have, say, *The Press-Enterprise*. The reporter could harbor little hope that he would win. He would know that the government would denounce him, with rage (as it has done to the skeptics, even prosecuting writer Jim Sanders and his wife).* He would know that he might be professionally iso-

---

*Sanders and his wife were prosecuted for asking NTSB investigator Terrell Stacey to supply them with "evidence stolen from a federal investigation," which was a piece of a seat with red residue on it that Sanders had tested and then publicly stated contained elements consistent with solid rocket missile fuel.

lated, that other reporters might well describe him as a lunatic. And even if he stuck to his guns, he could have little hope that he would be shown to be right. And meantime, to the extent that anyone did take him seriously, he could well be seen as affecting global markets and come under huge pressure for doing so. The right-wing nuts who always said that one-world government would affect our sovereignty have a point: global media companies have to be as concerned with what sells in Singapore as well as in Seattle, which is hardly good news for the old free market of ideas.

That free market is alive and well, but it's marginalized. You have a wild and free debate of these issues in the fringe press, and on the Internet, and no debate at all in the mainstream media.

This is hardly a new phenomenon, of course. The powerful have always published official truths. In Cuba they turned the cameras aside when Fidel fainted during a speech. In the kingdom of Tonga, where I've been to write a book, they do not allow public criticism of the king and members of the royal family. The old Soviet Union did not exactly embrace debate about communism. The American variant seems to be that in the headquarters of global capital, corporate media outlets cannot entertain serious questions about the legitimacy of the powers-that-be, even when spokesmen are shown to lie.

At least in our rich democracy, the alternative view is widely available. Anyone who doubts the government's findings on TWA 800 has the power to arm himself with a contrary set of facts. Just as Arkansas nursing home owner Juanita Broaddrick's assertion that Bill Clinton had raped her thrived on the Internet while it was virtually ignored among the agenda setters.

Still, I'd argue that this is not a healthy state of affairs. We have a split discourse: two sharply different worldviews existing alongside one another. There is almost no common ground between these belief systems, and a lot of stress on the social contract during crises. The famous red and blue map of the Bush and Gore vote in the 2000 presidential election—showing the Democratic vote concentrated in cities and on the coasts, and the Republican vote in rural areas and small towns—helps illustrate the information divide. Most well-paid reporters are urban liberals, firmly ensconced in the blue zone, physically and culturally. The country has weathered many such divides before, and will weather this one, too. But speaking personally, it's no fun. I've put some distance between myself and many of the liberal media friends I made at Harvard College, but now in my mid-40s, I still have to make a living. For me, the role of the corporate media is one of the most compelling ideological/political questions of our time. But the publications that pay don't care for me to write about it. Though God knows they are happy for me to do celebrity profiles.

My answer has been to pick my spots. When I had a column in a New York weekly, I piped up on my central issue there now and then, even though my paper's audience was a privileged one, and I didn't relish alienating those readers by going on about issues they didn't really buy. I'm working on a historical case that speaks to these questions, but happily in another time and place than millennial global America, where the First Amendment now seems to come second to how the markets closed in Japan.

And if a glossy magazine asks me to write about an actress, I'll do it if I need to. If she tells me she twisted her ankle on the set, I'll be sure to ask which one.

CHAPTER 16

STORIES WE LOVE, STORIES WE HATE

U.C. Berkeley School of Journalism

HELEN MALMGREN

Helen Malmgren is a producer for Ed Bradley at CBS News, where she works on 60 Minutes pieces as well as hour-long specials. During the last five years, she has produced stories about toxic dump sites, brutal police officers, dangerous hospitals, and the AIDS pandemic in Africa. She has won a number of awards for her work, including two Emmys, the Peabody Award, the Academy of Arts and Sciences Ribbon of Hope Award, and the Sigma Delta Chi Award from the Society of Professional Journalists.

Many journalists will tell you that, somewhere between Tonya Harding and the tobacco lawsuits, television reporting went into the toilet. Networks are spending most of their resources on the big, big stories now. If you're working on a story like O. J. or Monica or Elian, you're constantly rushing to get dishy little details on the air before scores of other reporters do. And if you're not working on this week's top story—if all you have is an exquisitely researched, nationally important story about, say, radioactive waste in

377

the water supply—well, good luck pitching it. And don't ask for any decent money to shoot it.

While all that may sound familiar, it's not the entire story. Every legal fiasco, every tabloid riot and factual screw-up on the national news not only embarrasses the networks, but also increases the stock of their best investigative reporters.

It's true. Remember the story about how Big Tobacco forced the networks to their knees back in 1995? Facing a $10 billion lawsuit by Philip Morris, ABC News apologized for a story about how tobacco companies manipulated the levels of nicotine in their cigarettes. Media critics ripped ABC for buckling to corporate interests. Everyone was talking about the chill effect and the death of investigative journalism.

In the middle of this mess, Peter Jennings proposed an investigative special about the tobacco companies' nasty, underhanded tactics: how they lie to the public, buy off politicians, and intimidate opponents. Network executives jumped on the idea, then bragged in the press how ABC News was still committed to the tobacco story. The show was given a huge budget and an hour of airtime. Nine people, including me, were assigned to it.

Then, while we were working on our tobacco hour, *60 Minutes*, under threat of a lawsuit, pulled its interview with tobacco whistle-blower Jeffrey Wigand. Media critics went crazy. The story was hotter than ever. The networks were on the defensive. And Walt Bogdanich, the producer whose story prompted the ABC lawsuit and apology, became the center of a sensational bidding war.

At the time, I was Walt's associate producer on the tobacco show, and we could hardly talk for half an hour without someone from *Dateline* or *60 Minutes* calling to recruit him, or someone from ABC calling to convince him to stay put. Even *I* started getting recruited, and I hadn't done anything. At one point, Walt and I went for a walk in Central Park to get away from his phone and do some work on our piece. We weren't there ten minutes when along came Forrest Sawyer, then an ABC anchor, running across the lawn to make Walt an offer to work with him.

This seemed miraculous to me. First, ABC apparently hung Walt out to dry. A few months later, they were practically groveling at his feet. But since then, I've noticed this kind of thing happen more than once. It seems that even the least liked, most disparaged news executives—the ones everyone blames for the decline of TV news—still want to be associated with good investigative reporters.

This is a good place for me to point out that, even though I'm talking about executive decisions at the networks, I have never been in any executive meetings about what will go on the air or when to pull the plug on a lawsuit or anything like that. I can tell you what I've observed, but I don't know why TV executives act the way they do. What's more, I don't want to know.

I was at an Investigative Reporters and Editors conference once where the biggest event, with at least fifteen hundred people in the room, was a talk given by Ira Rosen of *PrimeTime Live* and Neil Shapiro of *Dateline*. It was called something like "What the Bosses Really Want." With all due respect to the illustrious careers of Neil Shapiro and Ira Rosen, why would an investigative journalist want to go out and look for what pleases his boss? Pitch to your boss, argue with your boss, cajole your boss, even flatter your boss, but as soon as you start focusing on "what the bosses really want," then you might as well not have a brain of your own, and you are no longer a journalist, and you should get a job doing something else.

Even the truest believer has to admit that TV journalism has changed significantly, and not exactly for the public good. While Watergate and the Pentagon Papers and My Lai made investigative journalism seem glamorous and heroic in the '60s and '70s, the biggest stories of the last decade have put journalists just below used car salesmen on national popularity polls.

Tobacco was one of those stories. Walt Bogdanich won in the end—he went to *60 Minutes* and then to the *New York Times*—but that story ruined the trust between a lot of investigative journalists and their lawyers, and it sent the message that when the stakes are at their highest, the networks might abandon their public mission and turn on their own reporters.

Of course, another one of those stories was the Monica Lewinsky scandal. And then there was the Elian Gonzalez craze. But before all those stories, and bigger than any of them, was O. J. Simpson.

HOW I LEARNED TO LOVE THE O. J. SIMPSON STORY

No, really.

I know, I know, it's the story journalists love to hate, the shameful period in TV news, the story that went on and on dominating the headlines for so long that one word about Johnnie Cochran or Mark Fuhrman still provokes eye rolls in any newsroom.

I reported on *The People* v. *Simpson* from the day after the murders to the day of the verdict, sixteen months later, and I can confirm that some of the journalism on that story was shockingly bad. There were reporters buying stories and bookers buying pricey "thank you gifts" for their interview "gets" or subjects. There was a guy working for one of the networks who seemed to do nothing but eavesdrop on other journalists' conversations and then call into the bureau and pass on what he'd heard as if it were his own reporting.

And then there were the really, really stupid assignments. Example: For two weeks, I had to stake out a paralegal who was reported in a British tabloid to have had a fling with Nicole Simpson years before her murder. I didn't even have a car, but my boss wanted me to sit on the curb for eight hours a day in front of this guy's apartment building in Beverly Hills. After a few days, his neighbors started bringing me tea in the morning and lemonade in the afternoon, and I knew all their dogs' and children's names. I never saw the guy. I heard he was on vacation. He probably came back home about the time my boss lost interest in him and reassigned me.

So what exactly did I love about the O. J. Simpson story?

In spite of all the nonsense, I think O. J. was one of the great investigative stories of our time. O. J. wasn't just about murder or celebrity. So many people followed the O. J. Simpson story so closely that it changed life in America, and then it became a story about American life. Who couldn't tell you what they were doing and thinking during the "slow chase," when almost every television station in America went to a live shot of O. J.'s white Bronco heading south on the 405 freeway? How many people have told you that when the not-guilty verdict was announced, the white people in their office were stunned and the black people in their office were jubilant, and that made them all wonder how well they really knew each other?

Suddenly, the whole nation was talking about domestic violence, and how it affects even the superrich. They were talking about whether a mostly white police force can be fair to a black suspect. Whether a mostly black jury would convict a famous black man. Whether DNA evidence alone was enough to convict someone of murder. During those sixteen months, we did O. J.-related stories about battered women's shelters, secret police fraternities, drug dealing, real estate, jury selection, how many autopsies the Los Angeles County Coroner had botched (a lot), how many cases the FBI crime lab had blown (a lot), mafia connections to sports figures, and illegal domestic servants.

The real problem with the O. J. Simpson story was not that it was too tabloid or that it became a media circus. The real problem was that it gave the news media a new model for big-story coverage — saturation coverage. And saturation coverage doesn't leave a lot of airtime or resources for other stories.

One month into the O. J. story, ABC decided to be the first network to stop broadcasting live court hearings and put its soaps back on the air. Ratings dropped immediately, precipitously. I don't know exactly what impression that experience made on network executives, but a number of newspapers reported it, and everybody in the L.A. bureau was talking about it. The lesson was clear. Whoever covers O. J. the most, wins.

Months later, Jeff Greenfield, who was then ABC's chief political correspondent, was in the L.A. bureau. We were all watching the evening news show when he noticed a fairly obvious mistake in a political piece.

"Didn't anyone else hear that?" he asked, somewhat annoyed. "No one here caught that?"

"Hey," the L.A. bureau chief shot back. "You do politics. We do O. J."

Not exactly a high moral point for ABC's second largest national news bureau. But, at that point, she was right. We did O. J. We knocked other good stories off the air with O. J., and we pulled lots of good producers off other projects to work on O. J. ABC had an O. J. story on nearly every morning, evening, and late show, and tried to have an O. J. segment on every one of its weekly magazine shows. Even David Brinkley had a few flings with O. J. stories on Sunday morning. They were odd affairs, with Brinkley, Cokie Roberts, Sam Donaldson, and George Will setting aside politics to wonder aloud about things like Mark Fuhrman's use of the "N" word.

Even after the verdict was in and O. J. was let off, network newscasts still showed the influence of the O. J. model of coverage. The top story of the day almost always gets more time in the broadcast than it used to, and a big story might appear in one form or another on all the networks' shows during the week.

Of course, the O. J. story itself didn't end with the not-guilty verdict. Next came the civil trial, the custody battle for his kids, and a number of confessions from members of his legal team about how they had doubted his innocence all along. By then, I had already won my prize from the O. J. story, courtesy of Johnnie Cochran. Cochran had a habit, almost a verbal tick, of repeating your name over and over if you asked him a tough question. "Well, Helen," he'd say to me. "That's a good question, Helen. I'm not sure I can answer that right now, Helen."

After about a year of this, a few people at ABC headquarters began to notice that someone named Helen was showing up in all the field tapes and live shots, asking sharp questions for ABC News. I got invited for a round of job interviews back in New York, where I threw myself at the feet of every executive producer who would listen to me. In the end, I got a job on the Jennings tobacco hour.

UNDERCOVER IN CORPORATE AMERICA

These days, any journalist who wants to investigate corporate America really ought to take a look at the Food Lion case.

In 1992, ABC's *PrimeTime Live* ran a story about alleged spoiled food and unsanitary conditions at the Food Lion supermarket chain. As part of the story, *PrimeTime* sent a couple of associate producers wearing hidden cameras to work at Food Lion supermarkets in North and South Carolina. The footage they shot was the centerpiece of the show.

Food Lion sued ABC, focusing its legal argument not on whether *PrimeTime* had told the truth in its report, but on the techniques its producers used in the field: pretending to be food workers instead of reporters and taping their fellow employees without permission.

The argument worked. The Greensboro, North Carolina, jury ruled that ABC should pay Food Lion $5.5 million in punitive damages.

This verdict knocked the wind out of a lot of investigative reporters, and not just at ABC. If you can't conceal the fact that you are a journalist, then you can't get access to most places where people are doing illegal things. If you can't record illegal behavior, then you might not be able to prove it happened.

The punitive damage award was eventually cut down to two dollars by an appellate court. But before life got better for the Food Lion reporters, it got much worse. While ABC chose to keep its public comments about the case mostly in court, Food Lion hired a public relations firm and spun a story nationwide about how the ABC reporters had framed innocent employees, staged incriminating scenes, and withheld information favorable to Food Lion.

Personally, I can't help being suspicious of any story that comes from a public relations firm specializing in "crisis management" for giant corporations—those are the kind of public relations firms who brought us "scientific proof" that cigarettes are healthy and greenhouse emissions are good for the planet. But since I didn't work on the Food Lion story, I can't say what actually happened on it.

By the time the Food Lion verdict was announced in 1997, I was working with a small team of producers, doing investigative documentaries for Ed Bradley. And in 1998, we decided to undertake a major hidden-camera investigation in North Carolina, just down the road from where ABC got slammed in court.

Why did we do that? Honestly, I think my bosses at CBS actually liked the fact that we were taking on the Food Lion verdict.

"If we get sued, we'll be ready," said Linda Mason, the vice president in charge of the program, in a conversation.

"This is what we went to law school for," said Rick Altabef and Jonathan Sternberg, our CBS attorneys.

David Gelber, my executive producer and partner on the piece, was the one who suggested we go undercover in the first place.

And Ed Bradley—well Bradley has pretty much seen it all, I think. I'm not certain that he's afraid of anything, and he clearly wasn't nervous about *this*.

But the main reason we focused our story in North Carolina had nothing to do with pride or courage or legal tactics. Quite simply, North Carolina was the best place to do the story.

In 1998, I heard about a Greensboro boy who'd died in a mental hospital owned by Charter Behavioral Health Systems, the nation's largest chain of psychiatric hospitals. His death was awful: He suffocated after hospital staff members wrapped a towel around his mouth and a sheet around his head as they were strapping his arms and legs to a table.

Then I spoke to a father whose teenage daughter had been at the Charter hospital in Charlotte, North Carolina. This man told me that his daughter had run away from home for a few days, and when she came back, they took her to Charter for a "trial period." They got nervous when the doctor wouldn't return their phone calls and panicked when the staff wouldn't let them in to see her during visiting hours. He said when they finally saw her, she was woozy and bruised all over.

At that point, he said, he and his wife confronted a nurse and demanded to know what had happened to their daughter. He said the nurse looked at him seriously and told him she was a single mother and couldn't afford to lose her job. Then she pulled out a notepad and wrote him a warning: Get your daughter out of here as fast as you can.

Now, to me, that's a situation just screaming out for an under-cover investigation.

So we found a social worker, an excellent fellow named Terrance Johnson, and he agreed to get a job at a Charter hospital and wear a hidden camera for us. He didn't have to exaggerate his qualifications on his résumé because he was, in fact, overqualified for the job. We didn't make him a CBS employee—he was willing to do it for the experience.

Later, when he'd been wearing an eyeglass camera wired to a jock strap recorder every day for two months, he was a little less gung ho. But the footage he got was amazing.

Children were being manhandled and injured while staff members strapped them into leather restraints. Doctors lied on their patients' medical forms. One nurse even gave Terrance what amounted to a lesson in fraud, which she explained was the way to get insurance companies to keep paying for their patients.

"It's not like I'm *lying*," she told him. "I just focus on the negative . . . because that's how they get paid."

Everybody agreed that we had powerful material. Everybody agreed that we had to disguise the children's identities with the utmost care. And those were about the last two things we agreed on, until we went to air.

Editing that piece was torture, a months-long hair-splitting session with our lawyers about what to leave in, what to leave out, what constituted child abuse and what was just lousy care. At some point in the process, I realized that when our lawyers, Rick and Jon, screened our footage, they didn't see images of people. What they saw were potential lawsuits flitting back and forth across the screen.

Never mind that Charter might sue us. What about the doctor who lied on tape? He could sue us, too. What about the nurse who committed fraud on tape? So could she. And the unqualified coun-selors? And the underage patients and their parents? At some point, we were discussing a scene in which a child appeared to have been wrongly prescribed a dangerous medication, and we realized that we could incur a lawsuit from the pharmaceutical industry.

"Oh, I see lawsuits everywhere," said Rick, waving his fingers around his head. "They're floating all around us."

THE HOSPITAL WITH NO NAME

The first and biggest hurdle that we had to clear with our lawyers was whether or not we could name Charter hospital in the piece. I'm not kidding. After we spent months gathering evidence of fraud and abuse at Charter hospitals around the country, talking to whistle-blowers from Charter, and shooting inside a Charter hospital, we faced the serious suggestion of not telling our audience which chain of hospitals was endangering and ripping off patients. What would be the point of showing such a piece? What would be the point of watching it?

Realizing that we might lose the whole project if we didn't get past this issue, we put together a special "lawyers' cut" of our show — an hour and a half of experts and law enforcement officials and oversight agencies, all saying ad nauseum that Charter was breaking the law and shocking their consciences. It was all the boring stuff, the stuff that you try to keep to a minimum in the piece itself. But it worked. At the end of the day, Rick and Jon said we could use Charter's name, and we were back in business.

Another doozy of an argument was about "wuzzing." I had spent days and days at a postproduction house, artfully blurring the images of the children in our undercover footage. The lawyers rejected it in a minute. They wanted these kids to be unrecognizable even to their own mothers, they said. Not just their faces, but their bodies, their clothes — nothing could be identifiable.

I understood the privacy issues, but we had a little problem. How could we show that the hospital staff was physically abusing patients if we couldn't show the patients' bodies? For example, we had a scene where a boy with an injured arm is strapped down to a table, and a staff member wrenches the boy's arm and reinjures it. How do you show that without showing the boy's body?

In the end, we showed a wuzzed-out blob, with an arm sticking out of it. It wasn't exactly a graceful representation of the poor kid's suffering, but at least you could understand what had happened to his arm.

None of this happened through polite negotiations. We all argued, yelled, threatened, and whined. Sometimes we got on our high horses. On one late night conference call, I actually hung up on the lawyers and ran out of the room crying. (I can't believe I did that now. David later said that everyone was relieved when I, the only woman in the conversation, started crying because it gave all the men a face-saving way out of a nasty argument.)

And then, just before we went to air, Charter filed a lawsuit. Suddenly, we *loved* our lawyers. They were our champions, our heroes. They'd saved us from a thousand booby traps that were hidden in our story. We praised their judgment about cuts and adds, and even about wuzzing.

In fact, they had saved us. Charter tried to get a temporary restraining order to keep our show off the air, and failed. And after filing their suit, Charter never actually took us to court.

But if we had gone to court, I don't think we would have gotten an unfriendly, Food Lion type of jury, even in North Carolina. The week after the Charter piece aired, we were swamped with letters, nearly two thousand letters. All but a few dozen of them praised our show, and they especially praised the way we took care to be even-handed, and to be careful with the children's identities.

It was a complete surprise. We expected a court battle, and instead we got a love fest. Even a couple of the hospital staff who we exposed in the piece called to tell us how fair we'd been, and how they appreciated it.

PUBLIC RELATIONS

The next bout we had with Charter wasn't in court, but in the press.

After we aired our piece, the federal government started shutting down Charter hospitals here and there around the country. So CBS decided to rerun the piece that summer, with an update.

We notified Charter executives, who hired Powell Tate, a public relations firm in Washington, DC, to deal with us. Powell Tate's strategy was threefold.

First, they had a woman who called David and me constantly to yell at us. This isn't journalism! she'd yell. You aren't journalists! People are going to know about this!

Second, they swamped us with "evidence" to "disprove" what we had shown in our piece. My favorite piece of "evidence" was a document, signed by our own Terrance Johnson, claiming that he had undergone a formal training session. This was to refute our claim that Charter didn't suitably train its employees.

Unfortunately for Powell Tate, they forgot about our hidden camera. Terrance had been taping when he signed the document they later sent us. What happened before he signed was this: the head nurse told her staff that they weren't going to have any training session because the teacher hadn't shown up, but she wanted them to sign the paperwork saying they'd completed the class anyhow.

Powell Tate sent us pages and pages of this kind of material, none of it proving anything. Nevertheless, it caused a problem for us at CBS because we did not have time in our television program to repeat and refute all their allegations against us. And that was the third part of their strategy: They sent newspapers and TV stations around the country a packet of their material, entitled "The Facts That CBS Refused to Show."

That was very clever. Never mind that "The Facts That CBS Refused to Show" were actually a bunch of false allegations and empty excuses; as long as we didn't broadcast it, they could claim we were holding it back from the public.

That's what people always hear about television reporters, that they take a few things out of context, and leave all the rest—the "real story"—off the air. That was what Food Lion said about ABC.

But again, Powell Tate blew it. They forgot about the Internet. We didn't have the airtime for the pages and pages of stuff they dumped on us. But we had CBS.com, and we put it there. Every single word Powell Tate sent to us, we reprinted faithfully on our Web site, and then we refuted all of it, line by line.

It was a huge project, a giant headache, and I'm pretty sure almost no one read it. But we won. They lost. The only press I saw about "The Facts That CBS Refused to Show" was a *New York Times* article about how CBS had used its Web site in a creative new way to refute allegations against one of its programs.

WHEN NO ONE CARES

While I was working on the Charter story, one of my favorite moments in journalism happened, in Brentwood, on the O. J. story. By then, all the same producers and bookers and camera crews who had fought over every scrap of O. J. news for years were now staked out by Monica Lewinsky's father's house in Brentwood. Then, just after noon on February 9, 1998, an SUV drove into the middle of their media camp and O. J. Simpson popped his head out the driver's side window.

"Is that the Lewinsky house?" he asked. Then he stayed a while to chat.

You've gotta love these big stories, even if you hate them. These stories never really go away, they just show up in a different form. First, you've got a media frenzy, then the story seems quaint and amusing because everyone who was so worked up over it doesn't care anymore. In 1998, a bunch of reporters standing on the street in Brentwood could get an interview with O. J., but it would only run as a blurb on an inside page.

But by then, of course, Monica was dominating the headlines and leading all the broadcasts, and there wasn't much room for anything else.

CHAPTER 17

SHOUTING AT THE CROCODILE

Greg Cooke

MAURICE MURAD

Murad began his career at CBS News in 1962 as a film editor on The Twentieth Century *series with Walter Cronkite. It was there that he began working with the great journalists who invented television news. He became an associate producer in 1974 and then a producer in 1977. The next twenty years were spent almost entirely producing long-form documentaries and newsmagazine broadcasts. Murad has produced dozens of documentaries for the* CBS Reports *series, for the series* Our Times *and* Crossroads *with Bill Moyers, and for the* American Parade *with Charles Kuralt. In addition, he was the supervising producer on the magazine series* West 57th. *Most recently, Murad spent two years producing several two-hour documentary specials and producing for Mike Wallace at* 60 Minutes. *Murad has won numerous awards for his work, including Emmys for film editing, writing, directing, producing, and investigative journalism. He also received two DuPont/Columbia Journalism awards, the Edward R. Murrow Journalism Award, and the Peabody award.*

It was during the height of the Clinton impeachment frenzy. Larry Flynt, the publisher of *Hustler* magazine, was making the television rounds castigating the "puritanical Republicans" and promising a bombshell any day now — a juicy scoop exposing a Clinton enemy who was having an extramarital affair. I was sitting in Mike Wallace's office at *60 Minutes* going over a story when the executive producer, Don Hewitt, poked his head in. He looked at Mike and said, "If you want Larry Flynt, I can get him." Wallace didn't hesitate for a second. He said, "I have no interest in that, whatsoever." And Hewitt said, "Neither do I" and walked out of the room. I was astonished. Flynt was what we in television call a "get," a hot personality that could lift a broadcast's ratings. And I remember thinking that this is the only place left in the television news business where this conversation could have occurred. Here were two old veterans refusing to give in to the prurience of the times. I felt proud to have any association with them. Five minutes later I sat in my office knowing that, after thirty-eight years, it was time to put in my papers, that I would be leaving CBS News for good.

Africans have a saying: "Don't shout at the crocodile until after you've crossed the river." Well, I'm on the other side now, so I hope you'll forgive my shouting. I'll try to keep this from being a screed, but there are some things I need to vent about. I also ask forbearance for the occasional journey into my past. I want you to know where I came from, so you can get a better idea of why I feel the way I do about television journalism today.

I never wanted to be a journalist. I had majored in film production in college and I was trained as a film editor. I showed up for work in September 1962 thinking of CBS News as just another production company. My first assignment was for a broadcast called *The Twentieth Century* with Walter Cronkite, a historical documentary series. Each week we refought a battle of World War II or returned to the Roaring Twenties or regurgitated the Russian Revolution. It was a classy operation, done with impeccable research and attention to detail. If it weren't for the primitive graphics and some Cold War jargon, you couldn't tell those broadcasts were made four decades ago. Still, there was nothing about this series to disabuse me of the notion that this was just a stepping-stone for a career in film production.

Fourteen months later, President Kennedy was shot.

Cronkite stifled a tear, pulled off his glasses, and told us that the president was dead. It was only then that I realized that Walter had a day job. It was lunchtime. A buzz went through the cafeteria in the CBS Broadcast Center. People got out of their chairs and headed out the door. Others were already striding through the hallways with a sense of purpose. "Right," I thought, "this is CBS News." It was that weekend, watching the television coverage along with everyone else, that I began to understand where it was that I had come to work.

A year later I was temporarily reassigned to work for a documentary series called *CBS Reports*. By that time Edward R. Murrow, who had started the series, was gone, but his producers were still there. These were men (there were no women producers then) who had made their bones mostly at newspapers—good journalists who were still learning to communicate in this new, visual medium. I was trained visually but didn't have a clue about journalism. God! Did I get lucky.

The first *CBS Reports* I worked on was called "The Divorce Dilemma." It was a one-hour documentary on what were then the archaic divorce laws of New York State. The state legislature was, at the time, considering a divorce reform bill. The producer, Warren Wallace, was a friendly, sophisticated man whose way of working was that he would research a story for a few months, then film the interviews and situations that illustrated his research. With the research in hand, we looked at the raw footage together. Warren would then tell me what was important to show and which subjects he wanted to cover. I was left alone to construct the interviews and sequences in an order that I thought best told the story. Warren would then look at my cut and tell me what he thought was wrong or right about it and, most important, if it reflected the truth about what he had found out and filmed. Then, he wrote the script. It was like being in journalism school with myself as the only student in the class. I was to find out that most of the old-line producers worked this way, and, though it would be eight years before I went out into the field, my education as a journalist seemed assured.

And why suddenly did I want to become a journalist? Well, after the documentary aired, Warren called to say that a New York state senator told him that the broadcast had put the vote to change the divorce laws over the top. I had no way to know if that was true, but I was euphoric. One drag on the narcotic of influence and I was hooked. I learned only later what a terrible burden this kind of power can be.

In the '60s and '70s, CBS News was one of only four national outlets for public affairs. We had enormous influence and we knew it. But there was always a sense that we were a quasi-public institution with a duty to inform and be fair. In fact, we referred to ourselves as the "license to run the whorehouse" because, in those days, a television network was guaranteed to make a nice profit. But "fairness" and "information" are ill-defined terms. There has always been a fine line between an investigative piece and a polemic. A great deal of my sensibility in this regard was established during my early years, encouraged by those who led CBS News and a few great journalists who took the time to mentor me.

In the '60s there were two presidents of CBS News, Richard Salant and Fred Friendly. Friendly was the great pioneer and probably had more to do with the look of television news and public affairs than anyone. But for those of us old enough to remember, Richard Salant was the man. It was Salant who codified the standards and practices we follow today. Until he insisted on it, CBS News had no book of rules outlining proper journalistic method and behavior. To be sure, there were rules that we kinda, sorta knew from memos that had been passed down since the late '50s. But if you broke one of them, there was no real way to call you on the carpet. If you look at some of the old documentaries and newscasts, you will see moments that were obviously staged and interviews that were either somewhat rehearsed or edited in a way that distorted what the interviewee really meant. Ever since the Salant edict, every editorial employee at CBS News has been given a large white book that defines what a journalist may or may not do. For example, when there was only one camera available to film an interview, it would be directed at the subject. When the interview was over, often the camera would be redirected toward the correspondent, who would re-ask the questions for editing purposes. Salant's new rules required the interviewee to be in the room so that he or she could be sure that the questions were asked in exactly the same way. Another rule he insisted on was that no musical scores were to be used in documentaries. He was adamant that it was too easy to use music to editorialize. There were dozens of rules like these. If you got caught breaking one of them, you were in deep trouble.

My first contact with Richard Salant was at a screening of a documentary that was part of a series called *The 21st Century*. It was a science series that tried to predict what the future would be like thirty-five years hence. It was a difficult concept for television because there was so little we could film. Through editing, animation, and interviews with futurists, we were barely able to hold a viewer's attention. At the screening a sequence came on that was a ballet of the planets set to music. No big deal, but a tolerable visual concept that had some value. In the darkness of the screening room, Salant asked for some explanatory narration about what he was seeing. I was horrified. Narration would totally disrupt the aesthetic of the sequence. I said nothing, but when Salant left, I went into a state of high dudgeon. Why do we have to screen for this guy? What the hell does a goddamned lawyer know about filmmaking? Burton "Bud" Benjamin, my executive producer, put his arm around me and said, "You know kiddo, every morning Salant comes into work and sits at his desk. Right above that desk is a hole straddled by a big cow. And every morning, before he has his coffee, that cow shits all over his head. You never hear him complain. He never rubs any of the shit off on you. So, give him his two lines of narration and be grateful." The cow Bud was referring to was the corporation, CBS Inc. And what really made Richard Salant a great leader was his ability to keep the corporation off the news division's back. Not that Fred Friendly ever took any crap from corporate. He howled about their meddling all the time. It's just that Salant kept them at bay without anyone ever noticing. When I'm asked what it was like at CBS News back then, I always answer, "It was a sweet place to work." In retrospect, I realize that much of that sweetness was due to Richard Salant.

Another day, another screening. It was a documentary about Lyndon Johnson's plan to send wheat to India to relieve an impending food crisis. Salant suggested that we insert a map showing a ship's journey from Houston, Texas, to Poona, India. Winston Burdette, the correspondent on the broadcast cooed drolly, "Of course, we better make sure our audience knows that the earth is round." Emboldened, I chimed in "God, that would be so boring." Wrong! Salant almost never raised his voice. Nor did he this time. He simply turned around in his seat and said "Boring? Boring? Our franchise is to inform, not to entertain. I don't care if everyone falls asleep. I want the information in there."

I have often joked that Ed Murrow left CBS just as I came in, and the news division has gone downhill ever since. Truth be told, the fellow who runs it now, Andrew Heyward, is putting more and better news programming on the air for less money in real dollars than we ever dreamed of back then. But that statement, "I don't care if everyone falls asleep," could never be uttered today. The corporations are now pretty much in control of the network news divisions, and keeping audiences awake is paramount. If the information is going to put you to sleep, it isn't going to be there. A news broadcast gets ratings, or it is gone.

Want an example? *Nightline*, the paragon of television journalism, devoted five nights to a wrap-up of the Clinton presidency. Virtually all of the first four nights were devoted to scandals (Gennifer Flowers, Paula Jones, and Monica Lewinsky), a policy failure (universal health care), and a budget battle (the closing down of the government). A portion of the fifth night dealt with the bombing of Yugoslavia and subsequent capitulation by Slobodan Milosevic. All were hot topics, with personal anecdotes from White House insiders. ("When I heard the Flowers audio tape my heart sank," says George Stephanopolous.) In all five nights, there was nothing on Clinton's deciding to reject a compromise, thereby essentially destroying federal habeas corpus, nothing on the draconian immigration act he signed into law, nothing on his instant recognition that globalization was now the driving force behind foreign policy, nothing on his willingness to fight his own party on the North American Free Trade Agreement (NAFTA), nothing on putting teeth in the General Agreement on Tariffs and Trade (GATT) by backing the World Trade Organization, nothing on his bailout of the Mexican economy, nothing on his efforts to bring peace to Northern Ireland, nothing on his overtures to reduce tensions with North Korea, nothing on his gamble to back Boris Yeltsin—a move that may have thwarted a return of the Communists to power—and nothing on his fight against the evisceration of the Clean Water Act. I could go on. Why? you may ask. After all, they had five nights, and Ted Koppel and his executive producer, Tom Bettag, are without question the two brightest minds in our business. The answer is Jay Leno and David Letterman. Even at *Nightline* information goes begging when ratings are at stake. There's a reason why they aired over forty broadcasts on Jim and Tammy Faye Baker, and it had nothing to do with the public's need to know. I feel terrible picking on *Nightline*. It's far and away the best public affairs broadcast on television. I only do it to show that no one is exempt from the pressure of getting ratings. Everything you see on television today should be put in that context.

The problem is most apparent in local news. There, the slogan "If it bleeds it leads" has always applied, but today there is a subtler way of keeping you watching for the entire broadcast. In the nightly trailers and in the broadcast openings, an announcer will tease you with words that, in one form or another, say, "If you don't watch our newscast, you will die, you will die poor, and your mourners may not show up because of an impending storm." This usually takes the form of "Tonight on News 2 New York . . . Is there a killer hiding in your basement? . . . Your credit may be at risk without your knowing it. . . . Could there be snow in the forecast?" This is a formula that was first developed for sweeps (months when the ratings are measured) and is now used all the time. What kinds of stories actually run? Certainly any murders or fires will run first. Then teased story #1 about a mold called stachybotrous that occasionally is found in some buildings and can be, but is seldom, fatal—and could be, but is very unlikely to be, in your basement. Killer mold is a staple of local news and the story in one form or another is rerun three or four times a year. Teased story #2 is about credit card companies that can make mistakes on your credit report and cause you to have difficulties. This is another staple, rerun several times a year. It usually ends with the anchor telling you how to get a copy of your credit report. And . . . is there snow in the forecast? Well, not tomorrow but, on the fourth day of the five-day forecast, there's the possibility of snow with little or no accumulation. There are many variations available with this formula: killer shopping carts (there may be microbes on them from the previous user), killer chickens (improperly cooked chicken can make you ill), killer soda cans (a soda can top that has stickiness from another can that burst may harbor germs), and killer doorknobs (depending on the location, they can have everything on them from mucous to feces). Of course, since the World Trade Center attack, there has been a wealth of doom to use in the opening teases. Though an American is more likely to be struck by lightning than killed in a terror attack, you wouldn't know it by watching local newscasts. News directors learned quickly that terror sells.

Local stations will often hold you for the end of the newscast by promising a story with some cute animals in it. This is a holdover from an older formula used during the Vietnam War that, in those mostly male newsrooms, was referred to as "vets, pets, tits and tots." A war story, a dog story, a story about rearing children, and some cheesecake. The dogs, somehow, have survived.

I need to convey just a few more things about my journalistic upbringing. Most of what I became as a producer for CBS News I owe to two people, Tom Spain and Irv Drasnin. Tom Spain is a truly wonderful, award-winning documentary filmmaker whose greatest attribute is his courage. He always admonished me to do stories the way I thought best, then fight like hell to keep them that way. Though he's only a few years older than I am, he was my first mentor. From my early days in the editing room to the last segment I did for *60 Minutes*, his philosophy, attitude, and method have informed the way I do stories. Tom was James Fallows before there was a James Fallows, that is, above all a good journalistic citizen. His first lesson to me can be summed up as, "people are more important than television." It was really just the golden rule applied to journalism—that you should treat people and their stories the way you would want to be treated. Second, if you honestly reveal something of yourself and your intentions to people in your story, they will be more open and honest with you. Third, and most important, most stories aren't black or white. They are gray. This is something that most people directly involved in a story instinctively know and fear that you, the journalist, either don't know or worse, that you don't care. These maxims can even apply in many types of investigative stories. An example: Tom and I were assigned to work together on a film about mental institutions. Tom was to film the story, I was to be the film editor, and the two of us would coproduce it. Our associate producer, Peter Schweitzer, though a young man, already had a wonderfully developed sense of visual storytelling.

It was 1978, a time when mental patients were being released to live on the outside in the naive hope that facilities would be built to house and care for them. The common wisdom was that large institutions were ill equipped to care for the mentally ill. At the time, the image of most mental hospitals was somewhere between movies like *The Snake Pit* and *One Flew Over the Cuckoo's Nest*. None had a worse reputation than Creedmoor Psychiatric Center in Queens, New York. Creedmoor had lost its accreditation two years before and had just regained it. And so we chose Creedmoor as the place we would film to see if people might be better cared for on the outside. The first thing we did was spend a lot of time with the new director of the hospital, Dr. Bill Werner. Dr.Werner was responsible for regaining Creedmoor's accreditation, and we knew that there would be no access without his cooperation. Our first question to him was, "How did you get this hospital reaccredited so quickly?" He said, " I have only two rules for my staff: Don't hit the patients and don't fuck the patients. Other than that, be as creative as you like." I remember his eyes boring in on us to see our reaction. We were sizing him up and he was clearly doing likewise. After several visits during which we forthrightly explained our intentions, Dr. Werner told us we could have the master key to the acute ward, that we could come in unannounced anytime and were free to talk to anyone about anything. Naturally we were shocked and asked why he would take the chance in doing that. He said that he believed that patients would be better cared for in outpatient clinics and that if he were going to be the commandant of Andersonville (a notorious prison camp of the Civil War), he wanted the taxpayers to see just what it was they were paying for. It was clear to us that he had come to trust us. He believed that, if we spent time investigating the problems of large institutions, we would come to the same conclusions that he had. And by the way, to you nonjournalists out there, the best way to co-opt reporters is to give them full access. Bill Werner seemed to understand that. We spent the next four months at Creedmoor just watching what went on, getting to know the patients and staff, and finally getting permissions from everyone to film in the ward. Every so often, Tom would bring in his camera and just point it around so that people would get used to it. As we spent more and more time there, we began to realize how fuzzy this issue of deinstitutionalization was. The ward seemed to serve an important function for some of the more acute patients. When it all became gray, when we were sure we had no answers to the problem, we began to film. Our method was simple. Bill Moyers was our correspondent. He had come to Creedmoor from time to time during our research period but pretty much left us to do our work. While everyone knows Moyers as a thorough journalist and a great intellect, few may know that he's also a great street reporter. He can think on his feet better than anyone I've ever been privileged to work with. So we brought him to the door of the ward and told him to knock on it and just use his natural curiosity and his instincts. I said, "Don't turn around and say 'roll camera.' We'll be there." Things went well that first day, and the next, and the next. But I sensed that, despite all the months of our living on the ward, despite all the conversations we had with the staff, some of them were still wary of us. Then one day one of the patients, an elderly woman, had a psychotic episode. She became violent and had to be subdued. Two of the mental health therapy aides brought her to the ground quickly and softly, restrained her, and calmed her down. Tom was right there in the hallway. He had his camera loaded and ready, but he turned away from the incident and never turned the camera on. I could hardly believe it. Why? What Tom instinctively understood was that the two aides were the kindest, most devoted people on the ward; that this kind of incident wasn't typical and had not happened in all the time we had been there; that while the woman was let down gently, on film the action would appear violent, and that showing this incident would distort the basic sense of what the ward was like. Now, I realize that there's a whole body of thought that says to show everything and let the chips fall where they may. But a documentarian working for a network news division, with just one precious hour of airtime, has a responsibility to leave a viewer with a sense of what's typical and a duty not to sensationalize a story. In print you can give nuance with words. A camera shot isn't always what it seems and can leave a false impression. A film producer can hardly write a line asking the audience to not believe their eyes. At any rate, Tom's actions weren't lost on the Creedmoor staff. One of the aides involved, a woman named Mabel Taylor, told us she had been a little leery of us. Not any more. It was clear sailing from then on.

After almost a year of research, shooting, and editing, we came to the conclusion that the problems inherent in leaving people in or dumping them out of mental hospitals were caused more by the system than the people in it. The documentary, called *Anyplace But Here*, won four Emmys, the Christopher Award (the Christophers are a Catholic organization that honors programs that "light candles rather than curse the darkness"), the Monte Carlo Film Festival's International Critics' Prize for News Programs, and the American Mental Health Association Award. But that's not what I brag about. The real awards came from the people we filmed. Virtually all the patients, their loved ones, the psychiatrists, therapy aides, and social workers, none of whom could ever agree on anything, called to say we got it right. Unfortunately, Dr. Werner died of a heart attack just before the broadcast aired, but I want to believe that he, too, would have thought so. Best of all, we were told by people in the mental health field that *Anyplace* would be shown as a training film for prospective mental health workers to give them a realistic view of what they would be facing if they entered the field. That's what I brag about.

But, lest you think things were better in those "golden years" of broadcast news, the vice president in charge of documentaries called Tom Spain a few months later to complain that we had shot six thousand feet more film than the budget allowed for and demanded to know why. This, to a man whose previous two broadcasts alone had won every journalism and television award known to humankind. Tom calmly told him that he needed the extra two and a half hours of film to properly complete the job. He hung up the phone, turned to me, and said, "This is the last film I ever do for these guys." And it was.

Tom Spain is more of a documentary purist than Irv Drasnin. He tends to choose stories and issues that can be presented with little narration, using the principals in the story to carry the audience along. Drasnin is more of a gonzo journalist and a terrific writer. He came to documentaries from the hard news side of television and tends to tackle large issues that require enormous amounts of research and understanding before the fieldwork begins. I first worked with him in 1974 on a film called *The Guns of Autumn*, a ninety-minute documentary about hunting in America. I was the editor, and a woman named Meg Clarke was the researcher, a title that belied her huge contribution to the broadcast. Vowing not to film any "slob" hunters (hunters who didn't follow the basic rules of safety and sportsmanship) Irv, Meg, and the associate producer, David Lowe Jr., went out into America and filmed for three months. They filmed a buffalo hunt in Arizona (the culling of a herd by permit), deer hunting in the Colorado mountains (the idyll of the lone hunter), duck and goose hunting in Pennsylvania (again by permit and with limits), two bear hunts in Michigan—one with dogs and one at a garbage dump (most bears are hunted with dogs or with bait)—and the hunting of exotic animals raised for that purpose at a ranch in Texas. Through the entire editing process, Irv and Meg made sure I didn't distort in any way the sense of what happened in the field. Now, the stories I could tell about this broadcast would fill a book (I'll let Irv write it). I'll tell only one. This is how I learned that a journalist can never be too prepared and why one should never exaggerate, even a little.

The Guns of Autumn was completed, and all involved were sitting in the CBS Reports screening room. We had just shown the film to our boss, Bill Leonard, who, at the time, was CBS News vice president of public affairs programming. The lights came up, and Bill was effusive in his praise. Irv was properly humble, and I said, "Boy, the hunters are going to love this film." Bill said, "Are you kidding?" I replied, "No, This is what they do. This is their sport the way it really is." He said, "You're either the most naïve son-of-a-bitch who's ever lived or the dumbest." He was surely right on both counts. Before the film aired, we got five thousand letters telling us what a bad job we had done. After the film aired, we got ninety thousand letters saying the same thing. Many of the letters had the same exact wording, which led us to believe that the National Rifle Association (NRA) had orchestrated a large letter-writing campaign. I couldn't imagine what was making the hunters so upset. The only thing we showed that hadn't been on *American Sportsman* was the animals getting hit by bullets and falling dead. Then came a deluge of over $350 million worth of lawsuits against CBS News. Most of them, we believe, were encouraged or paid for by the NRA. As CBS prepared for the legal onslaught, they asked Meg and Irv to reproduce their research in a coherent form. Out of that came a 132-page paper on the kinds of hunting that typically went on in this country. It was here that I learned the lesson of preparedness, because after all the litigation was complete, CBS's liability came to one dollar. In just one case, the CBS lawyers opted not to put on a defense because, prima facie, there was no evidence of distortion. The judge, presiding in the plaintiff's venue, said that strategy was arrogant and instructed the jury to find against CBS. The jury's reply was to award the plaintiff a dollar, the traditional way juries have of saying that a case has no merit and should never have been brought to court. Through all of the turmoil that followed the broadcast, that 132-page research document held up. Every sequence in the broadcast was representative of hunting in America, and no one could show otherwise. After that, and for the rest of my working life, every time I wrote a line of script, I imagined Drasnin sitting on my left shoulder asking, "Are you sure you can back that up?"

Another lesson Drasnin taught me was to do my own digging and to believe my own eyes. It sounds ridiculously simple, but I'm always surprised by how many reporters don't do it. By 1976 I had already produced a television magazine segment and held the title of associate producer/editor. Irv asked if I would work with him as his associate producer on a film about the civil war in Zimbabwe, which was then called Rhodesia. Would I? Jesus! Exotic Africa! A civil war! Look out Hemingway, Murad has left the building. So, after reading everything that was available and spending ten days in London talking to people who knew the situation there, Drasnin, Meg Clarke, and I headed for Rhodesia. Now, there are a dozen great stories about the making of this documentary. Again, I'll let Irv write the book. But after we finished unpacking our stuff at the Monomatapa Hotel in Salisbury, our cameraman, David Green, suggested we go over to the bar at Meikle's Hotel. All the journalists hung out there, and he thought we could kind of get the lay of the land. Drasnin declined and forbade us to go over there, ever. I was crushed. Why? I mean, what good was it being on a foreign assignment if you couldn't kick back at the end of the day with others in the biz, have a beer, and tell war stories? The gist of his argument was that when you hang around with other journalists, be it in Washington, DC, or Shanghai, China, you all recirculate the same information. After a while that body of information becomes the common wisdom, which clouds your ability to process what you are seeing for yourself. Worse, when everyone is writing the same thing, a laziness sets in, and there's a tendency to accept what has been written as fact. Drasnin's idea was to put aside all we had read and everything we were told and try to find out for ourselves what was going on. I've noticed since that time that, whenever there's a large group of reporters covering a situation, all the stories that are filed read alike. This is especially evident in political campaign coverage. Everyone seems to have the same take on a story. Often, the result is bad information being given out. An example: When Al Gore rowed down a river in a kayak for an "environmental" photo opportunity, the Republican National Committee sent out a press release saying that a wasteful amount of water had been released from an upriver dam on orders from the Gore campaign, so that he might row his kayak. This calumny was repeated in all the newspapers the next day. As it turns out, water is released from that dam every day. And on the day the photos were taken, less water was released than usual. How did it happen that the story was misreported? I don't know, but I imagine that the reporters on the bus had a huge chuckle and decided it was too delicious to ignore. And if one reporter was going to go with it, they all had better go with it. There would be time for a correction at some later date.

This leads me to one of the biggest gripes I have about journalism today. I call it "The curse of the clips." I have no doubt that, twenty years from now, some fellow will be writing an article about the presidential campaign of 2000 and recount this event as one of the Gore campaign's blunders. He will have gone to old newspaper clippings (now in an archival base on the Internet), found the story, not seen the follow-up correction, and this libel will be given new and perhaps permanent life.

It's not easy fighting off the urge to piggyback on another reporter's work. In 1977, Tom Spain, Peter Schweitzer, and I were assigned to do a documentary about illegal Mexican immigration to the United States. We were in our offices in New York when we read a front-page story in the *New York Times*, the gist of which was that thousands of Mexicans were massed at the California border preparing to make a dash for the United States. The detention centers were supposedly full, and the Border Patrol was being overwhelmed. So we packed our bags and hightailed it for the Chula Vista Border Patrol Station on the California-Mexico border. There we found six rather bored Mexicans whose only concern was that they were running out of cigarettes, and who wanted to be tossed back to the Mexican side as quickly as possible. The Border Patrol guys said that it had been fairly quiet in recent weeks, a fact we could substantiate easily by riding with them. So how did this story get written? We called the *Times*, and they explained that it was done from information that was in the *Los Angeles Times* and would be corrected. But in the meantime, did some other reporter or columnist go to the clips and repeat this information? Were assignments made by other news organizations based on this story? I don't know. But, believe me, it happens. The *New York Times* has earned the right to be called "the paper of record." They have the best reporters and editors in the world working there. The problem lies not in their making mistakes. We all do. The problem is that many journalists take what they read in the *New York Times* as gospel — almost as if it were a primary source.

Here's an example. In 1980 I was assigned to produce an hour that was to be part of a five-hour documentary series titled *The Defense of the United States*. My assignment was to document the readiness and costs of our conventional (nonnuclear) forces. Part of the hour was devoted to what was then known as the Rapid Deployment Force (RDF). It was a combined force of army, marines, and airborne troops operating under the Southern Command. There was controversy over whether the force should exist at all, given that their mission was exactly that of the Marine Corps alone. The *New York Times* had reported that the RDF's budget was $5 billion a year, which seemed small given the large number of troops assigned to the force. Luckily my associate producer, Margaret Drain, became suspicious. Margaret (who is now the executive producer of *The American Experience* on PBS) was almost maniacal in her search for facts. She often said that we were lucky to find and deliver five new facts in any documentary hour, and she was right. Anyway, she found a source in the Pentagon who told her, off the record, that the actual cost was closer to $23 billion. After further inquiry she felt safe in saying the cost was at least $19 billion. I cannot, even now, tell you who that source was. He was promised confidentiality. Suffice it to say, he was a person who had some direct supervision of the RDF's budget. When the broadcast was completed, we screened for Roger Coloff, our boss at the time, and gave him a script. We got a call from him a day later saying that we had made an error in the cost of the Rapid Deployment Force, that the figure was $5 billion. He had read it in the *Times*. After we explained to him how we arrived at the figure and who our source was, Roger said, "Go with it." And we did. Now, I relate this story not to crow about how we got something right that the *Times* got wrong. I relate it because a few months later, we read in a weekly newsmagazine that the RDF cost the taxpayers $5 billion a year. Obviously that reporter had been bitten by the "curse of the clips." What's more, I have never seen the $19 billion figure in any subsequent story about the RDF. Everyone, it seems, likes to use the *New York Times* as a clip source. So, if the RDF idea is ever reborn and some reporter writes about the RDF experiment in the 1980s, which figure do you think he or she will use when citing the cost?

It's just so important for a reporter to disassociate himself or herself from the whole media whirl. At the time we were doing the *Defense* hours, stories were circulating in the media about the lack of readiness of our armed forces, with special significance attached to the low quality of recruits entering the service. The draft had ended, and there was no longer a war to fight. Morale was said to be at an all-time low. We spent a lot of time with the army, the marines, and the navy (the air force has an inordinate percentage of officers), and what we found was very high-caliber recruits being led by a disgruntled officer corps. (No war, no promotions.) Also, we had read in many journals that the Eighty-second Airborne, an elite corps, was in a state of unreadiness. Yet, when we went on NATO maneuvers called Operation Reforger in Europe, the Eighty-second Airborne troops acquitted themselves beautifully. They competed with crack German and British troops and kicked ass. So, why was this misinformation so prevalent? My guess is because the military establishment was looking to get more funding for pay and recruiting, and it was in their interest to promote such notions. Too often a reporter will take some expert's word for what's happening when that "expert" may have an agenda. In this case, I believe that a lot of reporters couldn't resist military men criticizing their own.

This phenomenon is most apparent when dealing with the issue of education in America. We have all heard lately about how poorly our public education system is working. In the autumn of 1996, I began producing a series of broadcasts featuring the students who would graduate in the year 2000. For research purposes I visited inner-city, suburban, and rural schools all over the country. I spent a term filming the freshman class in Joppatowne, Maryland. I spent another term filming sophomores in Franklin, Tennessee. I produced another hour involving students from many different places. If I learned one thing in all that time, it was that our public schools are working. Make that, working well. After a few months at Joppatowne High, I asked the school's principal, Tom Ackerman, what all this stuff was about the deterioration of the public school system. From what I could see, most teachers were creative and hardworking, and most students were well mannered and serious. He told me that it's in everyone's interest to badmouth the public schools. Teachers want higher pay, principals want budget increases, school boards want bond issues to pass, religious organizations want a voucher system to support their church schools, inner-city parents want charter schools, and the party out of power needs an issue with which to whip the party in power. It's no wonder you can't get an "expert" to tell you that the public schools are doing well. Tom Ackerman then asked me if I would be willing to believe my own eyes. That's funny, I thought. He asked me to look at America—look at how well we are doing compared to the rest of the world. If our system was so bad, why is it that each year our physicists, chemists, economists, writers, and medical researchers keep winning Nobel Prizes? We have the highest standard of living in the world for a reason, he asserted. "What about the fact that our students do poorly on tests compared to, among others, Chinese students," I asked. His answer was that while the Chinese may do better in tests at age eighteen, no one ever tests them again at twenty-three. By that age, those students have been burnt out preparing for tests, while American kids are just coming into their period of creativity. And after all, what's an education for? Certainly, beyond learning for learning's sake, it's to attain a higher quality of life. Indeed, when we asked some students in China what they thought about that, they readily admitted that the Chinese system allowed precious little room for creativity. Another complaint people have is that when American school kids are tested, they fall into the average range compared with other countries. Of course they do. An accurate statistical sample will take kids from superb districts to awful ones. Also, ours is a country that takes in tens of thousands of legal immigrants each year, and Lord knows how many illegal ones. Ten percent of the people living in the United States were born elsewhere. It might be informative to list some other countries that fall into the average range. How about England, Germany, Canada, Norway, Switzerland, Israel, Hong Kong, and Russia? And while on the subject of Russia, forty years ago Admiral Hyman Rickover predicted that Russia would bury us because its schools taught rigorous science courses whereas ours were too lenient. Back then, Rickover probably needed recruits with a physics background to build his atomic submarine fleet. If I learned anything in the two years I spent with the class of 2000, it's that America's future is in good hands, thanks largely to an excellent public school system.

Ah well, this treatise is about journalism, not public education, so let me get on with it. Here's an example of a misreported story that has been bugging the hell out of me. It shows what can happen when a piece of dramatic information is released and the story begins to snowball.

In October 1995, just before the fifth anniversary of the Gulf War, I was assigned to do an hour documentary that looked at that war and its consequences. To refresh your memory, the elder President Bush rather abruptly ended the war, even though his generals in the field were telling him that in one more day they could march unopposed into Baghdad. We now know that Saddam Hussein's family had already fled the country, and he had an escape plane fueled and ready for himself if the coalition forces kept advancing. Wafiq Samerai, Iraq's intelligence chief, was with Saddam when President Bush called off the war. He told us in an interview that Saddam "changed from a man who was sensing danger, sensing death was coming at any minute, to a man who had escaped drowning and got away unscathed." The upshot of the decision to stop the invasion at one hundred hours (a purely political move suggested by Colin Powell) was that nineteen million Iraqis had to continue living under a brutal dictator.

I had tried many times to get into Iraq. My mother and father (both Sephardic Jews) were born and raised in Baghdad, and I wanted very much to see my ancestral home. Each time I was rebuffed. The word "journalist" on my passport seemed to assure that I would never get in. As luck would have it though, just as I was assigned this project, Saddam invited journalists from all over the world to come to Iraq to witness the presidential election he was about to hold. We applied and were given visas. By that time, Iraq had been living under United Nations sanctions for five years, and the media was full of stories about Iraqi suffering. The most horrifying of these came from a UNICEF report claiming that a half million Iraqi children had died from starvation because of a lack of food resulting from the imposed sanctions. I have, at times, recused myself from certain stories because I felt too emotionally involved to be objective. This might have been one of them. The bastards, I thought, are killing my people. I just wanted very badly to see where my parents had come from, so I took the assignment.

At that time, no air traffic was allowed into Baghdad. The only way to get there was over land from Amman, Jordan, in a tedious twenty-five-hour journey across the Iraqi desert. We were pretty groggy as we motored into Baghdad, but almost instantly I began to feel something was odd. I turned to my colleague, Deirdre Naphin, and said, "This doesn't look like a place that's under sanctions." There was normal street activity, trucks carrying consumer goods, a huge amount of construction, an inordinate amount of traffic, food stalls piled high with fruit and vegetables, and people who were as well dressed as those in any place that I had been in the Middle East. What to make of it? We got to the al Rasheed hotel, unpacked, and headed straight for the Ministry of Information. Anyone who has ever covered the Middle East knows how hard it is, once in country, to get going on a story. We were lucky that our cameraman had been to Iraq before, and he guided me to the person in the ministry who tended to be the most cooperative. I was asked what I wanted. I said, "I want to see the starvation—any place it exists—in hospitals, the countryside, in city neighborhoods, up north, down south, in Karbala, Nejef, Mosul, Basra, or Baghdad. I need to bring this story to our viewers back home." He nodded. "Of course, of course. You shall have it, insha'allah." We waited for days. Nothing. But we had many other things to film around the city, and so we kept busy. I kept noticing food stands full of food, even in poor neighborhoods, and, Lord knows, we were eating well in restaurants and at the hotel. We also found that there was a food program being run by the government that allotted each family a ration of rice, cooking oil, tea, sugar, and, for those with young children, powdered milk. At one point, we got an interview with a gentleman who headed the World Food Program. He told us that there was no starvation in Iraq as yet; in fact, they didn't even have a feeding program going on at that time. I asked, "What about the half million dead Iraqi children?" He said that was the number of children that were at risk of starvation, but he had not seen any famine as yet. "What about in the countryside?" I asked. He said, because the people there were closer to the food supply, there was less risk for them. He also told us that Saddam had begun an irrigation program to grow food in the desert and that, as far as fruit and vegetables were concerned, the Iraqis were self-sufficient. We then interviewed a person from CARE (a private international relief and development organization), a woman most sympathetic to the Iraqis, who also told us that there were no current feeding programs but warned that children were at risk if the government ration supplement ever stopped.

Finally, we were given permission to visit Saddam Hussein Children's Hospital in Baghdad where, we were told, we would see the problems caused by the lack of food. There was a "minder" with us from the Ministry of Information, a man who kept tabs on what we did. Journalists go nowhere in Iraq without a "minder." Once at the hospital, the first thing I noticed was a lot of men standing around doing nothing. Odd, since the second thing I noticed was the dirt and cigarette butts all over the floors. We were brought up to a wing that was supposed to be where they dealt with malnutrition. There were three children on the ward, two premature babies and one boy about four years old. Each was attended by a woman from the child's family. The first woman, dressed in Western clothes, was leaning over an incubator looking at her child inside. She looked healthy, was obviously upper class, and luckily spoke English. I asked if the baby's early birth was due to malnutrition. She was reluctant to speak with me but said, "No, I had enough to eat." She didn't know why her baby was born prematurely. Next to the second incubator, a woman in traditional Muslim dress silently stared out into the ward. She spoke no English, and I didn't speak Arabic well enough to ask her about the baby. The doctors had already told us all three cases were due to malnutrition. The third child, a four-year-old boy, was, we were told, suffering from kwashiorkor, a condition brought about by severe protein deficiency. The boy had no orange discoloration of the hair associated with the condition, nor was his stomach distended. He did have scabrous brown marks the size of quarters over most of his body, and I knew that rashes were common in people suffering from kwashiorkor. Usually, powdered milk will help the condition, but perhaps the family hadn't gotten the ration. The woman who was tending him spoke no English, so I accepted the doctor's diagnosis at face value. I thought it was strange though that, in a city as large as Baghdad, there were only three cases — three dubious cases — of malnutrition. On any given day there would be more cases than that in any New York City hospital. So, I asked Deirdre to interview the doctor on camera knowing that our "minder" would concentrate on that. When the interview started, I backed out the door and began searching each floor of the hospital, looking for more cases of starvation or malnutrition. There were none, just what seemed to be ordinary pediatric patients.

So, we went to the countryside, ostensibly to cover the voting in the presidential election. We headed first to Nejef, then to Karbala. All the while I was looking for evidence of starvation. Because I had the heartbreaking experience of covering the famine in Ethiopia in 1987, I had a pretty good idea of what famine looked like. There was nothing. Not even in Karbala where the people had fought bitterly against the government and where Saddam responded by bombing the entire city, including the mosques. It was still in ruins with rubble everywhere. But no starvation. It's time, I thought, to start believing my own eyes.

What we finally figured out was that there was no food crisis in Iraq; there was a currency crisis caused by inflation. The problem wasn't finding food; the problem was paying for it. During the Iran-Iraq war, Saddam began to flood the market with Iraqi dinars to be used to purchase armaments. So much money was needed that they began printing it with color photocopy machines. By the time we got there, one hundred dinars was worth about seventeen cents. The deprivation, such as it was in Iraq in late 1995, was as much a result of the Iran-Iraq war as it was of the UN sanctions. Though food was plentiful, Iraqis were forced to pawn their worldly possessions or barter with others in flea markets for food money.

It turns out that what was happening in Saddam's Iraq resembled in many ways what happened in Mengistu's Ethiopia. This was nothing more than political deprivation. Control the food supply, and you control the people. Like Mengistu, Saddam could easily have ordered that food be distributed to his people at any time. But fear of starvation is a powerful political weapon. It was not lost on anyone that, during the Iraqi presidential election, government food ration cards were used for voter identification. As far as UN sanctions were concerned, anyone standing at the Jordanian or Turkish border could easily see them being broken. King Hussein of Jordan was diligent in not allowing anything to pass that could be used for weapons, but winked at everything else. I saw large earthmoving equipment piggybacked on flatbed trucks headed from Jordan to Iraq. At the Turkish border, vehicles weren't inspected at all. All day long one could see trucks with huge containers hanging beneath them. They were empty coming in and full of Saddam's oil coming out. It was clear that Saddam had plenty of money for medicines or anything else he might have needed to alleviate the suffering of his people as evidenced by the presidential palaces that were then under construction. Iraqi officials denied that this was proof of sanction busting, saying that the palaces were paid for in local currency. Imported steel reinforcement rods paid for in worthless currency? Hardly. And if you could smuggle in steel rods, how hard would it be to smuggle in antibiotics? While we were there, Saddam was building his fifty-second palace. Former Iraqi officials, now in exile, have testified to over $30 billion in personal wealth held by Saddam in foreign bank accounts. The reality is, this image of a starving people suited him. The doctors, in a kind of dog and pony show, would display gutted ambulances that were waiting for spare parts while right down the avenue there were car dealers showing Mercedes Benz, BMW, Lexus, and other luxury cars. At the car mart, a kind of used-car bazaar, there were hundreds of vehicles that could have been cannibalized to keep the ambulances running. The doctors told us there were no antibiotics available to treat infections but, by that time, Saddam had twice refused our offer to let him sell $2 billion worth of oil for, among other things, medicine. Saddam's whole strategy was geared to getting all the sanctions lifted. To do that, he had to elicit the world's sympathy. Smart man, that Saddam. It was working then. It still is. After the September 11 attack on the World Trade Center, the first message Osama bin Laden sent through al Jazeera cited our killing of children in Iraq.

So, five months after I see all this and report all this, what do I read in the *New York Times*? What do I see and hear on television, including on my own network? A half million Iraqi children have died because of the UN sanctions. It had been over a year since I first read that figure, but these reports were then still using the 500,000 number. Amazingly, though the sanctions were then still in place, not one child had died in the last year. At one point my boss, Linda Mason, sent me a rocket. "What the hell is going on?" she asked, "Did you miss something?" I have to tell you, even when you know you are right, when something like this happens, your mouth gets dry. I told her I would send her a detailed account of how I reported my story and what I had to back it up. Instead, what I did was send her a detailed rendering of what was wrong with all the other stories and told her to burn it after she read it. The last thing I wanted to do was get into a pissing match with broadcasts in my own news division. Even now I am loath to do it because most of the people involved are first-rate journalists who seldom get snookered. And anyway, they know who they are.

On May 20, 1996, the Iraqis and the UN reached a settlement allowing more Iraqi oil to be sold for money to purchase food and medicine. The *New York Times* began to hedge on its previous reports. They put the number this way. "Since the earlier deal broke down, hundreds of thousands of Iraqis (not Iraqi children) have become malnourished or ill, with many dying from lack of medication, United Nations agencies estimate." The parentheses are mine. Then, in the May 1996 issue of *Harper's*, Paul William Roberts wrote about a recent trip to Baghdad. In the article there is detail after detail about life in the city. No mention whatever of famine.

Finally, in the *New Yorker* of May 17, 1996, T. D. Allman, in a long article on his visit to Iraq, wrote, "I found no evidence that they were suffering and dying because of the embargo." He goes on, "All over Iraq, I made impromptu visits to hospitals and dispensaries. I talked with hundreds of Iraqis about the embargo. No one mentioned the rampant malnutrition and disease that was so widely reported." More, ". . . fresh fruits and vegetables were available everywhere. Every night there were traffic jams in front of Baghdad's most popular restaurants, as the jeunesse dorée flocked to them in their Nissans and Mercedes. One couldn't help noticing that there was no shortage of imported cigarettes. Aspen, a Canadian filter tip, and Johnny Walker Black [*sic*] seemed the most popular brands." He ends, "Under the new arrangements, access to food and medicine will remain a political, not a humanitarian matter. Saddam and his enforcers will decide who eats and who gets antibiotics."

Whooof! It was like the foreman of the jury had pronounced me "not guilty," or rather, "not crazy." Of course, we now know that American soldiers uncovered large warehouses of food during the initial invasion of the second Gulf War. And, while there were all sorts of problems with the subsequent pacification effort, lack of food was not one of them. Yet, as late as November 8, 2003, Nicholas Kristoff of the *New York Times*, in an op-ed piece condemning sanctions in general, quoted the 500,000 figure, while saying it was *probably* exaggerated (italics mine). No, Mr. Kristoff, it was completely false.

Next case. Of all the things going on in journalism today, none is more insidious than conglomerate ownership of journalistic enterprises. When Westinghouse bought CBS, I worried that there would be many stories that we at CBS News would be proscribed from covering. I have no evidence that this ever happened but, then again, no one ever asked to do a story about the atomic waste cleanup in Aniston, Alabama, that Westinghouse was involved in. When Westinghouse split off, then sold off their industrial assets, I was relieved. Then came the sale to Viacom, an entertainment-based company (*60 Minutes*, not surprisingly, then did the Aniston story). While Viacom is a better owner than Westinghouse, there's still a problem. The cross-promotion of entertainment on news broadcasts, which was once forbidden, is now so common that we hardly notice it. You can't turn on a news broadcast, local or national, without seeing some mention of *Survivor* or *Who Wants to Be a Millionaire* or the latest big television sports event or a story based on an original movie running that evening (meet the real twins that were separated at birth). Ask yourself, will Viacom ask Hillary Clinton for favors because of their $8 million book deal? Did Disney squash an ABC News report about pedophilia in its theme parks? When I watched MSNBC in the 1990s, should I have wondered if its brutal "bash Clinton all the time" programming had anything to do with Microsoft's fight with Clinton's Justice Department? Would Rupert Murdoch use the FOX News Channel to achieve his own personal goals? Certainly his newspaper, the *New York Post*, never slants the news toward Murdoch's business interests. Hmmmmm.

To get an idea of how pernicious it can get, you need look no further than Viacom's handling of two films it produced, the Bush docudrama *DC 9/11* and the Ronald Reagan biography. In *DC 9/11*, which ran during an election cycle, President Bush was depicted heroically by a writer who couldn't possibly have known what really happened on the days immediately after 9/11. At the time it aired, even the Senate Intelligence Committee members didn't know what happened. It ran without a whimper from anyone. On the other hand, the Reagan biopic, a less than flattering view of the Reagan years, caused a deluge of letters from Republicans and conservatives, chastising CBS and threatening its advertisers with boycotts. Viacom capitulated, saying the movie was unfair, and removed it from the CBS network schedule. Then, after demanding further cuts, Viacom moved it to its cable outlet, Showtime. Now, none of this is worrisome by itself. Consumer pressure is a hallmark of our democracy. Here's where the perniciousness comes in. At the time of the scheduled broadcast, Viacom had important business before the Bush administration. The Senate had just overturned an FCC ruling that allowed Viacom, among other large media, to own more television stations than it had been previously allowed to own. Big media's only hope of keeping their extra stations was a veto of the Senate bill by George W. Bush. Now, I'm a journalist, and I have to admit that I have no idea if there was a quid pro quo involved. (Full disclosure: I own a lot of Viacom stock.) I do know that, to the average American, this stinks like hell, and the news divisions, unfairly, will take a hit for it.

So you see, the concept of the liberal media or the conservative media is so much bushwa. The media is self-interested and market driven, period. Whatever sells suppositories gets on the air or in the newspaper. It's true that most of the people who run media businesses are conservatives, but that conservatism seldom trickles into the reporting. (Except at FOX News Channel where their mission is to capture the conservative audience.) I can think of only once in thirty-eight years that I was asked to change a sequence because of its political implications. In a documentary about Watergate, I was asked to remove George H. W. Bush from a scene in which he introduced Richard Nixon to a large gathering. Though Bush was head of the Republican National Committee during Watergate, the president of CBS News at the time, Eric Ober, said that using it was a cheap shot. It was certainly true in the early years of television news that most of the producers and reporters were liberals. Not any longer. Most people in editorial control nowadays are market-oriented centrists. For the most part, stories are chosen for their general interest and mass appeal. Station managers and news directors routinely define success or failure in ratings, demographics, and winning day parts, not in the importance of a story. That's not lost on young reporters who understand exactly what's expected of them. In producing stories, the biggest no-no is to offend a substantial chunk of the audience by reporting things in a way that goes against their attitudes. If you need proof of this, hark back to the coverage of the World Trade Center attack. Most on-air reporters behaved as either government cheerleaders or psychotherapists to the masses. One month after the attack, President Bush held his first formal press conference. In it, he gave virtually no information that wasn't already public. Regardless of the question asked, he kept repeating the same mantra about American resolve. Yet afterward, local and network anchors described him as "forthcoming" and "in command." Everyone had read the same poll numbers. On that day, President Bush had a 90 percent approval rating. No one was in the mood to hear him criticized, least of all, news directors.

By the fall of 2003, his approval ratings had dipped 50 percent and virtually every news outlet began questioning what the president knew before 9/11 and when he knew it. The same phenomenon occurred during the second Gulf War. At the beginning, news outlets were falling all over themselves to show their patriotism and confusing support of the troops with support for the war. As the president's approval ratings went south along with the pacification program in Iraq, reporters became emboldened to the point that President Bush began referring to them as "the filter," as if they hadn't been just that on *his* behalf in the early part of the war.

But don't be faint of heart. There are still ways to remain reasonably informed. The first thing to do is distinguish between information programming and the political mud wrestling that passes for public affairs. *Capital Gang, Hardball, Crossfire,* and the rest of the talking head spitting matches, whether network, syndicated, or on cable, are worthless. It is false conflict masquerading as serious discussion. The people who appear on these broadcasts are either trying to drive up their speaker's bureau fees or pushing their point of view with no respect for the truth. They are aware, as you should be, that the manipulation of perceptions is replacing reality as the governing principle in human affairs. So, as Chris Matthews starts shouting over his first guest, who is shouting over his second guest, turn to PBS where the *NewsHour* is parsing the day's events in a calm thorough manner. Don't worry, you'll get used to the pace.

Here's another tip. Don't get your information from entertainment programs. According to one study, a lot of people do. Jay Leno, David Letterman, and *Saturday Night Live* all do skits based on perceptions of people and events, not on truth. There are other admixtures of entertainment and current events that are perhaps more difficult to sort out. Rush Limbaugh and *Imus in the Morning* come to mind. Limbaugh's approach is pretty straightforward. Something like, Love me or hate me, I'm a conservative Republican. If you think I'm slanting the truth, I don't care, as long as you listen to my show. Imus, on the other hand, seems to be an equal opportunity destroyer. He will go after almost anyone. Bill Clinton has been his target of choice for many years. From a journalistic point of view, here's what maddens me about the Imus show. I've heard him refer to the former president as "a fat pantload," a "slime ball," and "a disgraceful human being" literally dozens of times. He constantly did skits referring to sex acts Clinton committed, both real and imagined. And *then* who appears on his show, in effect legitimizing this obscenity? Tom Brokaw, Jeff Greenfield, Dan Rather, Mike Wallace, Tim Russert, Barbara Walters, and virtually every journalist you've ever heard of except maybe Peter Jennings and Ted Koppel, all of whom treat Imus's loaded questions with great seriousness. Then, of course, they plug a book or an upcoming broadcast. A few weeks after George W. Bush took office, I heard Imus and Andrea Mitchell crapping all over Bill Clinton, and I began to wonder, just what kind of White House coverage I had been getting from Andrea Mitchell all these years? Speaking of Andrea Mitchell, the only real information I've been able to glean from the Imus show is how much the Washington "elite" hated Bill Clinton. I mean, Sally Quinn (who is so last century), commenting on Clinton's marital infidelity? Kill me!

So how do I stay reasonably informed? I rely on National Public Radio, the BBC World Service (which is still available on the Internet), C-SPAN, Britain's *Economist* magazine, and columnists whom I've read over the years—like Tom Friedman and Michael Lind. I also read the *New York Times* (I know, I know, so why do I keep griping about it?).

One other thing. Since I retired and have time to watch more live news feeds, I've been surprised at how well the network evening newscasts sum up the day's events.

That Dan Rather . . . he's still my fave.

Okay, so why after that glorious moment in Mike Wallace's office did I decide to call it quits? Because I shouldn't have been surprised at the decision to turn down the Flynt interview. Wallace and Hewitt were old-school guys who have been doing things on their own terms forever. I, on the other hand, though I was in the protective bosom of this great broadcast, had forgotten my upbringing. I had begun to equate ratings, demographics, and winning day parts with success. I had begun choosing stories that way. I had become as institutionalized as the people of whom I was critical. Screw it, I thought, by the time I shake this attitude loose, I'll be in a rocking chair dribbling oatmeal on my bib. I was gone.

CHAPTER 18

WHAT HAPPENED TO GOOD OLD-FASHIONED MUCKRAKING?

Sandra Scott Jensen

CARL JENSEN

Carl Jensen, PhD, founder and director emeritus of Project Censored, America's longest-running research project on news media censorship, has been involved with the media for more than fifty years as a daily newspaper reporter, weekly newspaper publisher, public relations practitioner, advertising executive, educator, and author. He is currently professor emeritus of Communications Studies at Sonoma State University. Jensen has written and lectured extensively about press censorship, the First Amendment, and mass media and has been a guest on many radio and television programs, including a Bill Moyers documentary entitled Project Censored; *a PBS Odyssey special entitled "Media Under Seige – Headlines or Hype?"; and a more recent PBS special,* Project Censored: "Is the Press Really Free?" *narrated by Martin Sheen. Jensen is the author of the 1990–1996 annual Project Censored yearbooks,* Censored: The News That Didn't Make the News . . . and Why, *as well as* 20 Years of Censored News, *and most recently,* Stories that Changed America: Muckrakers of the 20th Century. *He has won numerous awards for his work, including the Media Alliance Meritorious Award, the Society of Professional Journalists Freedom of Information Award, and the James Madison Freedom of Information Award for Career Achievement. His 1996 Project Censored Yearbook received the first national Firecracker Award from the American Wholesale Book Sellers Association for the best nonfiction alternative book of the year.*

417

At the start of the twentieth century, journalists such as Lincoln Steffens and Ida Mae Tarbell launched the twentieth century with what came to be called the Golden Age of journalism. They were investigative reporters who were derisively named "muckrakers" by President Theodore Roosevelt. The movement lasted only about a decade but resulted in social and legislative changes that improved the way of life for millions of Americans to this day. The movement also provided a startling revelation of the potential power of journalism.

About twenty-three years earlier, in 1877, John B. Bogart, an editor with the *New York Sun*, wrote, "When a dog bites a man, that is not news, because it happens so often. But if a man bites a dog, it's news." His definition implies the need for a sensationalistic ingredient in news and is used as a standard to this day. At the start of the twenty-first century, we may be witnessing the end of muckraking and the triumph of Bogart's man-bites-dog form of journalism.

The United States has a free press guaranteed by its constitution, it has the world's most sophisticated communication system, and it has more independent media outlets disseminating more information twenty-four hours a day than anywhere else in the world. Considering our autonomous press and the quantity of information that daily bombards us, we should be a very well-informed populace. Unfortunately, high technology and a free press do not guarantee a well-informed society.

The problem is not the quantity of information that we receive, but the quality. During the communist witch-hunts of the '50s, the media inundated the public with headlines of wild charges made by Sen. Joseph McCarthy, a Republican senator from Wisconsin who was a rabid anticommunist. McCarthy's accusations of communist infiltration in American institutions ruined the reputations and careers of many people, driving some to suicide. It created a national climate of terror that became known as McCarthyism. While the media provided extensive coverage of McCarthy's charges, they did not investigate whether those charges were accurate. Had the media fulfilled their responsibilities as "watchdogs" of society by investigating the charges, they would have saved many lives from being destroyed. The quantity of coverage during the McCarthy era was ample, but the quality was lacking. The media failed to provide the warning signals we needed. When a problem arises, there should be a warning signal—information—that alerts citizens that something is going wrong which needs attention and resolution. Given such a warning, an aware populace could then influence its leaders to act upon that information to solve the problem.

Few would deny that the United States has problems, serious problems, which need to be confronted and resolved if we are to succeed and survive in the future. Despite the economic boom of the late twentieth century, America is a nation beset by problems of homelessness, poverty, hunger, health care, pollution, violence, drug abuse, and environmental degradation. And yet, how many of our citizens are fully informed about, or even aware of, those issues? There has been a breakdown in America's early warning system. Only occasionally, when the problem gets totally out of control, such as was the case with the hazards of cigarette smoking in the mid-1990s, the electoral debacle in Florida in 2000, or the energy crisis in California in 2001, are the media inspired to provide the information the public needs to know. Even then, the media tend to provide too little too late.

In 1976, I launched a national media research effort, called Project Censored, to explore whether there is systematic censorship of certain subjects in our national news media. The primary goal of Project Censored is to improve media coverage of important public issues. It identifies and publicizes serious problems that the mainstream media have not sufficiently covered and educates the public by raising questions about censorship and the role of the media in a democratic society.

Project Censored was founded on the thesis that real and meaningful public involvement in public decisions is possible only if all ideas are allowed to compete daily in the media marketplace for awareness, acceptance, and understanding.

In brief, Project Censored defines censorship as the suppression of information, whether purposeful or not, by any method—including bias, omission, underreporting or censorship—that prevents the public from understanding what is happening in society.

The creation of Project Censored was stimulated by my personal bewilderment over how the American people could elect Richard Nixon by a landslide five months after Watergate, one of the most sensational political crimes of the century. The reason was very simple— Watergate was not a major news item before the November 1972 election. As Bob Woodward and Carl Bernstein subsequently pointed out, Watergate wasn't even a topic of discussion on election eve. The media did not put Watergate on the national agenda until 1973, months after the election.

Subsequent comparisons of the coverage given other critical issues in the mainstream media versus exposés in the alternative press persuaded me that, although the information might be available, the mass media do not provide the public with the data it needs to make informed decisions.

THE BAY OF PIGS COVER-UP

Critics of Project Censored claim there is no news media censorship. While Project Censored has exposed hundreds of stories that didn't receive the coverage they should have, the Bay of Pigs disaster provides a classic "smoking gun" example of how the media do censor some stories.

On April 17, 2001, hordes of US media, politicians, and old soldiers descended on Cuba to commemorate the fortieth anniversary of the Bay of Pigs invasion. With all the backslapping and laudatory comments, you would have thought they were celebrating a major US military victory. In reality, as we know, the Bay of Pigs was a national disaster, one of the most embarrassing foreign policy involvements in our history. It was also a disaster that could have been avoided.

When it came time to fix the blame for the Bay of Pigs, there were more than a few possible culprits. The guilt trail started with Vice President Richard Nixon's exuberant enthusiasm for a Cuban invasion in 1959. It was followed by President Dwight D. Eisenhower's formal approval of the aggressive action also in 1959, President John F. Kennedy's go-ahead and mea culpa in 1961, the US military's cautious cooperation, and finally ended with the CIA's 1998 public confession of its key role in the debacle.

But in all the millions of words speculating on who was to blame for the Bay of Pigs, there have been few raising the culpability of the news media in the fiasco. Indeed, forgotten in all the recriminations was the critical role of the press. The invasion plan was well known to many of the leading media, but after some heated discussions about whether they should or shouldn't go to print, the press decided not to tell the American people. This decision was made despite the fact that nearly everyone else knew about it, from politicians, to foreign governments, to Fidel Castro himself.

Media that knew but failed to expose the coming invasion included the *New York Times*, the *Washington Post*, *Newsweek*, the Copley News Service, and others. Not only did they censor the story, they ignored the urgings of other less mainstream media to tell the public what was going to happen. The *Nation*, in an editorial published November 19, 1960, five months before the invasion, documented the build-up for the invasion and urged the US media to check out the reports. But they didn't.

Only the American public didn't know about the coming invasion.

Perhaps the most culpable member of the press in the cover-up was the *New York Times*. The *Times* had full and potentially explosive information about the planned invasion. In early 1961, a *New York Times* journalist wrote an article that would have exposed the upcoming invasion of Cuba and the CIA's involvement. The story was originally to be published by the *Times* under a four-column headline at the top of page one. But when word leaked out in Washington that the *Times* planned to run the story, President Kennedy called James Reston, *Times'* Washington bureau chief, asking him to kill it. Reston told Orvil Dryfoos, the publisher of the *Times*, about Kennedy's call and suggested toning down the story and removing the references to the invasion.[1] As a result, a heavily edited version of the story, with a one-column heading, appeared with no mention of the CIA's involvement or that the invasion was imminent. Kennedy himself later told *New York Times* managing editor Turner Catledge, "If you had printed more about the operation, you could have saved us from a colossal mistake." It is generally agreed that if the *Times* had published the information it had, public opinion would have forced Kennedy to cancel the invasion.

The *New York Times* was not the only publication to censor the story. As David Halberstam pointed out in *The Powers That Be*, the media were "remarkably vulnerable to the seductive call of National Security." In an effort to absolve themselves of their failure, the media later said they saw the issue as a conflict between national security and national interest and were persuaded that this was a case of national security. In reality, the media failed to perform their responsibilities as the watchdogs of society. The Bay of Pigs was not a national security issue. It was a matter of national interest. And the media censored the story.

As the Bay of Pigs example shows us, news media censorship is not some kooky conspiracy theory. It is a fact of life.

THE RISE AND FALL OF MUCKRAKING

Before speculating on the future of investigative journalism, we should take a look at what happened to the golden era of investigative journalism over the course of the twentieth century. The beginning of the end may have started when President Roosevelt charged that the investigative journalists who were exposing corruption in society were "muckrakers."

There was a mixed response to the malicious terminology Roosevelt wielded at the journalists he attacked. Some, like Ida Mae Tarbell, were appalled at his satirical criticism of their research and writing. Others, like Upton Sinclair, responded to the challenge by accepting the label with pride. In the end, "muckraker" became a widely used vituperative term. Most modern-day journalists dislike the title and prefer to be called "investigative journalists." Yet, there are a few authors, like the late Jessica Mitford, who proudly wore the crown when *Time* magazine labeled her "Queen of the Muckrackers." Mitford, who successfully exposed a variety of society's "cherished" institutions, including The Famous Writers School, and Elizabeth Arden's Maine Chance spa in Arizona, is best known for *The American Way of Death*, a scathing indictment of the funeral industry.

In reaction to the muckrakers' criticism of corporate America, the fledgling fields of advertising and public relations rapidly grew in size and importance. The powerful propagandistic vehicles these growing fields provided gave corporate America the manipulative tools it needed to respond to the journalists' exposés. A loose corporate conspiracy ensued, one designed to discredit journalists, and along with the threat of World War I and other factors, the curtain came down on the Golden Age of journalism.

But there were some journalists who continued to dedicate themselves to exposing corporate crime, political corruption, and social injustice, and they did not disappear with the end of that sparkling era. However, the talent, energy, and impact of those dozens of investigative journalists concentrating their efforts in that first decade have not been seen since.

Research I did for *Stories That Changed America: Muckrakers of the 20th Century* (Seven Stories Press, 2000) provides an insight into the pattern of investigative journalism from those early days. The twenty stories selected for the book had to have a major, positive impact on society. They span a broad spectrum of critical issues, from corporate and political corruption, to the environment, population growth, and civil rights. They are an eclectic collection bound together by a common theme—they all helped make America a better place, which one might say is a proper goal for investigative journalism.

Consider, for a moment, the lasting impact of the words written by the following authors:

Ida Mae Tarbell broke up the Standard Oil monopoly.

Lincoln Steffens exposed political and corporate crime from the cities to the nation's capitol.

Upton Sinclair went undercover to expose corrupt meatpacking practices that led to the creation of the Food and Drug Administration.

Margaret Sanger fought politicians, the church, and censors to pave the way for birth control in the United States.

Rachel Carson's words exposed the hazards of poisonous chemicals and launched the Environmental Protection Agency.

Edward R. Murrow's telecast about Sen. Joseph McCarthy led to the downfall of the anticommunist tyrant and his reign of terror.

Betty Friedan's *Feminist Mystique* launched the women's liberation movement.

Michael Harrington's haunting description of America's invisible poor led to the War on Poverty and many of today's social welfare programs.

Ralph Nader first exposed unsafe cars and then went on to create a host of powerful consumer, political, and environmental groups that fight corporate and political crime.

BLEAK FUTURE FOR INVESTIGATIVE JOURNALISM

Based on my research for *Stories That Changed America*, I would say that the current outlook for investigative journalism in America is bleak at best. Four of the twenty stories were from the first two decades of the twentieth century. In the four decades from the twenties to the fifties, there were just three stories. The 1960s and 1970s were by far the most productive years in contemporary muckraking. Thirteen of the stories that changed America occurred during those turbulent years, a time of individual introspection, idealism, and social activism. The final two stories selected for the book were "Diet for a Small Planet," by Frances Moore Lappé (1971) and the Watergate coverage by Bob Woodward and Carl Bernstein (1972/1973).

Ironically signaling the end of that muckraking era was the assassination of Don Bolles, an investigative journalist with the *Arizona Republic*. Bolles was investigating local connections between business, politics, and organized crime, much in the manner Lincoln Steffens delved into corruption in the cities. Bolles was fatally wounded when a remote dynamite bomb was detonated in his car on June 2, 1976. His death contributed significantly to the growth of Investigative Reporters and Editors (IRE), a nonprofit organization founded in 1975 and based at the University of Missouri. It is a major resource center for investigative journalists in print, electronic, and online media.

The last quarter of the twentieth century did not produce any earth-shattering exposés that had the same impact as the stories cited above. Instead, it was a time when journalists became superstars, distracted by money rather than concerned with the public's right to know. As Don Hewitt, former executive producer of CBS's *60 Minutes*, once told Bill Moyers, "The 1990s were a terrible time for journalism in this country but a wonderful time for journalists; we're living like [General Electric's CEO] Jack Welch." Moyers astutely noted, "Perhaps that's why we aren't asking tough questions of Jack Welch."

While the early Golden Age of journalism was marked by a fortuitous congruence of dedicated authors, courageous editors and publishers, progressive politicians, and an outraged public, the circumstances are far different now. Today we have journalists dedicated to the pursuit of high salaries and prestigious awards, a paucity of courageous editors and publishers, a near reactionary political environment, and a public distracted by junk food news about O.J. Simpson, JonBenet Ramsey, and Monica Lewinsky.

Even television newsmagazine shows that built their ratings and reputations with hard-hitting exposé journalism appear to be fading now. Mike Wallace, award-winning correspondent for *60 Minutes,* conceded, "It's a question of time, money, and the ratings business." He added that newsmagazines are doing "damned little" significant investigative journalism and that what they do is "much softer than it used to be."[2]

SIX FACTORS DOOMING
INVESTIGATIVE REPORTING

There are at least six specific conditions contributing to the dearth if not impending death of investigative journalism in America.

1. The growing impact of litigation against the news media became an important variable in journalism in the late twentieth century. When ABC television used undercover journalists to explore meat hazards at the Food Lion grocery chain in North Carolina in 1992, they were sued and found guilty of misrepresenting themselves to get the story, a legal gambit used to avoid libel laws. While a jury initially awarded Food Lion $5.5 million in punitive damages, an appeals court overturned the verdict in October 1999, exonerating ABC of any fraud. But the time and cost of the litigation was not lost on media executives.

Upton Sinclair got his remarkable story for *The Jungle* by similarly misrepresenting himself in the meatpacking yards of Chicago in prelitigious 1905. As a result, the nation got its first food and drug laws. When ABC used the same basic technique to expose conditions at Food Lion, the issue of deadly meat was obscured by the lawsuit. There was no improvement in the nation's food and drug laws. In fact, there was an increase in deaths from E. coli–laden meat during the 1990s. Further, Professor Ronald Cotterill, an antitrust authority at the University of Connecticut's Food Marketing Policy Center, described the current working conditions in meatpacking as "now clearly more dangerous and debilitating than at any time since Upton Sinclair wrote *The Jungle* [in 1906]."[3]

Corporate America successfully fought the muckrakers in the early twentieth century with advertising and public relations and is now trying to do the same with lawyers and the courts.

2. Another factor that does not bode well for the future of investigative journalism is the growing censorship of sensitive or controversial subjects resulting from the monopolization of the media. As the publishing and broadcast industries are increasingly owned and controlled by conglomerates, there will be fewer and fewer media available to reformers. Media scholar Ben Bagdikian points out in *The Media Monopoly* (Beacon Press, 1997) that there were fifty major media corporations in 1993, and now there are only about half a dozen. It would be a truly naïve journalist at NBC who would expect his net-

work to air a report on the hazards of low-level radiation emitted by nuclear reactors built by General Electric, which also owns NBC.

While the Internet, a new medium purported to be a fount of information by some observers, provides a soapbox for all critics, it has to somehow authenticate its sources of information or misinformation before it can be taken seriously as a dependable news medium.

3. There is an ominous trend from individual investigative reporting toward a corporate group approach. Nineteen of the stories cited in *Stories That Changed America* resulted from dedicated individual efforts, often at the cost of personal sacrifice. Just one story, Watergate, in 1972, emerged from a group effort. This trend, from individual to group journalism, was confirmed when the Pulitzer Prizes were announced for 1999. In the eighty-two-year history of the prizes, the Pulitzer Prize board has overwhelmingly recognized the achievements of individuals. But in 1999, for the first time, a majority (seven out of thirteen) of the traditionally individual awards went to collectives such as newspaper and wire service staffs. The 2000 Pulitzers for breaking news reporting, explanatory reporting, national reporting, and international reporting all went to groups of two or more journalists.

Muckraking is most effective when done by individuals driven by social conscience who won't be deterred from their goals by corporate groupthink or allegiance to some corporate entity.

4. The future for investigative journalism also looks bleak because of the US Supreme Court's *Hazelwood School District* v. *Kuhlmeier* ruling in 1988. The decision gave high school administrators the power to censor student publications in advance, reversing a longtime trend of Supreme Court First Amendment support for freedom of expression issues on high school campuses. The case involved students of a suburban St. Louis high school who were prevented from publishing in the student newspaper articles about teenage pregnancy and the effects of divorce on high school students. Censorship by prior restraint—which was the case in this instance—is the most onerous form of censorship. Oddly enough, this apparent gross violation of the First Amendment has been generally ignored by the major news media. Despite ongoing student protest and a belief by many that *Hazelwood* is unconstitutional, the 1988 ruling still stands today. Now America's future journalists are being trained at an early age to acknowledge and acquiesce to censorship as a function of their profession. The 1988 ruling reversed a longtime trend of First Amendment support for freedom of expression

issues on high school campuses. Oddly enough, this onerous violation of the First Amendment has been ignored by the major news media. Despite a belief by many that *Hazelwood* is unconstitutional, and ongoing student protests, it is still unchallenged in 2001.

5. Another potential deterrent to the future of investigative journalism is that the public is losing faith in the media's ability to fulfill its role as a media watchdog. The public, concerned with the problems it sees around it, but bedazzled by junk food news, now questions not only the way the press does its job, but also its basic values and concerns. In 1985, a national survey found that 54 percent of the public perceived the press as "moral" and just 13 percent saw it as "immoral." In June 2001, a follow-up study revealed that 40 percent of the public now sees the news media as "immoral" while 38 percent sees them as "moral."[4]

If the people continue to lose faith in the news media, we can't expect them to trust what the press has to say, whether it's about tainted meat or corrupt politicians. In fact, the constitutional privilege of the press might itself be vulnerable to repeal. A national poll of public attitudes about the state of the First Amendment conducted by the Freedom Forum, a nonpartisan foundation dedicated to the research and study of a free press and free speech, revealed a significant deterioration in the public's support of First Amendment rights, including the rights of speech and press. Released in June 2001, the poll showed that an alarming 39 percent of the people feel that the First Amendment goes too far in the rights it guarantees. A year earlier, the figure was 22 percent.

6. In the final analysis, it is the media's bottom line—the profit and loss statement—that causes the greatest concern for the future of investigative journalism. Corporate media executives perceive their primary, and often sole, responsibility to be the need to maximize profits for the next quarterly statement and not, as some observers would have it, to inform the public. This attitude is not lost on journalists. An April 2000 survey of nearly three hundred journalists and news executives conducted by the Pew Research Center and the *Columbia Journalism Review* revealed that more than a quarter of the journalists surveyed admitted that they avoid going after important stories that might affect the financial interests of their news organizations or advertisers. Altogether, 41 percent of the respondents said that they either purposely avoid newsworthy stories and/or soften the tone of stories to benefit the interests of their news organizations.

Many of the stories Project Censored annually cites as "censored" do not support the financial interests of media corporations or their advertisers. Investigative journalism also is more expensive (it takes more time and requires more legwork and resources) than the "public stenography" school of journalism practiced at many media outlets. There also is the "don't rock the boat" mentality that pervades corporate media boardrooms and then filters down to the newsrooms. It doesn't take long for the bright young journalist at ABC to recognize that the chairman of the board at Disney, which happens to own ABC, does not appreciate aggressive journalists who might be tempted to investigate reported cases of employee discrimination at Disney World. This kind of corporate socialization has been exacerbated by the multibillion-dollar, megamedia mergers that created international giants such as AOL Time Warner, Disney, General Electric, News Corporation, and Viacom. The need to play it safe became more and more pervasive as the boats grew in size.

THE HISTORY OF STANDARD OIL—PART II

Who among today's establishment media would authorize and support an updated investigative report on Standard Oil's activities since Ida Mae Tarbell's investigation ended with the publication of *The History of the Standard Oil Company*?

The History of the Standard Oil Company, Part II, would have to hold Standard Oil accountable for its role in the conspiracy to destroy rapid transit systems in more than one hundred cities nationwide in the 1930s and 1940s, which has been described as perhaps the greatest economic crime in history. In 1949, Standard Oil of California and the other companies involved were convicted in the conspiracy and fined $5,000 each.

The History of the Standard Oil Company, Part II would have to reveal Standard Oil's traitorous but profitable relationship with Nazi Germany both before and during World War II. In 1933, Standard Oil of New Jersey invested $2 million in Germany to help them make gasoline for war purposes. After Hitler came to power, Standard Oil gave Germany the patents for tetraethyl lead, a crucial ingredient for one hundred-octane aviation fuel. And in 1942, after America entered the war, while Americans struggled with coupons and lines at the gas stations, Standard Oil was shipping fuel to the enemy through neutral Switzerland.[5]

The History of the Standard Oil Company, Part II would have to reveal that Standard Oil knew since the 1920s that leaded gasoline was a public health menace but continued to put lead in gasoline to prevent engine knocking until 1986 when leaded gasoline was banned. In the 1960s, Standard Oil of California marketed this lethal product with a gasoline additive called "F-310" as an antipollutant. Its marketing theme, "It cleans your engine as it runs," was so deceitful that the Federal Trade Commission issued a "cease and desist" order banning the advertising.

If some dedicated journalist ever wrote such a book, what media, outside of the alternative press, would have the fortitude to publish it?

The unseemly power of corporations like Standard Oil over the public's weal is not new. Several of our presidents warned us about it earlier. President Thomas Jefferson cited the aristocracy of moneyed corporations who defy the laws of our country; President Abraham Lincoln warned that wealth concentrated in a few hands could destroy the republic; and President Dwight D. Eisenhower feared the influence of the military-industrial complex. We didn't heed their warnings, and today the United States reflects the dangers they cautioned us about. But there are no investigative journalists to sound the alarm of this corporate takeover of our democracy.

What is needed to reverse the unfortunate trend away from investigative journalism is fairly evident. The critical first step is for the press to acknowledge it has a problem, something it has yet to do. The full extent of the see, hear, and speak no evil mentality can be seen in a special thirty-two-page report on investigative journalism published in the May/June 2001 issue of *Columbia Journalism Review* (CJR), the self-appointed monitor of the press.

The CJR report asks, "Are Watchdogs an Endangered Species?" and ominously answers, "The existence of investigative reporting isn't guaranteed." This remarkable admission, announced in the CJR, published by Columbia University's Graduate School of Journalism, could be expected to set off alarms in the profession. But it didn't, possibly because of the convoluted explanation CJR offered its readers.

TOO MUCH INVESTIGATIVE JOURNALISM?

The CJR article suggests the reason investigative reporting is in trouble is because there is too much of it, specifically by the television media. There has been a "diminution of watchdog reporting by dilution." Apparently this torrent of investigative reporting has "created a permanent infrastructure of news devoted to exposure." But the problem is that the local news teams, featured in "I-Team" and prime-time newsmagazines, "do not monitor the powerful elite and guard against the potential for tyrannical abuse." Instead, the CJR article charges, they merely inform the public of dangers to its personal safety or finances. In the best of all worlds, it would seem that this would be the proper role for the local media, on guard against the local elite and tyrannical abuse, while leaving the big crooks and tyrants to the major national media.

Thus, CJR appears to conclude that the real reason for the failure of investigative journalism in the future is that there is too much of it on too many insignificant issues. The article doesn't mention the possible threat to investigative reporting from litigation, monopolization, journalism student indoctrination, or the pressure to make a profit.

Meanwhile, this lengthy puff piece on mainstream media organizations and journalists fails to acknowledge the existence of a thriving alternative press in America. There are more than 250 alternative media ranging from the *Boston Phoenix* to the *Village Voice* to the *San Francisco Bay Guardian* where much of the investigative reporting that does occur takes place.

Nor did the magazine mention the Center for Investigative Reporting, an award-winning San Francisco–based group of investigative journalists founded in 1977 who have written hundreds of important exposés about money in politics, the environment, public health and safety, and government secrecy.

Nor, for that matter, did CJR mention my own foundling, Project Censored, the longest-running news media research effort in the world that regularly reports on the performance of major media (www.projectcensored.org). The project annually exposes the top twenty-five news stories that the mainstream media overlook, undercover, or censor.

The first step needed to correct the situation is for the major media and its monitor, CJR, to admit that there is a problem. Then, we need dedicated journalists giving us the facts, courageous publishers and editors providing the necessary soapbox, an outraged public demanding change, and responsible politicians to pass legislation where needed to solve the problems.

Fortunately, despite the many obstacles, there will always be some crusading individuals, be they investigative journalists, muckrakers, or whistle-blowers, who are willing to undergo great sacrifices, both personal and financial, to expose the crimes, the tricks, and the swindles cited by Joseph Pulitzer.

One person who saw the problem and was courageous enough to speak out about it was Jay Harris, the former publisher of the *San José Mercury News*. Harris resigned his position on March 19, 2001, rather than fire staff members to meet the profit demands of the paper's corporate owner, Knight Ridder. Harris said the constitutionally protected press "should not be managed primarily according to the demands of the market or the dictates of a handful of large shareholders." In a speech he made to the American Society of Newspaper Editors shortly after resigning, Harris warned, "The trend threatening newspapers' historic public service mission is clear — if we're willing to see it. And it can be challenged and reversed — if we're willing to speak out. Of course, many are unable, or unwilling, to see or speak the truth of the situation. One reason is that the high salaries many of our leaders receive, in newsrooms and business offices as well as corporate headquarters, have turned into golden handcuffs. And those handcuffs have morphed into blindfolds and gags as well." Harris rejected the golden handcuffs and spoke out. His voice should not remain a lonely one in journalism.

TEDDY ROOSEVELT HAD IT ALL WRONG

In an interesting footnote to the history of muckraking in America, we must note that the term "muckraker" is a misnomer as President Roosevelt used it when he spoke before the Gridiron Club of newspapermen in Washington, DC, in March of 1906. He called the investigative journalists muckrakers and likened them to the man with the muckrake in John Bunyon's *Pilgrim's Progress*, who, Roosevelt said, could "look no way but downward, with the muckrake in his hand; who was offered a celestial crown for his muckrake, but who would neither look up or regard the crown he was offered, but continued to rake to himself the filth on the floor."

The Gridiron speech was off the record. But a month later, on April 14, while dedicating the cornerstone of the House of Representatives office building, Roosevelt gave the same speech on the record, publicly labeling writers as muckrakers. He used the term in a pejorative sense to accuse them of being so busy stirring up the mud at their feet that they could not see the good things in America.

Ironically, it appears that Roosevelt misinterpreted the "Interpreter" of Bunyan's allegorical narrative. Bunyan's "Interpreter" was actually extolling the virtues of simple poverty. He described how the wealthy are obsessed with looking downward to rake more riches when they should have been looking up at the celestial beauty above them. The term "muckraker" would more accurately describe the robber barons of Roosevelt's time, not the journalists. John D. Rockefeller was king of the muckrakers, not Lincoln Steffens.

TODAY, IT'S "WATCH WHAT YOU SAY"

Shortly after the outbreak of the First Terrorist War of the twenty-first century, I was reminded of what US senator Hiram Johnson said during World War I: "The first casualty when war comes, is truth." This saying probably dates back to the earliest wars of any kind. But, this time there is a difference. If truth is the first casualty of war, this time the First Amendment may be the second casualty of war.

Post–September 11, 2001, the free flow of information in America is slowing to a carefully monitored trickle.

The president of the United States says he can only trust eight members of Congress.

The attorney general admonishes Congress to pass the controversial Anti-Terrorism Act without debate.

The national security adviser cautions television networks not to broadcast press conferences with Taliban leaders because they may contain hidden messages.

The military tells the press this is a "different war" and thus can't observe the 1992 agreement allowing the media more access to information.

The State Department tells the Voice of America radio network not to broadcast an interview with Taliban leader Mullah Muhammad Omar.

The president's press secretary warns the media and all Americans to watch what they say and watch what they do.

These are ominous signs for a democracy. We may be united in our effort to bring the terrorists to justice, but we should not be so willing to give up our civil rights and civil liberties.

We must not allow patriotism to become an excuse for censorship. This is where Project Censored, the national media research project headquartered at Sonoma State University, plays such an important role in our society.

Project Censored is an early warning system of the problems that plague us. Over the years it tried to warn us about many of the challenges we now face.

One of those challenges is the threat of biological and chemical attacks in the United States. In the past ten years, Project Censored raised the issue of biological and chemical warfare seven times. A 1981 story reported that while research on these weapons was banned in 1969 because of public pressure, the CIA still maintained biological warfare stockpiles. Further, a 1998 story revealed that the biological weapons materials the UN inspection teams were seeking in Iraq were supplied by US firms.

Another challenge is the possible Taliban use of American-made Stinger missiles against our aircraft. A censored story of 1993 told how the CIA was desperately but unsuccessfully trying to buy back hundreds of surface-to-air Stinger missiles that it secretly gave the Afghan guerrillas a few years earlier. The top censored story of 1997 said the United States was the principal arms merchant for the world and warned that American troops may be at risk from our own weapons.

In 1984, Project Censored reported that the United States had secretly given the Afghan rebels up to $300 million in covert aid, far more than the controversial $24 million it had given the Nicaraguan Contras. A censored story in 1989 revealed how CBS News broadcast pro-guerrilla biased news coverage of the Afghanistan war.

Ironically, one of the censored stories of 1983 reported how the Pentagon wanted to establish special "state defense forces" to prevent or suppress terrorism. The proposal failed. (For more information on these and other censored stories, please visit www.projectcensored.org.)

The tragic events of September 11 shocked many Americans who could not believe anyone could hate us that much. An explanation might be found in the number seven censored story of 1999. It reported how international news began to fade from America's newspapers in the 1970s following the Vietnam War.

Journalist Peter Arnett offered one explanation as to why Americans are less informed about what's going on in the rest of the world: "Most of the nation's newspapers and magazines and television stations, seeking greater profits through larger audiences, fed the public a diet of crime news, celebrity gossip, and soft features, choosing to exclude more serious topics that news managers feared would not stimulate public attention."[6]

All this is not to say that the terrorist acts would not have taken place if the press had provided us with more objective coverage of the Middle East, but perhaps it would have made us more vigilant and better prepared.

Unfortunately, instead of alerting us to these and other important issues, the news media distracted us with a phenomenon Project Censored calls junk food news—stories about O.J. Simpson, Y2K, Monica Lewinsky, Gary Condit, and "reality" television programs like *Survivor*.

Finally, we urge the press to be responsible in its coverage of this conflict. It is far easier but less responsible to beat the drums when jingoism runs loose in the streets than to carefully report events in a context that makes sense.

In the same way that we survived Pearl Harbor, we will survive the September 11 terrorist attack. In the meantime, let us not be terrorized into giving up any of our constitutionally guaranteed rights.

NOTES

1. David Halberstam, *The Powers That Be* (New York: Alfred A. Knopf, 1979), p. 447.

2. Neil Hickey, "Where TV Has Teeth," *Columbia Journalism Review* (May/June 2001): 46.

3. William Greider, "The Last Farm Crisis," *Nation*, November 20, 2000.

4. "Public Support for Watchdogs Is Fading," *Columbia Journalism Review* (May/June 2001): 52.

5. Charles Higham, *Trading with the Enemy* (New York: Delacorte, 1982); Jeffrey Udon, "The Profits of Genocide," *Z Magazine* (May 1996).

6. Peter Phillips, *Censored 2000: The Year's Top 25 Censored Stories* (New York: Seven Stories Press, 2000), p. 45.

CHAPTER 19

THE RISE AND FALL OF PROFESSIONAL JOURNALISM

ROBERT McCHESNEY

University of Illinois at Urbana-Champaign

Robert McChesney has written or edited nine books, including the award-winning Telecommunications, Mass Media, and Democracy: The Battle for the Control of US Broadcasting, 1928–1935 *and the multiple-award-winning* Rich Media, Poor Democracy. *His newest books are* The Problem of the Media: U.S. Communication Politics in the 21st Century *and, with Ben Scott, he has edited* Our Unfree Press: 100 Years of Radical Media Criticism. *Both were published in 2004. McChesney is currently research professor at the Institute of Communications Research at the University of Illinois. He is also the president and founder of Free Press, a nonprofit organization working to involve the public in media policy making and to craft policies for a more democratic media system. Since launching his academic career in the late 1980s, McChesney has made more than six hundred radio and television appearances and been the subject of nearly one hundred published profiles and interviews. He is the host of* Media Matters, *a weekly radio program on WILL-AM, the NPR affiliate in Urbana, Illinois. Prior to entering academia, McChesney was a sports stringer for UPI and was the founding publisher of the* Rocket, *a Seattle-based rock magazine.*

T he chapters in this book have provided a devastating account of the assault on democratic journalism that is taking place in the United States today. It is a dark picture, but the point of the book is not to depress people, or to immobilize them. The point is to show clearly what is transpiring and the troubling implications for a free people. In this concluding chapter I will locate this critique in a historical context, and argue that, ultimately, the problem is a result of the nature and structure of the media industries. Therefore, the solution will require changes in those structures.

Within democratic theory, there are two indispensable functions that journalism must serve in a self-governing society. First, the media system must provide a rigorous accounting of people in power and people who want to be in power, in both the public and private sectors. This is known as the watchdog role. Second, the media system must provide reliable information and a wide range of informed opinions on the important social and political issues of the day. No single medium can or should be expected to provide all of this; but the media system as a whole should provide easy access to this for all citizens. By these criteria, the US political system is in deep trouble. Contemporary journalism serves as a tepid and weak-kneed watchdog over those in power, especially in the corporate sector. And it scarcely provides any reliable information or range of debate on many of the basic political and social issues of the day.

In conventional wisdom, these flaws in the American political system and press are nearly incomprehensible. The profit-driven US media system is the only acceptable one for a free people. Whatever limitations for journalism the pursuit of profit might encourage are acceptable due to the manifold benefits of the market, and, anyway, there are professional standards to protect against degradation of the news by commercial pressures. If our journalism is floundering, it is because professional standards are not being rigorously adhered to, or because media consumers are sending the wrong message to media owners. The system works.

In my view, the conventional wisdom is misleading at best, and more likely dead wrong. It is a major impediment to our actually grasping the nature of journalism and its place in a truly democratic society. In this chapter I hope to debunk the conventional wisdom and show that the media system is, in fact, the source of much of the trouble with our journalism. I also intend to show that professional journalism is hardly a panacea, and, even at its best, it is seriously flawed. Specifically, I address the historical rise of professional journalism, its relationship to private media power and democracy, and its strengths and weaknesses.

The notion that journalism should be politically neutral, nonpartisan, professional, even "objective," is not much more than one hundred years old. During the first two or three generations of the Republic, such notions for the press would have been nonsensical, even unthinkable. The point of journalism was to persuade as well as inform, and the press tended to be highly partisan. The free press clause in the first amendment to the Constitution was seen as a means to protect dissident political viewpoints, as most newspapers were closely linked to political parties. It was understood that if the government could outlaw or circumscribe newspapers, it could effectively eliminate the ability of opposition parties or movements to mobilize popular support. It would kill democracy. A partisan press system has much to offer a democratic society, as long as there are numerous, well-subsidized media providing a broad range of opinion.

During the nineteenth century, the press system remained explicitly partisan, but it increasingly became an engine of great profits as costs plummeted, population increased, and advertising—which emerged as a key source of revenues—mushroomed. The commercial press system became less competitive and ever more clearly the domain of wealthy individuals, who usually had the political views associated with their class. Throughout this era, socialists, feminists, abolitionists, trade unionists, and radicals *writ large* tended to regard the mainstream commercial press as the mouthpiece of their enemies and established their own media to advance their interests. Consider, for example, the United States in the early 1900s. Members and supporters of the Socialist Party of Eugene V. Debs published some 325 English and foreign-language daily, weekly, and monthly newspapers and magazines. Most of these were privately owned or were the publications of one of the five thousand Socialist Party locals. They reached a total of more than two million subscribers. *Appeal to Reason*, the socialist newspaper that inspired Jim Weinstein to launch *In These Times*, alone had a readership of nearly a million.

From the Gilded Age through the Progressive Era (1870–1915), an institutional sea change transpired in US media not unlike the one taking place in the broader political economy. On the one hand, the dominant newspaper industry became increasingly concentrated into a handful of massive, multiple-paper owning concerns and all but the largest communities only had one or two dailies. The economics of advertising-supported newspapers erected barriers to entry that made it virtually impossible for small, independent newspapers to succeed, despite the protection of the Constitution for a "free press." The dissident press, too, found market economics treacherous and lost much of its circulation and influence throughout the first half of the twentieth century, far in excess of the decline in interest in "dissident" politics. At the same time, new technologies helped pave the way for the commercial development of national magazines, recorded music, film, radio, and, later, television as major industries. These all became highly concentrated industries and engines of tremendous profits.

At the beginning of the twentieth century, these developments led to a crisis of sorts for US media—or the press, as it was then called. Commercial media were coming to play a larger and larger role in people's lives, yet the media industries were increasingly the province of a relatively small number of large commercial concerns operating in noncompetitive markets. The First Amendment promise of a "free press" was being altered fundamentally. What was originally meant as a protection for citizens effectively to advocate diverse political viewpoints was being transformed into commercial protection for media corporation investors and managers in noncompetitive markets to do as they pleased to maximize profit with no public responsibility.

In particular, the rise of the modern commercial-press system drew attention to the severe contradiction between a privately held media system and the needs of a democratic society, especially in the provision of journalism. It was one thing to posit that a commercial media system worked for democracy when there were numerous newspapers in a community, when barriers to entry were relatively low, and when immigrant and dissident media proliferated widely, as was the case for much of the nineteenth century. For newspapers to be partisan at that time was no big problem because there were alternative viewpoints present. It was quite another thing to make such a claim by the late nineteenth and early twentieth centuries when all but the largest communities only had one or two newspapers, usually owned by chains or very wealthy and powerful individuals. For journalism to remain partisan in this context, for it to advocate the interests of the owners and the advertisers who subsidized it, would cast severe doubt on the credibility of the journalism.

During the Progressive Era, a criticism of the capitalist press reached fever pitch in the United States and was a major theme of muckrakers. Leading reformers, like Robert La Follette of Wisconsin, argued that the commercial press was destroying democracy in its rabid service to the moneyed interests. As Henry Adams put it at the time, "The press is the hired agent of a moneyed system, set up for no other reason than to tell lies where the interests are concerned." In 1919, Upton Sinclair published his opus, *The Brass Check*, that provided the first great systematic critique of the limitations of capitalist journalism for a democratic society. In short, it was widely thought that journalism was explicit class propaganda in a war with only one side armed. Such a belief was very dangerous for the business of newspaper publishing, as many potential readers would find it incredible and unconvincing.

It was in the cauldron of controversy, during the Progressive era, that the notion of professional journalism came of age. Savvy publishers understood that they needed to have their journalism appear neutral and unbiased, notions entirely foreign to the journalism of the era of the Founding Fathers, or their businesses would be far less profitable. Publishers pushed for the establishment of formal "schools of journalism" to train a cadre of professional editors and reporters. None of these schools existed in 1900; by 1915, all the major schools such as Columbia, Northwestern, Missouri, and Indiana were in full swing. The notion of a separation of the editorial operations from the commercial affairs—termed the separation of church and state—became the professed model. The argument went that trained editors and reporters were granted autonomy by the owners to make the editorial decisions, and these decisions were based on their professional judgment, not the politics of the owners and the advertisers, or their commercial interests to maximize profit. Readers could trust what they read. Owners could sell their neutral monopoly newspapers to everyone in the community and rake in the profits.

Of course, it took decades for the professional system to be adopted by all the major journalistic media. The first half of the twentieth century is replete with owners like the *Chicago Tribune*'s Colonel McCormick, who used their newspapers to advocate their fiercely partisan (and, almost always, far-right) views. And it is also true that the claim of providing neutral and objective news was suspect, if not entirely bogus. Decision making is an inescapable part of the journalism process, and some values have to be promoted when deciding why one story rates front-page treatment while another is ignored.

Specifically, the realm of professional journalism had three distinct biases built into it, biases that remain to this day. First, to remove the controversy connected with the selection of stories, it regarded anything done by official sources, for example, government officials and prominent public figures, as the basis for legitimate news. Then, if chastised by readers, an editor could say, "Hey, don't blame us, the governor (or any other official source) said it and we merely reported it." This reliance upon official sources gave those in political office (and, to a lesser extent, business) considerable power to set the news agenda by what they spoke about and what they kept quiet about. It gave the news a very establishment and mainstream feel.

To cite a more recent example, this bias explains the truly dreadful news media coverage of the Republican "victory" in the 2000 presidential election. Journalists were reduced to volleying between the official opinion in the Republican and Democratic camps. Republican sources were unified in their insistence that the White House was theirs, regardless of the vote count. The Democratic high command was unwilling to fight for what we now know they had clearly won—and many of them spoke of how perhaps it would be best if Gore threw in the towel—as that would have required mobilizing labor unions, feminists, environmentalists, and African Americans in massive demonstrations, something the party's big-money backers wanted to avoid like the plague. The press therefore accepted the debatable premise that Bush had won the election and Gore was grasping at straws to save his flawed position. For journalists to stick their necks out to press unwaveringly for a full and accurate tally of the votes—without Gore or other leading Democrats assuming an aggressive posture—would have left them exposed as being "partisan." So they retreated inside the walls of elite debate, and democracy was the loser.

Second, also to avoid controversy, professional journalism posited that there had to be a news hook or a news peg to justify a news story. This meant that crucial social issues like racism or environmental degradation fell through the cracks of journalism unless there was some event, like a demonstration or the release of an official report, to justify coverage. And even then, for those outside power to generate a news hook was, and is, often extraordinarily difficult. Combined with its obsession with "neutrality," journalism tended to downplay or eliminate the presentation of a range of informed positions on controversial issues. Instead, journalism produced the range of elite opinion on those issues the elite were debating. This produces a paradox: journalism, which, in theory, should inspire political involvement, tends to strip politics of meaning and promote a broad depoliticization.

Both of these factors helped to stimulate the birth and rapid rise of the public relations (PR) industry, the purpose of which was surreptitiously to take advantage of these two aspects of professional journalism. By providing slick press releases, paid-for "experts," neutral-sounding but bogus citizens' groups, and canned news events, crafty PR agents have been able to shape the news to suit the interests of their mostly corporate clientele. Or as Alex Carey, the pioneering scholar of PR, put it in his book *Taking the Risk Out of Democracy* (University of Illinois Press, 1997), the role of PR is to so muddle the public sphere as to "take the risk out of democracy" for the wealthy and corporations. Media owners welcome PR because it provides, in effect, a subsidy for them by providing them with filler at no cost. Surveys show that PR accounts for anywhere from 40 to 70 percent of what appears as news.

The third bias of professional journalism is more subtle but most important: far from being politically neutral, it smuggles in values conducive to the commercial aims of the owners and advertisers as well as the political aims of the owning class. Ben Bagdikian, author of *The Media Monopoly*, refers to this as the "dig here, not there" phenomenon. So it is that crime stories and stories about royal families and celebrities become legitimate news. (These are inexpensive to cover, and they never antagonize people in power.) So it is that the affairs of government are subjected to much closer scrutiny than the affairs of big business. Charles Lewis, founder of the Center for Public Integrity, notes that when his group releases exposés of government malfeasance, they receive far wider coverage from the press than when he provides similarly researched exposés of corporate crime. And of government activities, those that serve the poor (welfare, for example) get much more critical attention than those that serve primarily the interests of the wealthy (such as the CIA and other institutions of the national security state), which are more or less off-limits. The genius of professionalism in journalism is that it tends to make journalists oblivious to the compromises with authority they routinely make.

Professional journalism hit its high-water mark in the United States from the 1950s into the 1980s. During this era, journalists had relative autonomy to pursue stories and considerable resources to use to pursue their craft. But there were distinct limitations. Even at its best, professionalism was biased toward the status quo. The general rule in professional journalism is this: If the elite, the upper 2 or 3 percent of society who control most of the capital and rule the largest institutions, agree on an issue then it is off-limits to journalistic scrutiny. Hence, the professional news media invariably take it as a given that the United States has a right to invade any country it wishes for whatever reason it may have. While the US elite may disagree on specific invasions, none disagrees with the notion that the US military—and the US military alone, unless it deputizes some nation—needs to have a 007 (as in James Bond) right to intervene worldwide. Similarly, US professional journalism equates the spread of "free markets" with the spread of democracy, although empirical data show this to be nonsensical. To the US elite, however, democracy tends to be defined by their ability to maximize profit in a nation, and that is, in effect, the standard of professional journalism. In sum, on issues such as these, US professional journalism, even at its best, serves a propaganda function similar to the role of *Pravda* or *Izvestia* in the old USSR.

The best journalism of the professional era came (and still comes) in the alternative scenarios: when there were debates within the elite or when an issue was irrelevant to elite concerns. In these cases, professional journalism, with its emphasis on factual accuracy, could be sparkling. So important social issues, like civil rights or abortion rights or conflicts between Republicans and Democrats (such as Watergate), tended to get superior coverage to issues of class or imperialism, like the weakening of progressive income taxation, the size and scope of the CIA's operations, or United States–sponsored mass murder in Indonesia. But one should not exaggerate the amount of autonomy journalists had from the interests of owners, even in this "Golden Age." In every community there was a virtual Sicilian code of silence, for example, regarding the treatment of the area's wealthiest and most powerful individuals and corporations. Media owners wanted their friends and business pals to get nothing but kid-glove treatment in their media and so it was, except for the most egregious and boneheaded maneuver.

This is not so say that the organized activities of the mass of people do not have the ability to influence the shape of journalism. In moments of resurgence for social movements, professional journalism is malleable enough to improve the quantity and quality of coverage. In the 1940s, for example, full-time labor editors and reporters abounded on US daily newspapers, and there were several hundred of them. Even ferociously antilabor newspapers, like the *Chicago Tribune*, covered the labor beat. The 1937 Flint sit-down strike that launched the United Auto Workers and the trade union movement was a major news story across the nation. By the 1980s, however, labor had fallen off the map, and there were no more than a dozen labor beat reporters remaining on US dailies. (The number is less than five today.) The story was simply no longer covered. Hence, the 1989 Pittstown sit-down strike—the largest since Flint—was virtually unreported in the US media, and its lessons unknown. As the labor movement declined, coverage of labor was dropped. People still work, poverty among workers is growing, workplace conflicts are as important as ever, but this is no longer news.

It may seem ironic that, during the exact period that coverage of labor was disappearing from the news, a right-wing critique of journalism gained considerable momentum (fueled by conservative philanthropic dollars) that argued that US journalism was hostile to business and overly sympathetic to labor unions, government employees, feminists, peaceniks, environmentalists, civil rights activists, and the poor. This right-wing critique of "liberal" journalism was bankrolled by organizations obsessed with smashing labor, deregulating business, and putting corporations firmly in command of society. By the mid-1970s this critique of the so-called liberal media had established itself as the "official opposition" to professional journalism. The critique seems bizarre upon close inspection, but it actually makes perfect sense. The conservatives were criticizing the limited autonomy of professional journalists that gave them power to sway journalism away from the interests of owners and advertisers. Working journalists were hardly "leftists," but they tended to be more liberal, especially on social issues, than their bosses. The conservative critique also struck a resonant chord with many Americans insofar as it played on the elitism that was clearly a part of the professional culture of journalism.

The conservative critique of the "liberal media" remains in place, but it is far less persuasive than it was two decades ago. The conservative jihad against "liberal" media has been a success, as the dominant commercial media present a range of opinion from the center to the right. It is a tad ironic that Rush Limbaugh's blood boils over what he regards as rabidly pro-Clinton or pro-Gore coverage by the news media, when, in fact, on most of the core issues of state, Clinton and

Gore have pushed a solidly probusiness position. One need only look at the *New York Times* coverage of Ralph Nader in the 2000 presidential campaign—his treatment was roughly similar to how *Pravda* regarded Andrei Sakharov in the 1970s—to see how left-wing and radical the news media are.

This movement of journalism rightward is the result of many factors, but in the past quarter-century, and especially in the last decade, the most significant reason for this and much else that is happening with the news is the striking consolidation of the media from a number of distinct industries filled with scores, even hundreds, of significant firms to an integrated industry dominated by less than ten enormous transnational conglomerates and rounded out by no more than another fifteen very large firms. The first tier giants include AOL Time Warner, Disney, Viacom, News Corporation, Bertelsmann, Vivendi Universal, Sony, AT&T, and General Electric. This consolidation resulted from government deregulation of broadcasting, new communication technologies, and lax enforcement of antitrust statutes. To give some sense of proportion, in 2000, AOL purchased Time Warner in the biggest media deal ever, valued at around $180 billion. That was more than five hundred times greater than the value of the largest media deal in history that had been recorded by 1979. The nine or ten largest media conglomerates—few of which even existed in their current form in the mid-1980s—now almost all rank among the three hundred largest firms in the world; in 1965, there were barely any media firms among the five hundred largest companies in the world.

The consolidation and conglomeration of media ownership have ramifications that touch on every facet of media behavior. For example, the largest ten media firms own all the US television networks, most of the TV stations in the largest markets, all the major film studios, all the major music companies, nearly all of the cable TV channels, much of the book and magazine publishing, and much, much more. These firms are obsessed with finding ways to use their media empires to augment their profits. So, for example, movies that can spin off sequels, TV shows, soundtracks, consumer products, and books make the best sense, and the firms use their far-flung empires to promote all their wares. The logic of media industries is such that a firm can no longer compete if it is not part of a larger conglomerate. EMI is the last of the five music companies that sell some 90 percent of the music in the United States that is not part of a conglomerate, and it has attempted mergers with

AOL Time Warner and with Bertelsmann in 2000 and 2001. Likewise, General Electric's NBC is the only commercial TV network that does not own a major Hollywood film studio or even a music company or book publishing operation. General Electric will either become a full-fledged media conglomerate, or it will sell NBC to a firm that can place NBC into a larger empire. Moreover, these are truly global empires. Firms like Disney and AOL Time Warner have seen the non-US portion of their revenues double in the past decade—to around 20 percent—and expect continued rapid expansion into the foreseeable future.

But it is probably journalism, more than any other aspect of media, that has been affected the most by these developments. As nearly all the traditional news media became small parts of vast commercial empires, owners logically cast a hard gaze at their news divisions and were determined to generate the same sort of return from them that they received from their film, music, and amusement park divisions. The traditional deal—the separation of editorial from business—no longer made economic sense for these megacorporations. And since the "deal" was never in writing, it depended upon the magnanimity of the owners; it was only going to be honored as long as it served the economic interests of those in control. This meant laying off reporters, closing down bureaus, using more free PR material, emphasizing inexpensive trivial stories, focusing on news of interest to desired upscale consumers and investors, doing less overseas and investigative journalism, and generally urging a journalism more closely attuned to the bottom-line needs of advertisers and the parent corporation. The much-ballyhooed separation of church and state was sacrificed on the altar of profit.

This has meant that all the things professional journalism did poorly in its heyday, it does even worse today. And those areas where it had been adequate or, at times, more than adequate, have suffered measurably. Empirical studies chronicle the decline of journalism in numbing detail. Expensive investigative journalism—especially that which goes after powerful corporate or national security interests—is discouraged. Idiotic or largely irrelevant human interest/ tragedy stories get the green light for extensive coverage. These are cheap, easy to cover, and they never antagonize those in power. Then, when people consume these stories, the media companies claim they are responding to demand. It is a circular argument, especially when no other viable alternatives are on the "ballot."

Perhaps the most striking indication of the collapse of professional journalism comes from the editors and reporters themselves. As recently as the mid-1980s, professional journalists tended to be stalwart defenders of the media status quo, and they wrote book after book of war stories celebrating their vast accomplishments. Today the thoroughgoing demoralization of journalists is striking and palpable. One need only peruse the chapters of this book or go to a bookstore to see title after title by prominent journalists lamenting the decline of the craft due to corporate and commercial pressure. As Jim Squires, former editor of the *Chicago Tribune* put it, our generation has witnessed the "death of journalism."

In some respects we have returned to the world of the Progressive Era, when journalists and social critics alike lambasted journalism. And, as in the Progressive Era, the fault lines of mainstream journalism are clear: deference to business and a blind eye to problems of corporations and capitalism, as well as a much greater sensitivity to the needs of the affluent and privileged. In an economically unequal society like the United States, the rational course for commercial news media is to aim for the desired middle- and upper-middle-class target audience. Daily newspapers have effectively dropped the bottom quintile or perhaps third of the population from their "markets"; all the other major news media from magazines to network news and cable news channels are even more exclusive. The result of this recipe can be pulled out of the oven: mainstream news and "business news" have effectively morphed over the past two decades, as the news is increasingly pitched to the richest one-half or one-third of the population. The affairs of Wall Street, the pursuit of profitable investments, and the joys of capitalism are now presented as the interests of the general population. Journalists rely on business or free market–loving, business-oriented think tanks as sources when covering economics stories.

The dismal effects of this became clear from 1999 to 2001 when there were enormous demonstrations in Seattle; Washington, DC; Quebec City; and Genoa, among others, to protest meetings of the World Trade Organization (WTO), the World Bank, the International Monetary Fund (IMF), and other institutions of global capitalism. Here, finally, was the news hook that would permit journalists to examine what may be the most pressing political issues of our time. The coverage was skimpy, and paled by comparison to the round-the-clock treatment of the John F. Kennedy Jr. plane crash in the summer of 1999. News coverage of the demonstrations tended to emphasize property damage and violence and, even there, it downplayed the activities of the police. There were, to be fair, some outstanding pieces produced by the corporate media, but those were the exceptions to the rule. The handful of good reports that did appear were lost in the continuous stream of pro-capitalist pieces. In addition to relying upon pro-business sources, it is worth noting that media firms are also among the leading beneficiaries of these global capitalist trade deals (because they can buy assets overseas, and sell their products with fewer restrictions), which helps explain why their coverage of them throughout the 1990s was so decidedly enthusiastic. The sad truth is that the closer a story gets to corporate power and corporate domination of our society, the less reliable the corporate news media are.

In recent years, this increased focus by the commercial news media on the more affluent part of the population has reinforced and extended the class bias in the selection and tenor of material. Stories of great importance to tens of millions of Americans will fall through the cracks because those are not the "right" Americans, according to the standards of the corporate news media. Consider, for example, the widening gulf between the richest 10 percent of Americans and the poorest 60 percent of Americans that has taken place over the past two decades. Throughout the 1980s and 1990s, real income declined or was stagnant for the lower 60 percent, while wealth and income for the rich skyrocketed. By 1998, discounting home ownership, the top 10 percent of the population claimed 76 percent of the nation's net worth, and more than half of that is accounted for by the richest 1 percent. The bottom 60 percent has only a minuscule share of total wealth, aside from some home ownership; by any standard, the lowest 60 percent is economically insecure, weighed down as it is by very high levels of personal debt.

As economist Lester Thurow notes, this peacetime rise in class inequality may well be historically unprecedented and is one of the main developments of our age. It has tremendously negative implications for our politics, culture, and social fabric, yet it is barely noted in our journalism—except for rare mentions when the occasional economic report points to it. One could say that this can be explained by the lack of a news peg that would justify coverage, but that is hardly tenable when one considers the cacophony of news-media reports on the economic boom of the past decade. In the crescendo of news-media praise for the genius of contemporary capitalism, it is almost unthinkable to criticize the economy as deeply flawed. To do so would seemingly reveal one as a candidate for an honorary position in the Flat-Earth Society. The *Washington Post* has gone so far as to describe ours as a nearly "perfect economy." And it does, indeed, appear more and more perfect the higher one goes up the socioeconomic ladder, which points to the exact vantage point of the corporate news media.

For a related and more striking example, consider one of the most astonishing trends lately, one that receives little more coverage than O. J. Simpson's boarder Kato Kaelin's attempts to land a job or a girlfriend: the rise of the prison-industrial complex and the incarceration of huge numbers of people. The rate of incarceration has more than doubled since the late 1980s, and the United States now has five times more prisoners per capita than Canada and seven times more than the whole of Western Europe. The United States has 5 percent of the world's population and 25 percent of the world's prisoners. Moreover, nearly 90 percent of prisoners are jailed for nonviolent offenses, often casualties of the so-called drug war.

The sheer quantity of prisoners is not even half of it. Recent research suggests that a significant minority of those behind bars may well be innocent. Consider the state of Illinois, where, in the past two decades, more convicted prisoners on death row have been found innocent of murder than have been executed. Or consider the recent published work of the Innocence Project, which has used DNA testing to get scores of murder and rape convictions overturned. In addition, the conditions inside the prisons themselves tend far too often to be reprehensible and grotesque, in a manner that violates any humane notion of legitimate incarceration. It should be highly disturbing and the source of public debate for a free society to have so many people stripped of their rights. Revolutions have been fought and governments have been overthrown for smaller affronts to the liberties of so many citizens. Instead, to the extent that this is a political issue, it is a debate among Democrats and Republicans over who can be "tougher" on crime, hire more police, and build more prisons. Almost overnight, the prison-industrial complex has become a big business and a powerful lobby for public funds.

This is an important story, one thick with drama and excitement, corruption and intrigue. In the past two years, several scholars, attorneys, prisoners, and freelance reporters have provided devastating accounts of the scandalous nature of the criminal justice system, mostly in books published by small, struggling presses. Yet this story is hardly known to Americans who can name half the men Princess Diana had sex with or the richest Internet entrepreneurs. Why is that? Well, consider that the vast majority of prisoners come from the bottom quarter of the population in economic terms. It is not just that the poor commit more crimes; the criminal justice system is also stacked against them. "Blue-collar" crimes generate harsh sentences while "white-collar" crimes—almost always netting vastly greater amounts of money—get kid-glove treatment by comparison. In the year 2000, for example, a Texas man received sixteen years in prison for stealing a Snickers candy bar, while, at the same time, four executives at Hoffman-LaRoche Ltd. were found guilty of conspiring to suppress and eliminate competition in the vitamin industry, in what the Justice Department called perhaps the largest criminal antitrust conspiracy in history. The cost to consumers and public health is nearly immeasurable. The four executives were fined anywhere from $75,000 to $350,000, and they received prison terms ranging from three months all the way up to four months.

Hence, the portion of the population that ends up in jail has little political clout, is least likely to vote, and is of less business interest to the owners and advertisers of the commercial news media. It is also a disproportionately nonwhite portion of the population, and this is where class and race intersect and form their especially noxious American brew. Some 50 percent of US prisoners are African American. In other words, these are the sorts of people that media owners, advertisers, journalists, and desired upscale consumers do everything they can to avoid, and the news coverage reflects that sentiment. As writer Barbara Ehrenreich has observed, the poor have vanished from the view of the affluent; they have all but disappeared from the media. And in those rare cases where poor people are covered, studies show that the news media reinforce racist stereotypes, playing into the social myopia of the middle and upper classes. There is ample coverage of crime in the news media, but it is used to provide inexpensive, graphic, and socially trivial filler. The coverage is almost always divorced from any social context or public policy concerns, and, if anything, it serves to enhance popular paranoia about crime waves and to prod political support for tough-talking, "three strikes and you're out" programs.

Imagine, for one moment, that instead of being from the bottom quarter, nearly all the prisoners were from the richest quarter of the population. Imagine that the students attending Yale or the University of Illinois, for example, had half of their friends behind bars or dead from a confrontation with police, and that they had been hassled by the police for being "suspects" in some crime. Imagine, too, that their parents had the same experiences, and that they knew that many of those friends in prison were innocent. Imagine the donations the ACLU would receive! Would this be a news story then? Of course it would, but this is hypothetical because the problem would have been eliminated long before it could have reached that point, and it would have been eliminated because it would have been the biggest political and news story of our era.

Or perhaps not. On September 11, 2001, the news media encountered a story of even greater magnitude. Following the terrorist attacks on New York and Washington, DC, the United States launched a worldwide war against terrorism. The decision to go to war is the most important one any society can make. A war means many thousands, even millions, of lives will be lost, and immense economic resources must be diverted from peaceful uses to feed the war effort. In a society that is democratic, the decision to go to war must be made with the informed consent of the population. What that requires is a press system that provides the citizenry with the information and perspectives to make an informed decision. It is, in some respects, for the notion of a free press, its moment of truth.

Journalists had every reason to be skeptical about the rush to war immediately following September 11. Since the late nineteenth century, the US government has worked aggressively to convince the citizenry of the necessity of going to war in numerous instances. In cases like World War I, Korea, Vietnam, and the Gulf War, the government employed sophisticated propaganda campaigns to whip the population into a suitable fury. It was well understood within the establishment at the time—and subsequently verified in historical examinations—that the government needed to lie to gain support for its war aims. The media system, in every case, proved to be a superior propaganda organ for militarism and empire.

This is the context for understanding the media coverage since September 11. The historical record suggests we should expect an avalanche of lies and half-truths in the service of power, and that is exactly what we have gotten. Our news media has played along in toto, having learned nothing from history.

The Manichean picture conveyed by the media was as follows: A benevolent, democratic, and peace-loving nation was brutally attacked by insane, evil terrorists who hate the United States for its freedoms and affluent way of life. The United States must immediately increase its military and covert forces, locate the surviving culprits, and exterminate them; then prepare for a long-term war to root out the global terrorist cancer and destroy it. Those who do not aid the US campaign for justice—and logically, this would mean domestically as well as internationally—are to be regarded as the accomplices of the guilty parties, and may well suffer a similar fate. No skepticism was shown toward US military, political, and economic interests that might benefit from militarism and war. There was no hard questioning demanding evidence that the proposed war would actually reduce terrorism and bring to justice the terrorists responsible for the September 11 attacks. The mainstream press avoided those questions, which would have been asked of any other government that proposed to direct a world war.

The reasons for this grossly distorted coverage lie in the reliance on official sources that is written into the professional code, which I have discussed. The entire political establishment fell in line for the war effort, leaving little wiggle room for journalists to challenge the jingoistic sentiment without being accused of being unprofessional, partisan, or unpatriotic. Factual stories that challenged the official position appeared on the margins, but without official-source support, they died off from lack of oxygen.

Beyond the professional code, US media corporations play a large role in explaining the dreadful coverage. The number of overseas correspondents has been slashed, and international political coverage has plummeted over the past two decades, as that is expensive and generates little revenue. Whereas Americans once tended to be somewhat misinformed about world politics, now they are uninformed. The US citizenry is embarrassingly and appallingly ignorant of the most elementary political realities in other nations and regions. It is an unmitigated disaster for the development of a meaningful democratic debate over international policy, and highlights a deep contradiction between the legitimate informational needs of a democratic society and the need for profit of the corporate media.

American media corporations also exist within an institutional context that makes support for the US military seemingly natural. These giant firms are among the primary beneficiaries of both neoliberal glob-alization—their revenues outside the United States are increasing at a rapid pace—and the United States' position as the preeminent world power. Indeed, the US government is the primary advocate for the global media firms when trade deals and intellectual property agree-ments are being negotiated. Coincidentally, at the very moment that the corporate broadcasters are singing the praises of "America's New War," their lobbyists are appearing before the Federal Communications Com-mission seeking radical relaxation of ownership regulations for broad-casting, newspaper, and cable companies. Such deregulation will by all accounts lead to another massive wave of media consolidation. For these firms to provide an understanding of the world in which the US military and economic interests are not benevolent forces might be pos-sible in some arcane twisted theory, but it is incongruous practically.

The propagandistic nature of the war coverage was made crystal clear by AOL Time Warner's CNN a few weeks after the war began in Afghanistan. CNN is not only the leading US cable news network, it is the leading global cable and satellite news network. The war put CNN in a pickle. If it broadcast to international audiences the pro-US pabulum that it generated in the United States, those audiences would have reacted negatively. International audiences were getting a much more critical take on the war and the United States' role in it from their newspapers and other media, and they would not have watched CNN if they saw it as a front for the Bush administration. On the other hand, if CNN presented that same critical coverage to US audiences, it would have outraged the people in power here. CNN president Walter Isaacson solved this dilemma by authorizing CNN to provide two different versions of the war: a more critical one for global audiences and a sugarcoated one for Americans. Indeed, Isaacson instructed the domestic CNN operation to be certain that any story that might undermine support for the war be balanced with a reminder that the war on terrorism was a response to the heinous attacks of September 11.

The implications of this for journalism are self-evident.

The problems with our journalism are not because the people who run our newsrooms and media corporations are bad people. That is mostly irrelevant. They do what they do because they are rationally following the cues they are given. What we need to do is change the cues so it is rational to produce great journalism. That means we must redouble the efforts to support independent media. Some argue that with the rise of the Internet, the corporate media system and mainstream journalism will go the way of the dodo bird as billions of media Web sites offer a sumptuous feast of media. The track record so far, however, makes it clear that this will not happen. To the extent that the Internet becomes part of the commercial media system, it looks to be dominated by the usual corporate suspects. Their power is based not just on technology, but on political and economic muscle. To create and disseminate effective media requires resources and institutional support. Technology won't rescue us, although we do need to take advantage of it to the best of our abilities.

Ultimately, we need to press for the overhaul of the media system, so that it serves democratic values rather than the interests of capital. The US media system is not "natural," it has nothing to do with the wishes of the Founding Fathers, and it has even less to do with the workings of some alleged free market. To the contrary, the media system is the result of laws, government subsidies, and regulations made in the public's name, but made corruptly behind closed doors without the public's informed consent. The largest media firms are all built on top of the profits generated by government gifts of monopoly rights to valuable broadcasting spectra or monopoly cable franchises. The value of this corporate welfare, over the past seventy-five years, can only be estimated, but it probably runs into the hundreds of billions of dollars.

Our job is to make media reform part of our broader struggle for democracy and social justice. It is impossible to conceive of a better world with a media system that remains under the thumb of Wall Street and Madison Avenue, under the thumb of the owning class. It is nearly impossible to conceive of the process of getting to a better world without some changes in the media status quo. We have no time to waste.

INDEX